CW00927086

THE BUILDINGS OF ENGLAND

FOUNDING EDITOR: NIKOLAUS PEVSNER

THE ISLE OF WIGHT

DAVID W. LLOYD AND NIKOLAUS PEVSNER

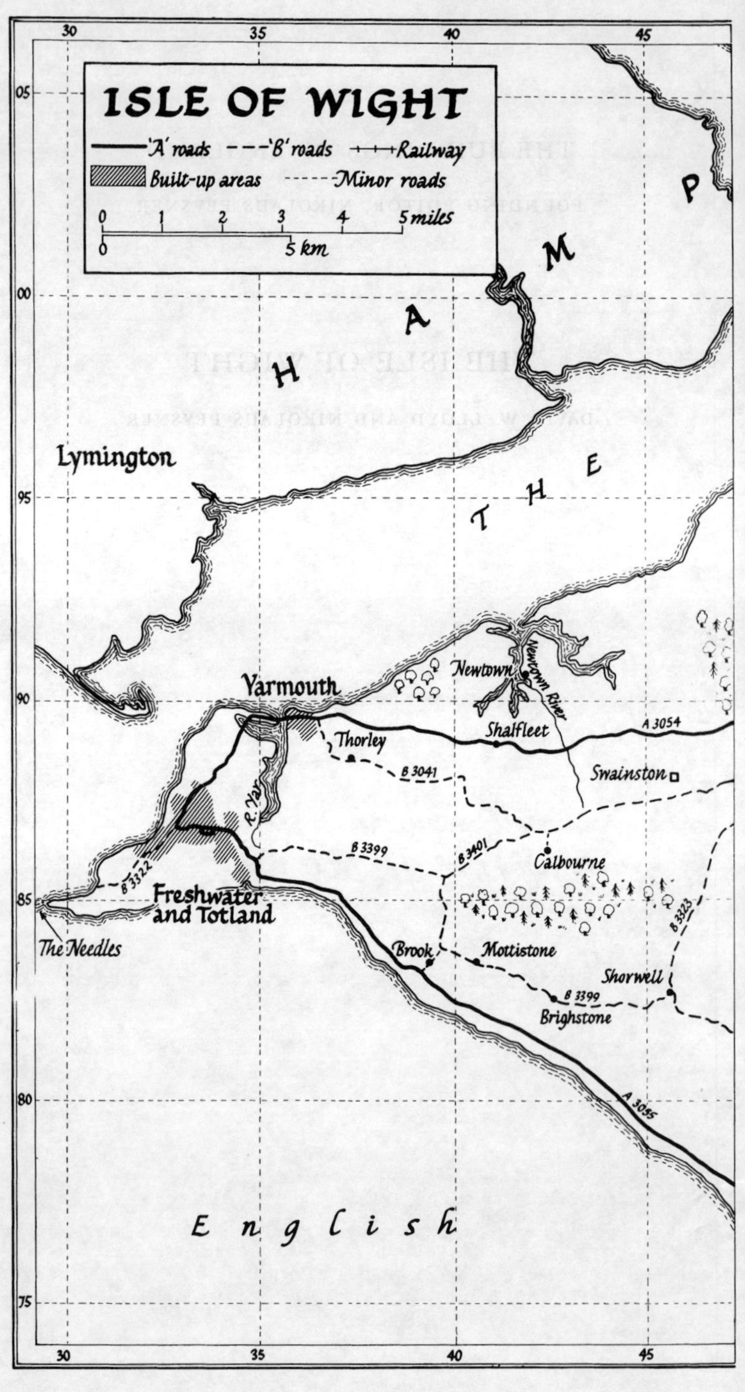
ISLE OF WIGHT
'A' roads
'B' roads
Railway
Built-up areas
Minor roads
0 1 2 3 4 5 miles
0 5 km
H A M P
T H E
E n g l i s h
Lymington
Yarmouth
Newtown
Newtown River
Shalfleet
Thorley
B 3041
A 3054
Swainston
R. Yar
B 3399
B 3401
Calbourne
B 3322
Freshwater and Totland
The Needles
Brook
Mottistone
Shorwell
B 3323
Brighstone
A 3055
30
35
40
45
05
00
95
90
85
80
75

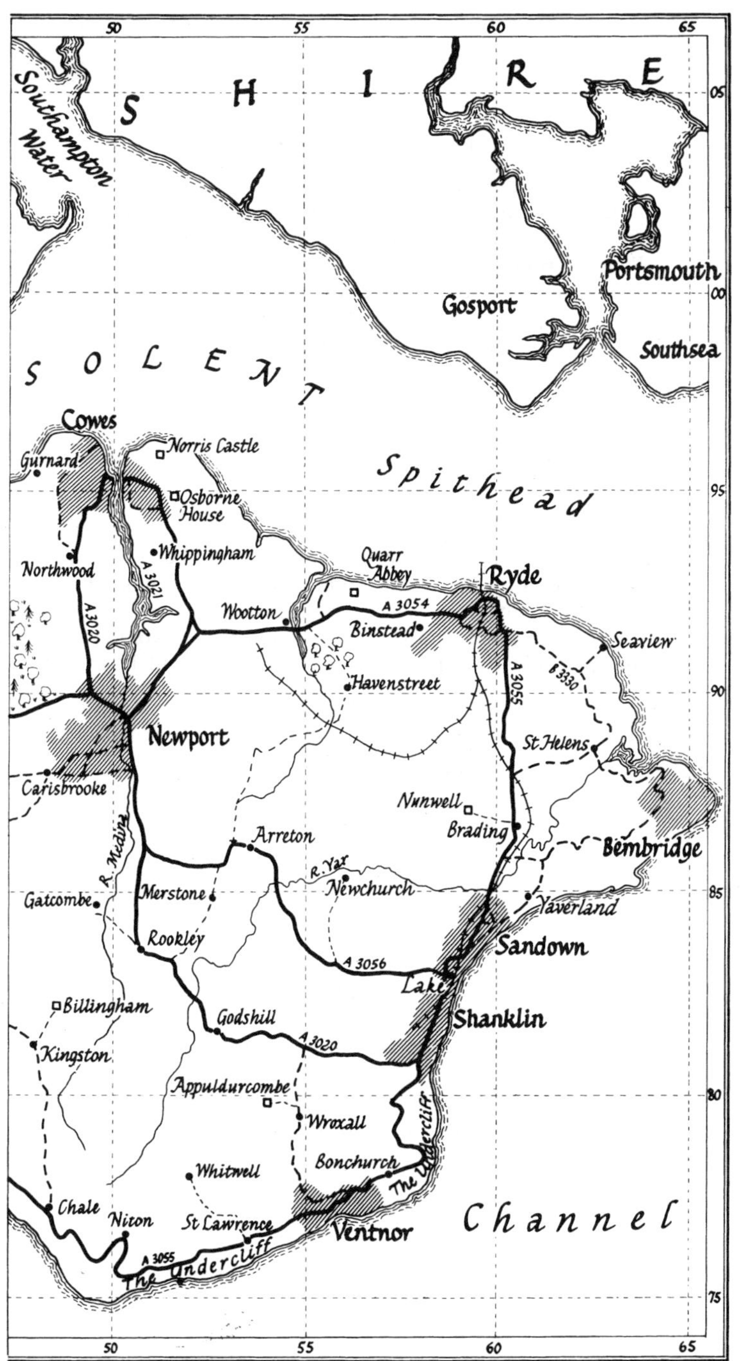

Southampton Water
S H I R E
Portsmouth
Gosport
Southsea
S O L E N T
Cowes
Gurnard
Norris Castle
Osborne House
Spithead
Northwood
Whippingham
A 3021
A 3020
Quarr Abbey
Ryde
Wootton
A 3054
Binstead
Seaview
B 3330
A 3055
Havenstreet
Newport
St Helens
Carisbrooke
Nunwell
Brading
R. Medina
Arreton
Bembridge
R. Yar
Newchurch
Merstone
Gatcombe
Yaverland
Rookley
Sandown
A 3056
Lake
Billingham
Shanklin
Godshill
A 3020
Kingston
Appuldurcombe
Wroxall
The Undercliff
Bonchurch
Whitwell
Chale
Niton
St Lawrence
Ventnor
Channel
A 3055
The Undercliff

PEVSNER ARCHITECTURAL GUIDES

The Buildings of England series was created and largely written by Sir Nikolaus Pevsner (1902–83). First editions of the county volumes were published by Penguin Books between 1951 and 1974. The continuing programme of revisions and new volumes has been supported by research financed through the Buildings Books Trust since 1994

THE BUILDINGS BOOKS TRUST

was established in 1994, registered charity number 1042101. It promotes the appreciation and understanding of architecture by supporting and financing the research needed to sustain new and revised volumes of *The Buildings of England*, *Ireland*, *Scotland* and *Wales*

The Trust gratefully acknowledges assistance from

ENGLISH HERITAGE

with photography for this book

a grant towards the costs of research and writing from

THE OPEN CHURCHES TRUST

and a grant towards the cost of maps and other illustrations from

THE C.J. ROBERTSON TRUST

The Isle of Wight

BY

DAVID W. LLOYD

AND

NIKOLAUS PEVSNER

THE BUILDINGS OF ENGLAND

YALE UNIVERSITY PRESS
NEW HAVEN AND LONDON

YALE UNIVERSITY PRESS
NEW HAVEN AND LONDON
302 Temple Street, New Haven CT 06511
47 Bedford Square, London WC1B 3DP
www.pevsner.co.uk
www.lookingatbuildings.org
www.yalebooks.co.uk
www.yalebooks.com
for
THE BUILDINGS BOOKS TRUST

Published by Yale University Press 2006
Reprinted with corrections 2007
2 4 6 8 10 9 7 5 3

ISBN 978 0 300 10733 3

Copyright © Nikolaus Pevsner, 1967
Copyright © David W. Lloyd, 2006

Printed in China
through World Print
Set in Monotype Plantin

All rights reserved.
This book may not be reproduced
in whole or in part, in any form (beyond that
copying permitted by Sections 107 and 108 of the
U.S. Copyright Law and except by reviewers
for the public press), without written
permission from the publishers

The 1967 edition of

Hampshire and the Isle of Wight

was dedicated

TO

THE MINISTRY OF HOUSING AND LOCAL GOVERNMENT,
WHOSE LISTS OF BUILDINGS OF ARCHITECTURAL
OR HISTORIC INTEREST
ARE ONE OF THE FINEST TOOLS
WE HAVE

2006 dedication

TO THOSE WHO HELPED ME
DISCOVER AND UNDERSTAND THE ISLAND
AND ITS BUILDINGS, ESPECIALLY
ROY BRINTON, ALAN FOSTER, MALCOLM PINHORN
AND CHARMIAN SHENTON

CONTENTS

LIST OF TEXT FIGURES AND MAPS

Every effort has been made to contact or trace all copyright holders. The publishers will be glad to make good any errors or omissions brought to our attention in future editions.

MAPS

PHOTOGRAPHIC ACKNOWLEDGEMENTS

We are grateful to English Heritage and its photographers Nigel Corrie and Pat Payne for taking most of the photographs in this volume (© English Heritage Photo Library) and also to the sources of the remaining photographs as shown below. We are grateful for permission to reproduce them as appropriate.

ABK Architects: 88 (© Terence Grimwood)
Brading Roman Villa: 9
English Heritage Photo Library: 1, 2, 3, 14, 15, 16, 17, 34, 37, 38, 67, 68, 69, 70, 71, 72
Newport Roman Villa: 8

MAP REFERENCES

The numbers printed in italic type in the margin against the place names in the gazetteer of the book indicate the position of the place in question on the index map (pp. ii–iii), which is divided into sections by the 5-kilometre reference lines of the National Grid. The reference given here omits the two initial letters (formerly numbers) which in a full grid reference refer to the 100-kilometre squares into which the country is divided. The first two numbers indicate the *western* boundary, and the last two the *southern* boundary, of the 5-kilometre square in which the place in question is situated. For example, Appuldurcombe (reference 5075) will be found in the 5-kilometre square bounded by grid lines 50 (on the *west*) and 55, and 75 (on the *south*) and 80; Yaverland (reference 6080) in the square bounded by the grid lines 60 (on the *west*) and 65, and 80 (on the *south*) and 85.

The map contains all those places, whether towns, villages, or isolated buildings, which are the subject of separate entries in the text.

EDITOR'S FOREWORD

This book is the first of three in the revised *Buildings of England* series which will replace the old *Hampshire and the Isle of Wight* volume of 1967. The mainland will be covered in two new volumes, *North Hampshire* and *South Hampshire*.

The 1967 edition was written jointly by Nikolaus Pevsner and David Lloyd, of whom the former undertook the Isle of Wight section. Major buildings received detailed attention, but the remainder were less closely covered, nor did the fifty-page treatment of the Island include very much to bring out the special character of its architecture. This imbalance extended to the illustrations, a mere eight of which were of Island subjects. The effect, however unintentional, was to present the Isle of Wight as the poor relation to the mainland county.

It is therefore very pleasing to be able to make good these omissions with the present volume. David Lloyd brings to the subject knowledge obtained by many years of investigation and close study, strengthened further by his own special interest in the growth and form of English towns. The physical changes and notable new architecture of the past forty years have of course been included, along with developments in scholarly understanding of the older buildings, which are now treated in much greater depth. The larger format of the revised *Buildings of England* series has also allowed the inclusion of many more text illustrations, including maps of the major towns. A wholly new Introduction, including a specially commissioned account of the early period, completes the survey, which is illustrated by a magnificent selection of photographs from English Heritage. For lovers of architecture, the Isle of Wight can now emerge as one of the most attractive and distinctive areas of England.

ACKNOWLEDGEMENTS

In the *Buildings of England* guide *Hampshire and the Isle of Wight* (1967) I wrote the entries for S and SE Hampshire, including Southampton and Portsmouth; I did not write those for the Island. When revision of the old volume started, my knowledge of the Isle of Wight was not extensive, and I was greatly helped by people who drove me round on many occasions, especially to remoter areas. This was particularly valuable when the need for investigation grew after it was decided to have a separate volume for the Island, which permitted a fuller account than was originally intended.

It was Malcolm Pinhorn, a genealogist with a special interest in Isle of Wight history, who first introduced me in the late 1960s to the qualities of its architecture. He was concerned with threats to the integrity of Newport as a historic town – not widely appreciated at the time. I had recently worked under Lord Esher (the architect Lionel Brett) in the preparation of his conservation report on York, and I was familiar with problems relating to historic townscapes. I undertook a preliminary study of central Newport, street by street. Although this proceeded no further, it formed the basis for my appreciation of the town when I described it for this guide. Mr Pinhorn later helped me over numerous buildings on the Island.

I met Roy Brinton in connection with a public inquiry in 1971 over the proposed destruction of the interior of the Royal Victoria Arcade in Ryde, one of the finest buildings on the Island. (After another inquiry in 1972, at which I also gave evidence, the arcade was finally saved). Mr Brinton, a former curator of Carisbrooke Castle Museum, has made an intensive study of the history and buildings of Ryde. The fruits of his researches, which he made freely available, have provided detailed information for innumerable buildings in the town and elsewhere. Several of the text illustrations also appear by his kind permission.

I owe a great deal to Charmian Shenton, a retired architect with long experience in conservation. She and her husband, established local residents, introduced me to the owners of many houses in connection with my study. She consistently encouraged me to continue and complete the work for this book. Alan Foster, also a retired architect, accompanied me on many visits. His knowledge and (sometimes) appreciation of modern as well as older buildings greatly stimulated me. Vicky Basford, who also wrote the introductory chapter and gazetteer descriptions relating to archaeology in this volume, was a great help with buildings and landscapes. Ian Smith, for long a conservation officer to local authorities on the Island, gave as much as he could of his time to help me.

As with other Pevsner Guides, much of the research was done in record offices and libraries. The County Archivist Richard Smout and his staff at the County Record Office in Newport were always helpful. I also visited the Hampshire Record Office, where the Winchester diocesan records contain files for faculties related to work on church buildings on the Island, including furnishings and features such as stained glass, before the formation of the Portsmouth diocese in 1927. The main collection of books on local history and buildings is in the Lord Louis Library, Newport; there is also material relating to the Island in the local studies libraries at Portsmouth and Winchester. At the national level, the archives of the Incorporated Church Building Society in Lambeth Palace Library relate to churches, especially furnishings, from 1818 onwards.

Among many people who have helped and welcomed me on my visits to Island buildings I should like to mention Colonel and Mrs Aylmer at Nunwell, Dennis Bacon at The Castle (St Helens), Mr and Mrs Crofts at Merston Manor, Martyn Davies at Ryde School, John Harrison at North Court (Shorwell), Mrs Laurence at Billingham Manor, A.C. Middleton at Mirables (St Lawrence), Fanny Oglander on the Nunwell Estate, Hugh Noyes at Lisle Combe (St Lawrence), Dr and Mrs Patterson at Wolverton Manor (Shorwell), Professor Picton at Kingston Manor, Mr and Mrs Rodley at Chale Abbey, Mrs Shine-Breaks at Puckaster (Niton), Mrs Smith at Gotten Manor (Chale), Robert Stigwood at Barton Manor (Whippingham), Colonel and Mrs Webber at Sheat Manor (Gatcombe), and the Mother Abbess at St Cecilia's Abbey (Ryde). Edward Roberts and Elizabeth Lewis, specialists in medieval and later houses, particularly in Hampshire, gave important advice on the significance of the manor houses at Chale Abbey and Swainston. Among many people with whom I have had fruitful correspondence, I should like to thank L.D. Butler, Brian Hinton, Robin McInnes, John Margham, B.F.J. Pardoe, and Michael Rainey, architect. As to churches, many on the Island are open, at least in summer, so that visiting them is less difficult than in some areas. I should like to thank clergy and lay people who have helped me over churches, including those at Binstead, Cowes (St Mary and St Faith), Freshwater, Havenstreet, Kingston, Newport (St John), Ryde (St Mary, R.C.), and Shanklin (St Saviour).

I owe a great deal to David Brock of English Heritage, who read my texts, made pertinent comments, and carried on valuable discussions about buildings including Appuldurcombe and Nunwell. Michael Turner, also of English Heritage, helped hugely over Osborne House. He read my draft entry and made suitable comments, and was particularly helpful over the former estate buildings, around Whippingham and elsewhere, which with their varied classical and romantic styles form a fascinating and little-known series. The entries on wall paintings at Bonchurch, Godshill, Shorwell and Whitwell were written by David Park, whose researches were assisted by Sharon Cather and Emily Howe. Finally I would like to thank Rodney Hubbuck, who greatly helped over the 1967 texts for the Hampshire mainland and who is also involved in their current revision, over his assistance with features in Isle of Wight churches, particularly stained glass.

On the publishing side, the book was edited by Simon Bradley at Yale University Press, and before that by Bridget Cherry at Penguin Books. The county map was drawn by Reg and Marjorie Piggott, other maps and plans by Alan Fagan; Emily Wraith oversaw the illustrations, and Emily Winter the production of the book. A further debt is owed to English Heritage, and in particular to Nigel Corrie and Patricia Payne, who generously undertook the photography.

As with every volume in the series, the author and publishers will be very grateful for information on errors and omissions.

INTRODUCTION

THE LAND

The Isle of Wight has a distinctive shape, roughly in diamond form, and extends for a maximum of 22 miles from E to W and 13 miles from N to S. It is separated from the Hampshire mainland on two sides by the waters of the Solent, which are generally around two to three miles wide, although they broaden towards the E and are narrower in the W. The land-form has great variety in relation to the Island's size. It is treated below in five geographical sections, beginning with the central chalk range which runs across the Island from E to W. This is followed successively by the area N of the chalk range, the sandstone belt to the S, the southern coastal hills, and finally the Undercliff and the rest of the SE coastline.

The CHALK RANGE which forms the backbone of the Island begins at its E end with the white Culver Cliff on the N side of Sandown Bay near Bembridge. Bembridge Down to the W rises to 345 ft (106 metres) above sea level. There is a gap in the chalk near Brading, through which flows a small river (the eastern Yar, *see* p. 3). From there towards the centre of the Island the chalk range forms a ridge, seldom more than half a mile wide, which rises to over 400 ft (123 metres) N of Newchurch. In the heart of the Island, S of Newport, there is a break in the chalk formation, accommodating the River Medina – here hardly more than a stream before it enters the tidal estuary further N. To the W of this gap the chalk range broadens southward to form an area of often steep-sided hills and valleys, rising in places to over 600 ft (185 metres) and extending for two or three miles towards Shorwell and Brighstone. Further W, the chalk range narrows again into a boldly formed ridge, which meets the coast near Freshwater Bay, a cove-like inlet. To the W of the bay (where the ridge is called Tennyson Down after the poet who lived nearby) there are grand white cliffs which form a memorable climax to views along the coast from further SE. Beyond this the ridge finally fragments as The Needles. There are few buildings on the chalkland, apart from scattered farms and houses in the valleys of its wider part. Adjoining settlements are related either to the spring-line on the N side, as at Calbourne, or to other land-forms to the N and S.

Newport and the Medina valley, engraving.
From W.H.D. Adams, *Nelson's Handbook to the Isle of Wight*, 1866

Much of the AREA NORTH OF THE CHALK RANGE is gently undulating and fairly well wooded, with surface soils that show a mixture of clays, gravel and sands. Underlying these is a very important, though intermittent, limestone formation which was extensively quarried in the past (*see* Building Stones, p. 7). Although still largely rural, the area contains the Island's three main towns, Cowes, Ryde and Newport – the last with historic Carisbrooke Castle on its SW outskirts.

The COASTLINES bordering the Solent, and the more open sea to the E, are deeply indented by tidal creeks and estuaries, into which flow small rivers or streams – two of which are, confusingly, called the Yar. At the far W of the Island is the estuary of the western Yar, with the small historic town of Yarmouth (now a busy terminal for ferries from Lymington in Hampshire) adjoining its entrance. The estuary, with the stream flowing into it from the S, almost makes a separate island of the western peninsula, which includes the seaside settlements of Freshwater and Totland Bay. These are flanked on their S side by the chalk ridge ending at the Needles. The peninsula's NW seaboard includes the colourful cliffs of Alum
2 Bay, where varied sands and clays are exposed. E of Yarmouth is the quiet, many-branching Newtown Harbour, with winding creeks that penetrate inland. On one of these was the medieval port of Newtown which declined to a hamlet (*see* p. 25). NE of Newtown is a stretch of generally low-lying coast which has been affected by erosion.

The most important tidal estuary is that of the River Medina, which extends for over four miles inland from the northern tip of the Island. The town of Newport was established in the Middle Ages beside the estuary head; it became very prosperous in Georgian times (as its architecture shows), and is now the Island's administrative and main commercial centre. Cowes developed as a port on both sides of the lower part of the estuary, and was notable for building and maintaining vessels, both large and small, from the C17 into the C20. Latterly it specialized in maritime aircraft including flying-boats, and eventually hovercraft. It is one of the main ports of entry to the Island, with car and passenger ferries from Southampton. The town's great importance as a yachting centre dates from the early C19.

E of Cowes is the Island's most famous building, Osborne 67
House. Queen Victoria was charmed with the Island when, as Princess, she stayed with her mother at Norris Castle near Cowes in the early 1830s. She and Prince Albert developed Osborne from 1845 – not as another royal palace but as a private country retreat (where, however, extensive provision had to be made for the associated royal household as well as for the conduct of affairs of state when she was in residence). The house, with a large part of its original grounds descending to the Solent shore, is now in public ownership. The royal estate formerly extended further SE over largely agricultural land, where many of its farmhouses, cottages, and other related buildings in distinctive styles remain.

Wootton Creek is a fairly small estuary, with an important terminal at Fishbourne for car ferries from Portsmouth. To the E of the creek, as far as Binstead, is an area where limestone was quarried from Roman times (*see* below); where the first Quarr Abbey (of which there are fragmentary remains) was founded in the Middle Ages; and where the second, architecturally remarkable, monastery of the same name was built 77
in the early C20. Beyond these is Ryde, which first grew as a resort and transit town in the early C19. It is now the largest town on the Island, with an extensive sandy beach and many fine buildings of the early to mid C19. It never had a harbour, but with its pier, first built in 1813–14, it became the point of entry to the Island for ferry passengers from Portsmouth. In the later C19 a railway was built along the pier, connecting with lines to other resorts on the Island. Today an electrified railway runs from the ferry landing to Sandown and Shanklin.

SE of Ryde, past the characterful Victorian village of Seaview, is Bembridge Harbour, busy with yachts. This is the relatively small surviving part of the once considerably larger Brading Haven, most of which was drained in the C19. Much of its former site is now marshland. In the past the haven, and the small eastern River Yar flowing into it, partly cut off the easternmost peninsula of the Island, including the originally small village of Bembridge. The peninsula ends at the rounded, low-profiled Foreland. From here the tumbled shoreline gains in height south-westwards into Whitecliff Bay,

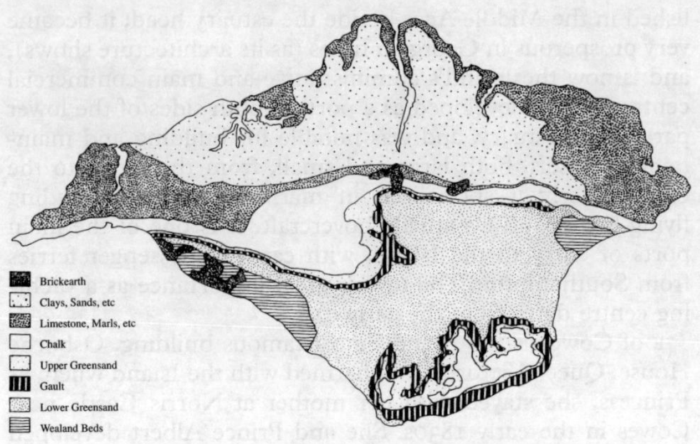

Geological map of the Isle of Wight.
After Marion Brinton, *Farmhouses and Cottages of the Isle of Wight*, 1987

with its irregular cliffs partly of sands and limestone. Beyond this bay is Culver Cliff, at the beginning of the chalk formation. The stretch of coast near the Foreland has been protected from the full force of the sea by limestone ledges, extensively exposed at low tide (*see also* Building Stones, p. 8).

The southern part of the Island is very mixed in character. It includes a relatively low-lying stretch of country, here called the SANDSTONE BELT, which extends up to three or four miles S of the central chalk range – though less towards the W. The land-form of this area is based on different varieties of sandstone, broadly classified as Upper Greensand and Lower Greensand, although these are largely overlaid by clays, gravels and other surface deposits. There is a narrow band of UPPER GREENSAND immediately S of the central chalk range, forming, intermittently, a subsidiary ridge below the chalk. Near Gatcombe this band broadens into a limited range of low hills. The stone from this formation is generally grey-buff, with occasional greenish tints. S of the Upper Greensand is a narrow low-lying belt of GAULT, a heavy clay which separates the Upper from the Lower Greensand. The greater part of the sandstone belt is within the LOWER GREENSAND formation. This is a generic term embracing stones of varying textures and colours – including carstone, which is coarsely grained and coloured brown; sandrock, more finely grained and buff to cream in colour; and ferruginous sandstones, which have traces of iron content, often giving rusty colour effects.

Much of the Sandstone Belt is fairly flat. The surface soils are often fertile, and parts of the area S of Arreton and Newchurch are highly productive, with specialized crops. (Ironically some of this area is now covered by greenhouses and similar buildings producing such crops internally.) Further to the S and SW the Lower Greensand landscape becomes more undulating, often quite boldly, with prominent eminences such as that on which Godshill church stands. To the W the Sandstone Belt narrows between the central chalkland and the converging coast.

Going SE, the undulations of the sandstone belt give way to the bolder land forms of the SOUTHERN COASTAL HILLS. These are essentially chalk downs (although with associated tracts of Upper Greensand), and are quite separate from the central chalk range. The typical land-form in these hills is one of sweeping round-topped slopes bordering fairly broad valleys – as around Whitwell, and in the vicinity of the former great house of Appuldurcombe. Stenbury Down, between the two, rises to nearly 700 ft (215 metres). St Boniface Down, NE of Ventnor, reaches 787 ft (242 metres) – the highest point on the Island. To the W the landscape comes to a climax at St Catherine's Hill near Chale, just over 780 ft (240 metres) above sea level, and crowned by a medieval lighthouse which 13
was attached to a now vanished chapel.

The coastal area on the SE and S side of the southern hills is known as the UNDERCLIFF. It has a highly irregular and dramatic form, due to landslides which took place several thousand years ago. They occurred because of the composition of the hills behind. On the seaward side of these hills the chalk overlays a fairly wide band of Upper Greensand, below which is a layer of Gault clay. These successive formations are tilted down towards the coast. The stone of the Upper Greensand sometimes develops fractures, while the Gault tends to have 'slippery' characteristics. Large sections of this Upper Greensand formation, together with the chalk above, probably broke away and slid over the Gault clay towards the sea. The process must have taken place over a long period; its time-scale is far from certain.

The result of these landslips is a tumbled coastal landscape extending for over six miles, from S of Shanklin to near Chale, W of the Island's southern tip. Behind the actual shoreline there is a series of cliffs, together with very steep hillsides that are almost cliffs, which extend fairly continuously about half a mile inland, roughly parallel with the shore. These mark where the landslips took place. Parts of the inland cliffs are essentially vertical and bare, showing vividly the successive formations, especially that of the Upper Greensand. But the adjoining steep hillsides that are less than vertical are often covered with vegetation. Between these inland cliffs and hillsides and the coast itself, the land-forms are very broken –

with short irregular slopes, often steep, and intermittent hollows. These tumbled land surfaces represent, in consolidated forms, the deposits of material that collapsed in the landslides. Much of the coastline itself consists of relatively low cliffs, which may be composed of fallen material, or are parts of the Lower Greensand formation which underlay the Gault clay and remained *in situ*.

The westernmost part of the Undercliff, around the southern tip of the Island, is still very unstable. A major landslide in 1928 largely obliterated Blackgang Chine (a gorge-like fissure in the cliffs), and destroyed a section of coastal road. There was a lesser, but still serious landslide in 1978. As a result parts of the coast in this area are almost inaccessible, and areas immediately behind it are wild, tumbled and difficult to reach. But the main part of the Undercliff, from St Lawrence eastwards, is at present subject only to occasional, relatively minor coastal cliff falls.

The most characteristic Undercliff landscape is in the St Lawrence area. The irregular land surfaces between the inland cliffs and the sea are in parts thickly wooded, but much of this coastal strip forms the grounds of large and medium-sized houses, mostly built of the local stone. St Lawrence merges into Ventnor, which grew from almost nothing in the C19 because of the salubrity of its climate as well as its picturesque setting. Alas, developers and builders have not always made the best of the latter. But parts of the town are attractively irregular, with buildings on tumbled sites backed by the steep inland hillsides, some of which are partly wooded and partly dotted with houses. The town's eastern appendage, *p. 86* Bonchurch, was developed more sensitively in the Victorian period. It was previously noted for its quarries in the deposits of Upper Greensand stone which fell in the early landslides (*see* Building Stones, p. 8). Bonchurch borders the NE end of the Undercliff, which has wider, more rounded land-forms than further W, and an irregular coastline subject to periodic, strictly localized, landslides.

At Luccombe, S of Shanklin, the curve of Sandown Bay begins. It is fronted for nearly three miles by cliffs which mark the seaward edge of the sandstone belt. They illustrate the components of the Lower Greensand formation, showing the various textures of its component stones. Shanklin Chine provides a gorge-like gap in the shoreline, with its waterfall set amid rocky, partly tree-grown slopes. It was this chine, with the surrounding landscapes, which first drew visitors to the small picturesque village of Shanklin in the early C19. It grew into a town after the railway reached it from Ryde in 1864, as did Sandown further N. Both towns became popular resorts, partly because of their splendid sandy beaches. Sandown has the only surviving pleasure pier on the Island, that at Ryde being purely for transit.

Shanklin Chine, engraving, 1843.
From George Brannon, *Brannon's Picture of the Isle of Wight*, *c.* 1844

The line of cliffs is broken at Sandown. For a mile or more the coastline is flat, bordering a stretch of originally marshy ground. Then, at Yaverland, sandstone cliffs begin again and curve along the bay; they culminate in the well-named Red Cliff, showing tilted layers of different formations of the Lower Greensand. Beyond, the coastline changes once more, with the white Culver Cliff marking the extremity of the central chalk range.

BUILDING STONES

Quarrying was important up to the C19, both for limestone in the N part of the Island and for different types of sandstone in the S. Although the use of these materials for building was largely local, substantial quantities – especially of limestone – were shipped to the mainland in the Middle Ages, often for important construction works.

BEMBRIDGE LIMESTONE is the general term used for the formation which underlies much of the N part of the Island (where it is usually topped by clays, sands and other soils). The largest area from which limestone was extracted is W of Ryde, around Binstead and Quarr Abbey (founded in the C12 and named after quarries which already existed). Other areas where limestone was found include Gurnard, to the W of Cowes; between Calbourne and Yarmouth; and, in the other direction, from St Helens to Bembridge. The term Bembridge

Limestone first arose because there are extensive ledges of the material, with irregular broken surfaces, off the coast near the Foreland at Bembridge, especially evident at low tides. But Bembridge is on the very edge of the area where the limestone occurs, and the term can be misleading.

There were two types of limestone in the 'Bembridge' formation. The harder type, which has come to be called QUARR STONE, was found in limited quantities in and around Binstead. It is creamy buff to greyish, occasionally green-tinted, with fragments of fossils. With its hard texture this stone is usually durable, but could not be used for delicately carved details. It was quarried by the Romans (who used it, for instance, in the fort at Portchester, Hampshire), and was used by the Saxons in churches in Hampshire and Sussex, as well as in the two Island churches with surviving Saxon remains, at Arreton and Freshwater. In 1079 Bishop Walkelin of Winchester obtained land at Binstead, from which stone was excavated for the new cathedral started in that year. Much of his work, and that of his immediate successors using the stone, remains in Winchester Cathedral. After *c.* 1090 Quarr stone was used in building Chichester Cathedral, and in rebuilding the great abbey church at Romsey, Hampshire. The stone was also used by the Normans in numerous parish churches in Hampshire and Sussex. Limited quantities went further afield – Quarr stone is found in work of *c.* 1100 and later in and around Canterbury.

The supply of Quarr stone was probably largely exhausted by the beginning of the C13. However, this type of stone formed only a small proportion of that in the Bembridge Limestone formation, most of which is rougher and less dense in texture. It often contains whole fossils of shells, not only fragments (as does the Quarr stone). Sometimes the fossils have eroded, leaving cavities in the stone. Its suitability for building work varied, and it was largely used as rubble for walling. However, stone from some parts of the formation was suitable for shaping into rectangular blocks, fairly roughly faced as ashlar. It was much used for defensive work, both as rubble and in blocks – particularly in the C13–C15 town walls and gateways in Southampton. It is found in a number of churches in Hampshire as well as on the Island. The coarser varieties of the Island limestone are sometimes called collectively Binstead stone, although it was quarried in a wider area (*see* above). Its use for domestic, farm and other buildings continued though the C16 and C17 (at least in the vicinity of the places where it was extracted), and was revived to some extent for buildings in and around Ryde in the Victorian period.

Among the various sandstone formations on the Island, that of the UPPER GREENSAND was the most valuable as building material. It was quarried in three general locations: in a narrow band S of the central chalk range, on the fringes of the Southern Coastal Hills, and in the Undercliff (for which *see* p. 5). The fallen stone of the last location was the most important source of supply. It was quarried in several places, particularly around Bonchurch and Ventnor; it came to be known as Green Ventnor stone, because it sometimes had greenish tints. This stone was widely used around the C14 and C15, when it was shipped to the mainland for several important buildings, including Chichester and Winchester cathedrals. It was much more suitable for detailed carving than the harder Quarr limestone, but it does not last well when exposed to the weather. The best available deposits were largely exhausted by the later C18, but it continued to be quarried, as rubble or in blocks, into the C19. Many Early Victorian buildings around Ventnor were built of it. Some of those in Bonchurch (including the Victorian church) are in the sites of hillside quarries, backed by what appear to be low cliffs but which were actually quarry faces. There were many quarries, often quite small, in the other sandstone areas, producing varied types of stones, including sandrock and, notably, the often rust-tinted ferruginous sandstone.

Sandstone in its various forms was the usual building material in much of the S part of the Island from the C16. Before then, stone was used on the Island only in special buildings, including churches, Carisbrooke Castle, and a few important houses such as the bishops' manor house at Swainston. Other buildings were of timber or of less substantial materials. But by the later Tudor and Jacobean periods, houses (including manor houses, farmhouses, and larger cottages), farm buildings and, in some areas, boundary walls were built of local sandstone over the S and SE parts of the Island; this continued for the rest of the C17. The great house of Appuldurcombe was rebuilt from 1701 using stone from the Under- 37
cliff, with Portland stone for fine details.

There is little evidence of the use of BRICK on the Island before *c.* 1600; it was first used on a significant scale early in the C17. Brick, made from varied local clays, became the normal building material on the Island by the end of the 52
C18.

It may be asked why FLINT was not more extensively used, particularly for smaller buildings, in the chalkland areas, as it was in similar locations on the mainland. The answer is that supplies of stone were seldom far away, and this was generally preferred to flint for building. However, some flint was used in the Ventnor area in the mid-Victorian period when supplies of the local sandstone were becoming exhausted.

The uses of local materials at different periods are discussed in later sections of the Introduction, pp. 23, 28 and 34.

THE ARCHAEOLOGY OF THE ISLE OF WIGHT

BY VICKY BASFORD

For a large part of its geological history, recorded in rock formations up to 120 million years old, the Isle of Wight was part of a much greater landmass that was periodically submerged. During the Pleistocene epoch, from two million to 10,000 years ago, glaciers expanded into much of Britain, although not as far S as the Isle of Wight. There were intervening milder periods, and major changes in sea levels accompanied these climatic fluctuations. During cold phases sea levels fell and the Island became part of mainland Britain, itself at times attached to the Continent. During milder phases the sea rose and the Island was separated.

The EARLIEST HUMAN ACTIVITY in Britain took place during the Pleistocene. On the Isle of Wight the oldest known site is at Priory Bay, St Helens, where flint hand axes and other implements of the Lower Palaeolithic period have been found, derived from the cliffs and dated by association with surrounding deposits to 425,000–300,000 years ago. Flint hand axes found at Bleak Down, near Rookley, also date from the Lower Palaeolithic. Gravel working at Great Pan, near Newport, located Palaeolithic hand axes that could date from 300,000 to 43,000 years ago. During the entire Palaeolithic (Old Stone Age) humans were hunter-gatherers who had a limited impact on the environment.

About 10,000 years ago, at the start of the Holocene geological epoch, the climate improved and sea levels again began to rise. Climatic improvement led to an increasingly wooded environment. During the MESOLITHIC (MIDDLE STONE AGE), between 8000 B.C. and 4000 B.C., humans were still hunter-gatherers, although the larger animal species had disappeared. Inland, Mesolithic implements have been found mainly on the Lower Greensand, but much of the archaeological material from this period occurs in the inter-tidal zone and in areas affected by coastal erosion and sea-level change. Mesolithic artefacts have been recorded within the truncated river bed exposed along the SW coast. Flint-working sites have been found at Newtown on the NW coast, and on the Medina estuary at Werrar, lying on inundated land surfaces. In 2000 marine archaeologists excavated a submerged woodland surface containing flint implements from the mid-seventh millennium B.C., buried beneath a peaty seabed in the western Solent at Bouldnor near Yarmouth.

The Wootton–Quarr Project surveyed 2½ m. of inter-tidal coastline from Wootton Creek to Ryde West Sands between 1989 and 1994. Analysis of plant and animal remains preserved in the submerged sediments suggested that the Island separated finally from the mainland by 4000 B.C. at the very latest, at the start of the Neolithic (New Stone Age), although the Bouldnor site suggests a possible earlier separation. Fifty-eight submerged trees dated by dendrochronology were part of a Neolithic woodland that had thrived during the period 3463–2557 B.C. These trees have helped to build a tree-ring chronology for southern England and are an important benchmark in reconstructing the history of shore-line change. Wooden trackways, radiocarbon-dated to the Neolithic, were recorded at extreme low water; they have been found elsewhere on the Island only at Newtown.

Farming was first practised in Britain during the NEOLITHIC, i.e. from *c.* 4000 B.C., and the earliest surviving MONUMENTS on the Isle of Wight date from this period. The Longstone, N of Mottistone, is situated on the Lower Green- 7
sand to the S of the central chalk ridge. This monument is thought to be the remains of a long barrow, i.e. a communal burial mound, with the stones marking the position of the former entrance portal. The other two surviving Neolithic monuments stand on the central chalk ridge on either side of Freshwater Bay. Afton Down Long Barrow is surrounded by a Bronze Age round-barrow cemetery and has been damaged by disturbance and early excavation. On Tennyson Down is the site of a mortuary enclosure, which has been confirmed as Neolithic following radiocarbon-dating of charcoal recovered from its ditch. This earthwork may have been used for the exposure of the dead, prior to burial within a long barrow. The three monuments at Mottistone, Afton Down and Tennyson Down indicate that some woodland had been cleared from the Chalk and Greensand in Neolithic times, but pollen evidence suggests a mosaic of agricultural clearances set within large areas of remaining woodland.

In the succeeding BRONZE AGE, from *c.* 2300 B.C. to *c.* 700 B.C., metal was utilized for the first time. Hoards of Bronze Age implements and weapons have been found throughout the Island; the first recorded find was on Arreton Down in 1735, the most recent at Yaverland and near Yarmouth in 2002 and 2003. Large-scale woodland clearance occurred during the period, leading to the creation of downland and heathland. The central and southern chalk downs contain many Bronze Age round-barrow cemeteries, often at the heads of combes. Few surviving ROUND BARROWS are situated away from the chalk, although there are notable examples at Headon Warren (Totland) and Mottistone Common. Over three hundred round barrows have been recorded on the Isle of Wight, although many no longer survive as earthworks, having been destroyed by ploughing and other activities. Most surviving earthworks are bowl barrows, but bell barrows and disc barrows occur on Brook Down and elsewhere, and may indicate burials of higher status and of women. Bowl barrows, the most common type, are simple mounds of earth or chalk with or without a surrounding ditch. Bell barrows have a berm or platform between the central mound and the surrounding ditch, whereas disc barrows have a small central mound on a wide platform surrounded by a ditch and an outer bank. A plough-damaged round barrow on Newbarn Down, Calbourne, excavated in the 1970s, provided evidence for the varying burial rites during the Early Bronze Age. The earliest was a contracted inhumation accompanied by a 'Beaker Culture' bowl. Other contracted inhumations, one in a deep shaft, were followed by an inhumation within a coffin and a contracted satellite burial in a wooden cist. In the final phase a miniature tree-trunk coffin and two cremations in 'food vessel' urns were inserted into the barrow. During the Later Bronze Age, from *c.* 1200 to *c.* 700 B.C., human remains were no longer buried within barrows at all but cremated and placed in flat urn cemeteries. At least four such urn cemeteries are recorded from the Island.

Prehistoric FIELD SYSTEMS have been recorded on the Chalk, indicating that some areas of chalkland were used for arable agriculture rather than for grazing. The best-preserved and recorded system lies within the C20 plantations of Brighstone Forest. Whereas land close to the chalk downland was important for settlement and agriculture, the clay soils N of the central chalk ridge supported much less intensive land use. Relatively few prehistoric sites and finds have been recorded from this area, although at Newnham Farm, Binstead, there is pollen evidence for woodland clearance and agricultural activity at the end of the Bronze Age. However, one area to the N of the chalk near Thorley and Wellow contains easily worked and relatively fertile soils overlying Bembridge Limestone. Air photographs reveal crop marks and soil marks here suggesting prehistoric activity, and a circular ditch proved on excavation to be a ploughed round barrow, sited away from the chalk. Few archaeological monuments survive on the arable land of the Lower Greensand, S of the central ridge, but crop marks and soil marks indicate areas of prehistoric activity here, as do concentrations of worked flint.

On the coast, the Wootton–Quarr Project found Bronze Age stakes thought to be the remains of fish traps, a rare survival that hints at the importance of the sea to the subsistence of Island communities. In the unique environment of the Undercliff, formed by a series of landslips that began up to 8,000 years ago, later prehistoric communities appear to have exploited coastal resources, since a number of middens (rubbish pits) have been recorded along the coastal cliff edge. Iron Age inhumations (*see* below) have also been recorded from the Undercliff, one with fragments of an iron sword and shield bindings.

In nearby mainland counties HILL-FORTS were prominent features in the Iron Age landscape, but on the Isle of Wight only one possible hill-fort is known, on Chillerton Down. There is also relatively little evidence for PREHISTORIC DWELLINGS. Only two Bronze Age hut sites have been recorded, located on the edge of the southern Chalk at Gore Down, Chale. Hut sites dating from the end of the succeeding Iron Age (*c.* 700 B.C. to A.D. 43) have been recorded from Sudmoor on the SW coast and from Gills Cliff at Ventnor. At Knighton, near Newchurch, a Late Iron Age enclosed farmstead on the Lower Greensand was excavated in the 1960s but remains unpublished. An earthwork at Castle Hill, close to the Mottistone Longstone, may be an Iron Age stock enclosure but has not been securely dated.

It is not known whether the Isle of Wight was occupied by an independent tribe at the time of the Roman Conquest in A.D. 43, or whether it formed part of the territory of one of the two tribes occupying the adjacent areas of the mainland: the Durotriges in the Dorset area and the Atrebates in the Sussex and Hampshire area. The Atrebates were friendly towards Rome whereas the Durotriges were hostile. A clue to the political allegiance of the Isle of Wight is provided by the Roman writer Suetonius in his biography of the Roman general and future Emperor, Vespasian. Suetonius records that Vespasian fought thirty battles in Britain, taking control of two powerful tribes, over twenty hill-forts, and the Isle of Wight. This is the first written reference to the Island, here called by its Roman name of 'Vectis'.

Some LATE IRON AGE OCCUPATION is associated with sites where Roman villas later developed. The Bowcombe valley, SW of Carisbrooke, was one focus of settlement. Finds made near Bowcombe Farm indicate Late Iron Age occupation and suggest the nearby presence of a villa. Slightly further E, a Middle Iron Age settlement on a chalk hilltop site at Mount Joy seems to have been abandoned in the Late Iron Age in favour of a site at the lowest fording point of the River Medina, close to the site of the later Newport villa, although the villa itself was not built until the C3. At Combley, N of Arreton, Late Iron Age pottery is associated with timber buildings erected shortly after the Conquest, although the earliest phase of the Combley villa dates from the C2. The site of *p. 5* the later Brading villa, on the western side of Brading Haven, a tidal inlet which at that time extended from St Helens as far as modern Sandown, was also settled in the C1. Part of a defensive enclosure excavated on the other side of Brading Haven in 2001, possibly of Iron Age date, was located close to traces of a later Roman building. However, Roman villas at Rock near Brighstone, at Clatterford in the Bowcombe Valley, and at Carisbrooke developed on sites where there is no evidence of Iron Age settlement.

Carisbrooke Roman Villa, mosaic.
Engraving from E.P. Wilkins, *A Concise Exposition of the Geology, Antiquities, and Topography of the Isle of Wight*, 1861

All known ROMAN VILLAS on the Isle of Wight are closely associated with the central ridge, except that at Gurnard, which is on the NW coast. Whereas the other villas were almost certainly farmsteads with wealthy Romanized owners, Gurnard may have been associated with the export of Bembridge Limestone, which has been found at mainland sites such as Fishbourne Roman Palace. Gurnard villa was destroyed by coastal erosion in the C19 and no trace now remains.

The villas varied in style and sophistication. Rock was a simple structure comprising five rooms entered from a hall running the length of the house. A mosaic floor was recorded at the Carisbrooke villa during C19 excavations. The 'winged-

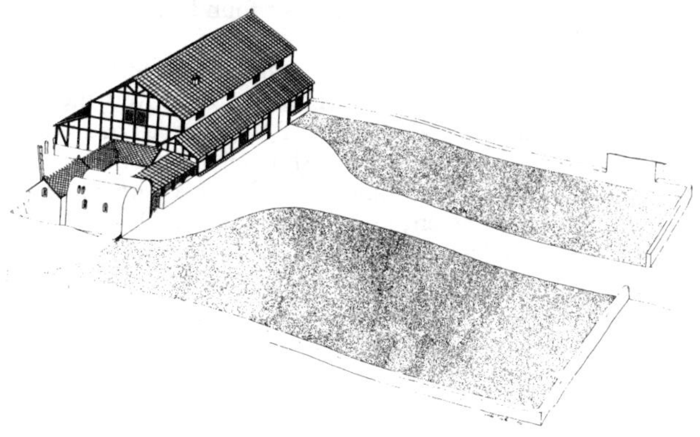

Arreton (Combley), Roman villa.
Reconstruction drawing from D.J. Tomalin, *Roman Wight*, 1987

corridor' villa at Newport had a range of rooms connected by a corridor with projecting wings at either end. One wing contained a bath suite with hypocaust and tessellated floors. An 8
aisled building was developed at Combley close to a simple twin-roomed cottage-type building. The aisled hall had two rows of posts supporting the tiled roof, and dividing walls separated living quarters of four rooms, containing a geometric mosaic and other simpler tessellated floors, from an agricultural area. Later, a bath-house extension was built with a dolphin mosaic. Brading was the most elaborate of the Island's Roman villas. Easy access to sea transport explains why it was so successful. When fully developed, *c.* A.D. 300, Brading was 9, *p. 97*
a courtyard villa planned around a square courtyard. As at Combley there was an aisled farmhouse with a bath house, but the main building was a winged-corridor house containing elaborate mosaics. There was also a separate bath house outside the courtyard. The Roman villas at Newport and Brading are open to the public.

Roman villas were akin to medieval manor houses, being the homes of high-ranking members of society, at the hub of agricultural estates which supplied provisions to the main house and produced a marketable surplus. The Isle of Wight appears to have functioned purely as an agricultural centre in Roman times and no traces of metalled roads or towns have been located. A field system on the S face of Brading Down may have been associated with Brading villa. Lynchets (cultivation terraces) on a steep slope close to Rock villa could be the remains of a field system associated with this villa. A corn- or malt-drying kiln of mid-C4 date excavated on farmland near Newchurch could indicate the presence of an unlocated villa; a Late Iron Age pottery deposit found nearby suggests a long period of occupation.

The collapse of stable government and the market economy in Roman Britain at the end of the C4 destroyed the villa system. Occupation of all the Isle of Wight villas had ceased by the early C5. However, the British inhabitants undoubtedly continued to live on the Island long after this date, whatever the truth of the statement in the Anglo-Saxon Chronicle that in 530 the Anglo-Saxon chieftains Cerdic and Cynric 'obtained possession of the Isle of Wight and slew many men at Wihtgarasburh'.

Past writers have associated Wihtgarasburh with Carisbrooke Castle, although this identification has long been suspect. The earliest fortification of this site is the Lower Enclosure underlying the medieval earthworks, until recently thought to be late Roman in date. However, extensive excavations at the castle, mainly between 1976 and 1980, found no evidence for Roman occupation.* The earliest definite use of the castle hilltop was found to be that of a SAXON CEMETERY in the first half of the C6; one of the three graves found was that of an important male, buried with drinking and table vessels, a gold-plated coin and a set of playing-pieces. For a fuller account of the castle *see* pp. 18 and 20.

Despite a lack of specific evidence for a late Roman presence at Carisbrooke Castle, the Bowcombe Valley and Carisbrooke area were certainly a focus for Roman activity, and continued to be significant in the Dark Ages when the Isle of Wight was occupied by Pagan Anglo-Saxon settlers of Jutish origin. The account of this occupation in the Anglo-Saxon Chronicle cannot be regarded as reliable, and a late C5 and C6 cemetery on Bowcombe Down, excavated in the C19, indicates that settlement had begun before the given date of 530. The earliest finds in the Bowcombe Valley indicative of settlement, recorded from SW of Carisbrooke Castle, are C8, but earlier settlement (i.e. contemporary with the Carisbrooke Castle and Bowcombe Down cemeteries) may have been here rather than in the present Carisbrooke village.

The most important Anglo-Saxon cemetery on the Isle of Wight is elsewhere, at Chessell Down N of Brook, on the chalk some 4½ m. SW of Bowcombe Down. Like Bowcombe Down, also excavated in the C19, this cemetery contained late C5 and C6 pagan graves. The collection of rich and exotic grave goods was subsequently acquired by the British Museum. Pagan Anglo-Saxon graves have also been found inserted into Bronze Age round barrows along the central chalk ridge. Rich C6 artefacts found recently in Freshwater parish, including a

*A new argument for the late Roman origins of the Lower Enclosure has since been made on the basis of the stone used in its construction.

perforated silver spoon and a rock-crystal 'oracle ball', are comparable to those found at Chessell Down.

Anglo-Saxon settlers on the Isle of Wight may have been independent from the mainland until the late C7. Bede, writing in the C8, attributes the original settlement to a distinct tribe called the Jutes, who also settled in Kent and southern Hampshire. Conquest of the Isle of Wight by King Wulfhere of Mercia in 661 and the subsequent donation of the Island to King Aethelwald of Sussex is recorded in the Anglo-Saxon Chronicle, which states that Christianity was brought to the Isle of Wight at the command of Wulfhere. However, Bede claims that the Isle of Wight accepted Christianity 'last of all the provinces of Britain' and dates this conversion to 686, after Caedwalla, the king of the West Saxons, had laid waste the Island, 'which was still entirely devoted to idolatry'. The establishment of large administrative units on the Isle of Wight may have followed conquest by the West Saxons and have determined the boundaries of Anglo-Saxon estates recorded in later charters; these estates formed the basis for the subsequent 'mother' parishes, at least some of which crossed the Island from the N to the S coast, encompassing the varying geological strata and soils.

Viking raids on the Isle of Wight in the late C9, late C10 and early C11 are recorded in the Anglo-Saxon Chronicle. There is no archaeological evidence of these raids, although isolated Scandinavian-style finds have been recorded, including a bronze cloak pin found during the Wootton–Quarr Project. Stake alignments of middle Saxon date on the Wootton–Quarr tidal foreshore may have been constructed as a coastal revetment or even, perhaps, for defensive purposes. The post-and-wattle remains of a large V-shaped fish trap of late Saxon date were also found in this area.

In LATE SAXON times the Island's 'central place' was probably at Carisbrooke, whether this central place was the defended *burh* on the site of Carisbrooke Castle,* on the site of the present village, or elsewhere. A church at 'Bowcombe' referred to in Domesday Book may have been on the site of St Mary, Carisbrooke, or elsewhere in the Bowcombe valley. It was one of ten churches recorded in Domesday Book, which also records approximately a hundred manors. Most medieval MANORIAL SETTLEMENTS probably consisted of the manor house and a few surrounding peasant dwellings, although one or two may have been associated with larger nucleated settlements. From the C11 lords established chapels close to their manor houses and some of these gradually achieved parochial status during the Middle Ages. The architectural remains of this period are discussed below.

*As suggested in C.J. Young, *Excavations at Carisbrooke Castle 1921–1996*, 2000.

THE MEDIEVAL PERIOD

The Early Middle Ages, to c. *1200*

3, 14–17, 34, *pp. 105, 108* CARISBROOKE CASTLE was an important focus for the Island's life and activities through much of its history. Its location is not particularly dramatic; it stands on a spur of land with a small but steep-sided valley to the N and lower ground to the W and S. It used to be thought that the site had been occupied by the Romans, but excavations have found no indication of this. The discovery of three important C6 graves is described above (p. 16). By the late C10 or early C11 the main part of the site was surrounded with earthen ramparts, later faced externally in stone – indicating that it formed a Saxon *burh* or defended place. It may have been a fortified town like Wareham in Dorset or Wallingford in Oxfordshire (formerly Berkshire), though smaller than either, but there is no mention of it in the Burghal Hidage of the early C10 which lists such places.

After the Norman Conquest William FitzOsbern became overlord. He was succeeded by his son Roger, who forfeited the lordship in 1078. The FitzOsberns formed the first castle in a corner of the Saxon *burh*, defended by ditches on the sides within the *burh*. The king granted the lordship in *c.* 1100 to Richard de Redvers, who held estates in Devon and around Christchurch in the Hampshire–Dorset borderland. His son Baldwin, who inherited in 1107, became Earl of Devon. Richard and Baldwin extended the castle to cover the whole area of the *burh*, heightening the old defences and crowning them with a stone curtain wall, much of which survives. They also formed an earthen motte at one corner, from which, by the 1130s, rose a stone keep. This, altered later, now forms an impressive ruin.

Several SAXON CHURCHES existed on the Island, but only
10, at Arreton and Freshwater is there structural evidence. At
p. 73 Arreton the W wall is largely Saxon, as is part of the N wall of
the chancel. These indicate that a relatively large Late Saxon church occupied the area of the present nave and part of the chancel. At Freshwater the W quoins of the Saxon nave remain amid later rebuilding and extension.

There are no complete NORMAN CHURCHES on the Island, but some have important Norman features. At
pp. 19, Shalfleet the broad W tower is like a small keep, with no access
259 except from within the church and only very small openings;
clearly built for defence. The church retains a remarkable C12
11 N doorway with a lively scene on a tympanum. At Yaverland
p. 310, are a complex Late Norman doorway and chancel arch; the
12 church adjoins the C17 manor house to whose predecessor it
was an appendage. The small church at Wootton had a similar relationship with an adjoining, vanished manor house; it has a fine doorway with zigzag and billet moulding. At Northwood

Shalfleet church, south elevation.
From Percy Stone, *The Architectural Antiquities of the Isle of Wight*, 1891

is a comparable doorway, and arcades of a characteristic late C12 Island type; they have round piers, capitals with square abaci chamfered at the corners, and pointed arches. There is similar work in arcades at Brading, Freshwater, Brighstone, *p. 139,*
Arreton and Whitwell. The arcade at St Mary, Carisbrooke, 18
of similar date, has round capitals that show a dense array of scallop decoration. This arcade cut through a wall in which the outlines of two small round-headed windows indicate that there was a substantial church here in early to mid-Norman times. Carisbrooke had one of seven Island churches the patronage of which was granted *c.* 1066–70 to the abbey of Lire in Normandy. In 1147 the latter established a small dependent priory alongside the church, which it shared with the parish until dissolved in 1415 as an 'alien' priory. Nothing remains of the C12 conventual buildings. The very small church at Bonchurch is of C12 origin and contains remains of a Romanesque WALL PAINTING, with draped figures and a tower – a remarkable, if fragmentary survival.

The Thirteenth Century

The Island has some striking architecture of the EARLY ENGLISH period.

The bishops of Winchester had a manor house at Swainston, E of Calbourne. It was not a regular episcopal residence, but formed a base for the estate which the bishops held around Calbourne, and provided accommodation for them on their visits to the Island. Much of it survives as part of the p. 279 present mansion (mainly C18 and later). A small wing contains C12 fabric, with a window of two round-headed lights – a rare survival of such a feature in an essentially domestic building. The main extant part of the medieval house is a large room over an undercroft, with a Geometrical E window and lancets (together with later windows) elsewhere. This was probably a chamber related to a former great hall which may have stood on the site of the main part of the present mansion.

Among CHURCHES with early work of the period, Calbourne has notable E windows to the chancel and S chapel. Each has a pair of lancets with a separate circular light above – a prototype for traceried windows. At Brading the W tower p. 169 has open arches to N, W and S. Newchurch has an impressive crossing with arches on three sides.

Quarr Abbey was founded in 1131 by Baldwin de Redvers for Savignac monks, who soon after merged with the Cistercians. It was the only full-scale MONASTERY on the Island. There are scanty remains, mainly C13, of the conventual buildings; some are incorporated into C19 structures on the site. Other monastic institutions on the Island were dependencies of abbeys on the Continent, including that at Carisbrooke already mentioned. St Cross Priory at Newport, of which nothing survives, was founded in the C12 as a cell to the abbey of Tiron in France. A small Cluniac priory was established in or before the C12 beside the coast at St Helens. Part of its small C13 tower survives in triangular form, having been sliced diagonally in the C18, and preserved as a landmark for vessels. There was another small priory on the site of the later mansion at Appuldurcombe. All these offshoots of Continental monasteries were closed as 'alien priories' by the early C15.

The successive members of the de Redvers family, earls of Devon, held the lordship of CARISBROOKE CASTLE until Baldwin de Redvers died in 1262. The lordship was inherited by his sister Isabella de Fortibus or Forz, then a young widow (of William de Fortibus, Earl of Aumale or Albemarle), reputedly the richest woman in England. Her daughter Aveline married Edmund (Crouchback), son of Henry III, but died in 1274; Aveline and Edmund are buried separately under sumptuous tombs in Westminster Abbey. Isabella made Carisbrooke her main residence and carried out many additions and improvements to the private apartments. Most of her work there does not survive, but in the W curtain wall is what amounts to a window seat: a polygonal vaulted recess with a two-light opening flanked by stone benches. In *c.* 1270 she 16, p. 110 added a private chapel, internal fragments of which are incorporated in the present staircase wing, including shafts, capitals and indications of vaulting. They show that it was a building of exceptional quality, comparable to the fine porch which she, as patron, provided for Christchurch Priory on the mainland.

Two Island CHURCHES, Arreton and Shalfleet, have delicate late C13 work for which Isabella may have had some 18, 19,
responsibility (Arreton was associated with Quarr Abbey of *p. 19*
which she was patron; Christchurch Priory held lands at Shalfleet). At Arreton the chancel was extended and a S chapel built; the windows are Geometrical with finely detailed shafting. The three-bay chancel arcade is a *tour de force* with tall slender Purbeck marble columns and arches which branch from cylindrical springing blocks a short distance above the capitals – a distinctive pattern found in the almost identical S arcade at Shalfleet. There is comparable work on a smaller scale in Hampshire churches, including Milford-on-Sea (associated with Christchurch) and Wymering, Portsmouth (a manor which had been held by the de Fortibus family). Isabella was evidently a notable patron of architecture, and stylistic affinities to work in Westminster Abbey may not be coincidental, given her connections with royalty.

The Later Middle Ages

There is little late medieval work of note in Island CHURCHES apart from TOWERS. That at Chale is a fine though simple composition of the early to mid C15. The very tall tower of St
Mary, Carisbrooke, *c.* 1470, has an impressive outline with 20
pinnacled parapet (reminiscent of some Dorset towers), and gargoyles under string courses, but it suffers from insignificant belfry lights. There is a smaller version at Gatcombe.
More remarkable is the tower at Freshwater, which began in 21
the C13 as a bellcote supported by a giant arched structure attached to the W front. In the C15 the bellcote was removed to make way for the top storey of a tower which incorporated the outside arch as its western support, and was built eastwards into the church. There are notable Late Perp ARCADES between chancels and chapels at Brading, Brighstone and Mottistone. Also remarkable are small PORCHES with pointed tunnel-vaulted roofs and transverse ribs at Arreton, Niton and Whitwell; their precise dating is uncertain. Mention must be made of the diminutive churches at Bonchurch and St
Lawrence in the Undercliff area, of mixed medieval and later *pp. 22, 249*
dates; these are still used for worship although superseded as parish churches by Victorian ones nearby.

The small S transept at Godshill has a roof with moulded arched braces, panelled in the West Country tradition. In the gable-head outside is an arched canopy for a sanctus bell. Very probably the transept was built (or remodelled) as a

Bonchurch, old church, aquatint by Charles Tomkins.
From Tomkins, *A Tour to the Isle of Wight*, 1796

CHANTRY CHAPEL for which a licence was obtained in 1520 by Sir John Leigh of Appuldurcombe (he died in 1529; for his monument *see* p. 155).

On the E wall of the transept at Godshill is a very unusual,
22 vivid, WALL PAINTING showing Christ crucified on a tree which divides into three branches, with foliage. On either side were representations of textiles (now showing only faintly), which probably framed a setting for sculptured figures attached to the wall (these are now lost). The whole composition must have made a dramatic background to the altar. It would have been appropriate for a chantry chapel commemorating the Leigh family, one of the richest on the Island at the time (their wealth descended to the Worsleys of Appuldurcombe, *see* p. 65).

Other wall paintings include the C12 one at Bonchurch (*see* p. 19) and, at Shorwell, an elaborate representation of St Christopher, *c.* 1470. This, unusually, depicts scenes from legends associated with the saint, surrounding his figure bearing the Christ child. MONUMENTS before the C16 are represented by BRASSES, of which the late C14 knights at Calbourne and Freshwater are the oldest. Others are at Arreton and Shorwell (early C16). Brading has an incised slab to John
p. 93 de Cherewin (†1441), which must once have been quite splendid.

Important building works continued at CARISBROOKE
15 CASTLE in the C14, especially in the GATEHOUSE. Two large round turrets, including cross-shaped arrowslits, were added

on each side of the entrance archway in 1335–6. The gatehouse was heightened in the 1380s as part of a series of operations for improving the defences of the Solent area, with which *Henry Yevele* and *William Wynford* were concerned. They were two leading master masons of the period; the first was responsible for the king's works at Westminster and possibly for the design of Canterbury Cathedral nave, the second for major work at Winchester. The heightening includes openings like inverted keyholes, suitable for primitive handguns – the earliest survival of such features on an English castle, although there are slightly older examples in the town walls at Southampton.

John de Langford, Constable of Carisbrooke Castle (an important post under the overlord) from 1334 to 1342, built a MANOR HOUSE at Chale, in stone, of which much remains in the house now called Chale Abbey. What survives is mainly *p. 117* an upper-floor room (now subdivided) over an undercroft, with a smaller room and undercroft at right angles. These together may have formed a solar wing to a vanished great hall, much as has been suggested for the bishop's house at Swainston. Nearby is a fine early C16 barn of stone, with one original truss remaining in the roof.

Little else remains of DOMESTIC BUILDING from before *c.* 1500 on the Island. Haseley Manor, Arreton, originally a grange of Quarr Abbey but now mostly C17 and later, has a truss in its S wing which has been dated 1440–60 by dendrochronology. Rew Street Farmhouse, near Gurnard, retains evidence of crucks, possibly of *c.* 1400, within a transformed building. The scarcity of surviving early timber-framed construction in Island buildings is discussed in the following section.

Mention must be made of one lost medieval house, Knighton Gorges to the N of Newchurch, demolished in 1821. *p. 24* An engraving shows it to have been large and complex, with many details, including gables and mullioned windows, clearly of C16–C17 date. However, because of the irregular ways in which these features were disposed, it is unlikely to have been built *de novo* during that period. Almost certainly it was a large medieval manor house altered piecemeal; this is confirmed by a description of a window which must have dated from the mid to late C13.

The Island possesses one late medieval building which is a unique survival. On St Catherine's Hill, half a mile from the coast near Chale, is a slender octagonal tower built in 1314 13 and used as a prototype LIGHTHOUSE. It was attached to a small oratory, of which foundations survive. The tower rises 35 ft (8 metres) above ground level and ends with an eight-sided pyramidal roof, below which, on each face, is a small square-topped opening through which light from a fire inside could be diffused.

Newchurch, Knighton Gorges, engraving.
From Sir Henry Englefield, *Description . . . of the Isle of Wight*, 1816

Medieval Towns

Four places on the medieval Island could be regarded as towns: Newport, Yarmouth, Newtown and Brading. The first three were founded as new urban settlements – among the 150 or more NEW TOWNS established in England by the king, or by feudal or ecclesiastical magnates, between the C11 and the mid C14. Newport, Newtown and to a lesser degree Yarmouth retain remarkable evidence of regular medieval street layouts.

NEWPORT was founded *c.* 1190 by Richard de Redvers, lord of Carisbrooke Castle, at the head of the Medina estuary over a mile from his stronghold. It was ambitiously planned, with two long E–W streets and shorter parallel ones, and a N–S thoroughfare which widened in its central part to accommodate a market. Another marketplace, St Thomas Square, was formed between the two principal streets, containing the church. A diagonal street led NE to the quay. This street pattern remains essentially intact; the most significant change resulted from market stalls being replaced by permanent structures, forming irregular islanded blocks in St Thomas Square on either side of the church. Such infilling of market areas was common in English towns and cities from the late medieval period onwards.

YARMOUTH was an earlier foundation (*c.* 1170) by the same Richard de Redvers, adjoining the wide estuary of the River Yar. It has a long wide N–S central space and a narrow street leading E, with offshoots from both. The town declined in the later Middle Ages, partly because of attacks by the French,

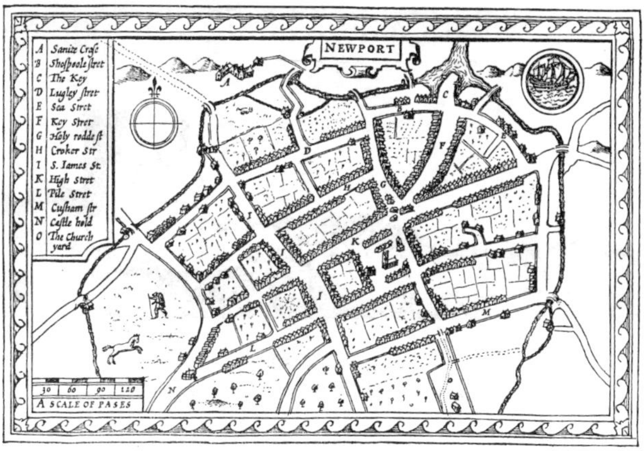

Newport, town map.
Detail from John Speed's map of Wight, 1611

but recovered in some measure by the C17. (Redvers also established the town of Lymington across the Solent; a ferry still connects the two towns.)

NEWTOWN (sometimes called Francheville) was established in 1256 by a bishop of Winchester, beside a navigable creek in his manor of Swainston: a late example in a series of towns founded or expanded by the bishops, in Hampshire and elsewhere, in the C12 and C13. There were two parallel E–W streets, and two wider N–S thoroughfares. The French devastated the town in 1377 and it never recovered; today it has a few houses within the pattern of former streets, parts of which are rough tracks.

THE SIXTEENTH AND SEVENTEENTH CENTURIES

Military Building

During the Tudor and early Stuart periods there were recurrent threats of attack from France and Spain. The Island was vulnerable as a potential base from which to attack the mainland. From 1538 coastal FORTRESSES were built from Kent to Cornwall, with a cluster around the Solent. These included Southsea Castle near Portsmouth, and Hurst and Calshot castles at the end of spits projecting from the mainland. On the Island, two relatively small forts were built on either side

Cowes Castle.
Engraving by Francis Place, *c.* 1690

of the mouth of the Medina. That on the W side remains, very much altered, as Cowes Castle, now the headquarters of the Royal Yacht Squadron. (A larger fort was built on the coast at Sandown, replaced in the C17 because of erosion, but no structural work from either period remains there.)

27 YARMOUTH CASTLE was built in 1545–7, a rectangle with strong curtain walls, which largely survive. Its most remarkable feature, now altered, is an angle bastion at the SE corner. This had flanks which faced along the lines of a former moat, and outer walls forming a sharp angle. Guns were mounted in two tiers behind gunports, and probably on the roof. Angle bastions had by then been developed in southern Europe, but this is the oldest extant example in England. They provided better protection than rounded bastions, which are features of many of Henry VIII's earlier forts. Yarmouth Castle was remodelled in stages over the century or so after it was built.

3 CARISBROOKE CASTLE was the hub of the Island's defensive system, for which its overlords – by late Tudor times called Governors of the Isle of Wight – had general responsibility (*see* p. 107). Sir George Carey (later Lord Hunsdon), a relative of Queen Elizabeth, was Governor from 1583. He strengthened its original perimeter and from 1597 employed *Federigo Gianibelli,* an Italian military engineer, to form an outer ring
p. 108 of earthen ramparts. These have a low profile, following the military practice of the period, with stone retaining walls, large polygonal bastions and an outer gateway with pediment. Carisbrooke Castle is therefore remarkable in retaining evidence of defensive work from Saxon to late Tudor times.

Around the 1620s there was a requirement that every Island parish should maintain a gun for local defence. This might be accommodated in a special building or even in an extension to the church. Examples of each are the small gun shed N of the church at Brading, and a W extension of the S aisle of Shorwell church.

Mottistone Manor, drawing by Reginald Blomfield. From Percy Stone, *The Architectural Antiquities of the Isle of Wight*, 1891

Houses

The later C16 and early C17 was a period of prosperity for the Island. This arose partly from the defence precautions, with building works and military placements, and partly from ships sailing along the Channel anchoring in the Medina estuary, or elsewhere off the Island coasts, to replenish their supplies. Agriculture was stimulated, bringing wealth to landowners. Nine MANOR HOUSES built or enlarged during this period substantially survive, all except one built of local stone. Most are E-shaped and gabled, with square-headed mullioned (and often transomed) windows, following the usual patterns of the period. Two of the grandest, North Court and Wolverton *p. 277* Manor, are at Shorwell. Wolverton was started by John Dingley (†1596) who, as Deputy Governor of the Isle of Wight, was partly responsible for defence precautions. It has a notable two-storey porch with flat roof and hollow angle columns. North Court was built *c.* 1615 by Sir John Leigh, a 28 former Deputy Governor. Unusually for houses of its size and date, it has only one wing. West Court nearby is smaller and *p. 276* more irregular. The main part of Mottistone Manor is thought to have been built *c.* 1567 by Sir Thomas Cheke, of a family with important Court connections. Another Cheke built Merston Manor, Merstone, *c.* 1615; unlike the others it is of brick, with stone dressings. Arreton Manor of 1637–9 is 29 a conservative work for the date, relatively little altered. Sheat *p. 151* Manor, Gatcombe, *c.* 1607, has a castellated porch. Yaverland Manor was built *c.* 1620 for a family which had made a fortune supplying ships; as on many of the other stone-built houses, the chimneystacks are of brick. Barton Manor, Whippingham, retains two impressive early to mid-C17 elevations, although the other frontages were rebuilt and the interior re-formed in the C19 under Prince Albert. A few other substantial houses retain C17 parts, including Nunwell, home of the Oglander family, where a wing of the period is partly of brick.

Mention must be also made of the C16 house on the site of the present C18 mansion at Appuldurcombe. This was the seat of Sir John Leigh (*see* p. 22), whose daughter and heiress married Sir James Worsley, a close associate of Henry VII and
p. 65 Henry VIII. A rough drawing exists of the Tudor house, which may have been enlarged from the buildings of the former priory on the site. It was irregular, with gables and mullioned windows.

By the beginning of the C17, stone, whether sandstone from the S of the Island or limestone from the N (*see* p. 7), was the normal building material for SMALLER HOUSES. Several substantial farmhouses were built or enlarged during the period. Typically they were symmetrical with central doorway and mullioned windows. Notable relatively unaltered examples include Lower House and Walpan at Chale, and Writtleston
p. 96 House (formerly Hill Farmhouse) near Brading. The last two have two-storey porches; that at Writtleston was added to the earlier house.

Because of the availability of stone, the history of lesser domestic buildings in the C16–mid C17 is markedly different from that of comparable buildings in southern Hampshire, where most houses were timber-framed until brick gradually became the principal material during the C17. The most remarkable TIMBER-FRAMED HOUSE on the Island where much original work survives is now part of the Wax Works Museum, S of the church at Brading. This was a jettied house of *c.* 1600 or before. The close studding of the upper storey, the moulded bressumer and its four supporting brackets are all original, but other details are mainly the results of C20 restoration. Other timber-framed houses survived W of Brading church until the late C19. The Old House at the S end of High Street, Ryde, is an interesting survival from the original hamlet of Upper Ryde. Some early C17 box framing is visible, infilled with brick nogging (probably original) in herringbone fashion. There is now nothing comparable elsewhere on the Island, apart from small amounts of timber-frame construction in a few otherwise unremarkable cottages (not recorded in this Guide).

Domestic Interiors

The larger houses on the Island dating from before *c.* 1700 are meticulously illustrated in Percy Stone's *Architectural Antiquities of the Isle of Wight* of 1891. His drawings are invaluable for internal details, especially of CHIMNEYPIECES, of which the Island has a notable series. They are typical of English designs of *c.* 1580–1660, derived initially from prints

Shorwell, Wolverton Manor, chimneypiece, elevation. From Percy Stone, *The Architectural Antiquities of the Isle of Wight*, 1891

or engravings from Flanders or elsewhere in Northern Europe, which were widely available from the later C16. Classical motifs and classically inspired patterns are used without overall understanding of the Orders (which of course did not become widespread in England until the mid C17). The local chimneypieces are good examples of their kind. Caryatids and similar figures abound, particularly on pilasters flanking the main panels, and less often to the sides of fireplaces. There are grotesque representations of humans and animals, and panels with writhing creatures or arabesque and foliage patterns. Merston Manor has three good chimneypieces, though none is in its original place; Wolverton Manor has two, recently repaired; Arreton Manor had two – one *in situ*, the other now at the Priory Bay Hotel, St Helens. Kingston Manor, a house of many dates, also has a good, fairly late C17 chimneypiece. A room in Arreton Manor retains PANELLING of the period, with Ionic pilasters decorated with vine stems; Merston Manor has simpler panelling. At Yaverland Manor the wood-framed archway into the stair hall has carvings in the same tradition.

pp. 77, 160

p. 311

No record of any craftsmen's names has been found for these features, but it is unlikely that all the furnishings in question were made on the mainland and shipped. There is no evidence that Southampton, Portsmouth or Winchester were centres for such craftsmanship, and there are few comparable furnishings of the period, extant or recorded, on the adjoining Hampshire mainland. Salisbury is one place where such features may have been carved, but journeys from there to a port, followed by sea crossings, would have been difficult. It is suggested here that there was a group of woodcarvers on the Island in the early to mid C17, probably based in Newport (as the chief town), who produced all or many of the works in question, and who may also have worked on church furnishings (*see* below). However, no evidence for such a local group has been found.

Churches

More building work was done in English CHURCHES in the century and a quarter after the Reformation than is generally supposed, and this is particularly evident on the Island. The church at Yarmouth, consecrated in 1626, is simple Gothic Survival. Much of it could have been built a hundred years before, apart from windows which are square-headed, mullioned and without cusps, as in contemporary houses; the E window (re-set in the C19) has six lights. St Mary, Cowes, built during the Commonwealth (1657) and since replaced, had a similar five-light E window. Shorwell is the most enigmatic 26, *p. 271* church for work of this period. Sir John Leigh of North Court promoted work of uncertain extent there in the early C17. He may have built the tower, with its short stone spire, and perhaps the five-bay arcades. Between the second and third bays of the N arcade (from the W) is a polygonal stone pulpit, with cusped panels. These arcades and pulpit are often cited as C15, but the capitals do not look medieval, nor is such a pulpit, particularly in this location, likely to have been a medieval feature in a small village church. The work probably dates from 1620, the year recorded on a fine wooden semi-octagonal canopy over the pulpit. The simple pews are probably also early C17, and are largely arranged laterally, much as in an Oxford or Cambridge college chapel. So we may have here an unusual example of an Anglican arrangement from the time between the Elizabethan Settlement and the Laudian period. Godshill church was altered in the early C17. The W window of the S aisle dates from then, and so possibly does *p. 153* the six-bay arcade running nearly for the length of the church (which has the unusual plan of parallel naves and chancels). It is more sophisticated than the Shorwell arcades, with moulded capitals and tall bases, which suggest that pews abutted when the arcade was first built. At Shalfleet the S *p. 19* aisle was widened, with very odd window tracery, probably in the C17. The nave arcades at Newchurch may have been

re-formed during the period. Other churches with post-Reformation Gothic-inspired work include Carisbrooke (simplified
Perp E window following demolition of the chancel), and
probably Niton with its W tower and short stone spire. Else- *p. 191*
where, C17 features including windows, recorded on old illustrations (as at Brighstone), were replaced in Victorian times.

The old St Thomas, Newport was rebuilt in the C19 but is *p. 173*
well recorded in engravings. It was altered and embellished in
the early to mid C17, with upper tiers of square-headed
uncusped windows in the aisles. These lit galleries, early examples of their kind. The wooden PULPIT, given by the mayor 33
in 1631, survives in the Victorian church – among the finest
of its period in England. The panels have figures in relief representing Virtues and other subjects; the canopy has figures
on the crest, a text on the frieze and a dove underneath. The
pulpit has been attributed to *Thomas Caper*, a craftsman of
Flemish origin associated with Salisbury, of whom nothing
more is known. It is obviously related to contemporary secular
woodwork, especially chimneypieces (*see* p. 28). There are
several smaller C17 pulpits on the Island, notably at Whitwell, *p. 300,*
Brighstone, Mottistone, Shalfleet and Wootton, the last with *32*
a fine canopy. At Shorwell a charming small font cover is
topped by a dove.

Church Monuments

The Island is notable for C16–C17 church monuments, thanks
largely to the series at Brading and Godshill, commemorating
respectively the Oglanders of Nunwell and the Worsleys of
Appuldurcombe. But the oldest of special quality is that to
Lady Wadham of *c.* 1520 at St Mary, Carisbrooke, with a large 24
canopy, densely cusped and panelled. She is a small figure
kneeling among six clearly disabled people, representing a
charity she supported. The monument to Sir John Leigh,
†1529, and his wife at Godshill must be by the same crafts- 23
man – it is equally busy in cusping and tracery, and has a
similar crest with angels and crenellation. The recumbent effigies are rigid, although hers has finely delineated drapery. The
tomb of Oliver Oglander, †1536, at Brading is related stylisti- 25
cally; there is no effigy, but the panels on one side have lively
sculptures of his family, while on the other are figures of aged
and infirm people – he too supported a charity.

With the tomb of Sir James Worsley, †1538, and his wife
Anne (daughter of Sir John Leigh), †1557, at Godshill we are
in a different world artistically to that of Sir John's tomb
nearby. No trace of Gothic, but a pediment, fluted pilasters
and arabesque frieze; the figures are small and kneel at desks.
The sophistication is not surprising since Sir James was
closely associated with Henry VIII. One assumes that the
tomb was executed nearer to Anne's death than to that of her

husband – by which time the effects of the Renaissance were
30 more established. The monument to Richard Worsley, †1565 (who organized the building of the Solent forts), is fairly similar but has no figures.

Back to Brading, and a different world again. The wooden
31 effigies of Sir William Oglander, †1608, and his son Sir John, †1655, are 'antiquarian' representations of medieval knights in armour. Both were in the possession of Sir John when he made his will in 1649, directing that they be used over his father's and his own tombs. The one on Sir William's tomb is stiffly

Newport church, Horsey monument (†1582), elevation.
From Percy Stone, *The Architectural Antiquities of the Isle of Wight*, 1891

recumbent, but Sir John's is in a lively posture. Stylistic details related to the mid C17 indicate that the effigy was carved then and is not a medieval survival. An earlier, more conventional representation of a knight in armour is that of Sir Edward Horsey, †1582, in alabaster, at St Thomas, Newport. The tomb of Elizabeth Leigh, †1619 (wife of Sir John Leigh of North p. 273
Court), at Shorwell has affinities with it.

THE EIGHTEENTH CENTURY

Country Houses

The dominant C18 country house on the Island was APPUL- 37, 38
DURCOMBE, built from 1701 by Sir Robert Worsley on the site p. 67
of the Tudor mansion; it was incomplete when he died in 1747. The designer was almost certainly *John James,* a leading architect who held posts including those of Clerk of Works to Greenwich Hospital and, later, Surveyor to St Paul's Cathedral; he was influenced by the Baroque tradition, though in a restrained way. Appuldurcombe is built of sandstone with Portland stone dressings; its main (E) front has broad wings under strong pediments, giant Corinthian pilasters, and a doorway in the centre which is not in itself prominent but is emphasized by flanking Corinthian columns. An engraving in *Vitruvius Britannicus* shows a broken pediment over these columns, making the composition more Baroque than it is now, but if it ever existed this feature had been removed by 1713. The S front was altered by Lord Yarborough (who inherited through marriage), *c.* 1820; he added a Tuscan colonnade. The house is now largely a shell, with a temporary roof over the great hall, which has been partly restored by English Heritage to a suggestion of its state after it was altered in the 1770s. The E front has been thoroughly repaired. The splendid Freemantle Gate ½ m. from the house, is probably also of p. 72
the 1770s; it has been attributed, with no firm evidence, to *James Wyatt.* It looks like a triumphal arch, flanked by Ionic columns under a majestic entablature. Appuldurcombe is set in a landscape of boldly rounded chalk and sandstone hills, which *Capability Brown* embellished for Sir Richard Worsley.

There are no other grand C18 houses, but several of moderate scale. The first properly CLASSICAL HOUSE on the Island may have been the present George Hotel at Yarmouth, probably built *c.* 1690 for Sir Robert Holmes, Governor of the Isle of Wight. It has been altered externally but retains fine panelled rooms and an impressive staircase. Thorley Manor nearby, 1712, has a deep modillion cornice to its hipped roof, and tall chimneys. Billingham Manor, a house of many periods, has a good N front in brick of *c.* 1720–2, with moulded

string courses and architraves, and an excellent staircase of the same date. Other houses with good early to mid-C18
39 STAIRCASES include North Court (Shorwell), Gatcombe Park and Nunwell; Wolverton Manor at Shorwell has, unexpect-
40 edly, an C18 Chinese Chippendale staircase with open square-patterned balustrading.

At Nunwell, the main part of the principal frontage was refaced in the mid C18 in mathematical tiles (an unusual material for the Island), with a notable rusticated doorway. The E front was remodelled *c.* 1768 in a very different way, in grey brick with sparse red dressings, with a central canted bay. The present library has a delicate ceiling of the same date. At Ningwood Manor (Shalfleet), a handsome balustraded front was built for a London banker, *c.* 1784. Swainston, the bishop's medieval house, was partly rebuilt *c.* 1750 and enlarged in 1798 by *William Porden* with a remarkable S front.

Houses in Towns

Newport was by far the most significant urban centre in the C18, and had the character of a substantial market town. Cowes developed during the period, with maritime yards on both sides of the Medina estuary. Newport has numerous C18 TOWN HOUSES fairly widely distributed along the principal streets and spaces; many now have shops at ground level. The
36 prototype is God's Providence House at a corner of St Thomas Square, dated 1701, with a shell-hood porch, modillion cornice and, inside, a fine staircase. Other early C18 examples include Seal House in Sea Street, Chantry House in Pyle Street with wavy-edged brick lintels, and Red House in High Street. In Cowes, No. 89 High Street has an impressive brick front of the mid to late C18. Claremont House on Market Hill and Ivy House on Sun Hill are free-standing houses of the same period, set at right angles to steep streets which climb W from High Street.

From the mid C18, grey header BRICKS with red brick quoins and window frames were frequently used on the Island (as over much of mid-southern England) – the term 'grey' covering shades of blue-grey, purple and grey-brown. By 1800 buff brick was coming into general fashion, on the Island as elsewhere. No names of local designers of C18 town houses are known; they were the works of builders with knowledge of classical motifs (partly, no doubt, obtained through pattern books), which they sometimes used in original or unorthodox ways.

BAY WINDOWS of the mid C18 to the early C19 are common, particularly in the towns. Sometimes they are rounded or canted projections with separate sash windows. Many others are almost continuously glazed – usually with three contiguous sashes (occasionally more). Where continuously glazed

bay windows are curved, the individual sashes usually follow the curves; such windows were notable feats of Georgian carpentry. Being constructed substantially of timber, they were uncommon in what is now central London because of the building regulations operating there from the early C18. For this reason, general studies of Georgian town houses tend to underestimate their importance during the period, particularly in many coastal and market towns in southern England. Bay windows are normally found on one floor of a façade (often the first floor), but sometimes they rise through two storeys, and occasionally three. Good examples in Newport can be seen on No. 54 Pyle Street facing St 51
James Square (first floor) and No. 43 High Street (first and second floors). There is an impressive series dating from *c.* 1800 or soon after in Bath Road, Cowes, where they rise through three storeys on Bars Hill House and through two on Exmouth House. Related to domestic bay windows are bowed SHOPFRONTS. There is a fine post-1800 pair on God's Providence House, Newport (*see* above), and elegant smaller examples in village settings at Godshill and on the post office at Shorwell.

Public and Commercial Buildings

Newport, Yarmouth and Newtown each sent two members to Parliament, with a limited electorate, until the Reform Act of 1832. C18 Newtown, a hamlet on the site of a vanished medieval town, retained a borough corporation which organized elections, and for this a TOWN HALL was provided in 35
1699 – a substantial building in brick with stone dressings, with a Tuscan portico added in 1813. It looks strange on its grassy site. The austere brick Town Hall of 1763 at Yarmouth is set, more appropriately, in the main street. It has the typical form of a small civic hall in a market town, with a main room upstairs, and a ground storey, originally open-arched, where market stalls could be placed. The smaller Old Town Hall at Brading had a similar form; the upper storey was rebuilt in the C19, but the C18 ground floor remains with open arches.

A HOUSE OF INDUSTRY was built in 1771–4 on the out- 42
skirts of Newport. It was a pioneer institution of its kind – serving as a workhouse for the poor and destitute of the whole Island, in place of the limited facilities previously provided in each parish. It was not until after the passing of the New Poor Law in 1834 that workhouses of this sort, serving areas wider than individual parishes, were introduced all over England. Much of the building of 1771–4 survives as part of the present St Mary's Hospital. Its main range, overlooking a courtyard, has a very large pediment with a lunette window.

Flour milling was an important trade on the C18 Island. Much of the product was shipped to the mainland, particularly Portsmouth. There was a cluster of WATERMILLS around Newport, powered by the Medina above its estuary head, and its tributary the Lukely Brook. The most impressive survival is Crocker's Mill of 1773 (now residential) on the latter stream. Several TIDE MILLS formerly existed beside estuaries and inlets; one (also now residential) survives at Yarmouth. A WINDMILL at Bembridge has been preserved by the National Trust. A former BREWERY AND MALTHOUSE of *c.* 1800 in Crocker Street, Newport, has been partly preserved through residential conversion. It has an impressive arched façade in grey brick with red dressings, including small iron grilles now adapted as windows. Similar grilles remain in another former commercial complex which included warehouses (now converted to the Arts Centre), adjoining the nearby Quay.

Churches

The Island has two C18 CHURCHES, both Roman Catholic.
57 St Thomas of Canterbury, Newport, of 1791, is claimed to be the first purpose-built Catholic church in England since the Reformation intended for a general congregation (i.e. excluding chapels built for foreign Catholics or privately); this was made possible by the Catholic Emancipation Act, 1791. It is a charming building of red brick with a Tuscan porch under a pediment and two tiers of windows, the upper lighting a gallery. In 1796–7 a church with the same dedication was built in Cowes by the same patron, Mrs Elizabeth Heneage. This
56 was badly altered in the C19, but the interior has a very fine termination with giant fluted pilasters containing a rounded arch behind the altar.

Little notable work of the period in Anglican churches on the Island survived Victorian restoration or rebuilding. Newchurch has a panelled pulpit of 1725, but its very large hexagonal canopy is now used as a table. There are two special MONUMENTS from the C18 or just before. Sir Richard Holmes, †1692, is commemorated in Yarmouth church by an over-life-size standing figure in Roman dress. The statue is said to have been captured, without a head, from a foreign ship; the head, of inferior quality, was added. In Godshill church Sir Robert Worsley, †1747, builder of Appuldurcombe, and his brother are commemorated by two busts with Roman drapery, under a sumptuous marble entablature supported by pink pillars. This has been attributed to *Peter Scheemakers*. The finest of many C18 and early C19 wall monuments are three at Arreton to members of the Worsley Holmes family, †1811, †1814 and †1825, with figurative scenes: the first two by *Sir Richard Westmacott*, the other, of comparable quality, by the little-known *J. Haskoll*.

Vernacular Building

Although most of the smaller C18 houses in the principal towns are of brick, farmhouses, cottages and farm buildings continued to be built in LOCAL STONE where this was con- 5, 41 veniently available (*see* pp. 7–9 and 28). Usually the stonework was in the form of rubble, sometimes roughly coursed, but cut stones of ashlar type were used for quoins and other dressings, and at times for stretches of wall. Occasionally hard varieties of chalk were used for simple buildings. Some small houses and cottages were built of two or more types of stone, including for instance pale and darker sandstones, to picturesque effect. THATCH, using straw, remained the commonest roofing material for small houses and cottages outside the towns throughout the period. Even some larger houses, including farmhouses, were thatched, especially in the early part of the C18. TILES, made locally in association with brickmaking, were the normal roofing material for more substantial buildings. There are a few instances on the Island of the partial use of STONE SLABS on roofs of larger houses, most notably on Mottistone Manor, where they form the lower *p. 27* courses of the covering of the main roofs, the upper parts of which are tiled. These slabs were probably shipped from the Purbeck area of Dorset.

THE EARLY NINETEENTH CENTURY

Romantic Houses and Landscapes

From about 1790 the Island was 'discovered' by wealthy, sometimes aristocratic people who built houses for periodic occupation on choice sites. At first these usually overlooked the Solent, where expanses of sea, fringed by wooded coastlines and enlivened by ships, provided compelling vistas. More adventurous people penetrated further, especially to the dramatic scenery in and around the Undercliff (*see* pp. 5–6). As ferry services from Portsmouth improved, more and more people came to the Island for holidays or for periodic or permanent residence.

Lord Henry Seymour commissioned *James Wyatt* to build NORRIS CASTLE on high ground NE of Cowes; started in *p. 195* 1799, a triumphant piece of Romantic design. The surrounding landscape was probably shaped by *Humphry Repton*; the drive approaching from East Cowes sweeps past a stables–farmyard block made to look like a smaller castle, a forerunner of the main building.

John Nash first visited the Island in the 1790s, and in 1798–1802 he built EAST COWES CASTLE as his country

Yaverland parsonage.
Engraving by George Brannon, 1823

retreat. It was at first fairly small, with a skyline formed by a round tower and taller thinner turret, on rising ground just behind the town. Nash repeatedly enlarged and embellished it; when he died at the castle in 1835 it was an architectural fantasy, with varied towers and turrets, two large conservatories, and richly decorated rooms of differing shapes. Alas, it was demolished in the 1950s–60s – the most serious architectural loss suffered on the Island in the last hundred years.

Nash displayed his versatility in numerous buildings on the Island. At his extensions to Westover, Calbourne, in 1813–15, one façade has broad bow windows, and another has a columned veranda extended at either end with delicate ironwork. Very different is his former rectory of the 1820s at Yaverland in an unorthodox Tudor-Jacobean style. Other buildings are attributed to him without certainty, including Hill Grove, Bembridge (now altered), built in 1827 to a most unusual design including a small dome.

Nash was associated with the Ward family at NORTHWOOD
50 HOUSE (originally called Bellevue), W of Cowes, where he designed two classical lodges, one of which remains. It adjoins St Mary's church, with *Nash*'s own remarkable tower (*see* below). Most of the present Northwood House is the work of *G.J.J. Mair* (who had been articled to Decimus Burton), *c.* 1836–46. It has a complicated external form, generally classical, including an entrance wing with a low dome. The interior is confusing, but has fascinating detailed work – notably

'Egypt Corner', where columns, entablatures and ceiling have 48
motifs and decoration of Egyptian derivation, painted in bright colours.

There are, or were, notable LANDSCAPES associated with *Humphry Repton*; that at Norris Castle has been mentioned. In about 1814 he was consulted by the Swainston Estate, where some extant features may survive, including a small curved lake, a stone-arched bridge and irregular groups of trees.

Cottages Ornés and Maisons Ornées

Humphry Repton was in professional partnership with Nash until about 1802. His son *George Stanley Repton*, aged only sixteen in that year, continued as Nash's assistant for a considerable time. Two of George Repton's notebooks survive, including drawings of what were already described at the time as *cottages ornés*. Strictly the term applied to very small dwellings such as estate workers' houses or lodges, designed as exaggerated versions of vernacular cottages. Typically they had elaborated roofs (often thatched), tall chimneys, windows arranged to Picturesque effect and, sometimes, rustic timberwork. Blaise Hamlet near Bristol has one of the best-known collections, designed *c.* 1810 by Nash. However, the term *cottage orné* is often applied to more substantial houses treated in this manner, for which the term *maison ornée* seems more appropriate.

The Island has many notable buildings designed in this way. Debourne Lodge stands at a crossroads W of Northwood House in Cowes (for which it was an entrance lodge). It has a gabled frontage and a side elevation with a recessed veranda fronted by a pair of rough tree trunks with small curved braces. These frontages are almost identical with those in an unnamed drawing in one of *George Repton*'s notebooks. Across the road
junction is the Round House, very much in the same manner, 43
although built as a toll house. It is circular, with a conical roof ending in a chimney and fringed by a wavy-edged bargeboard. Both buildings, which date from *c.* 1800 or soon after, must surely have been designed in *Nash*'s office. Nash's work at Westover, Calbourne (*see* above), included three lodges. The main one, in Calbourne village, is of knapped flint (unusual for the Island), with a slate roof. The other two, smaller and thatched, face the road towards Freshwater. (Another – classical this time – is at Cowes, as mentioned above.) 49

Shanklin is a good place to appreciate buildings in the 4
cottage orné tradition. Before the C19 it was a small scattered village, a little inland from a cliff-bound coastline from which
opened the gorge-like Shanklin Chine. The coast, the Chine, *p. 7*
the village itself and the surrounding scenery appealed greatly to early visitors. Barber's *Picturesque Illustrations of the Isle of*

Shanklin.
Engraving, 1870

Wight (1845) describes local cottages 'neatly built of stone, and thatched, standing in the midst of their productive, well-fenced gardens.' By this date the growing village included newly built Picturesque dwellings of varying sizes. Some accommodated lodgers in the summer season; others were rustic retreats for wealthy people. Typical of the latter category was Vernon
45 Cottage, built in 1817 (and later extended in keeping), with a thatched roof over many gables and bargeboards – essentially a *maison ornée* rather than a cottage. The centre of the Old Village is a tight-knit cluster of largely genuine old cottages and deliberately Picturesque early C19 houses.

To the SW of Shanklin is the beginning of the Undercliff with its dramatic scenery. Dunnose Cottage in this setting has typical thatch and bargeboards but, for a *cottage orné*, is disconcertingly symmetrical. Above the rugged coastline close to
44 Niton is Puckaster, built *c.* 1815–20 following a design by *Robert Lugar.* It has been altered more than once and is now a Picturesque, many-gabled composition with a tiled roof (at first it was thatched) and a rounded end elevation with an inset veranda, fronted by rough tree trunks with diagonal
46, braces (much as at the earlier Debourne Lodge). Swan's Nest
p. 240 in St John's Road, Ryde (originally in a rural setting) has a similarly treated veranda in a rounded end elevation. It was built in 1830 and, like Puckaster, was enlarged in Victorian times. On the E outskirts of Ryde is Puckpool House, transformed in 1822–4 by the architect *Lewis Wyatt* as his seaside retreat. Part of this work is still evident on the N side, which

had verandas on two levels, each with two trunk-like supports with angled braces; these survive on the upper floor. Wyatt retired to the house in the 1830s, when he enlarged it in the Gothic style, making it more like an early version of a Victorian villa.

The Growth of Towns

Ryde is an essentially early to mid-C19 town which developed from very small beginnings into an important resort and service centre. (It must be remembered that a seaside resort was not only a holiday location, but was also a place of residence or retirement, continuous or occasional, for people of independent means.) Cowes flourished as a maritime centre, and became a fashionable base for yachting as early as the Regency period. Several coastal villages started to develop as resorts in the early C19; of these Ventnor and Sandown as well as Shanklin grew into sizeable towns later in the century, as described in the next section.

Before *c.* 1800 Lower RYDE was a shoreside hamlet, with a few substantial houses on adjoining coastal sites. Upper Ryde was a small straggling village. In 1810 restrictions against the length of local leases were eased, and the main landowner promoted building on an urban scale. Boats from Portsmouth had previously landed on the beach, but in 1814 the first pier was built. Regular steam ferries were established in the 1820s.
The town developed very quickly – along the seafront, up par- *p. 219*
allel streets leading inland, and on the higher land around. Houses were built piecemeal, singly or in small groups. Union Street, originally linking Lower and Upper Ryde, became the main thoroughfare and was almost continuously developed by 1845, when many of the properties already had shops on the ground floors.

Some of the principal buildings in Ryde were designed by *James Sanderson* (1790–1835), a London-based architect who had trained under Jeffry Wyatt (later Sir Jeffry Wyatville). His
Town Hall of 1829–31 was an impressive classical building even 59,
before additions in the 1860s, with public rooms on the first *p. 228*
floor and space for markets at ground level. Sanderson also designed the only substantial residential TERRACE of the period
on the Island: Brigstocke Terrace, of 1826–9, set on a hillside; 54
twenty-seven bays long with articulated frontages on both sides. (He was not only a classicist; he designed St Clare, a
Romantic house E of the town, and Steephill Castle near Ventnor, *p. 289*
both demolished; his St Thomas church in Ryde, *see* p. 43, is Gothic.) Even more distinguished was *William Westmacott*, the only member of a family famous for sculpture who was
known primarily as an architect. His ROYAL VICTORIA 55,
ARCADE of 1835–6 (named after Victoria as Princess, to *p. 231*
commemorate her early visits to the Island) is internally superb,

with a shallow dome, clerestoried roof and original shopfronts. It is one of the best surviving arcades of so early a date in Britain, although the façade to Union Street has been altered.

No locally based architect's name is recorded for work in
47 Ryde before 1840 (the architect of the sophisticated Westmont House, 1819–21, is unknown). Its numerous early C19 houses and other buildings of quality must have been largely the
53 designs of local builders. They are usually stuccoed (though some are faced in the local limestone, which was still being worked at Binstead and elsewhere). Many have simple pilasters on the upper storeys, and there are several examples of tripartite windows. Bay windows are common, especially
51 ones with flat fronts and rounded angles (as also in Newport). Iron BALCONIES and VERANDAS remain on many houses; No. 23 Castle Street has fine examples on two storeys. Some villas of the period have façades which come out in bold segmental bows. Very few houses of before 1850 in the town are in Gothic or Tudor styles.

COWES continued to flourish, with the building and repair of quite large ships and smaller boats. Some were commercial; others were for the Royal Navy; a significant proportion were used for pleasure sailing. A Yacht Club was founded at Cowes in 1815; the Prince Regent became a member in 1817. It was named the Royal Yacht Squadron in 1833, with Lord Yarborough, owner of Appuldurcombe, as its first Commodore. The two parts of Cowes, East and West, separated by the estuary, had shipyards and wharves fronting the river, irregular streets behind, and outlying houses on the higher ground. At first the commercial activities were mainly in East Cowes, but they expanded on the W side in the C19. West
p. 119 Cowes then developed as the principal part of the divided town, and is generally called 'Cowes' as distinct from East Cowes. One of the focal buildings of the long High Street is the Fountain Hotel of 1803, which has a stuccoed frontage with arched recesses. Blenheim House further S, of 1835 in grey brick with red dressings, also has recesses in its frontage containing the first-floor windows. The firm of Ratseys, sailmakers, occupies a handsome ashlar-faced building – almost the only significant maritime-related structure remaining from the early C19.

60 In NEWPORT, *John Nash* designed the Guildhall of 1814–16 (then called the Town Hall; now the Isle of Wight Museum) on the site of an older civic building. There was a courtroom and a council chamber on the first floor and space for marketing at ground level. The exterior is stuccoed, with a tall Ionic portico facing W along High Street, but the symmetry is disturbed by the tower added to commemorate Queen Victoria's Golden Jubilee. Another significant building, formerly attributed to Nash but now known to be by *William Mortimer*,

is the County Club of 1810–11 in St James Square, with a 6 Doric façade in Portland stone.

The two earliest surviving SCHOOL BUILDINGS on the Island were built through aristocratic patronage. The former Free School in Melville Street, Ryde, founded in 1812 largely at the expense of the Countess Spencer (whose family had a seaside house nearby), is a long simple classical building with a teacher's house at one end. The oldest part of the present primary school at Godshill was rebuilt in 1826 by Lord Yarborough in a similar classical style, with a central doorway under a keystone. The larger, probably later, former teacher's house is almost Neo-Jacobean with dormer gables and hoodmoulds, but it has keystones over the windows. The school of 1833 at Bembridge (now part of a heritage centre) has a wavily bargeboarded gable and an intricate three-light Gothic traceried window. It was possibly by *T.E. Owen* of Portsmouth, who had worked with *Nash* a few years before in the erection of the nearby church, since replaced. Later C19 schools are described on p. 49.

Churches

The tower of St Mary, Cowes, was designed by *Nash* in 1816 58 to include a chapel and mausoleum for the Ward family of the adjoining Northwood House (*see* above). Pevsner found it remarkable, and unusual for the architect, with its sparse use of Neo-Greek motifs and little ornamentation. The rest of the church was rebuilt in Victorian times (*see* p. 51). Ryde did not have a parish church of its own before the mid C19; however, two proprietary chapels (privately owned places of Anglican worship) were opened in 1827. St Thomas, on the site of a *p. 225* rustic chapel built by the chief landowner in 1719, is by *James Sanderson*, normally a classical architect (*see* above). It is pre-Victorian 'Gothick' in local stone with brick quoins (a reversal of the usual respective use of these materials); now a public meeting place, it keeps its galleries. St James, the other pri- *p. 44* vately built chapel, was designed in gimcrack Gothick by an almost unknown London architect, *Greenway Robins*, but was 'restored' in 1968 and deprived of most of its external details. Inside, however, it retains a strong early C19 flavour, with side galleries and thin iron columns rising to four-centred arcades. Ventnor obtained its first church, St Catherine by *Robert* *p. 283* *Ebbels*, in 1836–7. It has an effective tower (formerly with a spire), well set against a hilly background, but the rest has been altered. The finest early C19 church on the Island is Holy Spirit, Newtown, built in 1835 on the site of a ruined medieval chapel in the former town by *A.F. Livesay* of Portsmouth, a sensitive architect whose Gothic had more in common with the seriously revived styles of the 1840s than with the

Ryde, St James.
Engraving, 1840

Gothick of the Georgian aftermath. (His greatest work is Andover church in northern Hampshire, rebuilt from 1840.) The Newtown church has a simple E.E. exterior in stone, and a fine plaster-vaulted interior with 'correct' details. Livesay also restored the medieval church at Calbourne in 1838–42, with an almost convincing Transitional Norman doorway.

Newport retains early NONCONFORMIST CHAPELS, variously altered. The Unitarian meeting house (formerly Baptist) was built in 1775 but enlarged, with a Gothick front, in 1825. The present Baptist church was built in 1812 but its impressive front dates from 1872 (*see* p. 54). The most interesting early Nonconformist building is the former Methodist church (now Apollo Theatre) in Pyle Street, built in 1804 and enlarged in 1833, from when the distinctive brick street front probably dates. It has a broad pediment into which rises an arched recess, containing the doorway, the central window above and a lunette in the arch. Little remains of the once fine galleried interior.

THE VICTORIAN PERIOD

The Queen at Osborne House

Princess Victoria stayed at Norris Castle with her mother in 1831 and 1833. She was charmed with its setting, particularly
p. 195 the views over the Solent with its array of shipping. In 1845 she bought the adjoining Osborne Estate, including an C18 mansion which, over the next six years, she and Prince Albert
67–69 *pp. 201, 203* replaced by the present Osborne House. This, although large and complex, was specifically a House or private residence –

not officially a Palace. No formally recognized architect was involved; *Thomas Cubitt*, the supremely successful developer of Belgravia and other parts of London, designed and built it in collaboration with *Prince Albert*, himself a well-informed authority on a wide range of arts and sciences, including architecture. The style of Osborne is Italianate, the anglicized version of Renaissance classicism which had been developed by Charles Barry in his London clubs and in mansions such as Trentham in Staffordshire (where the Queen had stayed). It is an amalgam of parts: the Pavilion or actual residence; the Household Wing, where the extensive royal household lived; the Main Wing containing the Council Room where constitutional meetings were held, and servicing and servants' accommodation. The skyline is dominated by two similar, but not identical, towers. As a composition, with symmetrical elements grouped asymmetrically, it is comparable to Barry's Houses of Parliament (though in a very different style and location). It is well related to its landscape setting, with formal garden terraces on and just below the crests of the slopes which descend towards the Solent. The house is mainly built of brick faced in stucco, as were most of Cubitt's major buildings in London (although the use of stucco to imitate stone in this way was going out of general favour in the 1840s). However, iron girders, supported on brick arches, were used at each floor level in accordance with the 'fireproof' means of construction then widely used for larger buildings. (This is entirely concealed by internal finishes and decoration.)

The internal work at Osborne was generally carried out by 70–72
Cubitt. For many features, including fireplaces and doors as well as basic equipment for sanitation and water supply, he provided material from his own workshops and stores in London. Much of the plasterwork in cornices, friezes and the like was carried out with patterns, generally of classical inspiration, used in his London houses. However, *Ludwig Grüner* from Dresden, appointed adviser in art to the Queen in 1845, was responsible for much of the more important decoration – for instance in the Grand Corridor of the Household Wing, the Council Chamber, and the principal rooms in the Pavilion. Prince Albert, Cubitt and Grüner together designed the formal gardens, splendidly restored in recent years under English Heritage. Down the slope to the E is a collection of buildings partly related to the upbringing of the Queen's children, including the Swiss Cottage of 1853–4 in imitation of Alpine vernacular building.

Cubitt ceased to work at Osborne in 1851. Responsibility for buildings on the estate passed to *John Blandford* as Clerk of Works (†1857) and then to his successor *J.R. Mann*, both surveyors. The architect *A.J. Humbert* began his association with Osborne when he worked with Prince Albert in rebuilding the local parish church at Whippingham (*see* below) from

1854. The Prince died in 1861, and Humbert designed his mausoleum in Windsor Home Park in conjunction with Grüner. Humbert was associated, certainly or possibly, with numerous ESTATE BUILDINGS related to Osborne, including houses, cottages and lodges, around Whippingham and in East Cowes. Many of these are in Romantic styles, with irregular outlines using variegated materials – in what can be called a development of the *cottage orné* tradition. The most fantastic
76 is Coburg, built in 1870–2 as a pair of cottages to the SE of Whippingham, but it is not certain whether Humbert was responsible for their design.

Resorts, Retirement and Commerce

At the beginning of Victoria's reign Ryde was well established as a resort, while Sandown and Shanklin were scattered villages attracting a few visitors. VENTNOR, in the Undercliff further to the SW, began to attract visitors and permanent residents in significant numbers from the late 1830s, because of its favourable climate as well as its scenery. Villas were built sporadically, some gabled and irregular, others mildly Ital-
p. 283 ianate. There was no overall planning, but there are many places in the town where individual buildings, often quite ordinary, stand in effective contrast to steeply sloping settings, and command extensive views. A town centre gradually developed along the present High, Church and Pier streets, where a few buildings are latter-day 'Regency' in character, sometimes with pilasters on their upper storeys. In 1847–8 an Esplanade was laid out along part of the seafront; it was soon lined with iron-balconied buildings (few of which survive). The first pier, built in the 1860s, was damaged in storms; a replacement was wrecked in 1881; another pier was opened in 1887. (Its successor was damaged in the C20, and finally removed in 1993.)

St Lawrence and Bonchurch, set in the Undercliff on either side of Ventnor, were developed on a smaller scale and with more sensitivity. ST LAWRENCE is widely scattered, with substantial stone villas, both plain and fanciful, in the tumbled
74 landscape; the many-gabled and bargeboarded Lisle Combe of 1839–*c.* 1850 is among the most fanciful. BONCHURCH had a long tradition of sandstone quarrying. There are a few large early C19 houses, including the Neo-Tudor East Dene designed by *Samuel Beazley c.* 1825 (extended later), but much of the village was developed by a sensitive landowner in the late 1830s and 1840s with villas on carefully chosen sites, including former quarries. The most unusual is Under Rock, rustic Italianate with diagonally set wings.

A railway from Ryde to Sandown and Shanklin was opened in 1864, and extended to Ventnor in 1866. This made all these places much more accessible from the mainland. Ventnor's

growth was accelerated, and SHANKLIN grew quickly from a picturesque village into a town. It has a two-tier coastline, with
a quiet, partly grass-bordered, clifftop promenade, and a 75
seafront below, with buildings set against the cliff, where an Esplanade was formed from 1873. A pier was built in 1888–91; its loss in a storm a century later deprived the seafront of its focal feature. The town centre developed inland, quite separately from the seafront.

SANDOWN was, before the railway came, a small place with a fort and barracks (one early C19 block survives from the latter, converted to offices). The fort, on the NE edge of the town, was relocated in 1866 and has since been dismantled, but parts of it survive in a present-day zoo. An Esplanade was laid out in 1889. Unlike Shanklin, the town is focused on its seafront, with the pier, originally built in 1887 but largely reconstructed in the C20, as the chief landmark.

By the end of the C19, PIERS were focal points of typical seaside resorts. They had two functions: pleasure promenades, usually with entertainment facilities, and landing places for passenger vessels. These might be regular ferries, or ships carrying visitors on excursions. The first pier on the Island was opened at Ryde in 1814 as a ferry terminal (*see* p. 41); it reached its present length in 1842. Following alterations and additions, the existing pier has little architectural interest. The losses of the piers at Ventnor and Shanklin in the C20 have been mentioned; Sandown is the only Island resort which retains a pier providing recreation and amusement. Yarmouth has a simple wooden pier built in 1876, which remained a ferry terminal until the early C20; it never had significant amusement facilities. Totland Bay has a very small pier. The most
remarkable pier on the Island was at Seaview, opened in 1881. *p. 256*
It was in effect a succession of three suspension bridges aligned out to sea, like the original Palace Pier of 1820 at Brighton. It was destroyed in a storm in 1951.

COWES flourished through the Victorian period as a centre for ship- and boat-building and related engineering. Many terraced streets, in locally produced buff and red brick, were laid out on either side of the Medina estuary to house the workforce (a relatively large proportion of whom would have been highly skilled, so that much of the 'industrial' housing is quite substantial). Larger houses were built for the continuing fashionable (or would-be fashionable) clientèle of visitors and residents – who were attracted after 1845 by the presence of the Queen at Osborne as well as by the landscape and maritime recreation. In 1842 (i.e. before the Queen bought Osborne), a scheme was proposed in East Cowes for what we now know as a garden suburb, with villas grouped round a central botanic garden. Only a few of these houses were built as intended. The site of the scheme bordered the grounds of Osborne House, and parts became associated with the royal estate. These included the Neo-Jacobean Kent House, a villa built in 1843, altered and extended for the Queen's mother, the Duchess of Kent, in 1864, and the complex Osborne Cottage, originally of 1856–7 by *A.J. Humbert.*

RYDE grew vigorously as the Island's main resort until the mid 1860s, when the opening of the railway to Sandown, Shanklin and Ventnor moved the emphasis more to those towns. Much of the mid-C19 expansion of Ryde was in the form of villas, sometimes paired. Until the later 1840s most
73 were built in the local Regency–Early Victorian manner. After that they tended to follow national trends. The influence of Osborne is occasionally seen in towers with low-pitched roofs over top storeys with grouped openings, which provided views over the Solent, e.g. at No. 77 West Street, built by the local architect *Thomas Dashwood* in 1865–6. Melville Street, leading E from the town centre, has villas in the earlier tradition towards its W end. No. 29 to the E is very different; it was built in 1855 for his own occupation by *Thomas Hellyer* (1811–94), the leading Island-based architect of the period, with highly individualistic features. St John's Park on the E outskirts of Ryde was developed from 1854 as a suburb with large villas, in interesting variations of mainly Italianate styles, facing perimeter roads (East Hill and West Hill roads) and backing on to a private–communal open space. *Hellyer* designed the layout, and probably some of the houses.

NEWPORT continued as the main marketing centre for the more rural parts of the Island. Prisons and other institutions were established on its N outskirts, and when the Island obtained its County Council in 1890 Newport became the administrative centre. There was some residential expansion with villas, but the most impressive Victorian thoroughfare is Carisbrooke Road, where a very long terrace of the 1860s has an alternating rhythm of canted bay windows and iron balconies. Finally, and appropriately, an elaborate memorial to Queen Victoria with eclectic, mainly Gothic details and Art Nouveau touches, designed by *Percy Stone*, stands in St James Square in the heart of the town.

Public Buildings and Institutions

The term TOWN HALL is ambiguous. Buildings so designated often had a council chamber, a courtroom, and a room suitable for assemblies and meetings, but not necessarily all three, and they were sometimes associated with markets. Nash's Guildhall in Newport is an impressive early example (*see*
59 p. 42), as was the Neoclassical Town Hall of 1829–30 in Ryde (*see* p. 41). This was altered and extended in an Italianate style by *Francis Newman* in 1867–8, and at the same time a tall cupola, by *Thomas Dashwood,* was added. Later town halls were often privately built, principally as places of assembly –

e.g. that at Sandown of 1868–9, set in an otherwise unimportant back street. It has a stylish frontage with giant pilasters and rounded pediments over windows. The Town Hall in Albert Street, Ventnor, by the local architect *T.R. Saunders*, 1878, was a similar private venture with a busy Italianate façade, which is all that survives, with redevelopment behind.

A SCHOOL BUILDING of the 1840s at Chale – part of the present primary school – has a gabled former teacher's house in the centre, flanked by the original schoolrooms. The former school of 1863 at Rookley has the same general form. The old village school at Bonchurch, set picturesquely above a steep bank, was built in 1848–9, largely at the expense of the Swinburnes of nearby East Dene, in a simple Neo-Jacobean style; it was enlarged in 1890. The Public Library and Technical Institute opened in Newport in 1904, in an elaborate building (now part of Nodehill secondary school) by *W.V. Gough* of
Bristol, is essentially Late Victorian. The former Frank James 81
Hospital at Cowes, by *Somers Clarke & Micklethwaite*, 1893, is more Arts and Crafts in character..

Prince Albert laid the foundation stone in 1845 of the Royal Victoria Yacht Club in Ryde, opened a year later. The former clubhouse (later Prince Consort Buildings, St Thomas Street) has a splendid Italianate frontage to the Solent, with nine round-headed windows on the first floor and a Tuscan colonnade supporting an iron-railed balcony. The more important Royal Yacht Squadron (*see* p. 42) moved in 1858 into Henry VIII's originally modest Cowes Castle, which had been much altered in the C18 and was remodelled for the Squadron by *Anthony Salvin*. He added a three-storey tower with a steep slated roof, rounded on the side towards the sea. Another institution deserving of mention here is the PRISON at
Parkhurst outside Newport, adapted and extended in Victo- *p. 188*
rian times from a barrack hospital built in the 1790s.

Domestic Building

References have already been made to the smaller and medium-sized Victorian houses in and near the growing towns and resorts of the Island. Around the middle of the century these generally reflected national trends. There were two basic types of urban or seaside villa, which could in the broadest sense be classified as Italianate and Romantic. Those in the first category were usually (but not always) symmetrical, with features derived, however remotely, from the classical traditions. They often had low-pitched roofs ending in eaves. Houses in the second category typically had gables (often with elaborate bargeboards), prominent chimneys, and windows of varied form. Substantial bay windows, usually canted, were characteristic of both types.

In 1853 the poet Alfred Tennyson took Farringford, a house near Freshwater (now a hotel) built *c.* 1806 and enlarged *c.* 1830 in a curious style with unorthodox Gothic features; he added a wing, including a study, in 1871. His presence attracted writers, artists and admirers to the western extremity of the Island. The painter G.F. Watts frequently stayed in The Briary, a house of 1870–2 W of Farringford, which *Philip Webb* designed for Watts's friends Mr and Mrs Prinsep, including a studio used by the artist. (The house was destroyed by fire in 1934.) The pioneer photographer Julia Margaret Cameron moved in 1860 into two villas near Farringford, which had been built a few years before and which she joined as a single house (more remarkable for her association than architecturally).

Not far from Farringford is Weston Manor, a very different house built in 1869–70 by *George Goldie* for W.G. Ward, a Catholic convert and nephew of the builder of Northwood House, Cowes (*see* p. 38). It is a somewhat rambling composition with Gothic and French château elements, remarkable mainly for its chapel with rich details partly inspired by A.W.N. Pugin's drawings, and for a screen by *Peter Paul Pugin.* At the other end of the Island, *S.S. Teulon* and other architects enlarged Woodlands Vale, E of Ryde, from 1870, giving it a variegated outline. Teulon built an impressive arched screen in the grounds.

Stephen Salter practised on the Island from *c.* 1885 into the C20. Like many architects of the period he was versatile; he designed the former Coachhouse to Woodlands Vale with a domed turret and terracotta decoration, a nearby lodge with a Venetian window, and several individual houses, including a group in Ryde Road, Seaview, with tall distinctive chimneys. He was one of the few local architects notably influenced by the Arts and Crafts movement, and by the revival of interest in vernacular classical architecture around the turn of the century.

Victorian Churches

Few major Victorian architects designed churches on the Island. The most important was *Sir George Gilbert Scott*, whose All Saints, Ryde, of 1869–72 is an impressive, fairly conventional work in a generally Decorated style, faced in rough Swanage limestone (a material commonly used for churches in mid-southern England at the time), with Bath stone dressings. The tower and spire were built in 1881–2 under his son *John Oldrid Scott.* Sir Gilbert's furnishings generally remain, with the elaborate reredos, pulpit and font. His more modest church of 1878 at St Lawrence was one of his last works; it replaced, as the parish church, the smaller medieval one which was retained. Much the same happened at Bonchurch, where a new church was built in 1847–8. The architect was *Benjamin Ferrey*, best known for Gothic churches. Here he used Neo-Norman, to a cruciform plan (the transepts were additions to the original design) – which is internally effective, with its almost convincingly Norman crossing arches. Also Neo-Romanesque is St Paul, Newport, of 1844 by *J. W. Wild*, better known for his much more ambitious Christ Church in Streatham, London. St Mary, Ryde (R.C.), of 1846, is an interesting work of *Joseph Hansom*, a versatile architect whose 65 works range from the Neoclassical Birmingham Town Hall to the High Gothic Arundel Cathedral. St Mary is Gothic, but defies categorization with its unorthodox W front, and arcades with low-pitched arches contained in taller arched recesses.

Thomas Hellyer was a remarkable locally based architect; his own house in Ryde has already been mentioned (*see* p. 48). He designed or altered several churches. St John, Ryde, of 1843 was cruciform with simple lancets (it has since been enlarged). His Holy Trinity, Ryde, has a beautifully proportioned 61 tower and spire completed in 1846; it is of broach form with slender pinnacles at the angles and acutely gabled lucarnes. Holy Trinity, Bembridge, of 1845–6, also by him, has a simpler broach spire. In 1868–70 Hellyer remodelled St James, East Cowes, a very plain church by *Nash*, retaining Nash's W tower and part of his exterior. Hellyer's arcades have Italian-Romanesque capitals, and the rounded window tracery is in a style of his own. His smaller St Peter, Seaview, 1859–62, has low-pitched arches to the N arcade with brick patterning.

The 1850s and 1860s were very active years for the building of churches on the Island. The most extraordinary is St Mildred, Whippingham, the parish church for Osborne. A 62 small medieval church which had been enlarged by *Nash* was rebuilt in two stages, 1854–5 (the E end) and 1860–2 (the rest), by *A.J. Humbert* (*see* above, p. 45) in association with *Prince Albert*. The style is broadly Transitional from Romanesque to Gothic, but highly individualistic – especially the central tower, which is open inside like a lantern. The church is full of royalty-related furnishings (including a font by a royal sculptor, *Princess Louise*). By far the best features artistically are the bronze screens between the N chapel and the chancel, by *Sir Alfred Gilbert*, 1897. The medieval and C17 St Thomas, Newport (*see* p. 31), was replaced in 1854–6 by *S. W. Daukes*. It is High Gothic with complex roof-line and skyline details, especially on the tower, which is very effective in its tight urban setting. Holy Trinity, Ventnor, of 1860–2 by *C.E. Giles* of Taunton, is High Gothic with a needle spire. St Mary, Cowes, was rebuilt, retaining *Nash*'s remarkable tower (*see* p. 43), in 1867 by *Arthur Cates* (of London). It is faced externally in Swanage stone but is polychromatic inside, with granite columns and variegated brick walling.

Apart from Thomas Hellyer, the most notable Victorian architect whose practice was based on the Island was *Richard James Jones* (*c.* 1835–1912). He designed the very remarkable St Michael, Swanmore, on the S outskirts of Ryde, initially in conjunction with the *Rev. William Grey* (a clerical amateur), from 1861. It is cruciform, externally in Swanage stone, but the central tower never received the intended spire. Internally
64 the walls above the nave arcades are faced in patterned polychromatic brickwork, but the crossing space has marble shafts and richly carved capitals. The polygonal vaulted chancel, designed by Jones alone, dates from 1873. Jones's other surviving work in Island churches relates to restorations (as at Whitwell in 1868), extensions, or part-rebuildings (including the chancel of 1865 at Gatcombe, which contains outstanding stained glass described later). On the Hampshire mainland he designed the small church at Clanfield (1875) with a memorable polychromatic interior.

Another significant local architect was *W.T. Stratton*, based in Newport, who designed the small church of 1871 at Thorley, with an intricately shaped turret. In 1875–6 he drastically restored the church at Freshwater, where the aisles were
p. 139 widened and the chancel lengthened. A similarly drastic restoration was undertaken in 1852 at Brighstone under the vicar, the *Rev. Edward McAll*, to his own designs. He reinstated a N aisle (restoring the blocked C12 arcade), remodelled the chancel in an almost convincing E.E. style, and altered windows on the S side from Perp to Neo-Dec, confusing the already complicated history of an otherwise Norman to C17 building.

There are few notable churches of the later Victorian period. St Saviour, Shanklin was begun by *Hellyer* in 1867, but the remarkable tower, octagonal at the belfry stage and topped by a spire with sharp lucarnes, was added by *W.O. Milne* in 1885–7. At the Good Shepherd, Lake by *Temple Moore*, 1892–4, the double nave (perhaps suggested by the medieval example at Godshill) opens into a chancel of one normal span, to odd internal effect. The two-gabled W front is unified visually by a central timber-framed porch, which contrasts with the smooth external stonework of the walls.

There are several notable former RECTORIES and VICARAGES of the C19. That at Calbourne (1838) has a stone Neo-Tudor façade, probably by *A.F. Livesay*, who restored the church (*see* p. 44). The old vicarage at Newtown may also be his. At Brighstone the *Rev. E. McAll*, who restored the church in 1852 (*see* above), also altered the rectory, which has a porch and other details in E.E. and Tudor styles. An elaborate vicarage was built at Bembridge *c.* 1860, with prominent trefoiled arches in the porch. The former vicarage of 1867 at Whitwell, studiedly irregular with mullioned windows and Gothic porch, was probably the work of *R.J. Jones*, who restored the church in the same year. *Sir George Gilbert Scott*'s old vicarage of 1871 survives W of All Saints, Ryde. Unlike the church it is of red brick, with dark bands and diagonals, and the windows are domestic: simple and square-topped. The finest former vicarage is that of St Saviour, Shanklin, of 1870–1 by *Henry Woodyer* (his only work on the Island). It has a tile-hung upper storey – a sign of the influence of the 'Old English' domestic style which was beginning at the time.

The Island is special for Victorian STAINED GLASS, notably because of works associated with *William Morris*. But there are many good windows by other artists, and several of quality for which the designers have not been established. One of the earliest with a recorded artist is the triple E window designed by *William Wailes* for the church of 1847–8 at Bonchurch. St Thomas, Newport, has a colourful E window, *c.* 1857, by *William Holland* of Warwick. In 1864 an absentee rector commissioned the firm of *Morris, Marshall, Faulkner & Co.*, established three years before, to design windows for the rebuilt chancel of the church at Gatcombe. All the five principal artists associated with the firm contributed to the outstanding three-light E window: *Dante Gabriel Rossetti*, *William Morris* himself, *Ford Madox Brown*, *Edward Burne-Jones* and *Philip Webb*, who co-ordinated the whole densely detailed composition.

In 1877 Morris & Co. provided windows for the chapel of the Royal National Hospital for Diseases of the Chest in Ventnor (demolished), much of which was re-set in 1974 in Sir Gilbert Scott's church at St Lawrence (*see* above). Figures by Burne-Jones, Madox Brown and Morris were placed in the S windows; other scenes by Madox Brown and Morris are in a hinged display within the church. But the most memorable window re-set at St Lawrence is probably that of 1892 by *W. Reynolds-Stephens*, showing a patient being treated within an angelic frame; its colours are more subtle and diffuse than those of the earlier windows.

Several windows on the Island were designed by *Clayton & Bell*, notably the very fine series at Holy Trinity, Ventnor (*c.* 1863), and the E window of Scott's All Saints, Ryde (*c.* 1872). The sanctuary of the latter church has walls and roof painted by *Clayton & Bell*, but this work has faded. *Lavers & Barraud* and their successors *Lavers & Westlake* are well represented, for instance in the windows of the apse of 1862 at Holy Trinity, Cowes. *Nathaniel Westlake* designed a series of windows for St Mary, Ryde (R.C.), including the E window of 1879. In 1894 he painted the very elaborate roof and the walls of the small Lady Chapel there, with richly detailed scenes and patterns. *Henry Holiday* is represented by two small windows in the Victorian church at Bonchurch. A window of *c.* 1900 at Brighstone,

66 depicting John the Baptist together with elaborate patterning, was designed by *William White* – a rare example of glass by that distinguished architect. At Chale is a series of windows by *C.E. Kempe* (mainly of 1897); there are others by him in St Saviour, Shanklin.

Victorian Chapels

Newport has the oldest NONCONFORMIST CHAPELS on the Island (*see* p. 44). The Baptist church, originally of 1812, has
63 a five-bay front of 1872 with Corinthian columns, the centre three under a pediment. The Baptist church in Cowes, of 1876–7, has a frontage with Composite pilasters and large pediment; the walls are of buff brick with round-headed windows arched in red. A simpler version of this design was used for the former Primitive Methodist chapel of 1889 in Cowes, now the public library.

From mid-century the separated Methodist sects generally preferred Gothic, often with elaborately traceried windows on their street fronts. The Methodist church at Yarmouth, 1881, has an octagon-topped angle tower ending with a short spire which complements the very different Anglican church tower nearby. The most elegant Methodist steeple is that on the church of 1901 in Birmingham Road, Cowes: slender and octagonal, ending with a small spire.

Numerous Nonconformist chapels were built in the growing seaside towns; not all survive. At Sandown they are on sites well behind the seafront. The most prominent is the Baptist church of 1882 by *S.E. Tomkins*, of polychrome brick in a generally E.E. style. In Shanklin the United Reformed (originally Congregational) church of 1888 by *J. Sulman*, also basically E.E., stands at a conspicuous corner in the heart of the town (the tower was reconstructed after bomb damage). The worst loss in the later C20 among Nonconformist buildings was that of the Congregational church in Ryde of 1870–2 by *R.J. Jones*, usually an inventive architect. Its tower changed from square to octagonal in long-drawn stages, and was topped by a tall thin spire. It was demolished in 1974.

THE TWENTIETH CENTURY AND AFTER

The first general impressions obtained from C20 and early C21 buildings on the Isle of Wight is that they are mainly mediocre or worse. In this the Island is typical of too many areas of Britain. But, as elsewhere, a few works of high architectural quality stand out. Others of special distinction are less conspicuous, and it is part of the purpose of this Guide to draw

Shanklin Congregational Church.
Drawing from *The Builder* vol. 44, 1883

attention to them. Some of these buildings are in styles influenced by the international Modern Movement in its various phases; others are in more traditional styles. A few are works of real originality.

Churches

The dominant architectural achievement of the C20 on the Island is QUARR ABBEY, the monastery established by exiled 77, 78
French monks in 1907 near the site of the ancient abbey of *p. 216*
the same name. The church was built in 1911–12 by *Paul Bellot*, a monk-architect who designed ecclesiastical buildings in Belgium, Holland, France and Canada. Not all of these

were completed according to his plans, and the church at Quarr (which, remarkably, was finished within two years) is probably his greatest achievement. He was influenced by the Expressionist movement current in Northern Europe in the early C20, which placed emphasis on the form and composition of buildings and architectural features, and the feelings and reactions induced by them. He admired especially the architecture of southern Spain, from Cordoba to Catalonia, but his own buildings have tremendous individuality. They are generally in brick, with some use of concrete; at Quarr he used ordinary Belgian bricks. Many of his details are related to the form and characteristics of the material, including stepped gables, straight-angled arches and patterns made by brickwork in relief. What makes Quarr stupendous is its sequence of spatial experiences – first the relatively small nave, then through the lengthy chancel, to reach the climax of the sanctuary, which is set unusually within a broad tower that is open to its roof. This has a wonderful vista upwards to the intersecting brick arches which support the roof structure.

After Quarr the most striking early C20 church is the
83 Roman Catholic St Saviour, Totland, by *W.C. Mangan*, 1923, of brick, in a basically Romanesque style influenced by early Modernism. Two interesting Anglican churches, each on a steep site, are St Alban, Ventnor, simplified Romanesque by *F.M. Coley*, 1922–3, and the incomplete St Faith, Cowes, by *J.S. Adkins*, 1909, the latter having transverse arches in concrete. *Percy Stone*, the meticulous draughtsman of the *Architectural Antiquities of the Isle of Wight* (1891), designed or restored numerous buildings. His work is sometimes mundane, but St Mark, Wootton, 1910, is inventive, with its internal brick piers supporting the timber structure of the aisle roofs. He also designed several WAR MEMORIALS, many of them in churchyards, e.g. at Brading.

CHURCH FITTINGS include the fine iron screen of 1909 by *Jones & Willis* which dominates the interior of St Peter, Seaview; it has intricate Gothic patterning, and might have been designed up to fifty years before. A statue of the Virgin and Child in St Mary, Carisbrooke, by *John Skelton*, 1969, is especially sensitive in composition and expression. St Saviour,
79 Shanklin, has STAINED GLASS by *Christopher Whall*, *c.* 1913, depicting the Nativity with the outline of a town in the background. The N chapel of Mottistone church was refurbished in 1948 by *John Seely* in memory of his father, the 1st Lord Mottistone; it has elegant partitions and pews, and an E window by *Reginald & Michael Farrar Bell*, largely opaque but including an angel holding a scroll. They also designed the main E window. The most memorable C20 stained glass in an
80 Island church is at Binstead, in two small windows by *Gabriel Loire* of Chartres, 1971 and 1987.

Houses, Traditional and Modern

The Seely family were landowners in the W of the Island from the mid C19. In 1925–6 General Jack Seely (later 1st Lord Mottistone) decided to restore Mottistone Manor, then a p. 27
farmhouse and partly ruinous; he had been persuaded to do so by Sir Edwin Lutyens. The task was undertaken by his son *John Seely*, newly established in partnership with *Paul Paget.* Seely altered the house again when he inherited it (and the title) in 1947. The result is a splendidly conserved C16–C17 mansion with an unmistakably Arts and Crafts feel. At the other end of the scale, *M.H. Baillie Scott*, one of the most distinguished architects influenced by the Arts and Crafts Movement, designed three small houses of 1936–7 at St Lawrence, two of them thatched – very much in the *cottage orné* tradition, of which they may be considered the last significant examples on the Island.

Oliver Hill was one of the most versatile of interwar architects. He designed Horstone Point, Seaview, a medium-sized holiday home of 1928, which combines elements of Modernism, Neoclassicism and the spirit of Lutyens. The first house on the Island in a style unmistakably influenced by the Modern Movement is probably the small seaside retreat built by *F.R.S. Yorke* for himself in 1946–51 at Luccombe, S of Shanklin. Most of the single storey is set behind a veranda under a flat roof, with a wing ending in a shallow bay window. In the same tradition, twenty years later, the local architects *Gilbert & Hobson* designed a two-storeyed retirement home called Chert on a steep rugged site SW of Ventnor, with large-scale glazing on its upper floor and servicing underneath. At 86
Gurnard, a house by *Colin Graham*, built in 2000, evokes the modernistic fashion of the interwar years in its irregular many-angled form. It stands out amid a series of much more typical seaside buildings of the C20.

Public and Commercial Buildings, 1900–1945

County Hall, the seat of local government, was built in 1938, by *Gutteridge & Gutteridge* of Southampton. Its frontage to High Street, Newport, is moderately monumental; Neo-Georgian with a suggestion of influence from 1920s Sweden. It has since been extended in less distinguished styles. There were a few fairly substantial developments in the coastal towns between the wars. In 1937–8 Osborne Court, by *R.W.H. Jones*, replaced a substantial part of the Georgian and Victorian waterfront at The Parade, Cowes. It is a block of flats in the modernistic manner (as distinct from the purer styles of the international Modern Movement) with varying building heights, curved corners, round-ended balconies and horizontal windows. The smaller Royal York Hotel, Ryde, by *Harrison & Gilkes*, 1937–8, with similar features, fits fairly well into the heterogeneous Regency and Victorian George Street. Internally it has a dramatic spiral staircase. The former Pavilion in Ryde, by *Vincent & West*, was built in 1926–7 on an open site by the sea. It now forms part of a larger complex, but its corner turrets with tiled concave sides remain important landmarks in a part of the Esplanade which has become visually confused.

Bembridge School was founded in 1919 by J.H. Whitehouse, a follower of the Arts and Crafts movement and an enthusiast for John Ruskin. The school is now amalgamated with another in Ryde, but the central building is still a boarding house. It was designed by *M.H. Baillie Scott* in the then well-established 'Old English' style, with tile-hanging, a touch of half-timber and tall chimneys. A room was added in 1929 to house Whitehouse's large Ruskin collection (transferred to Lancaster University in 1997). The chapel, with its sweeping tiled roof supported internally by intricate timberwork, was designed by *W.A. Harvey & H.G. Wicks*, architects of Bournville model village, Birmingham. Also in Bembridge is
84 the rare survival of a telephone kiosk of the early K1 type, 1929.

The influence of ART NOUVEAU is illustrated in one small
82 building in Cowes: Jolliffe's, a former shop in Shooters Hill, built *c.* 1917 with facing tiles in four shades of green, those on the first floor framing a window with a semicircular pattern of glazing, and stylized lettering.

Public and Commercial Buildings since 1945

The Isle of Wight County Council (and since 1995 its successor the Isle of Wight Council) have provided a series of PUBLIC BUILDINGS which have reached high standards in architectural design. An outstanding example is the Island's principal public library, the Lord Louis Library in Newport, opened in 1981, a complex, mainly single-storey building with slate roofs over low brick walls. The County Architect at the time was *Robert Smith*, but the project architect was *Michael Rainey*, who held the post of County Architect from 1983. Other architects in the county department were *J. Petrie* and *R. Whelan*. Between them they designed a series of SCHOOLS,
87 including Wroxall Primary School (1986), in buff brick with low-pitched roofs; its entrance is given special emphasis, with a canopy supported by slender columns. The larger Dover Park School, Ryde (1987–8) has similar characteristics; the entrance is through a prominent porch with round arch and low gable. Broadlea School at Lake (1993) is L-shaped; its striking feature is a continuous line of triangular shapes in dark colour along the slopes of the sweeping tiled roofs of both

wings. Adelaide Court, in the outer SW part of Ryde, is a very successful scheme of RETIREMENT HOMES with associated community facilities, built by the County Council in 1985–6, again with *Michael Rainey* as architect. The domestic buildings are grouped with studied informality, with variations in frontage and height.

The Isle of Wight County Council ceased to have an architects' department *c.* 1990. Many of its subsequent projects were designed by *Rainey Petrie Design*, formed by Michael Rainey and J. Petrie, previously his deputy as County Architect. Among them is a seaside shelter, circular with a turret, built in 1999–2000 over a pumping station on a prominent part of Ventnor seafront – providing it with an effective focal point, which had been much needed after the loss of the pier
in 1993. This was followed by Dinosaur Isle, a museum of 89
geology and prehistoric fauna, built at the N end of Sandown seafront in 2000–1. With the shape of its curving roof said to have been influenced by the form of a flying reptile, this is, again, a compelling landmark in a location where there was nothing comparable before.

At the S end of Sandown, an existing undistinguished Leisure Centre was extended in an interesting way by *Jenkins Milton Partnership* in 1991–2, making the most of a prominent site. It has a low pyramidal roof and polychrome walls.
Another seaside landmark is the lift connecting the clifftop 85
with the seafront at Shanklin. It was rebuilt in 1956, with an elegant concrete shaft in front of the cliff, linked to the upper promenade by a glazed passageway.

There is a series of notable buildings of varied modern character in the heterogeneous waterfront area of Cowes. The Island Sailing Club was designed in 1961 by *Howard Lobb*, with thin metalwork and glazing within a complex white-painted frame. It recalls interwar buildings such as the yacht club at Burnham-on-Crouch, Essex, but has been altered. Almost contemporary is Admiral's Wharf, with flats on two upper storeys lit by long windows under boarded fascias, and a ground floor with Corbusian concrete arches. Gloster Court, *c.* 1998 by *Richard Jones*, has upper ranges of flats set back above the main storey with its round-ended balconies. The climax of the area, socially and visually, is the Tudor to Victorian Cowes Castle. This was discreetly extended for the Royal Yacht Squadron by *Thomas Croft* in 2000, when a new pavilion wing was added to its NW. The wing is fronted by an elegant veranda with tent-like roof, but the new accommodation is partly set within the steeply rising ground behind.

By far the boldest architectural enterprise undertaken on the Island in the late C20 was the enlargement of St Mary's
Hospital, Newport, by *Ahrends, Burton & Koralek*, planned 88
from 1985 and opened in 1991 – a complex structure of many different elements with varying sizes, shapes and heights. Its

most innovative feature was the cladding of nearly all wall surfaces, and also roofs, with stainless-steel sheeting, providing insulation intended to reduce wastage in energy. This, however, has since been renewed. The hospital has pleasant internal spaces, with works of art, including murals, in prominent places.

The sequence of buildings of special quality ends with one from the beginning of the C21, covering the remains of the oldest extant building on the Island which can be considered as architecture: the Roman villa at Brading. This was done superbly in 2003–4 by *Rainey Petrie Johns.* It is built almost entirely of timber, with subsidiary metalwork internally.

Conservation and Adaptation

The record of conserving, restoring and adapting notable older buildings on the Island over the last thirty or forty years is on the whole impressive. English Heritage has splendidly restored Osborne House, including the terraced gardens. It and its predecessors have rescued the shell of Appuldurcombe from dereliction, and have restored its main front to pristine condition (as well as partly restoring the interior of the great hall to give a suggestion of its C18 condition). Houses which were for long in a bad state, including North Court and
28, Wolverton Manor in Shorwell, have been well restored
p. 277 (together with the gardens at North Court), as have Brig-
54, 55 stocke Terrace and the Royal Victoria Arcade in Ryde, both
once threatened with demolition. Historic streets in Newport have been uplifted through work on individual buildings, including the former malthouse and adjoining buildings in Crocker Street, as well as properties in other streets. Former warehouses and other buildings around Newport Quay have been imaginatively transformed into an arts centre (by *Tony Fretton Architects*, 1997–8). Such positive improvements – and many others of similar character – have on the whole outweighed major losses, such as those of Nash's East Cowes Castle and of piers which were the focal points of seaside resorts.

FURTHER READING

The outstanding publication devoted to older BUILDINGS is *Architectural Antiquities of the Isle of Wight* by Percy Stone, architect and archaeologist, published in 1891 (strictly, 1891–2) in two large volumes. His drawings, with those of collaborators, depict in meticulous detail the larger houses, churches and other buildings of before *c.* 1700. They are particularly valuable for internal details such as chimneypieces and church monuments. Other early views, with much additional information, are included in Sir Henry Englefield's *Description . . . of the Isle of Wight*, 1816. The best general history is *The Isle of Wight, an Illustrated History* by Jack and Johanna Jones, first published in 1987; the best wide-ranging architectural history, Johanna Jones, *Castles to Cottages, the Story of Isle of Wight Houses*, 2000. She is particularly good on smaller and medium-sized houses of the last hundred and fifty years. For vernacular building, *Farmhouses and Cottages of the Isle of Wight* by Marion Brinton and others, first published 1987, is outstanding, especially for building methods and materials.

The Victoria County History of Hampshire includes the main material on the Isle of Wight in vol. 5, 1912. Unlike more recent publications in this national series, it is fairly limited in scope, good for e.g. medieval CHURCHES, but not for later work. The Isle of Wight volume of the *County Churches* series, by J. Charles Cox, 1911, is excellent for medieval work. M. Lane, *Parish Churches of the Isle of Wight*, 1994 and later, has concise information about Anglican churches of all dates (occasionally in need of correction, e.g. Arreton). R. and P. Winter, *Village Churches of the Isle of Wight*, 1987, has superb photographs. There is no general history of Victorian or later work in Island churches, but D. Bond and G. Dear, *The Stained Glass Windows of William Morris and his Circle in Hampshire and the Isle of Wight* (Hampshire County Council, 1998) is excellent for the Island, especially for the Morris firm's windows at Gatcombe. G.K. Brandwood, *Temple Moore*, 1997, indicates the importance of this architect's church at Lake.

Guides to other individual churches vary greatly. Mention must be made of those by Jack Wheeler from the 1960s on C19 churches in Ryde (All Saints, Holy Trinity, St Thomas), Binstead, and Shanklin (St Saviour); by Janet Tudman on the Victorian St Boniface, Bonchurch; and more recently by Peter Clarke on St Mary, Ryde (R.C.). *Insula Vecta, the Isle of Wight in the Middle Ages*, by S.F. Hockey, a monk-scholar of modern Quarr Abbey, 1982, includes information about four small priories and the origin of parishes on the Island. His *Quarr Abbey and its Lands 1132–1631* covers aspects of the Island's only fully fledged medieval monastery, its possessions, and their fate after the Reformation. The architect of the modern abbey, Dom Paul Bellot, is the subject of an article by Charlotte Ellis in *Perspectives*, February 1997, and a book by Peter Willis, also 1997.

On CASTLES, Carisbrooke is treated in *The History of the King's Works* vol. 2, 1963, and vol. 4, 1982. Both are supplemented and partly superseded by C.J. Young, *Excavations at Carisbrooke Castle, Isle of Wight, 1921–1996*, 2000, with detailed accounts of many aspects of the castle's development. Vol. 4 of the *King's Works* also has references to Yarmouth and Cowes castles.

Among larger HOUSES, Appuldurcombe is admirably covered in English Heritage's guidebook by L.O. J. Boynton, revised 1986. Articles in *Country Life* on individual houses include two on Mottistone, by Christopher Hussey, 16 March 1929, and Alan Powers, 24 November 1994, and two on Nunwell by Marcus Binney, 19 and 26 February 1976. An article by D. Phillips-Birt, also in *Country Life*, 28 December 1967, covers Norris Castle and Nash's lost castle at East Cowes, which is treated in detail in Ian Sherfield, *East Cowes Castle*, 1994. Nash's work nationally is covered by Sir John Summerson, *The Life and Work of John Nash*, 1980, and Michael Mansbridge, *John Nash*, 1991, which includes references to several Island buildings. Osborne House is excellently covered in the English Heritage guidebook by Michael Turner, frequently revised as parts of the house and grounds are restored. Hermione Hobhouse, *Thomas Cubitt, Master Builder*, 1971 (new edn 1995) establishes Cubitt's rôle in the building of Osborne and in restoring the adjoining Barton Manor. An article by Mary Miers in *Country Life*, 29 March 2001, deals especially with Osborne's Indian-inspired Durbar Room.

Books on SPECIALIZED THEMES include the following. Seaside piers are covered nationally by S.H. Adamson, 1977, and locally by M. Lane in *Piers of the Isle of Wight*, 1996. E.F. Laidlaw, *A History of Isle of Wight Hospitals*, 1994, deals with several interesting examples, including the C18 House of Industry at Newport. Parkhurst and other Island prisons are covered in English Heritage's *English Prisons, an Architectural History*, 2002. P. Moore, *The Industrial Heritage of Hampshire and the Isle of Wight*, 1989, includes mills, some farm buildings, and public services such as electricity and water supply. F.T. O'Brien, *Early Solent Steamers*, 1973, is pertinent to Ryde and Cowes. B. Hinton, *Discovering Island Writers*, 2000, identifies places and buildings with literary associations.

The three planned medieval TOWNS are placed in context by Maurice Beresford in *New Towns of the Middle Ages*, 1967. Not all the Island towns are well covered by publications. C.W.R. Winter, *The Ancient Town of Yarmouth*, 1981, is good for medieval to Georgian periods. C. Tennant, *East Cowes, a Step into the Past*, 1992, and also *Discovering East Cowes*, 1994, are comprehensive. Shanklin is well covered by L. Boynton, *Georgian and Victorian Shanklin*, 1973, and A. Parker, *The Story of Victorian Shanklin*. Ventnor, together with Bonchurch, has a series of Town Trails published by the local history society, 1985 and 1999. A. Chapman, *Houses by the Sea, Buildings of the Undercliff, 1830–90*, 2000, has old illustrations and substantial text. R.G. McInnes, *Country Life*, 10 May 1984, describes buildings against the Undercliff landscape. M. Brandt, *The Story of Seaview*, 1999, is an excellent history of a seaside village. J. Margham, 'Freshwater, Man and the Landscape' in the *Proceedings of the Isle of Wight Natural History and Archaeological Society*, 1994, covers the western peninsula.

For a detailed account of the complicated LAND FORM of the Island and its evolution the best source is probably H.J. Osborne White, *A Short Account of the Geology of the Isle of Wight*, 1921 and later. Eric Bird, *The Shaping of the Isle of Wight*, 1998, has illustrations and descriptions of topographical features, particularly coastal. John Wolfenden, *The Countryside of the Isle of Wight*, 1990, has more emphasis on land use and settlement, with reference to buildings. Vicky Basford, *Parks and Gardens of the Isle of Wight*, first published 1989, covers man-made landscapes, particularly those of the C17–C19 related to houses. For BUILDING STONE the most valuable reference is in *Medieval Archaeology* 8, 1964: as a supplement to an article on the Saxon building-stone industry, there is an appendix with a note on the Quarr Stone by F.W. Anderson and R.N. Quirk concerning this variety of Island limestone, used for important mainland buildings in the early Middle Ages.

ARCHAEOLOGY is covered by H.V. Basford, *The Vectis Report, a Survey of Isle of Wight Archaeology*, 1980. More detailed works, whether by period, area or theme, include *Long Barrows in Hampshire and the Isle of Wight* (Royal Commission on Historical Monuments, England), 1979; D.J. Tomalin, *Newport Roman Villa*, 1977 (2nd edn) and *Roman Wight*, 1987; M. Tosdevin, *Romans on the Isle of Wight*, 1992; R. Loader, D. Tomalin and I. Westmore, *Time and Tide, an Archaeological Survey of the Wootton–Quarr Coast*, 1997; and C.J. Arnold, *The Anglo-Saxon Cemeteries of the Isle of Wight*, 1982; also in articles in the Isle of Wight Natural History and Archaeological Society's *Proceedings*. Worth a mention in this connection is A.D. Mills, *The Place-names of the Isle of Wight, their Origins and Meanings*, 2001.

As in other areas which were visited for their picturesque qualities, numerous GUIDEBOOKS were published in the early to mid C19, illustrated with romanticized views. The most prolific were published by George Brannon (1784–1860) and for a time by his sons; there were many editions, often revised. The Brannons' depiction of buildings was usually reasonably accurate, but their scenic backgrounds were often romanticized, even falsified, so that they made the Undercliff, for instance, appear more dramatic than it was. Several are reproduced in this volume.

Buildings of national importance are covered by GENERAL ARCHITECTURAL HISTORIES. Good starting points are John Summerson, *Architecture in Britain 1530–1830* (Pelican History of Art), last revised 1991, *Victorian Architecture* by R. Dixon and S. Muthesius, 1978, and *Edwardian Architecture* by A. Service, 1977. Standard works on other building types include J. Earl and M. Sell, *Guide to British Theatres, 1750–1950*

(Theatres Trust), 2000, Kathryn Morrison, *English Shops and Shopping*, 2003, and Harriet Richardson (ed.), *English Hospitals 1660–1848* (Royal Commission on Historical Monuments, England), 1998.

INDIVIDUAL ARCHITECTS can be followed in H.M. Colvin, *A Biographical Dictionary of English Architects 1600–1840*, 1995 (3rd edn), the *Directory of British Architects 1834–1900* (British Architectural Library), 1993 (expanded edn 2001, up to 1914), and A.S. Gray, *Edwardian Architecture, a Biographical Dictionary*, 1985. For sculpture, the standard works are Margaret Whinney, *Sculpture in Britain 1530–1830* (Pelican History of Art), revised by John Physick, 1988, R. Gunnis, *Dictionary of British Sculptors 1660–1851*, revised 1968 (3rd edn forthcoming), B. Read, *Victorian Sculpture*, 1982, and Susan Beattie, *The New Sculpture*, 1983. INDIVIDUAL BUILDINGS can sometimes be investigated in contemporary periodicals, *The Builder* and *Building News* (later *Architect and Building News*) for the C19, the *Architectural Review*, *Architects' Journal* and *RIBA Journal* for the C20 and C21.

A database of recent PERIODICAL ARTICLES is available at the British Architectural Library (RIBA), and on-line at *www.architecture.com*. A FULL BIBLIOGRAPHY of general works, including much on individual architects and artists, can be found at the Reference section of the Pevsner Architectural Guides' website, *www.lookingatbuildings.org.uk*.

THE ISLE OF WIGHT

APPULDURCOMBE 5075

Godshill

The shell of a mansion, once the grandest in the Isle of Wight, set amid swelling hills behind the rugged SE coastland. A small monastery was founded *c.* 1100 as a cell to the Benedictine abbey of Montebourg in Normandy; it was suppressed as an alien priory in 1414. In 1498 the site was leased to Sir John Leigh, whose daughter and heiress Anne married Sir James Worsley in 1512. The Worsley family originated in Lancashire; James was knighted by Henry VIII soon after his accession, and in 1511 was appointed Constable of Carisbrooke Castle and military captain of the Island. He took possession of Appuldurcombe in 1527, and was succeeded in 1538 by his son Richard (†1565), who also became the military captain and who supervised the building of Henry VIII's forts on the Island.* 37

The Tudor and Stuart Worsleys lived in an irregular house, probably the biggest on the Isle of Wight at the time. A rough drawing of the house was published by Sir Robert Worsley in 1720, well after its demolition. The drawing shows a central block of two storeys with tall mullioned windows, narrow

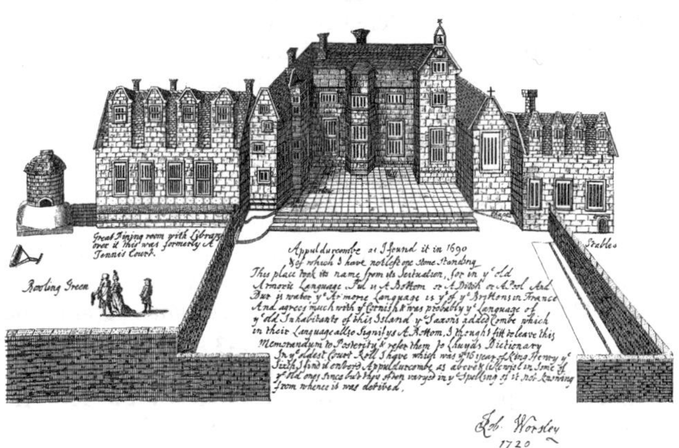

Appuldurcombe, old house.
Drawing by Sir Robert Worsley, 1720

* The tombs of Sir John Leigh and Sir James and later Worsleys are in Godshill church (q.v.).

irregular gabled wings, and flanking ranges with dormer windows.

Sir Robert Worsley, the 4th baronet and creator of the present house, succeeded as a minor. He came of age in 1690, and married Frances Thynne, daughter of Lord Weymouth of Longleat, Wiltshire. Sir Robert started to rebuild in 1701, beginning with the NE corner, followed by the central part including the hall. *Joseph Clarke*, probably a London mason, undertook masonry work in 1705–6. Work continued on the S side of the house until about 1711. Almost certainly his architect was *John James*. Little work took place between *c.* 1711 and Sir Robert's death in 1747.

Construction on a substantial scale resumed under Sir Richard, the 7th baronet, who inherited in 1768. Sir Richard started work on the house and grounds after his return from the Grand Tour in 1772. The great hall was transformed, and the house was completed on the unfinished N side, generally according to the originally intended external form. It is not known who was his architect, but *Capability Brown* was employed for the surrounding landscape. Sir Richard became a Privy Councillor and Governor of the Island. Following a matrimonial scandal in 1782 he left the country for five years, travelling in SE and E Europe. He amassed the largest collection of Greek antiquities made by an Englishman before the time of Lord Elgin. He accommodated these and other works of art at Appuldurcombe, which became, *inter alia*, a major private museum.

Sir Richard died in 1805. The heiress was his niece, who in 1806 married Charles Pelham, 1st Baron Yarborough, of Brocklesby Park, Lincs (created 1st Earl of Yarborough in 1837; †1846). Appuldurcombe became Lord Yarborough's subsidiary home, which he visited frequently as the first Commodore of the Royal Yacht Squadron at Cowes. He carried out substantial alterations, giving it a new entrance and forming a large library where works of art could be displayed. The 2nd Earl sold Appuldurcombe in 1855, when much of the collection was moved to Brocklesby. Appuldurcombe was used *c.* 1867–90 as a boarding school, and in 1901–7 by Benedictine monks from Solesmes, France, who moved on to Quarr House, near Ryde, and established what became the modern abbey (*see* Quarr Abbey). In 1943 a bomb fell nearby and caused severe damage to the unoccupied house.

In 1952 Appuldurcombe was taken over by the Historic Buildings and Monuments Commission for England, the predecessor of English Heritage, which now manages the house and surroundings. It was then decided to remove what remained of the roof and structural timberwork, preserving the building as a shell. A further stage of restoration began in 1986. Roofs were constructed over the eastern part – sheltering the Great Hall, where replicas of former classical columns were introduced. External stonework details were meticulously restored, and sashes of Georgian design inserted in the E elevation – Appuldurcombe has regained its C18 appearance on its most significant side.

THE EARLY C18 HOUSE

It is best to describe the house first from the E or GARDEN SIDE, where it looks largely as it did in the early C18, almost certainly as designed by *John James* (*see* below). The main five-bay block is of two storeys with tall attic, focused on a central doorway between giant Corinthian columns. Two-storey pavilions, each of three bays under a prominent pediment, project boldly as wings. A modillion cornice continues round the whole frontage at the level of the attic floor on the central block and of the bases of the pediments on the wings. The walls are basically of sandstone (from quarries in the Undercliff near Bonchurch), with Portland stone for important features and dressings. 37

Work started on the northern pavilion in 1701. The central part of the old house survived in some measure until it was replaced *c.* 1705–6 by the present main block, including the Great Hall. The entrance doorway itself is quite 38
modest; square-headed under a shallow bracketed hood. Above is a circular window crowned by the figure of a satyr amid contorted foliage, and flanked by hanging drapery – all exquisitely carved. Doorway, circular window, foliage and drapery are contained by the giant Corinthian columns which rise to a projecting part of the main cornice. The two

Appuldurcombe, east front.
Engraving from Colen Campbell, *Vitruvius Britannicus* vol. 3, 1725

main storeys, including the central range and wings, are of even height. The windows have raised frames with triple keystones. The inner faces of the wings have pairs of concave niches on each floor, contained in raised frames which are narrower versions of those of the windows. Giant Corinthian pilasters, rising from just above ground level, are special features of the composition, particularly on the wings. Two pairs of chimneystacks, each pair linked by arches (very much in the manner of Vanbrugh), punctuate the skyline. As part of the restoration in the 1980s, sash windows of early C18 form were inserted throughout the E frontage.

Many of the features cited are characteristic of the English Baroque tradition around the beginning of the C18. An engraving in the third volume of *Vitruvius Britannicus* (1725) illustrates the E elevation, including details not now existing, which make it seem more Baroque than at present. The central composition, including the giant Corinthian columns which flank the entrance and rise to the main cornice, is surmounted on the engraving by an open pediment with a prominent cartouche. Nothing now exists of this pediment. Other non-existing features shown are urns and statuettes on the parapet where there is now a balustrade, and large urns at the angles of the pavilion pediments. In 1713 the mason *James Clarke* was paid for altering the pediment over the hall door, and it may have been then that the pediment and cartouche shown on the engraving in *Vitruvius Britannicus* were taken away; or they never existed.

John James (*c.* 1673–1746) was associated with Wren, first as Master Carpenter at St Paul's Cathedral, then, from 1715, as Assistant Surveyor there; he became Surveyor to the fabric after Wren's death in 1723. He was also connected with the building of Greenwich Hospital from 1705, and in 1718 became joint Clerk of Works there. The evidence for James's involvement with Appuldurcombe is based partly on questions of style, and is supported in correspondence at Longleat House between Sir Robert Worsley and his father-in-law Lord Weymouth. James is known to have had reservations about some of the tendencies of English Baroque design in his early career, and came to show sympathy for the growing fashion for Palladianism. Sir Howard Colvin's *Biographical Dictionary of British Architects* notes that James's buildings 'are for the most part plain and unadventurous', but cites Appuldurcombe as an exception.

James's design for the house was not fully achieved, since Sir Robert largely suspended building work after 1711, and the part of the house built by then was much modified in the later C18 and C19. The central block as designed by James consisted largely of the hall, occupying its whole width, with rooms above. This was intended to be flanked by long wings, projecting to the E with the pavilions as at present, and extending for greater distances W, where they would have bordered a large open courtyard. Little was built of James's N wing during his lifetime, but his S wing was largely complete by 1711; it was much altered about a century later. The S ELEVATION of this wing had the same general form as the E frontage, with a recessed central part and flanking pavilions, but was longer, simpler in detail, and had different proportions. The central block was of seven bays and two storeys with attic topped by a balustrade; the upper part of this façade largely survives, above a seven-bay Doric colonnade added by Lord Yarborough between the pavilions in the early C19. To the r. is the side elevation of the SE pavilion, which is duplicated to the l., at the SW corner. The pavilions are of only one wide bay on their S sides, with eaves cornices formed by the roof slopes behind the pediments. These arrangements give somewhat awkward effects in the general composition. The colonnade formed the front of a veranda to Lord Yarborough's new library (*see* Interiors). The veranda roof does not survive, but a simple iron balustrade over the colonnade indicates the former presence of a balcony. Glazed windows were not replaced on the S frontage during the 1980s, so that the house appears clearly as a shell from this direction.

Sir Richard added a range of rooms on the W side of the hall following his return from the Grand Tour in 1772 (altered in the C19 and now unroofed). These encroached on the space which would have formed the open courtyard if both of James's long wings had been fully built. In fact, Sir Richard completed the N WING on James's intended alignment, largely following his external design. It included service accommodation, and at its N termination is a pavilion which originally contained the kitchen. This was built in general imitation of James's pavilions at the other corners, although its stonework is of different character.

Lord Yarborough's PORTE COCHÈRE, added at an uncertain date between 1806 and 1846, is a prominent and (at least in its present roofless state) ungainly feature. It projects from the alignment of the NW and SW pavilions, with carriage entrances to N and S; it has a blank W frontage (which of course would not have been seen on the approach). The carriage entrances are fronted by handsome shallow Doric porches, with free-standing columns and plain entablatures. Entrance towards the house from the porte cochère was through a smaller doorway with simple pilasters. This is of stone, but the flanking walls are now of exposed brick, the plaster having been removed.

The architects of the 1770s alterations and of the C19 work for Lord Yarborough are unrecorded. There is slight evidence that *James Wyatt* may have offered advice in the 1770s.* More definite is the involvement of *William Dunn* (or *Donn*), who supervised much of Sir Richard's work, but it is uncertain to what extent he was more than a craftsman or artisan. He was employed at Claydon House, Buckinghamshire, in 1770–1, in connection with architectural work there.

INTERIORS

The entry for present-day visitors follows the same route as in the mid C19, but under very different conditions. They go through what remains of the porte cochère, into a small space, and past denuded rooms into the partly restored

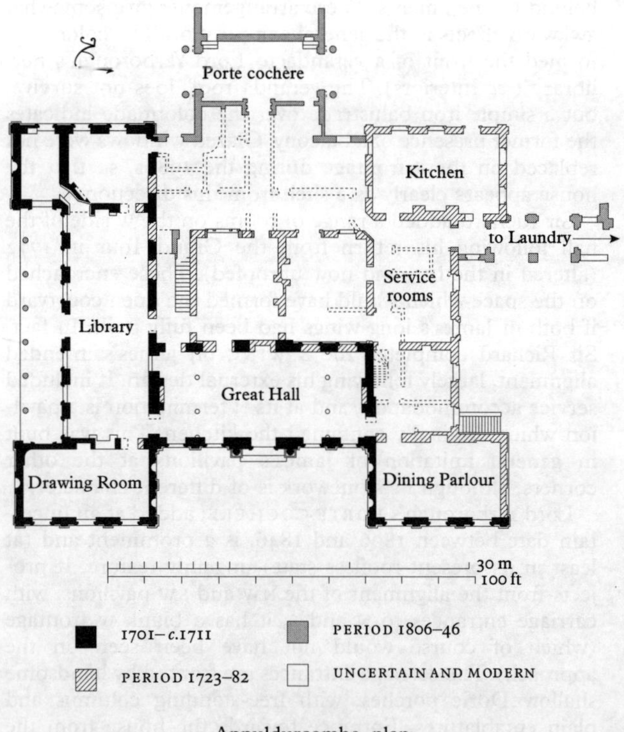

Appuldurcombe, plan.
After English Heritage

*The suggestion derives from records of payments to 'Mr Wyatt'. The payments were small, and the Wyatt in question was probably a local builder or craftsman.

Great Hall. This gives an impression of the house as it is today very different from that obtained on the garden side, looking towards the splendidly restored E front. It is the latter impression which ought to remain in the memory.

The doorway from the porte cochère now leads into a small COURTYARD, representing the W part of the large open courtyard envisaged in James's design, reduced through Sir Richard Worsley's late C18 alterations. The wall fronting the range of rooms which Sir Richard built on the W side of the Great Hall forms the E boundary. It is in a somewhat battered state, and the rooms behind, which were altered in the C19, have of course been stripped. It is hardly possible to recapture the form and appearance of the entrance to the house from the porte cochère after Lord Yarborough's alterations were completed. The courtyard itself was subdivided in the later C19 (presumably when the house was used as a school), and now shows the remains of demolished partition walls.

Sir Richard Worsley transformed the GREAT HALL. James's hall was quite low, being contained in the ground storey. Sir Richard heightened the hall, encroaching into the space of the floor above. An open screen of four Ionic columns faced in scagliola (two free-standing, two engaged) was inserted towards each end of the remodelled hall. When the house was reduced to a shell after the Second World War the columns were removed. Since the 1980s the block has again been protected by a roof, not at the level of the previous ceiling, but in a higher position over the spaces formerly occupied by the first-floor rooms and attic. In 1987 replicas of the Ionic columns at the S end of the Hall were inserted in their original locations, together with a beam, with plaster frieze, in the position where it would have spanned the room under the ceiling. Scagliola columns, without capitals or a cross-beam, were also erected at the N end. The marble floor of the 1770s, with tiles set diagonally and a simple geometric pattern in the centre, has survived. So something of the character and appearance of the later C18 Great Hall can once again be appreciated.

The history of the staircases at Appuldurcombe remains a mystery. Before Lord Yarborough's alterations the main staircase was probably S of the Great Hall, in part of the area in the S wing which Yarborough converted into a library. The present staircase, SW of the Great Hall, evidently dates from Yarborough's alterations, but is strangely unimpressive. It is in simple dog-leg form with plain stone steps and thin moulded iron balusters. Its modest scale may be a reflection of the status of Appuldurcombe as Lord Yarborough's secondary home.

LANDSCAPE AND SURROUNDINGS

Sir Richard Worsley commissioned *Capability Brown* in the 1770s to improve the already fine landscape. Few detailed features survive from his planting, but the whole setting, with its sweeping but not awesome hill-slopes and informally disposed clusters of trees, has a generally late C18 feel. Two skyline landmarks have been lost. An obelisk erected in 1774 on a crest ½ m. to the NW was struck by lightning in 1831; a pile of stonework marks the site. A 'Gothick' folly, Cook's Castle, built *c.* 1773 on a hilltop over a mile to the E, was demolished in the mid C20.

FREEMANTLE GATE, about ½ m. N of the mansion, is a triumphal arch probably built by Sir Richard in the 1770s; it spans the carriage drive at the entrance to the former park. The name of no architect is known, although that of *James Wyatt* has been suggested (*see* p. 70). On the outer side the large, simply moulded arch, with heraldic keystone, is flanked by pairs of engaged Ionic columns, under an entablature with broad frieze and prominent cornice. The inner elevation is similar, without the keystone and with pilasters instead of columns. The scale of the carriage arch is emphasized by small pedestrian arches on either side. The original wrought-iron GATES survive in all three arches; they have slender balusters and curved tops reflecting in reverse the curvatures of the arches.

The CARRIAGE DRIVE to Appuldurcombe left what is now the Godshill–Shanklin road about 1 m. N of Freemantle Gate, passed through it, and took a serpentine course to the

Appuldurcombe, Freemantle Gate, elevation.
Drawing by Alan C. Pennell, 1948

mansion. Although now generally closed to traffic, the drive provides a magnificent approach for walkers from Godshill.

ARRETON 5085

A large parish (once even larger), stretching S from the chalk ridge over the Island's central vale. Arreton Manor and its related buildings group with the church under the slope, and the village straggles SE along the main road towards Haseley Manor. There are several outlying farmsteads and smaller manorial centres.

ST GEORGE. One of the most remarkable churches on the Island, possibly the successor to an earlier Saxon 'mother church'. It has impressive late Saxon work at the W end (seen only internally), and mid- to late C13 architecture of outstanding quality in the chancel and S chapel. At first the 18
church appears quite homely as we approach from the SW. This is due partly to the relatively small W tower, with disproportionately large angle buttresses, and partly to the catslide roof sweeping over nave and aisles. One must go inside to appreciate fully the scale and quality of the building.

The W wall is essentially late Saxon. The W doorway is 10
well preserved on its inner side, with typical long-and-short work in the jambs, and thin imposts flush with the wall but chamfered under the arch. There are no rebates for a former door, indicating that the doorway must have opened at the

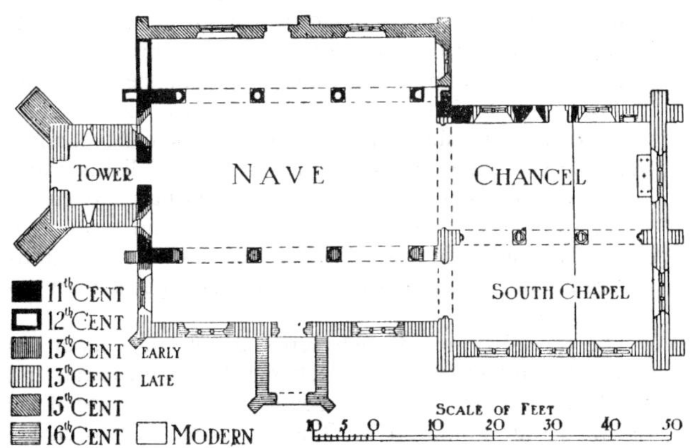

Arreton church, plan.
From *The Victoria County History, Hampshire and the Isle of Wight* vol. 5, 1912

start from a roofed space further W. High above the doorway is a round-headed aperture of similar date, splayed inside, which has no evidence of groove or rebate, showing that it too must have opened from a room. So there was a two-storey W porticus, which was evidently replaced by the present tower in the C13. A short time before the latter was built, two lancets were inserted in the W wall to either side; they were later blocked (being very close to the corners of the tower), but were reopened in the C19.

Another feature of Saxon character is a deeply splayed round-headed window in the N wall of the chancel, showing that the W part of the chancel is of early origin: Saxon, or at least late C11. (This window was blocked in the C13 but reopened in the C19.) So the pre-1100 church must have occupied the space of the present nave without the aisles (an area of 49 by 23 ft, 15 by 7 metres), plus part of the chancel. This was large for a Saxon parish church.

18 A N aisle was built in the late C12. The three-bay arcade has slightly pointed chamfered arches. Its capitals and responds have thin squared abaci chamfered at the corners, as on several arcades of the period on the Island (*see* Introduction, p. 19). One capital has scallop decoration. A S aisle was added in the early C13, with widely chamfered arches of two orders with simple rounded capitals. At some time in the mid to late C13 a clerestory was built above the arcades on both sides, with quatrefoiled circular openings. This is now covered by the catslide roof.

Arreton church was closely associated with Quarr Abbey (q.v.), which received the rectorial tithes from *c.* 1150, making it responsible, in particular, for the fabric of the E part of the church. The chancel was extended and the S chapel built in the mid to late C13 in exquisite E.E. style. It is suggested in the Introduction (p. 21) that this was one of a series of works carried out under the influence of Isabella de Fortibus, who held the lordship of the Isle 1262–93 and
19 was patron of the abbey. The windows in the chancel and S chapel are Geometrical; the E ones are of three lights, those in the side walls of two. The main lights have no cusps; above are traceried circles – three in the E windows, one in each of the side windows. The slender shafts to the jambs and mullions – internal and external – are specially attractive features.

The three-bay arcade between chancel and chapel has graceful, slender piers of Purbeck marble. Their capitals and moulded bases are models of beauty, the latter being of the so-called waterholding type. The arches are of two chamfered orders and do not rise directly from the capitals in the normal way – there are short cylindrical blocks above the capitals from which they spring. Such features are also found in the nearly identical arcade at Shalfleet (q.v.), and in churches on the Hampshire mainland. The wide chancel arch is similar in style, with slender jamb shafts rising from restored corbels a few feet above the floor. The arch from S chapel to S aisle was a smaller version of this but has been altered. Above it is a blocked two-light C13 window which must have opened over the roof of the original S aisle, but was filled in when the aisle was heightened.

Important alterations took place at the end of the Middle Ages. A wide rood loft was erected against the chancel arch on its W side; it does not survive, but there is a reopened archway which contained the stair to it between the E respond of the S arcade and the jamb of the chancel arch. A two-light square-headed window at clerestory level must have opened onto the loft. Both aisles were probably reconstructed and heightened at the same time; they now have two three-light square-headed side windows. A S porch was built then or later, with broad parapet and angle buttresses; it has a remarkable vaulted roof with chamfered cross-ribs, similar to those at Niton and Whitwell (qq.v.). It shelters the S doorway which has a complex series of delicate mouldings, extending from the jambs into the arch with no intermediate capitals. This is probably mid- to late C13 (though shown as C16 by the VCH). There is a similar but much simpler W doorway to the tower, which was built around that time. The upper storey of the tower was rebuilt *c.* 1500 or later, with simple paired belfry lights and battlements.

The catslide roof is the most disturbing feature of the church architecturally, since it covers the clerestory. Its date is uncertain; it must be post-Reformation, since it also covers the small two-light window which lit the rood loft. There is reference to unspecified work on the roof in 1649, and in 1738 the nave roof was ceiled in plaster. The latter is the latest possible date, since the ceiling plaster remained until removed in *Ewan Christian*'s restoration of 1886. This was the second of two Victorian restorations; the first, in 1863, mainly affected the chancel; the second was more thorough and resulted in most of the furnishings being renewed.

FURNISHINGS. FONT, 1886. Square bowl of grey marble, with round corner shafts; the design is based on remains of a C13 font found during the restoration. – PULPIT, 1924 by *Percy Stone*; of wood with arched panels, incorporating some Jacobean details. – SCULPTURE. On the E wall of the N aisle, a beautiful fragment of a C13 Christ in Majesty in an elongated quatrefoil, pointed top and bottom, rounded l. and r. It was recovered at the church's restoration. – MONUMENTS. Brass to Henry Hawls, S chapel. Early C15, a 2 ft 6 in. figure, headless. – N aisle, Henry Roberts, †1754, cartouche with cherubs. – Along the S aisle is the most notable series of early C19 wall monuments on the Island. Henry

Worsley Holmes, †1811, by *Sir Richard Westmacott.* A youth, like St John on Patmos, seated among rocks. From the l. comes an eagle, from the r. a female genius. – Sir Richard Fleming Worsley Holmes, drowned in 1814. Also by *Westmacott,* and even more Baroque than the other. A woman in despair, a wrecked ship on the r., a broken anchor on the l. – Sir Leonard Worsley Holmes, †1825, by *J. Haskoll.* The wife seated like a Grecian matron by a wreathed pedestal with an urn. Two children stand on the other side, mourning also. A very fine work by a little-known sculptor.

The CHURCHYARD is attractive, not over-tidied, with several minor Georgian tombstones. It contains the WAR MEMORIAL by *Percy Stone,* 1919; slender octagonal shaft with shield on the cross.

ARRETON MANOR. Built 1637–9, on the site of an earlier house, by Humphrey Bennett (who had bought the property in 1630).* A typical and well-preserved example of an early to mid-C17 Island manor house (conservative for its date in national terms), retaining much contemporary woodwork within. It is H-shaped, two-storeyed, built of
29 limestone rubble with freestone dressings. The main (S) elevation has gabled wings and two-storey porch; a small W extension of 1812 in similar style disturbs the symmetry. The windows are mullioned in ranges of three to five. The porch, with the date 1639, has a moulded three-centred arch; the inner doorway is four-centred within a square frame, and has a fine studded panelled door. Three pairs of brick chimneystacks with moulded bases and tops.

The porch opens into the SE corner of the hall. This has panelling of which some was originally in an upstairs room, but was sold in 1938, and bought back by a later owner. It has a simple pattern of panels with fluted pilasters and foliage frieze. The stone fireplace is restored (the chimneypiece originally in the hall is now at the Priory Bay Hotel, *see* St Helens). On the E side of the hall is a plain but substantial screen of C17 date (it has been claimed to be earlier) which conceals the staircase.

The finest room is in the wing W of the hall; it has richly detailed woodwork, much of which is probably *in situ* from the time of building, but some features have been added. Above the stone fireplace, with its nearly flat arch, is a three-panelled wooden overmantel. The central panel has the Bennett coat of arms in an arched frame; the outer two have cross patterns with small carvings in relief, supposedly of Mars and the Goddess of Plenty. At the top is a foliage frieze, and flanking the fireplace are pilasters with drapery

*Information about the building of Arreton Manor from a draft history of Island properties by Clifford Webster, former Archivist at the Isle of Wight County Record Office.

Arreton Manor, chimneypiece, elevation.
From Percy Stone, *The Architectural Antiquities of the Isle of Wight*, 1891

and garlands, suspended from lions' mouths. The room has fine panelling, especially on the W wall, where Ionic pilasters and parts of the frieze have carvings of vine stems and grapes. Some of the panelling on the E wall must have been rearranged; a pilaster there has a stylized figure under a cocked hat. This is one of the most memorable ensembles of work by the C17 Island carvers (*see* Introduction, p. 30), using motifs typical of domestic internal work of the period. The simple staircase, E of the hall, has rounded newels and widely spaced balusters. Upstairs, a room retains a stone fireplace with four-centred arch; this room contained some of the panelling now in the hall.

SE of the Manor, between it and the church, was an impressive group of ancillary buildings. The principal one, a BARN, is now a ruin, its fine roof lost, but an early C17 stone DOVE HOUSE remains – rectangular, two-storeyed, *p. 78* with hoodmoulds over the doorway and over the pigeon entrance below the end gable.

HASELEY MANOR, ¾ m. SE. Originally a grange held by Quarr Abbey. From 1538 the home of George Mill (son of John Mill who demolished the abbey), and then of his widow Dowsabel. In 1609 it was bought by Sir Thomas Fleming, Lord Chief Justice, and it remained in Fleming ownership until the early C19. It became a farmhouse, and by the 1970s was derelict. It was restored from 1977 and was open to the public, with varied exhibits, for several years.

The house is set round an irregular courtyard open to the E. The long S wing shows a mixture of stone and brick with assorted windows; it was built in more than one stage, the

Arreton Manor, dove house, drawing by A.L. Collins.
From *The Victoria County History, Hampshire and the Isle of Wight* vol. 5, 1912

N part from the mid C15, on internal evidence (*see* below), the rest evidently later. The main (W) range, partly faced in C18 brick, has a bulky porch of the 1990s with a four-centred doorway and flat roof-line. The small N wing is of 1778 but its windows have been altered.

The main range is of composite and uncertain dates. It contains three rooms which possibly reflect medieval or Tudor planning, but no visible features (except in the roof) look earlier than C17. Two massive chimneystacks project from the W elevation, with brick chimneys set diagonally – paired to the S, single to the N. There are square-topped fireplaces, simply moulded but without arch shapes. The former kitchen to the N has a very large brick fireplace with elliptical arch, probably C18. The southernmost room in the range was fitted modestly as a drawing room in the late C18, with a Venetian S window – set in a wall externally of smooth-faced stone, with mathematical-tiled gable above. The roof structure over the S part of the main range has curved wind-braces, suggesting a C16 date, but that over the rest is C17 or later.

Part of the roof over the S wing, towards its western end, has been dendro-dated 1440–60. One exposed truss, probably the central feature of a former upper-floor chamber, has a collar-beam with arched braces. Re-set on the external N wall of the wing is a SCULPTED FRAGMENT including the arms of Henry VII, placed in a broken part of what was clearly the angle of a former arch, with foliage in the spandrel. Where the arch was originally is not known.

LITTLE EAST STANDEN, ¾ m. NW. Adjoining the house is a picturesque group of FARM BUILDINGS, C18 or earlier, with walls of limestone, chalk, sandstone and weatherboarding.

GREAT EAST STANDEN MANOR, ½ m. WNW. C18 front of five bays, irregularly spaced, with grey headers and red brick dressings; the windows have slightly segmental tops. At the N end a very massive chimneystack, dated 1768.

STANDEN HOUSE, facing the A3056 N of Blackwater, 2 m. W. Fine seven-bay mid-C18 brick front; the porch has engaged Doric columns and triglyph frieze. (Inside, a fine STAIRCASE probably contemporary with the house.)

MERSTON MANOR. *See* Merstone.

GREAT BUDBRIDGE MANOR. *See* Godshill.

BARTON MANOR *see* WHIPPINGHAM

BEMBRIDGE 6085

The name Bembridge applied at first to the whole of the wide peninsula S of the original Brading Haven. A significant village did not develop until the early C19. It is now large and sprawling, related both to the curving coastline E and SE, and to the fairly small harbour on the NW side, which is the remaining part of the once extensive Haven.

HOLY TRINITY. 1845–6 by *Thomas Hellyer*, replacing a church of 1826–7.* Of Swanage stone externally with W tower and spire, S aisle and short S chapel, the windows mainly lancets except in the chancel with its three-light E window. In 1896–7 additions were made by *A.R. Barker*, a transeptal organ chamber to the N, and a large SE vestry which abuts on to the E wall of the S chapel and extends a little further E than the chancel, with a gabled elevation. Internal details mainly of Bath stone; substantial chancel arch of two orders, the outer order moulded and without capitals. S arcade with round piers of stone darker than the rest. – REREDOS by *F.E. Hansard*, *c.* 1900; gilded oak, with traceried niches filled by (partly later) figures. – FONT. Tall circular bowl with trefoiled and shafted arches.

Several interesting features around and near the small GREEN (now almost more a traffic intersection), SE of the church. The present Heritage Centre was built as a school in 1833, possibly by *T.E. Owen* of Portsmouth, with wavy-edged gables and an arched three-light window with intricate

* The 1827 church has been attributed to *Nash*, but Incorporated Church Building Society documents in Lambeth Palace Library are signed by *Jacob Owen*, who like his son *T.E. Owen* was a noted Portsmouth architect.

tracery. WAR MEMORIAL by *Percy Stone*, *c.* 1920; tall cross on stepped base. S of the Green some stuccoed cottage-villas of *c.* 1830, and WATERLOO COTTAGE of 1784 in local limestone – one of the few houses in the village built of the stone misleadingly named after it (*see* p. 7). Further S is a
84 TELEPHONE KIOSK, a rare survival of the early K1 type, installed 1929; concrete frame with heavy canopy and spidery metal finial. E of the church is the VICARAGE, Gothic of *c.* 1861 in stone with square-headed windows, gabled wings, and a porch with trefoiled arches between the wings; later Victorian S extension. Further E in SHERBOURNE STREET is a remarkable row of houses, *c.* 1980; contrived irregular effect with the alignment receding in stages from S to N; gables and windows of different sizes and decorative bargeboards to the porches. Between King's Road and Ducie Avenue is HILL GROVE, the remaining part of an early C19 stuccoed house attributed to *Nash*, which had a central dome and main entrance flanked by pairs of giant Ionic pilasters set diagonally – a surprising and successful motif.* Alas, the dome and entrance features were lost, following partial collapse in the 1960s, and what remains includes the fairly ordinary S façade with bowed centrepiece and thin end pilasters.

BEMBRIDGE HARBOUR dates in its present form from 1877–8, when a causeway carrying a branch railway was built across the former Brading Haven, enabling a large part of the once extensive sheet of water to be drained (*see* Brading). The railway station of 1887 and a hotel of 1882, which made an impressive group, have been demolished, but the FOUNTAIN of 1910 which adjoined them survives; exuberant Free Baroque with bulging brackets, dome and iron finial. Of the flats that now border the harbour the best group is well to the N in St Helens, q.v.

Other notable buildings are scattered. BEMBRIDGE WINDMILL, ⅓ m. SW, has a simple circular stone shell with wooden cap, gabled at the opposite end from the sails; wooden machinery in working order. (BEMBRIDGE LODGE, set back from the E side of High Street at its far end, N of the windmill, is of three bays, *c.* 1820–30, with lower wings since heightened, and a doorway renewed in the C20.) STEYNE LODGE, ½ m. S, is early C19, extended in the mid C19; the extended part was largely rebuilt *c.* 1900 by *John Belcher* for the marine engineer Sir John Thornycroft. Early C19 stuccoed E frontage of three bays with shuttered windows under a broad-eaved hipped roof, and a tent-roofed iron veranda. *Belcher*'s S front has a slightly

*The attribution is uncertain. The house was built (or enlarged) in 1827 by Edward Wise, a local landowner who may have known Nash and was also associated with the building of the first church.

higher profile; it has small-paned windows and an off-centre projection with a Venetian window under an open gable pediment.

The former BEMBRIDGE SCHOOL was founded in 1919 by J.H. Whitehouse, an admirer of John Ruskin, on a coastal site off Hillway Road, ¾ m. S. Whitehouse was associated with the Arts and Crafts movement, and with schemes for social reform including Bournville model village in Birmingham. He made a large collection of material associated with Ruskin, which he kept at the school, and bought Brantwood in Cumbria, Ruskin's home, in the 1930s. The school ceased to be a separate institution in the 1990s, when it merged with Ryde School (*see* p. 244). The Ruskin collection was moved to Lancaster University in 1997.

Most of the school buildings are now put to other uses, but NEW HOUSE, in the centre of the complex, remains a school boarding house; built 1925 as the Warden's House by *M.H. Baillie Scott* in association with *Whitehouse*, including dormitories and school accommodation. The main elevation faces S; basically of brick but with three sets of canted bay windows rising through both storeys, tile-hung between the casements on each floor, under a wide-eaved roof with flat dormers. To the W is a larger-scaled addition built in 1929 to house the Ruskin collection. The E frontage is irregular, with a short centrepiece containing three entrance arches and half-timbered upper floor; to the NE is a wing with complicated hipped roof and a two-storey bay with herringbone brick, contained in timber framing, in the space between the windows. Further N is the CHAPEL, now not used, 1931–3 by *W.A. Harvey & H.G. Wicks*, the architects of Bournville, and extended to the W (liturgical E) in 1961–2; it is of brick with a sweeping tiled roof and a plainly detailed porch-tower at the (liturgical) W end. Above the entrance, under the tower, is a SCULPTURE in relief of St George by *Alec Miller*, 1949. Attractive interior with wooden aisle-posts, collar-beams and curved braces; simple panelled pews partly arranged sideways. A cottage at the entrance to the site, originally CULVER COTTAGE, with broad gabled upper storey, was built in 1920 following a design of 1914–15 by *Baillie Scott* for a miner's dwelling in Scotland.

BEMBRIDGE FARM, Centurions Lane, 1 m. SW. Adjoining the simple early C19 farmhouse is an impressive group of FARM BUILDINGS, including a barn, stables and former brewhouse. Many are from the C18, with C19 accretions and extensions; they are largely in limestone rubble with ashlar quoins.

MONUMENT on Culver Down, about 2 m. S, to the 1st Earl of Yarborough, †1846 (*see* Appuldurcombe). A massive obelisk of granite with vermiculated rustication, set on a square base with family arms carved on two sides. Originally erected in 1849 on a site ½ m. W, but moved in the 1860s when the old site was taken by BEMBRIDGE FORT, an outlying defensive work in earth and brick, capping the chalk ridge from which there are huge views. The S face of this ridge is partly formed by the sheer white cliffs which mark the N side of Sandown Bay.

4580 BILLINGHAM

Shorwell

BILLINGHAM MANOR is set back on the E side of the Newport–Chale road, where the downland gives way to lower-lying country. It developed from a substantial early to mid-C17 house of stone, which was greatly extended in brick in the early C18. (There is a date, usually interpreted as 1631 but which may be 1651, on the W front, and one of 1722 above a window on the E front.) There was much alteration in the late C19 and C20. The most famous resident was the writer J.B. Priestley from 1933; he moved to Brook Hill, Brook (q.v.) in 1948.

The four frontages are very different. The description begins with the W side containing the entrance, and continues clockwise. The main W elevation is of stone, basically C17, and retaining a two-light mullioned window on the ground floor. On the first floor are two early C18 sashes, and a large five-light transomed window of uncertain date (lighting the staircase) in between. Entrance to the house is through a severe C18 porch (off-centre to the r.) with pediment, triglyph frieze and rusticated pilasters. At the S end a service wing, mainly C19–C20, projects to the W. In the angle between this wing and the main W front is what may have been a two-storey C17 porch, refronted and altered in the C18 and later. A small gable and finial, rising above the present W parapet of this feature, was possibly the top of a larger gable to the original porch.

The fairly short N front of four bays has the finest external details. It is of *c.* 1720–2, in excellent brickwork with stone quoins, but stands on a C17 stone basement (of which the top part is above ground level), with two-light mullioned windows. The main windows are sashes in broad wooden frames, taller on the ground floor than on the first floor. The two end windows on the first floor have raised brick surrounds. Between the floors is a wide, cornice-like string course in moulded brick.

The garden front (E), also of brick, has deep wings with stone quoins and hipped roofs, but is not as purely C18 as at first sight it looks. The space between the wings was infilled around 1900, and J.B. Priestley added a pavilion 'like the bridge of a ship' over the infill. This provided extensive views – he wrote much of his autobiographical *Rain Upon Godshill* there. The infill was removed in 1955 and the three-bay central part restored to a modified version of the C18 original, with the upper-floor windows smaller than before. But the one-bay E elevations of the wings, under hipped roofs, are of *c.* 1720–2; with upper-floor windows similar to those on the N front.*

The S elevation, always a service frontage, has confused features of different dates. Much of the ground floor, essentially a raised basement, is C17 and stone-built, with a two-light mullioned window and a simple four-centred doorway. Sadly, the effect of these was, at the time of visiting, overwhelmed by drainage pipes.

Inside, the finest feature is the main STAIRCASE of *c.* 1720–2, of well form. It has slender spiral balusters and scrolled and foliated treads, delicately carved. (A wooden C17 SECONDARY STAIRCASE, of winder form in a panelled oak frame, leads up from the service doorway in the S elevation. In a corner of the NW room on the ground floor is an early C18 ROTATING BOOKCASE, set behind a vertically sliding panel within an arched frame.)

To the NE of the house is an C18 GAZEBO; square, of brick, with one window. This was a shell in the C19; in the C20 it was re-roofed in tiles, and topped by a white wooden turret with ledges, making it appear as a dovecote.

LITTLE BILLINGHAM (or West Billingham). Handsome farmhouse of 1720 (date over doorway), across the road to the W of Billingham Manor. The five-bay E front is of limestone ashlar. The windows are C19 casements, but set in openings which are obviously C18, taller on the ground floor than on the first, with keystones on the lintels. The central doorway has a similar lintel and keystone. The keystones of the outer windows of both floors, as well as those of the central upper window and the doorway, are fluted. (Presumably the original windows were sashes, matching those of *c.* 1720 on the Manor.) The sophistication of the frontage does not extend to the other elevations, which are simply of rough stone.

BINSTEAD *5590*

Ryde

In 1079 a tract of land including Binstead was granted to the Bishop of Winchester as a source of stone for rebuilding his

* Percy Stone's drawing in *The Architectural Antiquities of the Isle of Wight* (1891) shows that the windows on the central part of the early C18 garden front had framed architraves, much as on the wings and the N front. The restored windows on this part of the frontage do not have them.

cathedral – the hard limestone, later known as Quarr stone (after the abbey founded ¾ m. to the W in 1131, q.v.), which was largely exhausted in the C13. However, the rougher, fossil-shelly Binstead stone continued to be quarried, especially in the C14, and sporadically until Victorian times (*see* p. 8). The village was small until the C19, when it developed along the Ryde–Newport road (chiefly in brick), with the church in relative seclusion to the N. To the W of the church are hollows overgrown with trees, the sites of quarries from which material for cathedrals and many other buildings was taken.

HOLY CROSS. Of the small medieval quarrymen's church the chancel survives; the nave was rebuilt in 1845 by *Thomas Hellyer*. Much of the chancel walling is in herringbone masonry, suggesting an early date, but the windows (three-light E, two-light S) are mid- to late C13; uncusped lights with trefoiled upper circles. Their finish is sophisticated, with outside and internal hoodmoulds and deep rere-arches. Also remarkable is a tall rectangular lowside

Binstead church, east window, elevation.
From Percy Stone, *The Architectural Antiquities of the Isle of Wight*, 1891

window, unblocked in 1884; this has a deep internal splay with a blind trefoil above the window, and rere-arch with moulded hood ending in carved stops. *Hellyer*'s nave has lancets; over the two in the W wall are small stones with weathered carvings from the older nave showing long-tailed beasts, one with wings, the other sucking its tail. Above the archway of Hellyer's porch is another small carving, a bird and cross symbolizing the Holy Spirit. The N aisle with four-bay arcade was added in 1875. The small W bellcote dates from 1925; a shaft in the W gable, resting on a head-corbel, was presumably related to the previous bellcote.

FURNISHINGS. A fire in 1969 destroyed the nave roof (since replaced in light hammerbeam construction) and damaged fittings, especially at the W end. The chancel furnishings escaped. The wooden ALTAR has seven carved panels, probably late C16 or early C17 Flemish. The central scene is of the Last Supper with the Presentation and Nativity below; it is flanked by subjects in arched panels including the Purification of the Virgin.* – PANELLING and other features were brought into the chancel in 1932 from Winchester College Chapel, attributed to *William Butterfield* and presumably removed from the chapel when W.D. Caröe restored it in 1913–21. Dark oak with traceried panels and, to the W, single stalls with pinnacled canopies. The rector's stall on the S side has a separate LECTERN in front, with a lively carving of Moses, his arms outstretched, supported by two other prophets; it is C19 but of unknown provenance (not part of the Butterfieldian ensemble). – FONT, 1844. Octagonal, with richly carved roundels of biblical scenes, ringed with stylized foliage. Designed by the *Hon. Henry Graves*, 1844 (church guide). – STAINED GLASS. In the N aisle two outstanding windows, in single lancets, by *Gabriel Loire* of Chartres. St John Baptist, with red background 80
around the head, 1971; Our Lady of Quarr, figure against blue background with de Redvers crest, 1987. – NE lancet of chancel by *Lawrence Lee*, representing the Holy Spirit, 1972. Also by *Lee*, two lancets in the W wall, and one in the SE of the nave with a symbolic cross.

The CHURCHYARD has been cleared of most of its TOMBSTONES, a deplorable practice in a place with a tradition of stone carving. A few remain, including some with Georgian cherubs and strapwork, and one showing a masted boat commemorating Thomas Sivell, a ferryman shot in 1776 in the mistaken belief that he was a smuggler. At the SE entrance to the churchyard a GATEWAY incorporates the late Norman arch from the N doorway of the

*The altar may have been made up (it was last modified in 1956), but the three central panels, and the four flanking ones, each belong together, though the two series are not necessarily from the same original source.

original nave; it has a simple roll moulding. Above it yet another re-erected medieval SCULPTURE, a crouching figure. Near the SW entrance of the churchyard is the former RECTORY, like a large cottage of local stone under a thatched roof.

5575 ## BONCHURCH

Ventnor

At the E end of the Undercliff (*see* p. 5), its buildings scattered amid the hillocks and hollows formed by the huge landslip several thousand years ago, with the very steep wooded slopes of St Boniface Down looming behind. From the later Middle Ages stone was quarried from the fallen parts of the Upper Greensand formation, often known as 'Green Ventnor', but the better deposits were exhausted by the late C18. The village was very small until the early 1830s when the main landowner, the Rev. Charles White, was constrained by terms in a will which forbade new development, but these were revoked in 1836. Many medium-sized villas were built in the next twenty years or so, with evident sensitivity in their siting and design. Apart from sometimes unfortunate infilling, Bonchurch has changed relatively little since then.

p. 22 ST BONIFACE (old church). One of the few medieval churches in England dedicated to this Saxon monk (†755), originally from Devon but later based in a monastery at Nursling near Southampton, who helped spread Christianity in Germany and became Archbishop of Mainz. A tiny building; nave and chancel, of Norman origin – see the simple S doorway, of two plain orders. The Norman-style

Bonchurch and setting, engraving, 1808.
From J.L. Whitehead, *The Undercliff of the Isle of Wight*, 1911

chancel arch was, however, largely renewed by *Percy Stone*, who restored the church in 1923 and 1931; old illustrations show a simple rounded arch. The chancel is C13 with N and S lancets, but the two-light E window and others in the church are late medieval or Tudor. The studded S DOOR is possibly C17. The square stone W bellcote appears to date from *c.* 1830, when repairs were carried out – it was not there in 1825. – WALL PAINTINGS.* Seemingly remains of more than one period high up on the nave N wall, though difficult to decipher. The earliest and most complete appears to show (from l. to r.) parts of two draped figures, a tower-like architectural feature, and swags of draperies decorated with stars. The top of this painting was destroyed later when the height of the wall was reduced, but doubtless the scheme originally occupied much of the nave. The draperies are Romanesque in style, and the architectural feature particularly reminiscent of the towers used to divide scenes in such early wall paintings in Sussex as those at Hardham of *c.* 1100. Other good parallels are provided by the Bury Gospels of *c.* 1130, so the painting can be dated to about the first third of the C12, i.e. most likely coeval with the building. It represents the only survival of Romanesque painting on the Island. – C17 Flemish wooden CROSS behind the altar, on base with winged cherubs, scrolls and floral swags; brought here in the early C19. – Very attractive CHURCHYARD with old headstones.

ST BONIFACE (new church). 1847–8 by *Benjamin Ferrey*. His first design was for a large nave and chancel in Neo-Norman style; he incorporated a N transept to provide more accommodation, but the matching S transept was not added until 1873. Outside, however, it is more like an Early English than a Romanesque church, with lancet windows that are rounded instead of pointed. Those on the W and transept-end elevations are paired with circular openings above; the E window is triple with similar circle over.*

Inside, the cruciform plan – although not originally intended – results in an impressive spatial form, with emphasis on the crossing arches which are in almost convincing Late Norman style. Chancel arch of two orders with roll moulding, scalloped capitals and shafts. The arches to the transepts are a little simpler. The lightly constructed roofs make a nice contrast. – PULPIT by *H. Bryant*, 1920. Stone with round-arched panels. – ROYAL ARMS, Queen Victoria. – FONT. Octagonal bowl with scallop decoration on the underside angles; black marble shafts. – The STAINED GLASS is collectively impressive; not all the artists are known. E windows by *William Wailes*, 1848. Crucifixion

*Descriptions contributed by David Park.

*The upper circle of the E window was enlarged *c.* 1898.

and other scenes with rich background detailing. The single side windows in the S transept are by *Henry Holiday*; that to the E, 1877 or later, shows St Benedict Biscop under a Gothic canopy; his folded robe is specially effective, although the colours have faded a little; the opposite window shows St Edith. Both have smaller scenes under the main figures. The westernmost side windows in the nave are by *Shrigley & Hunt* of Lancaster: St Faith on the S side, *c.* 1913, in flowing robes against a plain background; St John to the N. – TABLET to the 1st Earl Jellicoe, †1935; grey grained marble with coat of arms.

The CHURCHYARD was an old quarry site, its edges lushly landscaped, with a cliff-like face to the N. It contains the graves of Algernon Swinburne and other writers, and an Egyptian-style MAUSOLEUM of the Leeson family (dates 1864–72).

The itinerary of Bonchurch (not a Perambulation) begins in the vicinity of the old church, goes generally W, then turns S, and finally ascends the slope to the N.

The church is a little inland from the start of the stretch of rugged coast, subject to landslips and largely undeveloped, which extends N for two intensely scenic miles towards Shanklin.

A narrow road leads up to EAST DENE, the most remarkable house in the village – passing first its annexe Turret House (the description of which follows that of the house itself), and then the LODGE, essentially a *cottage orné* with a fretted bargeboard and a little oriel on the ground floor.

East Dene was built *c.* 1825–6, on the site of a former farmhouse, by *Samuel Beazley* for W.H. Surman, in an irregular 'Elizabethan' style. It was leased in 1836 to Captain (later Admiral) Charles Swinburne, who bought the property in 1841. His son Algernon, born in London in 1837, spent much of his childhood at East Dene. He returned to live there in 1863 (when he was beginning to be recognized as a poet), but in 1865 Admiral Swinburne sold the property to his son-in-law John Snowdon-Henry M.P. It was used as a convent *c.* 1910–14, housing nuns originally from France, and is now a holiday centre for young people.

The house of *c.* 1825–6 was enlarged, mainly eastwards, in *c.* 1854, roughly doubling its size. It is built in smooth, irregularly coursed sandstone under slate roofs. The entrance is in the unremarkable W front (*see* below), but it is best to look first at the S frontage, which faces a large lawn extending towards the sea. This frontage is of six bays, of which the W three are of *c.* 1825–6 and the others of *c.* 1854. Each part has a central gabled bay, slightly projecting, with a large mullioned-and-transomed window in the ground floor and a small oriel above. The later part has a slightly lower roof-line, but it is a little longer and more prominent – mainly because the ground-floor mullioned window breaks forward as a canted bay. The E frontage is irregular, with open-bargeboarded gables of different sizes and heights. A small bellcote over one of the gables is a relic of the use of the house as a convent.

The W frontage is confusing. Entrance to the house is through a nondescript porch (with a geometrically patterned tiled floor). Much of the INTERIOR is sumptuous, with features including chimneypieces, doorcases and panelling which were introduced at different times by both the Swinburnes and the Snowdon-Henrys. It is not always clear which is mid- or late C19 work and which was, at least in part, brought from elsewhere. There are two main ground-floor rooms on the southern side. That in the older part of the house is smaller but is more elaborately decorated, having a chimneypiece and doorways with motifs generally reminiscent of Artisan Mannerism. The fireplace is flanked by tapering panelled pilasters (of wood) with Ionic capitals. The wide doorway leading into the eastern room also has panelled pilasters and an intricately shaped architrave. The narrower doorway on the N side is similar, with roundels on the door panels. The flat ceiling, with shaped patterns formed by thin intersecting bands, may be a feature from *c.* 1825–6. The room to the E has large wall panels with beaded edges, and a relatively simple fireplace flanked diagonally by strongly coloured tiles in diamond patterns. The ceiling is in three sections divided by beams; each has panel patterns and a central roundel with colourful decoration. The mullioned bay window (described above from outside) gives a fine view to the sea. A room in the NE part of the house has a low-pitched roof with arched tie-beams and a large mullioned bay window facing E with heraldic stained glass (relating to the Snowdon-Henry family) in the upper lights. To its W is the STAIRCASE HALL, lit by another tall window with stained glass in small diamond-shaped patterns in largely opaque glazing. The well staircase has scrolled wooden openwork between the balusters, and the ceiling has a colourful panel with classical celestial figures.

TURRET HOUSE, SSW of the main house, was built after 1865 by John Snowdon-Henry as a stable and coachhouse block; it is now residential. Of stone, in two storeys round a courtyard. Its main feature is a GATEHOUSE, with a four-centred arch flanked by very large circular towers, each topped by a tall conical roof.

The former SCHOOL lies W of the entrance to East Dene and S of the C19 church; it is seen above a steep bank from the road. Built in 1848–9, largely at the expense of the Swinburne family, and enlarged in 1890 with a substantial W wing. The older part is domestic Jacobean with mullioned windows; the small E wing contained the master's house. Central wooden turret with short spire.

W of the school, across the road, is the entrance to COMPTON UNDERMOUNT – a complex house, now divided. The entrance is guarded by a LODGE of 1857, partly built of flint. The drive passes through a short TUNNEL (also of 1857), cut into a rocky outcrop of sandstone. An older farmhouse was replaced by (or enlarged into) a Picturesque villa called Undermount in 1827. It was embellished and extended from 1851 by Sir John and Lady Pringle (she had been Mistress of the Bedchamber to the Queen). The wing, later called Compton as a separate house, was added in 1857 and has a large, opulent Music Room with a heavy coffered ceiling and a central medallion depicting Aurora, possibly designed by *David Roberts*. The cornice frieze has festoon scrolls, with figures at the end of the ceiling ribs, while over the end bay window – in odd contrast – is a pattern of fan-vaulting. Elaborate chimneypiece with white marble fireplace and wooden surround. Opening from the terrace to the W was a conservatory or winter garden, added in 1863 and largely demolished in 1995; it was reconstructed in 2001 by *Charmian Shenton*, architect and owner, to a third of its original length – the end being rebuilt, as before, in polygonal form. Sloping roofs rise to a flat-topped clerestory supported by iron hoops and braces. The original house to the E, the present Undermount, has openwork bargeboards, curved with Rococo effects, and a mullioned staircase window filled with partly heraldic stained glass. Both parts of the present complex have chimneystacks in brick with moulded patterns.

The village street leads W. To its N is PEACOCK VANE, formerly Uppermount, enlarged *c.* 1830 with bowed W front embraced by a two-tiered iron-columned veranda under a tent roof. Beside the entrance to the house from the street is a GROTTO, also of *c.* 1830, with archway under a hood-mould with small gable, and iron gates leading to a vaulted chamber with waterspout. Beyond is a tree-shaded POND, formed *c.* 1800 and meticulously landscaped. SHORE ROAD leads S past villas in large grounds, many of them of *c.* 1835–50. The most remarkable is UNDER ROCK, two-storeyed to an unusual plan – basically polygonal with wings projecting at 45 degrees to each other; the walls are of ashlar with rough stone bands, under low slate roofs. The larger WESTFIELD, further S, has similar banding on its N side; the garden front looks earlier, with central bow and iron veranda. THE GRANGE to the E is an older house gabled and bargeboarded in the C19, with ugly later additions.

To the N of the village street and Victorian church is THE PITTS, where several more houses were built *c.* 1835–50, some since replaced. The gardens of those on the N side back on to cliff-like slopes which are the results of old quarrying. Cliff Cottage has two gables with fretted edges and a simple ground-floor veranda. Further E, Bonchurch Shute leads steeply uphill past The Cottage and Myrtle Cottage – simple rough stone houses, remarkable for having paired chimneys of flint.

BRADING 6085

Before the C19 Brading was the principal place in the E part of the Island. It was a small port at the head of a large tidal harbour most of which, after several previous attempts at reclamation, was drained in 1882, leaving the present smaller Bembridge Harbour (q.v.) well to the E. The church is by tradition an early foundation but is not firmly recorded before the C12; its large parish included what are now Sandown and Bembridge.

St Mary. Standing prominently at the N end of the town, with spired W tower, aisled nave, and N and S chapels under separate gables; in rough local limestone with finer dressings. An impressive church with an outstanding collection of monuments, especially to members of the Oglander family of Nunwell (q.v.). The early C13 tower makes a fine composition, with three open arches N, W and S, originally allowing a public way or a processional path to pass through. They are of two chamfered orders which die into massive semicircular jambs with thin imposts. Wide angle buttresses rise through two storeys of the tower, leaving a clear profile to the upper stage with its small paired belfry lights. Parapets project over simple corbel tables, and behind them rises a moderately high splay-foot spire, showing slight entasis. The spire itself is perhaps later than the tower, but of uncertain date.

Entered through a plain doorway under the tower, the interior seems quite grand, with well-proportioned five-bay arcades, *c.* 1190–1200, of the Island Transitional type (*see* p. 19): square abaci with canted corners, pointed chamfered arches. Most of the capitals have simple scallop decoration, the scallops varying in width (two capitals have only plain mouldings). The church had two restorations: 1864–6 by *Thomas Hellyer*, and 1875–6 by *A. W. Blomfield* when the chancel was extended and given a triple-lancet E window. The chancel arch could go with either restoration.

The N and S chapels are late C15 or early C16. The S or Oglander Chapel is the more sophisticated. Its two-bay arcade has a remarkable pier: eight engaged shafts alternate with rounded hollows to form an undulating effect; the four-centred arches have a pattern of squared and rounded mouldings. The N chapel arcade has a pier and responds of simple octagonal form, but its arch mouldings are similar to those opposite. The N aisle retains a W lancet; other aisle windows are restored, but those of the chapels have their original forms of three lights within four-centred frames. The S porch, disused as such, is mainly C19.

FURNISHINGS. REREDOS, by *Powell's*, 1908. Elaborate Gothic canopy with a representation in *opus sectile* of Christ at Emmaus; the dado on each side has panels with formalized leaf patterns in deep reds. – Wooden Jacobean ALTAR TABLE, now in the S chapel, with bulbous legs and inscription round the top. – PAINTING. Under the E window of the chapel, a copy of a C16 Pietà by Francia. – Wooden SCREENS in the W arch and western N arch of the Oglander Chapel, designed by *Hellyer*, 1866; broad low-arched openings with bands of tracery above. – Brass CHANDELIER in the chancel, 1798. – FONTS. Two; one is a plain square bowl with scallop decoration on the underside edge, set on a short round stem with rim moulding; presumably, but oddly, of *c.* 1200. The other is smaller and octagonal, probably C17. – In the chancel a STOUP (not *in situ*), with a square projecting bowl, roughly carved, on a rounded corbel. – STAINED GLASS. Triple E window by *Clayton & Bell*, 1876. In the Oglander Chapel the E window is by *Powell's*, 1900; the two S windows are C19 heraldic. In the S aisle, the three-light window W of the doorway is by *Powell's*, 1910; the next W, also three-light, is by *Clayton & Bell*, 1926. By the latter firm also, the four-light W window of the S aisle, 1885, and the W lancet of the N aisle, 1886.

MONUMENTS. The prolific monuments are described first in the chancel, then in the N chapel, culminating with those of the Oglanders in the S chapel. – On the chancel floor a once splendid incised slab, possibly Flemish, to John de Cherewin, †1441; full-length figure in armour, dogs at his feet. An elaborate canopy with Geometrical tracery (strange for the date in an English context) has vaulting seen in perspective; an octagonal turret rises at the top; saints stand in canopies at the sides; long borderline inscription. His face and clasped hands must have been detailed in brass or other material which has disappeared. – Table tomb, N of the chancel, under the E arch of the arcade, of William Howlys, †1520. Cusped panels with inscriptions or emblems on three sides. – Similar tomb of Helizabeth (sic) his wife, against N wall of chapel.

Now for the S chapel monuments. The oldest is to John Oglander, †1483, against the S wall. Table tomb with marble
25 top and thick entablature; traceried panels. – Oliver Oglander, †1536, in E arch of arcade. Table tomb with details of special quality. On the S side are three-dimensional kneeling figures of him, his wife, sons and daughters in lively pos-

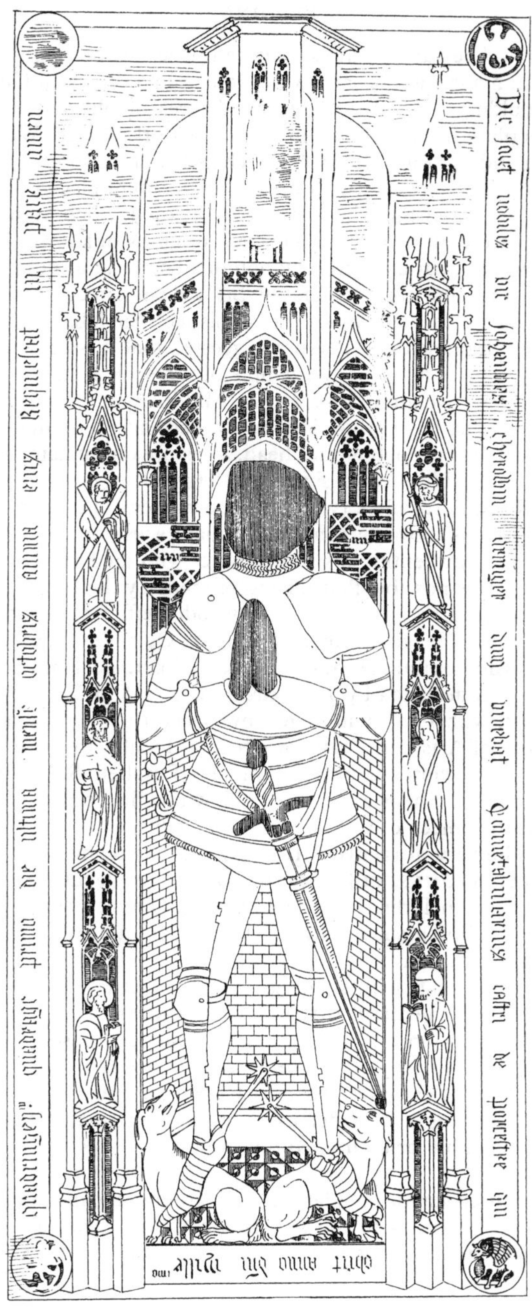

Brading church, Cherewin monument, drawing by R.W. Paul, 1884.
From Percy Stone, *The Architectural Antiquities of the Isle of Wight*, 1891

tures. They are set in four cusped panels of varying width, within a frame of carved vines rather than the usual Gothic mouldings. On the N side are figures of old and infirm people – he was active in charitable works.* – Sir William
31 Oglander, †1608, SE corner of chapel, and his son Sir John, †1655, NE corner. Two wooden effigies were placed on the tombs under Sir John's will made in 1649, when both effigies were in his possession. Their origin is unknown. Each is an antiquarian representation of a knight in armour with a sword; that commemorating Sir William is recumbent, on a half-rolled mat, with a lion at his feet. Sir John's effigy is more remarkable – Pevsner suggested that it is of national importance as an early example of romantic historicism in retrospective admiration for the Middle Ages. It is robustly carved; he lies on his side on another half-rolled mat with an elbow propping up his head, a gesture out of date by the mid C17. His sword, shield and crossed legs are those of early C14 crusaders (with a little ornament of *c.* 1650). Set in a recess above the tomb is a miniature version of the same effigy, representing his son George (who died in his twenties). It is possible that they were made by the local school of woodcarvers (*see* p. 30); the wooden effigy at Gatcombe (q.v.) may be connected. – Sir Henry Oglander, †1874, and his wife Louisa, †1894. Tomb-chest of marble, alabaster and mosaic, designed by *J.C. Powell* (i.e. *Powell* of Whitefriars), 1897, with two small angels by *Henry Pegram*; a sensitive piece of Arts and Crafts Jacobean. – Finally, in the N aisle is a small white marble monument to Elizabeth Rollo, †1875 in infancy. She is asleep on a pillow in a flowing gown – an effective piece of Victorian sentimentality.

The very attractive CHURCHYARD has many weathered GRAVESTONES, C18 to early C19, with vernacular Rococo carvings including occasional figures. One of 1747 to the S of the church shows angels, cherubs and drawn drapery. – WAR MEMORIAL by *Percy Stone*, S of the church tower; tapering shaft with small gable and crucifix. – Part of the shaft of a medieval CHURCHYARD CROSS with a sundial dated 1815 on top, set on a circular stepped base. – Abutting the churchyard to the N is the GUN SHED, probably built in the early C17 when each Island parish was required to have a gun as a defensive precaution; small, of rough stone with a brick-framed doorway.

The church stands on relatively high ground; the narrow High Street descends to the S, twists, and rises again at its far end. Few buildings in the town date from before the C19.

*The tomb has affinities with those of Sir John Leigh at All Saints, Godshill, and Lady Wadham at St Mary, Carisbrooke (qq.v.). The latter also has figures representing the recipients of charities which the person promoted.

The oldest lies S of the churchyard, forming part of the Wax Works. Despite its prettified appearance, it is substantially a two-bay jettied timber-framed house of *c.* 1600 or before. The upper storey has original close studding with mid-rail and herringbone brick nogging painted over; the bressumer is moulded and the four curved supporting brackets are original. The two gables of the thatched roof, the upper-floor windows and the external ground-floor arrangement are the result of restoration in the 1960s – as is the massive stone chimneystack to the W, built on the foundation of an older stack. The small OLD TOWN HALL, now a museum, abuts the churchyard; it has open pairs of C18 brick arches to the S and W; the N part of the ground storey is of rough stone. Restored 1875–6 when the upper floor was rebuilt. (Old illustrations show a row of timber-framed houses N of the Old Town Hall and backing on to the W end of the church; they were demolished in the later C19.)

HIGH STREET is remarkable less for its simple, mainly Victorian houses than for its townscape effects, with the twists, slopes, and views northward towards the church. The RED LION on the W side has a simple stuccoed exterior and partly C17 timber framing inside. The street curves to the SW and opens into the irregular BULL RING, with the small NEW TOWN HALL by *James Newman*, 1902–3; gabled front with two-tiered mullioned window, slightly in the Arts and Crafts tradition. The main road leads to the SE; the quieter MALL ROAD continues uphill S, with houses notable for their varied materials. ROSEBANK on the E side is a weatherboarded cottage, unusual for the Island; the main part is late C17 or C18 in origin, the N extension later. Opposite, STONEHAM has an early C18 frontage to an older house, in grey header bond with red brick string course and dressings; the N elevation is of stone – a mixture of large rectangular blocks and rubble. Past a plainly stuccoed Victorian house, then BEECHGROVE, dated 1699 on a gable, with a chequered front in Flemish bond and C20 cross-shaped windows; the side elevation is of rubble. A long way to the S, Nos. 1–2 Mall Road on the W side is a castellated stuccoed pair with bold bows and sashes.

WRITTLESTON HOUSE (formerly Hill Farmhouse), 1¼ m. *p. 96*
NNE. A substantial two-storey early to mid-C17 farmhouse of local limestone, with gabled porch of two storeys and attic. The porch was an addition (it blocked a window) and has a 'Tudor' arched doorway. One original mullioned window l. of the porch.

MORTON MANOR, 1 m. S, W of the Sandown road. A fairly small older house of varied materials was refurbished and extended from *c.* 1903 in an Arts-and-Crafts-influenced style. The best room has early C20 panelling and a stone fireplace with *William de Morgan* green-glazed tiles.

Brading, Writtleston House, elevation.
From Marion Brinton, *Farmhouses and Cottages of the Isle of Wight*, 1987

BRADING ROMAN VILLA, 1 m. S, W of the Sandown road. The new COVER BUILDING is of 2004 by *Rainey Petrie Johns.* The main building is necessarily large, as it shelters the entire remains of the main villa, without intruding on the surviving structural and decorative features, and allowing for circulation of visitors and adequate presentation. It is built almost entirely of timber, with subsidiary metalwork internally. The principal elevation is striking, with a central circular feature, or rotunda, marking the original entrance to the villa (though it did not have that shape). This is flanked by long elevations with eaves, which gently slope up from the rotunda. The roof rises at a slight pitch behind the rotunda to an even roof-line in the background. All the buildings are clad in boarding (vertical on the rotunda). Inside, there is impressive structural timberwork, especially within the rotunda, as well as intricate timberwork and metal-work associated with the display of the remains.

The site was occupied from the late Iron Age, but the VILLA was in its heyday during the early C4, when it was the focus of a prosperous farming estate. The main winged corridor-house was one of three buildings linked by a wall enclosing a courtyard. On the N side was an aisled farm-house with many living rooms, and on the S was a range of farm buildings. The main house, occupied by the owner, faced E towards the main gate. The important mosaics at Brading show that the owners of the C4 villa were rich and well educated.

In the front corridor is the ORPHEUS MOSAIC. At its centre is a small square panel with a medallion showing Orpheus playing his lyre to charm the surrounding animals. In the room at the S end of the corridor is a mosaic con-

Brading, Roman Villa, reconstruction drawing.
From D.J. Tomalin, *Roman Wight*, 1987

taining in the central panel the figure of Bacchus, holding
his staff or thyrsus. Below Bacchus are two sparring gladi-
ators. Another panel shows a strange cock-headed man 9
beside a building approached by steps, with two griffins
beyond. The symbolism of this panel is uncertain.

In the northern wing is a large room divided into two parts where the mosaics are particularly fine. The mosaic in the W half contains representations of the Seasons at the corners. Spring is decorated with a wreath of flowers, while Summer has poppies in her hair. The panel once showing the face of Autumn is destroyed, but Winter is graphically depicted with a warm hood, carrying a stick on which dangles a dead bird. Another surviving panel of this mosaic shows Perseus and Andromeda. Perseus has slain the snake-headed gorgon, Medusa, and holds up her head but both he and Andromeda avert their eyes from the gaze of the gorgon which could turn them to stone. The two parts of the room are linked by a panel depicting a bearded man seated in front of a globe with a bowl and sundial set before him. This figure may represent an astronomer. In the E half of the room is a mosaic with a central medallion containing another representation of Medusa. Her face is set slightly askew in relation to the surrounding panels, suggesting that the central medallion was prefabricated away from the villa. Four square panels surround this medallion. One depicts Ceres, the goddess of corn, handing an ear of corn to Triptolemus, credited in mythology with the discovery of agriculture. Another panel depicts Lycurgus, King of Thrace, in the process of being strangled by Ambrosia, who has been transformed into a vine by Mother Earth so that she may escape the advances of Lycurgus. The third panel depicts a shepherd and a water nymph while the fourth badly damaged panel shows a girl fleeing from a male figure. Triangular panels set between the square panels represent the four winds. At the E end of the mosaic a long panel depicts sea nymphs (nereids) riding on the backs of tritons who are half human, half fish.

NUNWELL. *See* p. 197.

4080

BRIGHSTONE

5 A village between the SW coast and the central chalkland. Despite C20 development, parts remain picturesque, with cottages and houses built in mixtures of local sandstones (varying from buff to rusty brown), and sometimes chalk; typically thatched. The church dominates at one end of the village.

ST MARY. The embattled W tower, with pudding-like walls of mixed local stones, is of uncertain date; the lower part may be C14, with C15 belfry stage and stumpy spire of 1720. However, the W door is C13, with roll mould and shafts with capitals; it shows signs of having been inserted from elsewhere. Otherwise the church as seen on its N side is almost all the result of a restoration under an enthusiastic rector, the *Rev. Edward McAll* (probably to his own design), in 1852. Internally the story is more complicated. The three-bay N arcade is late C12 with round piers, square thin abaci and slightly pointed, thinly chamfered arches. The original N aisle was demolished and the arcade blocked at some time, but the arches were reopened when the present aisle was built in 1852. The wide S aisle is of *c.* 1500; simple four-bay arcade with octagonal piers. A trefoil image niche set on a bracket, integrated with the stonework of the arcade, is attached to the W side of the westernmost pier. Unfortunately the windows of the aisle were altered to Dec in 1852 – but the S doorway is late medieval, with no capitals and fine moulding; set in a porch with a four-centred outer archway. The S chapel is probably slightly later than the aisle; its three-bay arcade is more sophisticated, with piers of four-shafts-and-four-hollows section and moulded four-centred arches. Again, the windows in the chapel are Victorian Dec, while the four lancets in the N wall of the chancel are also of 1852, with traces of stencilling on the splays.*

*An old illustration shows a curious E window to the S chapel, probably C17; of five lights, the outer two square-headed, the inner three contained in a rising rounded arch; a hoodmould followed the curve of the arch.

FURNISHINGS. PULPIT, a fine Jacobean piece, octagonal with two tiers of panels. The top panels have arches in false perspective with obelisks under them; the bottom ones have strapwork cartouches. Brackets carry a book-rest; the base is a short stem which broadens elegantly with curved ribs. – LECTERN. 1876 by *William White*. Of wood; stepped cruciform base; octagonal stem; pivotal eagle. – FONT. Octagonal, Perp, with small cusped panels. – STAINED GLASS, a remarkable series. In the S aisle, E of the doorway, a three-
light window of *c.* 1900 with scenes relating to John the 66
Baptist; patterning above and below, including circles of different sizes. A drawing in the faculty papers is signed *William White*, an unusual example of work by him in this medium. – The next window to the E, by *Powell's*, 1892, depicts the Good Samaritan. – The SE window of the S chapel is of 1897 (although commemorating the Rev. E. McAll, †1866); angels play musical instruments. By *W.G. Sutherland Ltd* of Manchester, a rare known work of this firm. – The main E window, and that of the S chapel, are by *James Bell*, as are the windows in the three easternmost lancets on the N side of the chancel. – MONUMENTS. Tablet to the Rev. William Heygate, †1902, by *Powell's*, on the N side of chancel arch. Elegant rectangle with mottled brown border and panels in dark green with flower and stem patterns. – Similar smaller tablet near S door to his son Bernard, †1898; also by *Powell's*.

The OLD RECTORY, S of the church, has a mainly Georgian exterior of mixed stone and brick, with evidence of older structure; Early Victorian embellishments were presumably made by the *Rev. E. McAll* (*see* St Mary, above). He added a broad canted bay window in the form of a porch on the W side, with castellated parapet, four lancets on each of the diagonal sides, and two more flanking the doorway, which has a 'Tudor' arch. (Internally the porch-bay opens into the hall-lobby through three depressed arches.) Prominent on a corner is a brick Neo-Tudor chimneystack with spiral decoration. WAYTES COURT, off Broad Lane SE of the church, is a C17–C18 house built of motley materials under a thatched roof.

BROOK 3580

Brighstone

The short village street descends towards the coast. Inland, the ground rises towards the central downland, with the church standing by itself on a spur above the main road.

ST MARY. Rebuilt in 1864, after a fire in 1862, by *Willoughby Mullins* (cf. Mottistone). The S porch-tower which largely dated from *c.* 1730 was retained, but was reconstructed in 1889 by *A.R. Mullins* with doorway in E.E. style, new upper storey with paired belfry lights, and short shingled spire. The body of the church has lancets, plain in the nave but cusped in the chancel, including the triple E window with taller central lancet. The oldest feature is the arch from the porch-tower into the nave, probably C13; of one order, chamfered, with thin abaci. It may originally have led into a S chapel on the site of the tower.

Internally the walls were never plastered, and the visual effects arising from their varied materials are fairly striking. The nave walls are of coursed sandstone rubble, with a few bands of darker stone. The chancel is faced in blocks of lighter stone, with chequer patterns partly of a darker shade above the chancel arch and around the E window. A two-bay arcade with foliated capital leads off the nave into the strange N transept, which is divided by a N–S arcade of two arches (and has a double-gabled N elevation). This transept was a replacement of a family chapel related to Brook House.

FURNISHINGS. FONT. Bowl of trefoil shape in white marble with carved band under the rim; short stem of three clustered columns. By *Farmer*, as is the PULPIT, octagonal, of stone with dark marble columns between Gothic arched panels with figures in relief.* – STAINED GLASS. Grisaille glass in many windows, attributed to *Lavers & Barraud.* E window, a war memorial, by *Clayton & Bell*, 1920.

The former BROOK HOUSE, W of the village street, is of C18 origin, much altered in the C19 and C20 and now subdivided. The E front still appears Georgian, of two storeys and seven bays with a taller round-headed central upper window under a small pediment. Originally there was a substantial attic floor with dormers, but there is now a low roof profile, with the pediment standing up on its own. The house was bought *c.* 1860 by Charles Seely, the first of the family to settle on the Island (*see* Mottistone).

BROOK HILL HOUSE, ½ m. NE, on the brow of a hilltop with superb views S and W. Built from *c.* 1901 for Sir Charles Seely, son of Charles Seely of Brook House (*see* above), but not finished until 1916 (a year after Sir Charles died). The architect was *Sir Aston Webb*, but the house hardly seems typical of his work. It is an irregular, eclectic composition, in coursed rubble with fine stone dressings, mainly two-storeyed, but rising on the S and (to a lesser extent) W sides from a high plinth faced in rough stone. It seems almost modernistic in general outline, with flat roof-lines and many right-angled projections, but the details are oddly assorted

*Attributions from the church guide. It is not clear whether this refers to William Farmer of Farmer & Brindley or, more probably, to *Thomas Farmer.*

(there have been alterations, and the house is now subdivided). On the S side the dominant feature is a wide segmental arch at ground-floor level opening from a recessed veranda, with a balustraded balcony projecting over the plinth. Otherwise the S façade has projections and recessions; the windows are narrow tall sashes grouped singly or in twos or threes; the parapet has intermittent balustrading. A tower, with a third storey, rises behind the NE corner. The shorter W front has a projecting lower storey. At each end, facing N and S, are wide openings with flanking columns, broadening downwards in a Neo-Egyptian way. That on the N side forms the porch entrance, with a coat of arms over. Otherwise the N frontage, with an E service wing at right angles, is strangely disjointed. The writer J.B. Priestley lived here for eleven years from 1948; he married Jacquetta Hawkes, archaeologist and writer, in 1953.

(LITTLE BROOK is a charming Neo-Georgian house of the 1930s by *Seely & Paget*; two-storeyed in whitened brick with shutters and, on the main frontage, two short verandas with tent roofs. THE RED HOUSE, *c.* 1938, is also by *Seely & Paget.*)

BROOK DOWN BARROWS, 1m. NW. Although popularly known as Five Barrows, there are actually eight Bronze Age round barrows here, forming a cluster around the summit of the down. They comprise one of the best-preserved round-barrow cemeteries on the Island, despite past disturbance. The monuments include bowl barrows, one or more bell barrows and a disc barrow (a small central mound on a wide platform surrounded by a ditch and an outer bank). The largest monument, a bell barrow, is 10ft (3 metres) high; the smallest 3ft (0.5 metres) high.

CALBOURNE 4085

A big parish with three separate historic centres. Swainston (q.v.), 1½m. E, was the main manorial centre, held by the bishops of Winchester until the late C13. The shrunken medieval town of Newtown (q.v.) is 2½m. N. Calbourne itself has a triangular Green which descends gently to the SW, towards the entrance to the Westover Estate with its Georgian landscaping. The church is near the SE corner of the Green.

ALL SAINTS seems a complex building when one approaches from the Green, with its main entrance through an elaborate C19 N porch. Before entering, it is especially worth walking round the W and S sides. The W end of the nave, with a large lancet, is at least early C13. The base of the SW tower, where a doorway and two small windows have shouldered tops, is *c.* 1300 or later, but the top of the tower was plainly rebuilt in 1752. The S aisle and chancel are mid-C13, and are best seen from the churchyard well to their E. The E window is remarkable. Two large lancets, each with external chamfer and roll moulding, and a trefoiled circular opening above them. The E window of the gable-ended S aisle is similar on a smaller scale, except that the circle contains a quatrefoil. Back to the N porch, which forms part of extensive work done by *A.F. Livesay* (*see* Newtown) during a vigorous restoration in 1838–42. It has an almost convincing Late Norman outer doorway with zigzag arch and a roll-moulded inner order, resting on paired shafts. The inner doorway is a simpler version, but the porch itself is vaulted with wide diagonal ribs, which have zigzag decoration. Inside the church, the tall three-bay S arcade is Livesay's, with slender piers of pale marble, possibly inspired by the arcade at nearby Shalfleet. The C13 chancel arch has no capitals and a distinctive shape; its curve begins sharply but straightens towards an acute apex (the arch was restored by *W.T. Stratton* in 1873). Finally there is a large N chapel, transeptal to the nave from which it is screened off; rebuilt by *Livesay* in 1842 for the Simeons of Swainston on the site of a chapel associated with their predecessors there, the Barringtons. It had a fine Neo-E.E. interior with two bays of plaster vaulting and blank arcading against the walls, in a style derived from the Winchester Lady Chapel. Alas, this was largely destroyed in alterations of *c.* 1970, leaving an internally elaborate N window of two trefoiled lights with shafts and upper quatrefoil, flanked by single-light windows with similar mouldings, all containing heraldic and patterned glass. – PEWS by *Livesay*, 1839–41, with panelled pointed ends. – FONT. Strange – it looks as if the bowl was originally square with simple carvings, but the angles were later cut off to make it octagonal. – BRASS to a knight, later C14, with excellent details; over 4 ft (1.2 metres) long, placed on a wall in the S aisle, but originally set on a table tomb which has disappeared. Another curious brass in the chancel to Daniel Evance, 'Reverend Religius and Learned Precher', †1652, with engravings of a winged Father Time and a skeletal figure of Death.

W of the church and S of the Green is a succession of very different buildings. First the stone-built OLD RECTORY of 1838, probably by *Livesay*, with Neo-Tudor mullioned windows. Then the NORTH-EAST LODGE to Westover (*see* below), presumably by *Nash*; a two-storeyed, partly octagonal *cottage orné* with canted top corners to the windows and slate roof; built, unusually for the Island, in dressed flint. There is a view (in winter) to the house across the park. Round the corner to the W is WINKLE STREET, a well-established tourist sight; up to a dozen genuinely vernacular cottages, C18 or later, face a stream. They are mostly in local rough limestone but one has dark ironstone and others are in whitish clunch. Some are thatched.

BRASS TO DANIEL EVANCE IN CALBOURNE CHURCH
BLEST IS THE IVST MANS MEMORY
BOTH HEERE AND TO ETERNITY
BEING DEAD HE YET SPEAKETH
HEB XI IIII
IN MEMORY
OF THE
REVEREND
RELIGIVS
AND
LEARNED
PRECHER
M DANIEL EVANCE
WHO WAS BORN AT LONDON MARCH 2 1613
AND DYED HERE AT CALBOVRNE DECEMB 27·1652
THS MONVMENT WAS ERECED BY HANNA HS MOVRNFVL RELICT
DANIEL EVANCE ANAGRAM I CAN DEAL EVEN
Who is sufficient for this thing
Wisely to harpe on every string
Rightly divide the word of truth
To babes & men to age & youth
One of a thosand where's he found
So learned pious wise and sound
Earth hath but few there is in heven
One who answers I CAN DEAL EVEN
SCALE
10 INS

Calbourne church, brass to Daniel Evance, †1652.
From Percy Stone, *The Architectural Antiquities of the Isle of Wight*, 1891

WESTOVER. An older, smaller house was reconstructed in 1813–15 by *John Nash.* Two-storeyed and white-painted; the main (E) front has seven original bays with a summary pediment over the central three. But on the ground floor broad bow windows span the widths of three bays on either side, and in between is a Doric porch with triglyph frieze. An interesting composition – but two bays added to the N in the later C19 spoil the symmetry. The S front is of seven bays; the centre three are more widely spaced and come forward slightly under a pediment similar to that on the E side. The ground floor has a veranda of which the centre part has wooden square-sided columns and a triglyph frieze, with iron railings forming a balcony. The flanking parts have arches in delicate ironwork, with slender paired columns supporting tent canopies, and open circles between the columns and in the spandrels; to charming effect. The veranda continues round to a short stretch on the W elevation. Inside, there is a delicate spiral staircase with simple ironwork, under a glazed flat dome.

The former STABLES to the NW (now residential) belonged to the older house; large two-storey courtyard in local stone with tall, elliptical, keystoned N entrance under a simple pediment; there is a balancing composition on the opposite range with a single-storey arch.

There was already a landscaped PARK by the 1790s with a small lake near the entrance from the village (*see* above for the lodge there). A BRIDGE crosses a stream where it enters the lake from the N; the side facing the lake has a central rounded arch with smaller blank arches to the sides; the N face has a single simple arch.

FULLINGMILLS, ¾ m. W on the Freshwater road. A former farmhouse built of rubble with substantial ashlar quoins, which must have been quarried locally in an outlying part of the Island limestone deposits. A wing of *c.* 1620 has gabled end elevations, each with four-light mullioned windows on both floors and double attic lights. Further along the Freshwater road are two outlying lodges to the Westover estate in the *orné* tradition, presumably associated with *Nash*. SWEETWATER LODGE is one-storeyed in rough stone with a thatched roof; part is half-octagonal and the windows have canted corners like those on the North-East Lodge already described. WHEELBARROW COTTAGE, a little further W, is simpler.

4585

CARISBROOKE

Newport

3, 14 Carisbrooke was the focal centre of the Isle of Wight in early medieval times, with its castle on an older fortified site. The village centre lies to the N of the castle, from which it is separated by a small steep-sided valley. It is now on the western outskirts of Newport, the town which was founded in the late C12 (*see* p. 171) in a location more suitable for trade and urban development than that of Carisbrooke. Despite its partly suburban setting, the old village retains a strong identity.

CARISBROOKE CASTLE was an important fortress and feudal centre; the only medieval castle on the Island. It was enlarged in late Tudor times, and royal connections have continued almost to the present day. But it does not look immediately impressive from the approach road leading SW from Newport. It occupies a flat-topped hill of modest height, the older part contained within a stone curtain wall which rises above grassy ramparts. This is surrounded by lower, later defences, also grass-grown but partly faced in stone. Only when one reaches the gatehouse in the W side does one appreciate the grandeur of much that survives of the medieval castle. It is a splendid place to visit – a

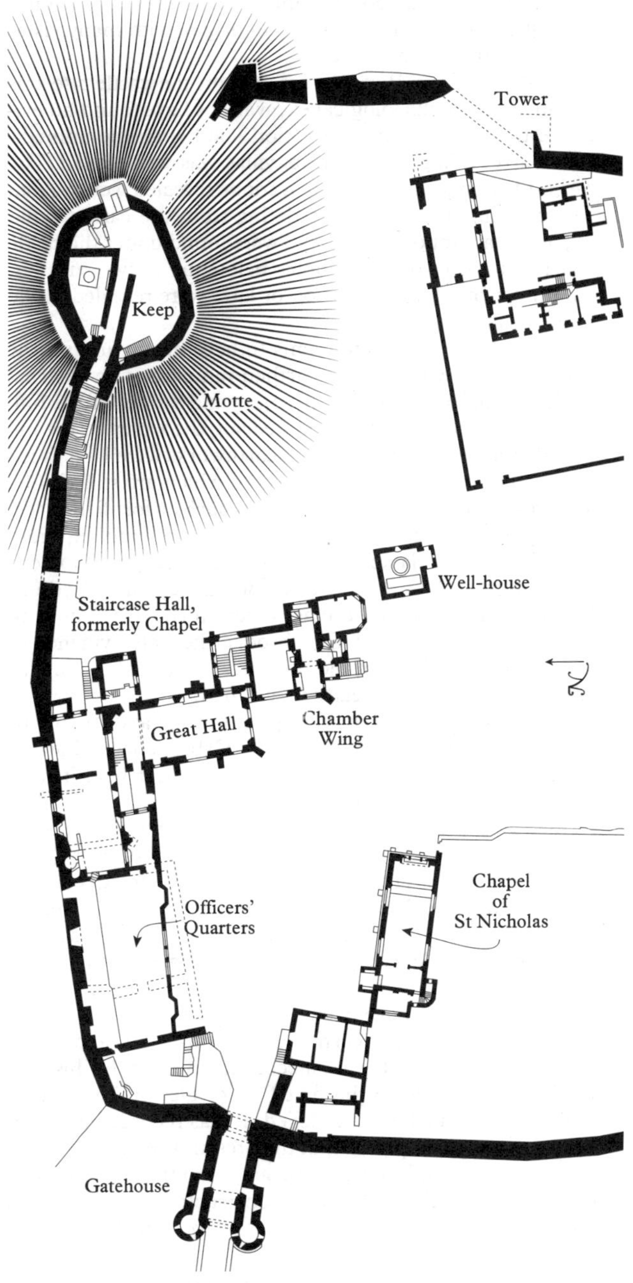

Carisbrooke Castle, plan showing main buildings. After C.J. Young et al., *Excavations in Carisbrooke Castle 1921–96*, 2000

combination of ruined and intact structures, some once domestic, others purely military in origin, with many vistas over attractive countryside.

Until recently a Roman presence on the castle site was assumed, but archaeological excavations have found no evidence there of Roman occupation – although the immediately surrounding area with its villas was well settled. The earliest features which the excavations revealed were Saxon. The remains of three graves dating from the early to mid C6, one of an important person, were found under the castle courtyard (*see* p. 16). Post-holes belonging to two substantial timber buildings of *c.* 1000 or later were revealed in the same locality.*

Fortification of the site seems to have begun around the late C10 or early C11, when earthen ramparts with external ditches were formed round the N, W and S sides of the hill, and across it on the other side (leaving the E part of the hill outside the defended area). The earthworks were later faced externally with a stone wall, parts of which are still visible. This resulted in a substantial Saxon *burh* or fortified place, of roughly rectangular form, its defences resembling those in other, larger, Saxon *burhs* such as Wareham (Dorset), Wallingford (Oxon., formerly Berkshire) and Lydford (Devon). However, these places were fortified towns with streets and buildings; at Carisbrooke the only evidence of Saxon settlement within the ramparts is that of the remains of the two buildings already mentioned.

Soon after the Norman Conquest the site and surroundings were granted to William FitzOsbern, later Earl of Hereford; he died in 1071 and his son Roger held it until he rebelled unsuccessfully against the king in 1078. They formed a simple castle mainly in the NE quarter of the older fortifications, defended within the *burh* by ditches (long since filled). In *c.* 1100 the site was granted to Richard de Redvers, who held extensive estates in Devon as well as around Christchurch on the Hampshire–Dorset border. He enlarged the castle, taking over the whole area of the Saxon *burh*; he formed the existing motte over the NE corner, which may at first have been topped by a wooden keep; he made new perimeter earthworks within and above the Saxon ones. Richard was succeeded in 1107 by his son Baldwin, who became the first Earl of Devon. Under him the castle was further remodelled. It was recorded as being of stone in 1136, implying that the present keep (now ruined and reduced from its original height), and the curtain walls, had been built. The latter were constructed over the earlier Norman ramparts; they largely survive, much repaired.

*The evidence obtained from excavations on the castle site is summarized in C.J. Young, *Excavations at Carisbrooke Castle 1921–1996*, 2000.

Little is known of other buildings within the Norman castle; the present Great Hall probably dates from the mid C13, incorporating part of an earlier smaller building, and there was a chapel on the site of the existing one.

The last of the de Redvers was Isabella de Fortibus, who inherited the estates and title (as Countess of Devon) in 1262. She was a widow aged twenty-five, reputedly the richest woman in England (*see* p. 20). She made Carisbrooke the main residence of her far-flung estates; she built a private chapel, extended the hall range to include chambers, and probably built the central part of the gatehouse. What survives of her work at Carisbrooke indicates that it was of very sophisticated architectural quality. Carisbrooke passed to the king at Isabella's death in 1293. Later overlords were royal appointees; an important one was William de Montacute, Earl of Salisbury, in 1385–97. They were regarded as lords of the Island as well as of the Castle; from the early C16 they were called Captains, later Governors. In 1583 Sir George Carey, a relative of Elizabeth I and later Lord Hunsdon, became Governor; he improved the castle both as a residence and a stronghold. With threats of invasion continuing after the defeat of the Armada, *Federigo Gianibelli*, an Italian engineer, was commissioned in 1597 to elaborate the defences. In 1647–8 Charles I was a prisoner in the castle; he tried twice to escape. In 1648 he was taken to London for his trial and subsequent execution.

Governors of the Isle of Wight continued to be appointed; Carisbrooke was their official residence, although not all lived there, even occasionally. In the C18 and early C19 many of the main buildings were maintained and modified; others fell to ruin. The Great Hall and adjoining buildings were restored from 1856 under *Philip Hardwick*. Further alterations took place after 1889, when Prince Henry of Battenberg became Governor. He was succeeded seven years later by his widow, Princess Beatrice, †1944, Queen Victoria's daughter. She was the last resident of Carisbrooke. Since 1951 the Great Hall and adjoining rooms have housed a museum, with the rest of the castle open to the public.

DESCRIPTION

The GATEHOUSE is one of the castle's finest features. It is 15
almost intact in its medieval external form, built of pleasantly weathered stone with just enough ruination – e.g. in the parapet – to indicate the absence of drastic restoration outside. We approach across a dry perimeter ditch and through an outer gateway with (surprisingly) a pediment, and an inscription ER 1598 – this is part of the work of *Gianibelli* (*see* p. 112). The gatehouse itself rises in front of

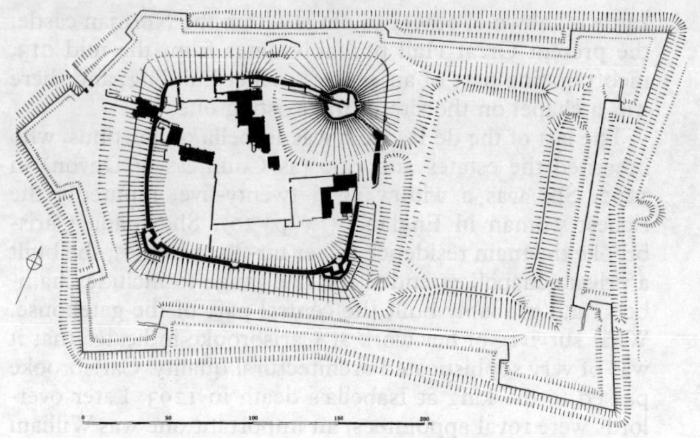

Carisbrooke Castle, plan including Tudor extension.
After English Heritage

the grassy ramparts which are topped by the curtain wall, with parts of the defensive stonework of the Saxon *burh* visible at the bottom of the banks. Nothing is evident of the Norman entrance; the core of the present structure is C13. The existing front was largely formed in 1335–6 when massive round turrets were added, rising in three stages between string courses; on the lower two stages are cross-shaped arrowslits with rounded extremities. The gatehouse was heightened in 1380 under *Henry Yevele*; the tops of the turrets contain keyhole openings with round apertures at their bases, shaped to accommodate very early guns.* There are contemporary or slightly earlier keyhole openings on the Southampton town walls and the Westgate at Canterbury, but these are the earliest such features surviving on a British castle. Between the turrets is a machicolated parapet with five arched openings.**

The entrance archway between the turrets is four-centred and heavily moulded. It leads into a small rib-vaulted chamber in front of a simpler, chamfered arch, which is deep enough to contain a portcullis groove. Beyond this a passageway leads to the rear arch of the gatehouse, which

* In *English Mediaeval Architects* (1984) John Harvey wrote that *Henry Yevele* was commissioned in 1380 to impress workmen for Carisbrooke Castle, notably for the heightening of the main gatehouse. Yevele, with *William Wynford* and *Hugh Herland* (the master carpenter at Westminster Hall), drew up a contract in 1384 for carpenter's work at Carisbrooke, but nothing survives of this.

** A shield on the parapet with the arms of Anthony Widville, lord of the castle around 1470, must relate to work (of uncertain extent) during that period.

has another portcullis groove. The gatehouse was for long a shell; the interior was restored, with roof and floors at old levels, by *Percy Stone* in 1898. It abuts the CURTAIN WALL, which is basically Norman, built of limestone rubble, much patched later with sandstone and other materials. The wall-walk is continuous and accessible.

The gatehouse opens into the NW part of the courtyard. To the r. is the chapel of St Nicholas, to the l. are seriously ruined buildings backing on to the curtain wall (these are described later). In front, eastwards, is the GREAT HALL – which at first sight does not look impressive. But the top of the keep behind is visible over its roof and helps to make this a memorable view. The Hall stands on an undercroft (the latter is below ground on the W side but above on the E, owing to differing levels). The undercroft incorporates C12 work, but the hall was constructed to its present floor dimensions at some time in the mid C13 – possibly before Isabella de Fortibus's inheritance in 1262. There were alterations *c.* 1390 under William de Montacute; from 1592 by Sir George Carey (he inserted an upper storey); in *c.* 1700, when the floor was lowered; and from 1856 under *Hardwick* – but the present plain transomed windows date only from *c.* 1888–1904. We enter the Hall at its NW corner through a small wing built by Carey; the external doorway in the S wall of the wing, with stone hood and brackets, dates from *c.* 1700.

Inside the hall, the dominant feature is a stone CHIM- 17
NEYPIECE of *c.* 1390 on the E side, long concealed behind later work but revealed in the C19 without subsequent over-restoration. The fireplace has a straight top with several orders of moulding, which continue down the jambs. The main part of the hearth is blocked between diagonal flanks with trefoiled panels. The mantelpiece has twelve cinquefoil panels in pairs, divided by pilasters. The original treatment of the top and sides does not survive. Immediately to the S is a small C13 two-light window with a thin Purbeck shaft, behind a moulded rere-arch – long blocked and fairly recently reopened.

Opening E off the Hall at its S end is the present Stair- 16
case Hall, originally a private CHAPEL built by Isabella de Fortibus from 1270. It was converted and heightened by Sir George Carey; his floor was taken out *c.* 1700 and the staircase inserted; good ordinary work with turned beaded balusters. When panelling was removed in the C19, details of Isabella's chapel were revealed. It had been an exquisite piece of E.E. design with two vaulted bays, the side of each bay subdivided by two arched recesses, of which one on either side contained a lancet window. On the N side the arched recesses largely survive, simply chamfered, with moulded responds and thin Purbeck shafts; the

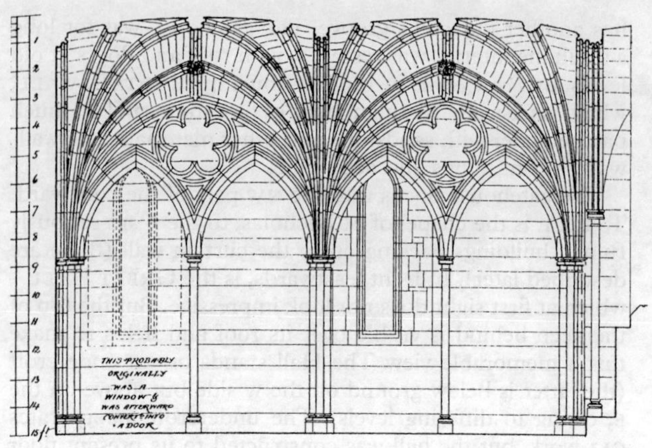

Carisbrooke Castle, former private chapel, reconstruction. From Percy Stone, *The Architectural Antiquities of the Isle of Wight*, 1891

intermediate shaft for the vaulting remains, including its capital, as well as the lancet. At the E end there was a six-light window which must have had Geometrical tracery; the top of the marble shaft and capital on the N side of its rere-arch remain. Percy Stone drew an imaginative reconstruction in his *Architectural Antiquities of the Isle of Wight* (1891), and pointed out similarities with the porch of Christchurch Priory, Hants (now Dorset), built under Isabella's patronage.

14 To the S and SE of the Great Hall is the CHAMBER WING, an irregular block of three to four storeys, difficult to interpret because of successive alterations. It may have begun with a chamber added by Isabella. It was reconstructed by William de Montacute *c.* 1390, enlarged probably in the C15, altered by Sir George Carey *c.* 1600 and – especially – restored in 1856 (under *Philip Hardwick*) and subsequently. Montacute's main chamber was in a gabled range aligned E–W, which now has a fine five-light W window with two tiers of slightly ogee-headed lights, presumably by *Hardwick*. The basement on the W side has two restored square-headed mullioned windows of three lights. To the S of this is a taller T-shaped block, of which the W part was built by Montacute as a tower wing formerly holding a staircase; its corner buttress has his coat-of-arms. The rest of the T-shaped range may have been built *c.* 1470–80. However, many of the windows in the wing are Hardwick's, to an interesting design – two-light, square-headed and transomed, with arches under the transoms but plain square

openings above. He may have taken this design from a window from Carey's time of which he could have found evidence.

In 1272 Isabella de Fortibus built private rooms N of the Great Hall, extending up to the curtain wall; they were remodelled under Sir George Carey. Their roofs and floors have gone, but a very interesting feature remains from Isabella's time – a window recessed in the thickness of the curtain wall, unblocked in 1891. It has two trefoil lights with transom; the recess is broadly angled with rere-arch and transverse rib, containing steps which bend to relate to the shape of the recess. Stone window seats, diagonally aligned, suggest that this was a vantage point from one of the rooms. To the W Carey built a two-storey domestic range (sometimes called the OFFICERS' QUARTERS) against the curtain wall; little survives except ruinous sections of internal walls and the remains of Tudor fireplaces. A hint of a previous building is provided by the base of a shaft set against the curtain wall; this must have related to a vaulted roof. SE of
the gatehouse (*see* above) is the CHAPEL OF ST NICHOLAS 14
(the main chapel of the castle, as distinct from Isabella's private chapel). This was rebuilt on the old foundations in 1738 but unroofed in 1856. It was rebuilt again by *Percy Stone* in 1905–6, and embellished internally by him after 1919 as a war memorial. It is a simple rectangle outside with Perp-style windows under segmental arches, the E one with elaborate tracery. The bases of the buttresses and the flanks of the plain S doorway remain from the C13. The lavish interior has traceried panels between the windows, figure sculptures on the cornices, painted panels on the polygonal wagon roof, a painted reredos under an elaborate openwork canopy, continuous stalls on either side and, at the W end, a vestibule containing a statue of Charles I. – STAINED GLASS in several windows by *J. Dudley Forsyth*.

Returning eastwards, the steeply roofed stone WELL- 34
HOUSE dates from 1587, with a restored treadwheel for drawing water. The early C12 MOTTE overlays the line of the older ramparts at their NE angle. On it is the stone
KEEP, built by the mid 1130s and altered in the C14; it 14
was formerly taller than now. The keep is an irregular dodecagon, approached from the W by a flight of seventy-one steps abutting the curtain wall. The steps end at a two-storey gatehouse, in domestic terms a porch; its entrance arch, with a portcullis groove, leads to a one-bay vaulted space, with diagonal ribs springing from plain corbels. This is probably coeval with the work of 1335–6 on the main gatehouse. Beyond is a taller space – actually within the thickness of the keep wall – with a longitudinal vault spanned by three transverse ribs which die into the walls without capitals. The keep was a shell-keep, i.e. never wholly roofed over

but with distinct structures within it. The NW part was walled off in the C16 to enclose a deep well, and an incomplete stretch of wall to the S has the remains of two fireplaces. But the most interesting feature here is the garderobe: a projection with a drain, probably C14, entered through an arch on the E side of the keep.

Part of the eastern CURTAIN WALL, S of the keep, was rebuilt in the C14; it is linked to a small square TOWER at the foot of the motte, with an embattled top altered *c.* 1600. Set in the bank under the curtain wall on its E side is another revealed stretch of stonework related to the Saxon *burh*.

Sir George Carey's improvements from 1587 started with enlarging, in canted form, two small, previously rectangular towers at the SE and SW corners of the curtain wall. Under *Federigo Gianibelli*, commissioned in 1597 (*see* above), the fortress was greatly enlarged through forming an outer rampart, enveloping the medieval castle and extending the defended space E to incorporate an area which later became a bowling green. The new outer line consists largely of grassed earthworks in low profile, shaped according to the principles of military engineering when artillery had come to dominate siege warfare. It is bounded by an outer ditch, towards which the earthworks are faced in stone. There are four polygonal flanker bastions or bulwarks to the NE, SE, SW and W (and a much smaller one to the NW). They are in arrowhead form, those on the S and E sides having recesses behind 'ears' on their flanks; these contained stone-built batteries, later largely demolished.

Altogether Carisbrooke is exceptional in providing examples of defensive works of successive periods from Saxon to late Tudor.

The VILLAGE of Carisbrooke is centred ¼ m. N of the castle, with a dominant church at the upper (W) end of a long main street.

ST MARY. The early parish was large, and there was an important Saxon church, the site of which is uncertain. The Domesday Book records one at Bowcombe, now a hamlet to the SW – but the name then had wider territorial significance. Wherever it was located, this church and six others on the Island, with their revenues, were granted soon after the Norman Conquest by William FitzOsbern to the Benedictine abbey of Lire in Normandy, which he had founded. A church existed on the present site by the mid C12, and a priory was established *c.* 1147 as a subsidiary cell to Lire (never with more than six monks). This was closed as an alien monastery in 1415.

The medieval St Mary's was at least as much a parochial as a monastic church. It has a nave with S aisle in two parts, and a tall late medieval W tower; the chancel was demolished *c.* 1565. The monastic buildings abutted on the N side. Internally the dominant feature is the late C12 S arcade of five bays with circular piers. The capitals and abaci are round, with unusually thin and dense scallop decoration; the arches are pointed, with two slight chamfers. But there is evidence of an earlier aisle-less church, seen in the outlines of two small Norman windows: one in the spandrel between the two western arches, the other at the W end of the arcade near the tower. The part of the aisle corresponding to the two W bays of the arcade is much narrower than the E part. The former probably represents the width of the late C12 aisle; the wider part is a rebuilding of the early to mid C13 – on the evidence of a trefoil roll-moulded piscina, and also of an arch leading into the narrower part. This arch has shafts with rounded responds, and abuts in a curious way the adjoining pier of the arcade, which has a flat profile on its S side. The S doorway, opening from a C16 porch into the narrow part of the aisle, is also early C13, its outer order shafted with trefoil leaf carvings on the capitals.

The church has an interesting series of later Gothic windows. Of the three in the S wall of the wider part of the aisle, all of three lights, the E is transitional Dec–Perp to a complicated design; the W is more normal Perp; the middle one is square-headed. Two four-light windows in the nave N wall have ogee-headed lights and plain upper tracery; they must have been inserted after the removal of the abutting buildings of the priory. The four-light E window in the infilled chancel arch dates from the demolition of the chancel *c.* 1565; it is simplified Perp with no cusps, under a four-centred arch. The E window of the S aisle is similar, set within the otherwise blocked frame of a taller, older window.

The tower (dated 1471 on a renewed stone) is majestic; 20
the tallest on a medieval parish church in Hampshire or on the Island. It has affinities with towers in Dorset. It is built of greenish sandstone, in five stages divided by string courses which go round the diagonal buttresses and the SW stair-turret, with heads on their undersides. The embattled parapet has slender pinnacles. The chief defect of the design is the absence of sizeable belfry windows; there are only two small openings on each side. Inside is a tall tower arch with ribbed inner order; angle buttresses to the tower are ruthlessly built into the nave. The tower space has a star vault with central circle.

On the external N side of the nave are two arched recesses which must have faced the destroyed cloister and presumably contained tombs. The W one, *c.* 1200, is quite low, with a rib-moulded rounded arch and short shafts with delicate foliate capitals. The other, mid-C13, is taller and deeper, with two orders of moulded arch, and shafts with rounded capitals to the W; its E end is obliterated.

FURNISHINGS. SANCTUARY remodelled 1967 by *Seely & Paget*; ALTAR RAILS with turned balusters. – PULPIT, dated 1658, with a tier of round-arched panels of Jacobean type and plain squared ones below; canopy with diamond pattern on the cornice. – SCULPTURE. Virgin and Child by *John Skelton*, 1969, in a medieval niche to the l. of the S aisle E window. A fine composition: slender, attenuated; strong face; the curve of her arm, holding the child, continues in the fold of the drapery. – ROYAL ARMS, Queen Anne. – FONT. Early C17. Octagonal bowl with receding moulding below, on a bulbous stem; simple conical COVER dated 1602. – MONUMENTS. Engraved figure of a prior with crozier, possibly C12, on marble slab in S aisle. – Lady
24 Wadham, wife of the Captain of the Castle, *c.* 1520, a sumptuous piece. Panelled table tomb; wide canopy with depressed arch, cusped and sub-cusped, in a rectangular frame; panelled octagonal columns, and a foliated frieze topped by an angel and shield. She kneels, a small figure in simple robes, in the centre of the recess. Set in trefoiled panels on either side are six crippled figures representing a charity she supported.* – William Keeling, †1619, an East India adventurer, is commemorated both by a small brass in the nave floor (a shield surrounded by scroll pattern), and by a painted wall board setting out his exploits, in distinctive lettering, under a roundel showing a vessel at sea. – Sir William Stephens, †1697, N wall. A curious design. Broken pediment with scrolls and shield; oval tablet under suspended drapery with zigzag patterns to the sides; flanking Tuscan columns.

(PRIORY FARMHOUSE, a short distance N of the church, is partly early C16, incorporating older fragments from the medieval priory. It retains a C16 roof of three bays, with collar-beams and curved wind-braces.)

HIGH STREET is pleasant, despite traffic; two-storeyed and low-key, with the church rearing to the W. Among the modest houses, Nos. 69–71 on the S side are C18 with grey headers and bow windows on the ground floor, while No. 63, *c.* 1800, of buff brick, has windows under segmental arches on the lower storey.

ALVINGTON FARMHOUSE, ¾ m. NW of the church. Five-bay house of the early to mid C18, in rough stone with strongly emphasized brick window frames and string course; hipped roof with broad eaves.

MOUNTJOY CEMETERY, off Whitcombe Road, E of the

*The monument has an affinity with that of Sir John Leigh at Godshill (*see* p. 155), particularly in the cresting, frieze, cusping and panel patterns, suggesting the work of the same craftsman. There are also comparable details in the tomb of Oliver Oglander at Brading (*see* p. 92).

Castle. Opened in 1858. The LODGE is a small Gothic fantasy with rough stone walls, long-and-short quoins, a canted bay with trefoil lights, and a broad main gable with a smaller one over the porch.

ST DOMINIC'S PRIORY (former), Whitcombe Road, SE of the castle. Built for Dominican nuns in 1865–6 by the Countess of Clare (*see* St Mary, Ryde, p. 226). Closed as a convent in 1989, and now a Christian healing centre. Designed by *Gilbert Blount*, mostly in domestic Gothic. Irregular ranges in coursed stone with long slate roof-lines and some gables. Chapel with polygonal apse. The most striking feature as one approaches is a first-floor oriel with two-light traceried windows in an embattled tower at the end of the range to the l.

GREAT WHITCOMBE MANOR, Whitcombe Road, ¾m. S of the castle. Mid-C18; main (E) façade of two storeys and five bays, in red brick with stone quoins in long-and-short pattern; doorway with simple hood; hipped roof. It stands on a slope, so that the N façade, visible from the road, is three-storeyed.

WHITECROFT HOSPITAL (former), 1½m. S of the castle. Built as the County Lunatic Asylum in 1894–6. Large, but mostly unoccupied at the time of writing. The main buildings, by *B. Jacobs* of Hull, are not notable, but the TOWER, built as a water tower in 1898–1902, with clock turret on top, is a landmark. Six main storeys in red brick, plain except for the top stage which has three rounded arches on each side, under a widely projecting cornice with large dentils. Tall square-shaped turret, in brick and stone with ogee-shaped leaded top, capped by a weathervane.

CHALE 4575

Set amid spectacular scenery on the SW side of the Island's
southern tip. The steep chalk slopes of St Catherine's Hill end
about ½m. from the coast with its crumbling cliffs (*see*
Niton); the original chasm-like Blackgang Chine nearby,
which attracted C19 and early C20 sightseers, has largely disappeared through landslips and erosion. To the W the coast- 1
line sweeps magnificently to the chalk cliffs of Freshwater ten
miles and more away. To the N and NW is more placid country,
into which the long-drawn village extends loosely.

ST ANDREW. Splendidly set on a brow with a view along the coast to the Freshwater cliffs. Outwardly it is Perp, with a two-gabled E end, S aisle and chapel under a continuous roof-line, and W tower. One has to go inside to try to understand its history. The first chapel was dedicated in 1114, but nothing is evident from then. The arch from chancel to chapel looks late C12: rounded, with slight chamfer and flat responds. The S arcade has three assorted bays; the E bay is *c.* 1200, with plain slightly pointed arch, square abacus and rounded columns. The second bay is slightly narrower; the arch of two chamfered orders dies into a flat surface above the abacus – presumably C13. The W arch is narrower still and lower. It is part of an early to mid-C15 reconstruction in which the church was extended W, the aisle rebuilt and the tower added. In 1872 the chancel was enlarged to align with the S chapel (which had previously extended further E than the chancel itself), and the present chancel arch was formed. The tower is the finest feature. It is two-tiered, the set-back buttresses ending at the top of the lower tier; the upper part is plain save for small belfry lights with stone tracery; battlemented top; NE stair-turret. The W window is C19, but round the base of the tower are C15 panels with tracery patterns.

PULPIT, 1861. Wooden, with a panel of Christ with his disciples, carved locally by *Millicent Johnson* (church guide). – STAINED GLASS. Several windows by *Kempe*, including W tower window of 1891, and five others donated in 1897 by E.A. Hearn of New York to commemorate his ancestors, including the three-light E window of the S chapel and smaller windows on the N side of the nave. – MONUMENTS. Rev. Richard Burleigh, †1734, aisle wall. Open pediment with the outlines of informally stacked books on top, and an urn at the apex. – Sir Henry Worsley, †1841. S chapel. Gothic details, including cusped arch with carved spandrels; frilly frieze, and coat-of-arms at top flanked by figures of Bengal Lancers. – In the churchyard are weatherworn Georgian TOMBSTONES with vernacular carving.

SCHOOL, NE of the church. 1840s. Small; two-storey centre part with plaque in gable; single-storey wings.

METHODIST CHURCH, ¼ m. N. 1888. Gabled front with three-light Gothic window flanked by turrets.

CHALE ABBEY, ¼ m. NNE. Never a monastery, but in origin a substantial manor house, built by John de Langford who was Constable of Carisbrooke Castle in 1334–42. The surviving medieval work is in two stone-built two-storey ranges in L-form. The main range is aligned N–S; a narrower wing runs E–W from its N end. There was substantial remodelling in the mid to late C16, possibly in more than one stage. In the C19 (by which time the building had the status of a farmhouse) there were alterations and extensions, principally to the NW and W. Recent restorations have resulted in the stripping of many internal details of the last two centuries, revealing or emphasizing older features.

The N window of the upper floor of the main medieval range is prominent outside; tall, two-light and transomed, without cusps and with a wide dagger-like upper light.

Chale Abbey, engraving.
From Sir Henry Englefield, *Description . . . of the Isle of Wight*, 1816

Underneath, the ground floor was lit at this end by two two-light ogee-headed windows which are visible inside (they are obscured outside by a lean-to addition); their mullions have been replaced by metal supports. Otherwise all the windows in the medieval parts are C16, C18 or later insertions, except for one small single light in the W wall of the upper floor of the main range, recently reopened. A restored medieval shoulder-headed doorway survives on the first floor, leading from the main range into the W wing. The ground floor of the main range has two old doorways on the E side. They now lead to an annexe built in the C16, containing a staircase. It has been suggested that, like similar surviving medieval domestic buildings of stone with main rooms on the upper floors, the existing early fabric is that of a solar or chamber block originally attached to a former great hall – which is presumed to have been timber-framed and of which nothing survives.* If this suggestion is correct, the hall probably abutted the present main range on the E side, and the two old doorways would have connected with it, leading from service accommodation in the ground floor of the solar block. In the C16 alterations, the

*Mr Edward Roberts first made this suggestion. Something similar may have happened to the partly medieval house at Swainston (q.v.).

S part of the ground floor was remodelled as the kitchen, and a large, impressive fireplace with a low straight-angled arch was inserted there, with similarly shaped smaller openings on either side. The upper floor of the main medieval block was subdivided, and a fireplace with a straight-angled arch similar to that in the kitchen was inserted in the W wing.

To the W is a fine stone-walled BARN, C16, with diagonally stepped buttresses, and one original truss – a raised cruck with collar-beams and braces.

LOWER HOUSE, Chale Street, ½ m. N. Small C17 stone house, little altered. Symmetrical front with mullioned windows and doorway with almost flat arch; axial brick stacks.

GOTTEN MANOR, off Gotten Lane, 1½ m. NNE, under the W slopes of St Catherine's Down. Three-bay S front of *c.* 1854 with the upper windows under fretted bargeboards. Internal features including fireplaces and roof beams indicate that the building is of at least C17 origin (it is probably on the site of a medieval manor house). To the E is a smaller annexe with external steps to the first floor, and a C17 fireplace with cambered stone top. In a linking block is a remarkable PUMP with bowl-shaped leaden top bearing the date 1800, and a figure, presumably Diana, with hunting dogs.

WALPAN, off Military Road, ¾ m. WNW. C17 stone-built former farmhouse; mullioned windows; two-storey porch; thatched roof.

On ST CATHERINE'S HILL, ¾ m. E, is the shell of a medieval
13 LIGHTHOUSE, the only one surviving in England; it was built in 1314 and abutted an earlier oratory of which only the foundations remain. It is a slender octagonal tower 35 ft (11 metres) high, with an eight-sided pyramid roof which, to Pevsner in the 1960s, made it appear just like a rocket. Inside it is a square-sided shaft; at the top are eight rectangular openings which diffused light from the fire maintained within. The four buttresses to the lower part were added in the C18. To the N is a circular stump forming the base of a new lighthouse started in 1785 but never completed. (The present St Catherine's Lighthouse, of 1838–40, is much nearer the coast; *see* Niton.)

On the SE side of the lighthouse, straddling the boundary between the parishes of Chale and Niton, is a Bronze Age ROUND BARROW excavated by G.C. Dunning in 1925. 55 ft (17 metres) in diameter, 4 ft (1.2 metres) high.

(HOY'S MONUMENT, on the crest of St Catherine's Down, 1 m. N of the medieval lighthouse. Built in 1814 by Michael Hoy, a merchant with Russian interests, to commemorate a visit to England by Tsar Alexander I. Tall round column on a square base, ending with a square-shaped capital surmounted by a large ball; altogether 72 ft (22 metres) high.)

CHERT *see* VENTNOR

CHILLERTON *see* GATCOMBE

COWES 4595

Cowes is a dual town. Cowes proper (sometimes called West Cowes) and East Cowes are separated by the estuary of the River Medina; they are connected by a chain ferry. There was no significant settlement before the C16 – the site of West Cowes was in Northwood parish and that of East Cowes in Whippingham. In 1539–40 Henry VIII built two small forts on either side of the estuary where it opens into the Solent. That at East Cowes was abandoned a few years later, but the one on the western side survives, greatly altered, as Cowes p. 26 Castle. Hitherto shipping trade on the Medina had been focused at Newport at the head of the estuary, but in 1575 a custom house was established at East Cowes. Port trade developed through the C17 and C18, much of it transient; ships sailing along the Channel, naval and civilian, sometimes stopped at Cowes to replenish their supplies. Vessels of various sizes, some quite substantial, were built and maintained in yards along the estuary, many of them for the Navy. At first this activity was largely at East Cowes, but it developed too on the western side, where a chapel (the predecessor of St Mary) was built in 1657.

Substantial settlements grew along the riversides, and by the early C19 fashionable villas and country houses stood on the higher ground to either side. There was already yacht

Cowes, view of West Cowes.
From W.H.D. Adams, *Nelson's Handbook to the Isle of Wight*, 1866

racing in the late C18; a Yacht Club formed in 1815 became the Royal Yacht Squadron in 1833. Vessel building developed through the C19 from wood and sail to iron and steam, and in the early C20 Cowes came into the forefront for the building of maritime aircraft. Seaplanes evolved into flying-boats, whose development reached a peak after the Second World War. After their abandonment for general service in the 1950s attention was focused on hovercraft. Shipbuilding and related engineering continued to a significant extent until the 1960s. The scaling down of its technological industries in the last part of the C20 left Cowes largely dependent on leisure facilities; it remains one of the greatest yachting centres in Europe.

Cowes has never known formal urban planning. Both parts developed from the C17 to the C19, often densely, along the riverfronts, and more loosely up the hillsides behind. House building in quantity, associated with the development of industry, took place on either side of the river in the later C19 and very early C20 – usually in local buff brick with some variegation in red.

Cowes is treated in its two parts separately: first Cowes town (West Cowes), then East Cowes. Osborne House, on the edge of the latter but never dominating it, is described under a separate heading, as are Norris Castle and the older villages of Northwood and Whippingham.

COWES TOWN (WEST COWES)

The town centre is based on the long, narrow and slightly tortuous High Street and its continuations, running roughly parallel to the estuary shore. Except to the N, where there is an open Parade ending at the Castle, there is little public access to the waterfront in the central part of the town. Outside this inner area, maritime and commercial activities extend for some way along the riverside to the S. In the opposite direction a fairly informal Esplanade borders the Solent shore beyond the Castle. Streets and lanes, often steep, lead W and SW up the hillsides to an area of generally mixed development, including the park adjoining the early C19 Northwood House.

Following the church descriptions, the interesting parts of the town are covered in two Perambulations, after which there is a description of Northwood House and its vicinity.

ST MARY, Church Road, off Union Road, near the entrance to Northwood Park. The chapel of 1657 was consecrated in 1662 and altered in the C18 and early C19, with a W tower added in 1816. It was rebuilt, except the tower, in 1867. Illustrations before the rebuilding show aisles with two tiers of windows, the upper ones related to galleries, and a five-light square-headed E window without cusps. The last must

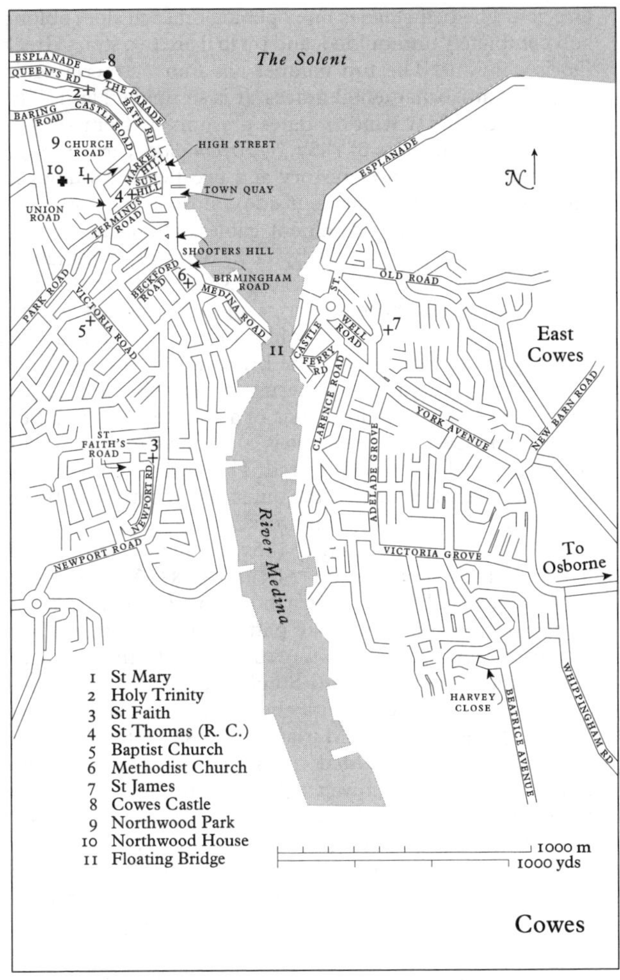

have been a survival from the C17 building; it resembled that of a few decades earlier at Yarmouth (q.v.).

The tower, of Portland stone, was designed by *John Nash* 58 for George Ward of Bellevue (now Northwood House; *see* p. 129). The ground storey was the family chapel with a burial vault underneath. Pevsner found the tower 'astonishing' because of the ways in which classical motifs were used: 'It is so radically Grecian that one thinks at first rather of C20 Grecian disguise for modern . . . than of the early C19

Grecian. The bell-stage is one opening on each side, oblong and completely unmoulded, and set in it are two short Greek Doric columns. The top parapet has four acroteria again devoid of any ornamental graces. It is so unlike Nash.' The intrusive Gothic W window dates presumably from 1867.

The nave and aisles of 1867, by *Arthur Cates*, are of rough Swanage stone, with clerestory and two-tiered windows in the aisles (there are galleries inside), those in the upper tier of dormer type with prominent gables. The chancel, with polygonal apse, was rebuilt by *H.R. Lloyd* of Birmingham in 1900. The nave interior is a surprise; spacious, with walls and arches of polychromatic brick, piers of polished granite, stone capitals with acanthus-like foliage – and galleries, unusual for so late a date. The brickwork in the spandrels is buff with geometric patterns in red; the arches are rimmed in red brick with bands of alternate black and buff on the outsides. The chancel is also polychromatic, with two-light windows arched in red. The tower arch, renewed by *Cates*, is of three orders, the outer one in patterned brick, the other two in ornate stonework.

FURNISHINGS. PULPIT, *c.* 1867, octagonal, stone, with figures in arched panels. – STAINED GLASS. Apse windows by *Horwood* of Frome. – W window by *Heaton, Butler & Bayne*; deep colours, intricate patterning; prominent Risen Christ in roundel at top. – MONUMENTS. In the N gallery, several wall tablets: Richard Stephens, founder of the first chapel, †1671, cartouche with cherub and intricately draped border; to its r. and l. Maria Stephens, †1768 and John Stephens, †1774, moulded ovals each with a small cartouche. – Under the tower a large monument to George Ward, †1829, with representation of a chest supporting a sarcophagus with carved panel, flanked by female figures; obelisks with wreaths on either side. – N wall of tower space, two tablets with angels in relief, each tapering to a pediment with acroteria: Charity Frances Ward, †1851, r.; Emma Ward, †1880, l.

The large CHURCHYARD is attractive, much of it semi-wild, with C18 and early C19 tombstones.

HOLY TRINITY, Queen's Road, on a hillside SE of the Castle. By *Benjamin Bramble* of Portsmouth, 1832. Rectangle of buff brick with W tower; tall pointed windows with later tracery; buttresses ending in spiky pinnacles. The tower has a good outline with embattled top. The small apsidal chancel, by *R.J. Jones*, 1862, is of buff brick banded in red, with Romanesque windows and conical roof. Inside, the nave is a broad space, formerly ceiled (the roof was renewed in 1910). The apse is internally polychromatic; in buff brick with black bands, and black and red patterns round the windows – which have STAINED GLASS by *Lavers & Barraud*, 1862.

ST FAITH, Newport Road and St Faith's Road; by *J.S. Adkins*, 1909. A church easy to underestimate. It is built on a slope, which steepens down eastwards; the intended chancel with lower storey was never built. The nave is roughcast, with three-light square-headed windows, battered Voysey-like buttresses and a white turret on the W gable, with two round-headed bell-openings and a cross. The interior is unexpected; transverse arches, in pre-stressed concrete rendered over, rise from sill-level bases; a narrower chancel arch opens into a shallow polygonal sanctuary.

ST THOMAS OF CANTERBURY (R.C.), Terminus Road. Built 1796–7 at the expense of Mrs Elizabeth Heneage – very early for a Catholic church in England, but five years later than the church she founded at Newport (q.v.). The designer was probably the *Rev. Thomas Gabb*, the first priest. The S façade (the church is oriented E–W) must have been impressive: of buff brick, with five rounded arches containing four windows; the E arch, over the entrance, is blank. A three-storey priest's house is attached at the (geographical) W end, the whole being under a continuous parapet with cornice. Unfortunately tracery with paired rounded lights was inserted in the windows in the C19. Handsome porch, with Ionic columns and dentilled pediment, at the E end of the S side.

Memorable interior, with the interest concentrated on 56
the W (ritual E) end. The altar is backed by a RETABLE with giant Doric pilasters, a frieze with triglyphs and *paterae*, and a keyed arch between the pilasters. On either side are smaller arched recesses. At the opposite end of the church is a GALLERY with triglyph frieze and balustrade, curving forward gracefully at its centre.

BAPTIST CHURCH, Victoria Road, 1876–7. Façade in buff brick and stucco with moulded cornice and pediment, Composite pilasters, arched windows and doorway brought out in red brick, topped with keystones. A more elaborate version of the later West Hill Chapel, now Public Library, in Beckford Road (*see* Perambulation 1, p. 124).

METHODIST CHURCH, Birmingham Road, 1901, by *Bell, Withers & Meredith*. Eclectic street front facing E, in red brick and stone dressings, with a big Perp window. The best feature is the octagonal tower at the NE corner, in brick with three stone stripes at first-floor level (echoed by a similar pattern on a two-storey porch to the l.). The tower narrows to a graceful upper stage with thin windows on each side of the octagon, topped by a frilly stone parapet and ending with a short spire. Such architectural treatment does not continue round to the N side. For the previous chapel *see* Perambulation 1, p. 124.

COWES CASTLE. *See* Perambulation 1, p. 127.

PERAMBULATIONS

Perambulation 1 covers the streets close to the river, where most of the pre-C19 town was sited. This route begins at the Floating Bridge (the river crossing from East Cowes) and goes N to Cowes Castle, the headquarters of the Royal Yacht Squadron. Perambulation 2 extends up the slopes to W and SW.

1. Floating Bridge to Cowes Castle

The FLOATING BRIDGE, a chain ferry, provides the only public crossing of the estuary. It was established in 1853 and has been renewed several times – one of the few of its kind still operating in Britain. A succession of thoroughfares leads N parallel to the estuary: Medina Road, Birmingham Road, Shooters Hill, High Street and Bath Road (the last three narrow and sinuous). Many of the properties fronting the E sides of these streets originally backed directly on to the river, but this pattern has been modified by subdivisions, amalgamations, rebuildings and reclamation.

Opposite the ferry, RATSEYS provides an appropriate introduction: a three-storeyed building in ashlar of *c.* 1800 used for sail-making, with segment-headed doorways, small windows and larger openings which contained hoists. MEDINA ROAD leads N and continues into BIRMINGHAM ROAD, where WESTBOURNE HOUSE on the r. (No. 42) is the N part of a once larger house of *c.* 1752; of grey headers with red brick dressings, including moulded cornice, string course and pilaster at the N end. A plaque commemorates the birth therein of Thomas Arnold (the famous headmaster of Rugby School), the son of the collector of customs at Cowes. The site of the S part is occupied by C20 housing. ALEXANDRA HALL, further on the r., was built in 1831 as a Methodist chapel; it is now residential. The ashlar front has a pediment, but the windows are 'Gothick' with four-centred heads. (The present Methodist church is across the
52 road; *see* above.) On the r. again is BLENHEIM HOUSE (Bekens), 1835, of two bays and three storeys, with a striking façade in grey and red brick above the later shop. The first-floor windows are set in blank arches with broad, short pilasters, and the tall parapet has a moulded cornice.

BECKFORD ROAD, leading W, was laid out in 1888–9. The PUBLIC LIBRARY was built in 1889 as West Hill Chapel (Primitive Methodist); of temple form, mainly in buff brick, with round-headed windows and pilasters between them – a simpler version of the earlier Baptist church (*see* p. 123). Along the road are several Late Victorian bargeboarded houses in buff brick, sometimes with red dressings.

Birmingham Road is continued by SHOOTERS HILL, curving

and descending to the r. On the l. is JOLLIFFE'S (No. 1), 82
rebuilt *c.* 1917 under Art Nouveau influence. Facing tiles in four shades of green; big first-floor windows with a semicircle in a rectangular frame, and the name spelt twice in stylized lettering with thick horizontal strokes.

Shooters Hill turns N into HIGH STREET, long, narrow and twisty, partly pedestrianized and generally picturesque. Much of it is lined with small shops under modest C18 and later upper storeys, interspersed in places by more pretentious buildings. The VECTIS TAVERN, on the corner with Town Quay, is a small-scale C17 survival; timber-framed, plastered in front, and partly jettied and weatherboarded on its side elevation. In contrast is the FOUNTAIN HOTEL immediately to the N, built in 1803 when the town was beginning to be fashionable. It has a three-storey stuccoed frontage, with the principal windows and doorway contained in arched recesses.

The Pontoon, behind the hotel, is the landing place for passenger ferries from Southampton. The ARCADE is a passageway behind Tuscan columns, under a partly recessed upper storey, connecting the Pontoon with High Street to the N of the Fountain Hotel. It has features which look generally of *c.* 1890–1900, including an oriel window in a projecting gabled bay, but it may be of earlier origin. If it were sensitively restored, it could once again provide a discreet prelude to the town for people arriving from the ferry.

One passes under an archway from the Arcade into one of the narrowest and most attractive stretches of High Street. No. 94, on the r. going N, *c.* 1800, has a slightly convex upper frontage with a dentilled cornice. Nos. 41–41a across the street, of similar date, have two tiers of canted bay windows on the upper storeys. No. 89 on the r. is grander – a five-bay late C18 house of red brick with pedimented doorway, reached up steps. The three central bays come slightly forward under a pediment. No. 88, abutting to the N, is a former malthouse which extended back towards the riverside. Its street frontage, in brick with a broad gable, looks mid-C19. A two-light ground-floor window has a spiral iron mullion. Above are two small round-headed openings and a circular light under the gable, which contain patterned iron grilles similar to examples in Newport (as on former quayside warehouses, and the converted malthouse in Crocker Street, p. 183). Part of the side wall of No. 88 High Street is of older brickwork, probably C18, and its lower section is in rough stone. Next, to the N, is the HSBC BANK of 1924; Neo-Georgian with bracketed pediment over tall doorway.

Further on, the street narrows, bends to the l. and opens up with ADMIRAL'S WHARF on the r.: a Corbusian block with frontages to street and river, *c.* 1961 by *David Stern &*

Partners. The ground floor has shallow concrete arches, partly used as car ports; upper parts have horizontal glazing and white boarded fascias. The irregular space where Market Hill joins High Street from the W was formerly the Market Place. Buildings around it were destroyed by bombing in 1942, including the Town Hall of 1816. Many of the replacements are not right for the location, especially the staggered flats on the NW side. W of these, an alley passes Ward's Cottages, built in the early C19 for retired servants from Northwood House (*see* p. 129), to reach MACNAMARA ALMSHOUSES, 1881, with frilly parapet and bargeboards over the doorways.

Further N along High Street, No. 70, r., is the former Lloyds Bank, converted in 2000–1 for living accommodation. The lively Free Baroque ground-floor frontage of *c.* 1900 has round-headed windows between engaged columns, a segmental hood over the doorway, and curving sections of balustrade. The upper part of the exterior is plain Late Georgian. Facing the river nearby is the ISLAND SAILING CLUB, built in 1961 to a design by *Howard Lobb*, probably influenced by the inter-war Royal Corinthian Yacht Club at Burnham-on-Crouch in Essex, but has been much altered. White fascias and thin metalwork are evident.

BATH ROAD takes a curving course NW from High Street, forming an attractive townscape with bow windows and slightly convex frontages to some of the buildings. The nicest group is at the far end, including EXMOUTH HOUSE and BARS HILL HOUSE, the latter on the S corner of Bars Hill itself. They both date from *c.* 1800–10 and are distinguished by bow windows with three curved sashes – a local and regional speciality (*see* p. 34). Bars Hill House has such windows on all three floors, Exmouth House on the lower two storeys only. In the latter house the central sashes are four panes wide, while the flanking ones have single panes – to striking effect. PRINCES HOUSE, on the N corner of Bars Hill, was built in 1885 as offices; the upper storeys are of brick with quoins, but the ground floor is stone-faced with fluted pilasters flanking the doorway under a bold pediment.

Bath Road enters THE PARADE, a shoreside space where the Medina estuary opens into the Solent – the most accessible public place for viewing yachts and shipping. The seafront was formerly focused on the Victoria Pier, opened in 1902 but demolished in 1961. The balustrade of 1902 survives on the shoreline. The dominant feature on the landward side is now OSBORNE COURT by *R.W.H. James*, 1937–8; a modernistic essay in painted concrete, with flat roof-lines at differing heights of up to ten storeys. Its centre part is set back above a podium, between long, irregularly shaped wings. Angles are curved, with inset balconies; open balconies with rounded ends project from the central range. (The entrance hall, within the podium, is roof-lit with panelled glazing between segmental cross-arches.) To the NW is a surviving C19 house with iron balconies, and then GLOSTER COURT, *c.* 1998 by *Richard Jones*, in a pleasant scaled-down version of the style of Osborne Court. There are four storeys above a ground-level basement, the upper two floors recessed; and the main storey above the basement has balconies in short round-ended sections. It stands on the site of the Gloucester Hotel, where the Royal Yacht Squadron was based before it moved to the Castle in 1857.

COWES CASTLE. The fort built by Henry VIII in 1539–40 consisted of a round tower of two storeys, low square wings, and a semicircular gun platform which survives on the sea (NE) side. The master mason may have been *Thomas Bertie*, responsible for Calshot Castle and the slightly later Hurst Castle, both on spits jutting out from the Hampshire mainland. Much of the stone came from the dissolved Beaulieu Abbey. In 1716 most of the tower was demolished, and further remodelling in the C18 and later left the building largely domestic in appearance. The Royal Yacht Squadron employed *Anthony Salvin* to remodel it in 1856–8; there have been later accretions. Salvin's work is externally modest except for the tower at the NW end, rounded towards the sea, with a steeply sloping slated roof. On the SW side a segment of the lower part of the 1540 tower survives, pierced by windows and containing the entrance; it has a later upper storey. The adjoining round stair-turret is C18. The gun platform has a low outer stone wall, broadly castellated. In 2000 a new PAVILION by *Thomas Croft* was added on the NW side; simple and elegant, set behind a veranda with steel columns of square section, all under a concave-sided tent-like roof. It stands on slightly rising ground; the main accommodation is provided partly within the sloping land behind. In the background is Holy Trinity church (*see* p. 122). *p. 26*

2. *The Esplanade to Northwood Park*

THE ESPLANADE begins as a sinuous footpath twisting between Cowes Castle and the sea. It straightens and continues W past PRINCE'S GREEN, a public space opened in 1863. The DRINKING FOUNTAIN, 1864, set between two shelters, has an elaborate domed iron canopy with four fretted arches resting on thin iron columns, richly painted. It was provided by *Macfarlane's* of Glasgow (cf. Ryde, p. 238). Turning E along QUEEN'S ROAD, which borders Prince's Green on the landward side, one passes a series of early to mid-C19 houses on the r. MARINERS has a porch with a tent-like canopy and round-headed first-floor windows, the centre one in an elliptical-headed recess. BELMORE HOUSE, *c.* 1810, has a tall porch with columns and triglyph frieze. Further E are Holy Trinity (*see* p. 122), and its former vicarage on the opposite side. The first vicarage was built with the church (1832), but the present house, in buff brick with red and black bands, is probably of *c.* 1862 when the chancel of the church was rebuilt by *R.J. Jones* using similar materials.

Queen's Road joins CASTLE HILL, which climbs steeply S. At the top is an impressive GATEWAY of 1841 to Northwood Park (*see* p. 130 below), with an arched entrance set between pairs of Tuscan columns with balustrade above. It is flanked by quadrant walls with blank niches and rusticated ends. One can walk through the park to Northwood House, but the Perambulation goes l. along CASTLE ROAD, curving to the SE round the brow of a slope which descends towards the riverside. On the l. are three pairs of stuccoed houses of *c.* 1840 which face towards the river; their road frontages are given prominence by large round-arched porches.

The middle stretch of Castle Road was largely developed in the later C20, but the part S of the junction with Bars Hill, continuing to Market Hill, has an oddly mixed sequence of C18–C19 houses, forming one of the pleasantest pieces of townscape in Cowes. No. 11 Castle Road is prominent on the l., facing Church Road which comes in from the W; it is a plain plastered house of *c.* 1810, three-storeyed at one end, with a long lower wing to the N. Its most striking features are two sharply pointed Gothic doorways. No. 9, *c.* 1830, has its main frontage at right angles to the street. It too is idiosyncratic, with pilasters, moulded cornice, porch with pediment, and paired sash windows under almost Jacobean hoodmoulds with headstops. By contrast, No. 12 across the street is big-boned Victorian, *c.* 1860–70, with canted bay windows. The nicest in the group is No. 2 on the W corner with Market Hill, Mid-Georgian and timber-built. The weatherboarding on the main frontage is a rare survival in Cowes; the ground-floor windows have raised wooden frames with the outlines of keystones.

MARKET HILL (into which Castle Road leads) rises steeply westwards from High Street – *see* Perambulation 1, p. 125. CLAREMONT HOUSE, late C18, faces E down the hill; its side elevation partly closes the view along Castle Road. Its main front is of grey headers and red brick dressings with a deep bracketed pediment over the doorway, which is approached sideways from the street up a short flight of steps. Going up Market Hill, Nos. 15–16 on the r., C18, are also in grey and red brick, but altered. SUN HILL joins

Market Hill at a sharp angle from the l. A simple C18 or early C19 building in the angle facing W, partly three- and partly two-storeyed, forms an effective marker in the street scene when seen from the opposite direction. No. 32 Sun Hill to its S, built by the Foresters' Friendly Society in 1865, is grander than the adjoining buildings. It has a rusticated ground storey, with representations of sea creatures in a small rounded pediment above the doorway. In the centre of the parapet is a plaque showing a working forester watched by a pelican. Sun Hill descends steeply to High Street, with an attractive jumble of houses on the l., and a glimpse of the sea beyond. IVY HOUSE on the r., mid- to late C18, faces eastwards on a brow – a position comparable to that of Claremont House on Market Hill. It too is fronted in grey and red brick, with a boldly pedimented doorcase, and three storeys of bow windows at the far end.

The Perambulation continues W along UNION ROAD. Nos. 5–7 on the l. are late C18 urban cottages with pairs of casement windows and simple door hoods. No. 17 is mid-C19 with frilly gables and a fantasy porch. Nos. 21–23 have a uniform Late Georgian front of buff brick with broad canted windows on both floors. No. 25 was built as a Masonic Hall in 1846 by 'Mr Wyatt', evidently the locally based builder *Frederick Wyatt*. Handsome stuccoed façade with four pilasters, triglyph frieze and tall pediment with urns. Opposite, CHURCH ROAD leads past St Mary's (*see* p. 120) to CHURCH LODGE, a little-known work of *John* 49
Nash. It is faced in ashlar, with a recessed portico of Tuscan columns, a broad frieze, and an attic with three shallow windows. Pevsner wrote that it 'has much of the ruthlessness of [Nash's] tower of St Mary'. It must have been intended to relate to an entrance to Northwood Park, but there is no evidence of the existence of a drive from here to the house. The date of the lodge is not known. *Nash* designed another entrance feature at the junction of Union Road and Park Road, near the present approach to Northwood Park; this was demolished in 1938. It was an open tetrastyle Tuscan portico with pediment; again, no date for it is known.

NORTHWOOD HOUSE AND PARK

In 1783 George Ward, a London merchant, bought an estate called Bellevue, W of Cowes. By 1800 he had built a new house, later renamed NORTHWOOD HOUSE. Ward died in 50
1829; his son George Henry consulted *John Nash* about improving the house. Preparatory work was carried out, including unsigned drawings of 1832 now in the British Library which were probably by *James Pennethorne*, who visited Northwood in that year and who took on many of the

commitments of the last years of Nash's practice. In *c.* 1836–7 Ward commissioned *George J.J. Mair* as architect.*

The present building seems to be largely to *Mair*'s design, and has the date 1837 on the pediment of the main N elevation. However, it is evident that there were changes to Mair's plans before the building was completed. He displayed drawings for work in different parts of Northwood House at the Royal Academy four times in 1838–46.

George Henry Ward died in 1849; his nephew built Weston Manor, Freshwater (q.v.). Northwood House passed in 1929 to the local council, together with some of its grounds, for a public park. At the time of writing it is used for gatherings and meetings, including those of Cowes Town Council. It is a strange house outside and stranger within, with some exceptional internal features.

The house is largely two-storeyed and rendered, with a main E–W axis, a large N wing containing the entrance, and a S wing which is aligned a little westward from its northern counterpart; the W side of the house contained the services. The important S frontage is asymmetrical because of the wing to its l., and the elevation of the main block on this side is a slightly awkward nine-bay composition. Its three central bays are brought forward under a pediment and project further on their ground storey, with a balustrade above four engaged Ionic columns *in antis*. The rest of the ground floor has banded rustication – a characteristically French motif. The E side of the wing is in matching style (discussed below). The short E frontage of the main block has a large central bow. The seven-bay N elevation is similar to the S but simpler. The N wing is very different, but is part of the *c.* 1837–46 composition. It is single-storeyed with a dome visible behind parapets; on the E and W sides are tetrastyle Ionic porticos *in antis*. The E portico is blind, but that on the W side has a porch with paired columns and low pediment. The main entrance is through this porch.

The entrance opens into a spacious ROTUNDA, where eight columns of a simplified palm type support a coffered dome with top light. Arches in the encircling walls contain doorways or niches. A corridor leads S, which, like others in the house, has small domes between cross-arches. It meets the wide E–W passage of the main block, which to the W has a roof glazed between segmental beams. This leads to the spectacular focal point of the interior; the brilliantly

*There are drawings in the British Library which relate to the house of *c.* 1800 and proposed alterations to it. These indicate that the present house is likely to be a complete replacement, except for parts of the basement. *Mair* is otherwise known for work at Kneller Hall, Whitton, Richmond upon Thames, and Flass House, Crosby Ravensworth, Westmorland.

decorated 'EGYPT CORNER' in the angle of the E–W corri- 48
dor and one leading S. Four red-painted ribbed columns with palm capitals support a square canopy, enriched with Neo-Egyptian devices in bright colours. A red star in the centre of the canopy ceiling is a compelling feature. On the W wall of the canopied space is a doorcase-like frame, with battered sides and gilded details. The opening to the corridor leading S has a concave hood and more painted decoration. The ETRUSCAN ROOM, SE of Egypt Corner, has engaged columns and a ceiling with a shallow dome, with patterns and devices having supposed Etruscan references. Beyond, in the S wing, is the simpler OCTAGON ROOM with an eight-panelled ceiling.

The largest room in the house is the former BALLROOM at the E end, focused on the bow window which is prominent in the elevation, but this room is less memorable than some of the smaller ones. The ceiling has a central panel with a ring of small medallions depicting literary and philosophical figures. Leading off the Ballroom to the NW is the former DINING ROOM, with more Egyptian or Etruscan references. The corresponding room to the SW – the former DRAWING ROOM, now Council Chamber – has a grander effect, with arched recesses, a thickly decorated frieze, and coffered ceiling with large central circle and roundel. The STAIRCASE HALL is in a confined position on the N side of the main corridor, lit by round-headed windows at upper level; the well staircase is surprisingly modest, with slender round-patterned iron balusters.

The S wing has a complicated form, which must have been reached in more than one stage. Its E side has two floors, but the corridor leading S from Egypt Corner, which runs along the W side, has no upper storey. At the S end is a substantial single-storey projection, a little wider than the wing. The Tithe Map of 1844 suggests that the wing then included the corridor but not the two-storey E range, and that the S projection already existed to its present width. However, the buildings depicted may have been altered before the map was published, and it is probable that the wing was completed in its present form around 1844. The details of the four-bay E elevation of the wing match those of the main S frontage, to which it is set at a right angle. The single-storey S projection of the wing has a remarkable E façade. It is an aedicule with Ionic columns flanking a large niche which contains a statue. A balustraded parapet is broken by turrets with ball finials. Very probably this aedicule was originally designed as the setting for an important entrance to the house, rather than the niche which it now contains. This would have opened into a lobby within the E part of the present projection of the wing.

An undated lithographed drawing signed by *Mair* shows

what was evidently a major proposed extension of the house to the W. The view is from the SE, showing the E and S elevations of the house as they are now, including the S wing with the aedicule. But to the W of these the drawing shows a three-storey tower, and further still to the W a long single-storey range with columns and arches, ending with a second tower similar to the first. None of this was carried out except, evidently, the ground storey of the first tower. This seems to have been modified to incorporate the present S entrance – a round-headed doorway between vertical bands of rustication which would have continued upwards to form the quoins of the tower. This doorway now leads into a vestibule at the beginning of the corridor leading N to Egypt Corner. The vestibule abuts, to its E, a room which was probably first designed as the lobby inside the intended main entrance within the aedicule, in the way suggested above. The vestibule and the intended lobby together form the present S projection of the wing. In the absence of comprehensive documentation it must be presumed that there were major changes in the intended plan and form of the house during construction. A reasonable presumption is that it was intended that the main entrance would be in the S wing, through the elaborately designed aedicule and into a lobby, from which the corridor led N to Egypt Corner – designed and decorated as the focal point of the interior. Later it was decided to site the main entrance in the N wing, facing W. This presumed change may have been related to the formation of the long drive from the NW, as described below.

The former SERVICE QUARTERS on the W side (where the intended grand extension, shown in the drawing already described, never took place) are now a hotchpotch, following piecemeal additions and adaptations. However, an impressive N elevation to the service area was built, presumably *c.* 1840–5. It has blank arches with keystones and, in the centre, a tall rusticated archway between Tuscan columns. This façade bordered the carriage approach to the main entrance. But the archway is blocked, and irregular smaller-scale buildings abut it behind. Parts of these look older than the archway or façade, and may be survivals from the pre-1837 house.

A PARK was formed around the older house from *c.* 1810. This extended over the large area between the present Park Road and Baring Road. Debourne Lodge (*see* below) stands at the junction of these two roads, about ¾ m. WSW of the main house. From this lodge a sinuous drive was formed to provide the principal approach, ending at the entrance in the N wing. The length and alignment of the drive gave visitors a favourable impression of the extent of the estate, in a way typical of the time. The E part of the park became public space in 1929, and provides a pleasant setting for the house and the adjoining church of St Mary (*see* p. 120), although there are few significant surviving features of the C19 landscape. The greater part of the former park was developed during the C20.

Two small but remarkable buildings stand beside the junction of the present Park Road, Baring Road and two other roads, on the edge of the original park and well to the W of the house, from which they are now separated by development. Debourne Lodge stood at the entrance to the carriage drive. The other, across the road junction, is the conspicuous Round House. Both are important examples of self-consciously Picturesque buildings in the tradition of the *cottage orné*. The ROUND HOUSE is circular, with rough 43
limestone walls and a conical tiled roof which rises to a decorated brick chimney. A wavy-edged eaves fascia projects over an inset segmental veranda. The building probably appears on an estate map of 1801 (the indication is not quite clear), and was described as a Turnpike House in 1846. The parts of DEBOURNE LODGE seen from the roads are not specially notable, but the elevation on its E side (which faced the carriage drive) was shown by Nigel Temple to be closely related to a drawing by *George Repton* in the Pavilion Notebook (located in the Royal Pavilion Art Gallery, Brighton) of *c.* 1805–18, when Repton was chief assistant to John Nash. It has walls of rough limestone under a sweeping scale-tiled roof. There is a wide central veranda flanked by rough tree trunks with branch-like brackets, just as in Repton's drawing. The lodge retains a fine trio of decorative brick chimneys on a stone stack, but they have lost their moulded tops. It is reasonable to assume that both buildings were associated with *Nash*'s office.

EAST COWES

In the C19 and early C20 the contrasts between the maritime riverside and the more genteel hinterland were more marked in East Cowes than in Cowes proper. Industries related to the sea and, later, partly to the air came to dominate the waterfront. A little behind was *Nash*'s East Cowes Castle, and beyond that was Osborne (with Norris Castle, q.v., further in the background). Smaller mansions and villas occupied sites with choice views. In 1842 a scheme for a 'garden suburb' (the term had not yet been coined) called East Cowes Park was launched, with villas bordering an approximate rectangle of roads on the lines of the present Victoria Grove, Adelaide Grove and York Avenue, some of them backing on a central botanic garden. The E fringe of the scheme was affected by the development of Osborne. A few villas were built on other sites. But the scheme did not proceed as intended, and the area near the waterfront was covered with terraced housing from the 1870s. The botanic garden site was eventually built over.

ST JAMES, Well Road. Originally by *Nash*, 1831–3. His was a simple church with nave, broad transepts and embattled W tower. The tower survives, with lancets as belfry lights; a quatrefoil opening on its S side is an original feature. The rest was largely rebuilt by *Thomas Hellyer* in 1868–70, with aisles and longer chancel, retaining Nash's outer transept walls. Hellyer's style was his own. His two-light windows have rounded arches and no cusps; the wheel-like clerestory windows have six small circular lights surrounding an open roundel; a similar, larger window in the S transept has eight outer circles. The chancel windows are nearer to conventional Gothic. The interior is just as individualistic. The four-bay arcades with slender piers and simple arches have capitals derived from Italian Romanesque. There are galleries in the shallow transepts and across the two E bays of the aisles surprising for 1870 (but cf. St Mary, Cowes).

FURNISHINGS. FONT. 1869, of stone. Big square bowl with chamfered angles; sides and angles have carved figures; frilly undersides to the bowl; short marble columns. – REREDOS by *Heaton, Butler & Bayne*, 1905–6. Five trefoiled recesses with mosaic; elaborate frieze with lacy openwork. – Wooden SCREEN of 1933, entirely Gothic. The statues are later. – STAINED GLASS. E window by *Abbott & Co.* of Lancaster, 1949; colourful figures against plain background. (Older windows were destroyed in the Second World War.)

TOMB of *John Nash*, †1835, and his wife, †1851, in the churchyard S of the tower. A stone sarcophagus with angled lid. The base, with lettering different in style from that of the older inscription, must be part of *Seely & Paget*'s C20 restoration. The tomb itself may date from the time of Mrs Nash's death.*

Worthwhile buildings are scattered and are described in two groups: those near the waterfront, and others on higher ground towards Osborne. These cannot be called Perambulations in the normal sense because of the often haphazard distribution of the buildings covered.

From the Floating Bridge, crossing from Cowes proper, FERRY ROAD passes the former CONGREGATIONAL CHURCH of 1829, an odd mixture; a Gothic entrance projects from a gable-pedimented front with round-headed windows. The small former TOWN HALL near the junction of Ferry Road, Clarence Road and York Avenue is by *James*

* As suggested by John Summerson, *The Life and Work of John Nash*, 1980.

Newman, 1896–7; debased Italianate with French references. It has segment-headed windows, a balustrade with spikes, and a central feature with clock. This road junction is, if anywhere can so be called, the focal point of East Cowes. In the first part of CLARENCE ROAD leading S is some sense of urban quality lacking elsewhere, with a twelve-bay three-storey terrace of *c.* 1846–50 on the E side; the corner is rounded and recessed (cf. examples of this treatment in Ryde), and the first-floor windows have architraves. There were shops on the ground floor from the start; one on the corner has paired plate-glass windows with thin intermediate columns.

York Avenue leads E uphill towards Osborne (*see* below) and, in the opposite direction, returns to CASTLE STREET, on the edge of the industrial waterfront. On its W side is a commercial range of *c.* 1900 with polychrome patterned brickwork on the upper storeys. Castle Street leads N past factories to the beginning of OLD ROAD, which, ascending E, was the original road to Newport, narrow and awkward for pedestrians. About ½ m. along on the r. is NORTH LODGE, the only remaining feature of *Nash*'s EAST COWES CASTLE, built 1798–1802, later enlarged, and demolished in stages 1956–62. The lodge has one-and-a-half storeys with fretted bargeboards, elaborated roof tiles and prominent coved hood. The Castle stood to the SE; its site and surroundings are covered with suburban houses.

Returning to the waterfront, THE ESPLANADE extends N of the industrial frontage, with fine views over the estuary mouth. Set back to the E are the former COASTGUARD COTTAGES built in 1881–2, a long range in buff brick with red brick window heads; generally two-storeyed but with four gables rising at wide intervals to include small attics. Nearby, a PROPELLOR from HMS *Cavalier*, built locally in 1944, forms a sculptural feature. CAMBRIDGE TERRACE stands at right angles to the shore; it is three-storeyed with two levels of delicate iron-framed verandas extending for eleven bays. Each bay is arched at both levels between the columns. It dates from as late as *c.* 1870.

Back to the Town Hall and up YORK AVENUE. In ADELAIDE GROVE, leading S, is the former FRANK JAMES HOSPITAL 81
by *Somers Clarke & Micklethwaite*, built as a seamen's home in 1893. It is a charming Arts and Crafts composition of one-and-a-half storeys round an open courtyard, mainly of red brick with sweeping tiled roofs, dormers, and tall chimneys in twos and threes; the wings end with stepped gables and prominent chimney-breasts. The centrepiece is a square cupola with lantern and gilded vane. Further up York Avenue, two villas from the East Cowes Park scheme remain on the r. KENT HOUSE, built in 1843 as Powlesse House, was bought by Queen Victoria in 1864 and altered.

It is Neo-Jacobean with simple gables, the central part brought forward with an oriel over a four-centred doorway. The smaller POWYS HOUSE adjoining has a simpler version of the Kent House centrepiece.

York Avenue bends to the S, and a short way along a turning to the l. is *Thomas Cubitt*'s ROYAL ENTRANCE to Osborne House, *c.* 1845–6, a grand but simple rusticated archway under a prominent modillion cornice, with small round motifs in the spandrels; it is flanked by single-storey lodges. This was the Sovereign's entrance, some way N of the house itself. From here S to the present entrance to Osborne, York Avenue passes on the l. a strip of land bought by the Queen, which had previously been on the edge of the newly established residential scheme, East Cowes Park (*see* above). A few houses already stood there. ALBERT COTTAGE, in the angle with New Barn Road SW of the Royal Entrance, is an irregular Italianate house mainly built in 1848, but incorporating a smaller villa (on its SW side) of the earlier 1840s. OSBORNE COTTAGE further S is very different. It replaced a *cottage orné* of before 1813. The present building of 1856–7 is by *A.J. Humbert* in association with *Prince Albert* (cf. p. 202). It is generally in buff brick with variegated red brick patterning, small gables, and prominent chimneystacks. The S wing was added in 1867. A covered corridor linking with Albert Cottage was built in 1898, and in 1901–2 the house was altered for Princess Beatrice, the Queen's daughter. A charming ORANGERY was added – a small square greenhouse with arch-patterned framework and two-tier roof with iron cresting. Since 1950 the house has been a retirement home, with modifications on the E side. VICTORIA COTTAGE further S was built in 1843, and was occupied for a time by Thomas Cubitt while he supervised the building of Osborne House. It is a simple stuccoed villa with a strange wooden balcony, including a fretted frieze and tall balustrade, over the entrance.

York Avenue then turns towards the present entrance to Osborne. In the angle is ARTHUR COTTAGE, 1868–9, simple Italianate with low-gabled wings. On the opposite side of York Avenue, Nos. 201–203 (Upper Park Cottages) are a plain Italianate pair erected in 1852 by the local builder *Richard Langley* with walls of cement using shuttering – one of the first examples of this technique. Finally, along a lane leading W from Beatrice Avenue (S of Harvey Close) is the former KINGSTON FARMHOUSE, built in 1866–7 for the Osborne Estate by *A.J. Humbert*. It is typical of his work (cf. the houses associated with him further S, in Whippingham), but in red brick with patterns in buff – the reverse of the usual relationship between the two shades.

EAST COWES *see* COWES

FARRINGFORD *see* FRESHWATER AND TOTLAND

FRESHWATER AND TOTLAND 3085

The West Wight peninsula is almost an island in itself, nearly 1
cut off by the River Yar and its estuary. The estuary extends S from Yarmouth to within a mile from the S coast. The Yar itself rises a few hundred yards from the shore and flows as a small stream to the estuary head. The peninsula has dramatic coastlines, especially the sheer chalk cliffs to the S and the shorter range to the N, which together mark the extremity of the central chalk range of the Island before it disintegrates into the rugged fragments that form the Needles. Alum Bay curves northwards with colourful cliffs, mainly of sandstone, which give way to the irregular NW coast of the peninsula with its broken and often wooded slopes. To the SE, Freshwater Bay is an inlet of the sea, like a large rounded cove between ranges of cliffs. The whole area was in Freshwater parish until that of Totland was formed in 1894. However, there is no clear distinction between the two places, and the peninsula is treated as a single entity.

There was no substantial village before the C19. Freshwater church, of Saxon origin, stands near the head of the estuary with, for long, only a relatively small group of houses beside it. (The estuary is, of course, tidal; the name may have derived from the freshwater stream which flows into it.) The rest of the population was scattered in and around outlying hamlets, some of which were based on greens. One of these hamlets, sometimes called School Green, grew into a sizeable though irregular settlement during the C19. It became, in effect, the town centre of Freshwater as the area developed, loosely but extensively, through the C20 – especially towards Freshwater Bay. There were few buildings around the latter before the C19, but the bay is now the main focus of Freshwater as a seaside resort. Totland Bay was established by *c.* 1880 as a separate resort on the irregular NW coast of the peninsula, with an informal promenade and a very small pier. It has a distinct identity, but there is now no break between it and the main part of Freshwater.

Alfred Tennyson occupied Farringford, an early C19 house, from 1853. His presence attracted writers, artists and other creative people, either for permanent or partial residence, or as visitors. Many were close friends, including the artist

G.F. Watts and the photographer Julia Margaret Cameron.* The poet is commemorated by a monument on Tennyson Down (renamed after him), a chalk ridge adjoining the coast S of Farringford. This is part of the extensive stretches of fine countryside which fortunately survive around Freshwater and Totland, despite late C19 and C20 development.

The area is treated in three sections: Freshwater and Freshwater Bay; Totland Bay; and Norton, the northern part of Freshwater parish. Nowhere are sustained Perambulations practicable as the interesting buildings are so scattered, but they are described as far as possible in topographical sequences.

FRESHWATER AND FRESHWATER BAY

21 ALL SAINTS, Church Place. The W tower looks very dramatic at the end of a street in the original village settlement, on the NE periphery of the present town. It has an unusual C13 giant arch rising through two storeys, and a late medieval upper stage. Otherwise the church looks largely C19 outside, due to a restoration in 1875–6 by *W.T. Stratton*, in which the aisles were rebuilt and the chancel extended E. One has to go inside to appreciate the building's historical complexity.

There was a late Saxon church with aisle-less nave, from which some of the quoins at its NW and SW angles have survived subsequent accretions, and are visible internally; they show long-and-short work typical of the period. In *c.* 1190–1200 aisles with three-bay arcades were added to the Saxon nave, and chapels were formed to the N and S of the original chancel. There were further works in the mid to late C13, including part of the chancel, a new W bay to nave and aisles, and the start of the remarkable W end. In 1875–6 the medieval lean-to aisles were replaced by wider ones under separate gables, and the church was enlarged eastwards, with substantial alterations to its internal arrangements. What had been the W part of the chancel became an extension of the nave, and a new chancel arch was built to the E of the older one. The older arch was reconstructed to greater height. The presence of these two transverse arches helps to give a confusing first impression of the complex interior.

The three-bay late C12 nave arcades are of the type found elsewhere on the Island, with round piers, square abaci and pointed arches with slight hoodmoulds. E of the arch on the site of the original chancel arch are single arches which led

*After 1867 Tennyson lived during the summer in a house in Sussex, to avoid the crowds on the Island. But Farringford remained his main home until his death in 1892.

Freshwater church, interior, drawing by Percy Stone.
From Stone, *The Architectural Antiquities of the Isle of Wight*, 1891

into side chapels. They are similar in detail to the main arcades apart from the E respond of the N arch, which has a simple version of waterleaf carving under the abacus. The former chapels are medieval in outline, but restored. The old S chapel has a remarkable late C13 TOMB RECESS (the back of which projects externally). This has a broad, finely moulded arch with an outer dogtooth band, and four large cusps with pierced quatrefoil circles and rather crudely carved ends. One of the cusps has been partly broken.

The present chancel is largely *Stratton*'s work of 1875–6. His chancel arch (the eastern of the two transverse arches) is of two orders, the inner order resting on corbels; his E window is Geometrical. The W part of the chancel S wall is adapted from the E part of the side wall of the medieval chancel. It retains a fine C13 window with two tall slender lights, without cusps but with a trefoil above. E of this is an identical window, re-set by Stratton from the opposite side of the chancel (where it was displaced by the present organ chamber). These two windows provided models for

Stratton's new windows in the aisles, giving the misleading first impression that the present aisles are medieval ones restored.

In the C13 the nave and aisles were extended one bay westward. The newer arches are not continuous with the late C12 arcades, since a few feet of masonry from the old fabric were retained (including the Saxon quoins already described), between them and the earlier arcades. The added arches are wider and taller than the earlier ones but surprisingly plain, with simple moulding and flat jambs. The climax of the C13 W extension is external: the giant arch, deeply recessed and narrow for its height, which projects from the W wall and is still such a dramatic feature as one approaches the church. It probably first supported a stone bellcote, for the detailed form of which there is no evidence. In the C15 or early C16 this upper structure was demolished and the present tower formed. This incorporates the giant arch on its western side and extends eastwards into the nave (blocking parts of the C13 western arches). The tower's top storey above the arch is quite plain, with small square-headed belfry lights and a tall castellated parapet. Within the arch is the C13 W window, with two uncusped lights and a trefoil circle above, similar to the windows in the S wall of the chancel. The moulded C15 doorway below was brought here from the former S porch at the restoration of 1875–6.

One further feature remains to be described: the N doorway, not now easily seen since it opens from a small Victorian porch which is generally kept locked. It is late C12, with three orders of zigzag facing outwards, and plain imposts. It was moved by *Stratton* from the medieval S aisle, where it opened into the S chapel.

FURNISHINGS. FONT, *c.* 1190–1200, of polished Purbeck marble. Plain square tapering bowl, round stem with shafts. Restored and set up at the W end of the N aisle in 1894 by *F.L. Pearson* (son of the great architect J.L. Pearson). It now has a stepped base behind brass rails on openwork iron brackets. – PULPIT. Probably of 1875–6. Stone, circular; moulded trefoil arches on short black columns; rounded base with larger black column. – The chancel was refurnished by *F.L. Pearson* in 1894; his CHOIR STALLS have traceried front panels. – STATUES of St Peter (N) and St John (S) flank the E window, the latter in memory of Lionel Tennyson, the poet's son. – STAINED GLASS. Three-light E window with scenes in strong colours, and patterned decoration in the cinquefoil lights above; probably of *c.* 1876, but by whom? In the S aisle a two-light window of 1913 by *Morris & Co.*, executed by *J.H. Dearle*. It is based on a painting by G.F. Watts showing Sir Galahad on a horse on the l., and again in armour on the r. (In the original paint-

1. The south-west coast, looking from near Chale towards the cliffs of Freshwater (pp. 115, 137)
2. Newtown, harbour, looking north (p. 190)

3. Carisbrooke Castle, aerial view from the south-west (p. 105)
4. Shanklin, old village, looking north (p. 262)

5. Brighstone, village (p. 98)
6. Newport, town centre, with former Isle of Wight Institution (now County Club), by William Mortimer, 1810–11, and Queen Victoria Memorial by Percy Stone, 1903, right (p. 171)

7. Mottistone, Longstone, Neolithic (p. 166)
8. Newport, Roman villa, hypocaust, C3 (p. 189)
9. Brading, Roman villa, mosaic, C4 (p. 97)

7 | 8
9

10. Arreton, St George, west doorway, late Saxon (p. 73)

11. Shalfleet, St Michael the Archangel, north doorway, mid-C12 (p. 260)

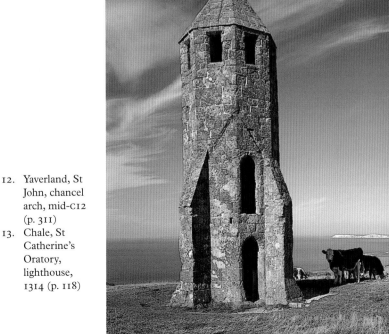

12. Yaverland, St John, chancel arch, mid-C12 (p. 311)
13. Chale, St Catherine's Oratory, lighthouse, 1314 (p. 118)

14. Carisbrooke Castle, including chamber wing (centre), chapel of St Nicholas (left) and keep (right), various dates (from the south-west) (p. 110)
15. Carisbrooke Castle, gatehouse, remodelled 1335–80 (p. 107)
16. Carisbrooke Castle, Staircase Hall, showing remains of private chapel, *c.* 1270 (p. 109)
17. Carisbrooke Castle, Great Hall, mid-C13 and later (fireplace *c.* 1390) (p. 109)

14	16
15	17

18. Arreton, St George, chancel, mid- to late C13, looking through to nave north aisle, late C12 (p. 73)
19. Arreton, St George, detail of south chapel window, mid- to late C13 (p. 74)

20. Carisbrooke, St Mary, west tower, dated 1471 (p. 113)
21. Freshwater, All Saints, various dates, west tower C13 and later (p. 138)

22. Godshill, All Saints, painting of Crucifixion, *c.* 1520 (p. 154)
23. Godshill, All Saints, monument of Sir John Leigh †1529 and wife (p. 155)
24. Carisbrooke, St Mary, monument of Lady Wadham, *c.* 1520 (p. 114)
25. Brading, St Mary, monument of Oliver Oglander †1536 (p. 92)

22 | 24
23 | 25

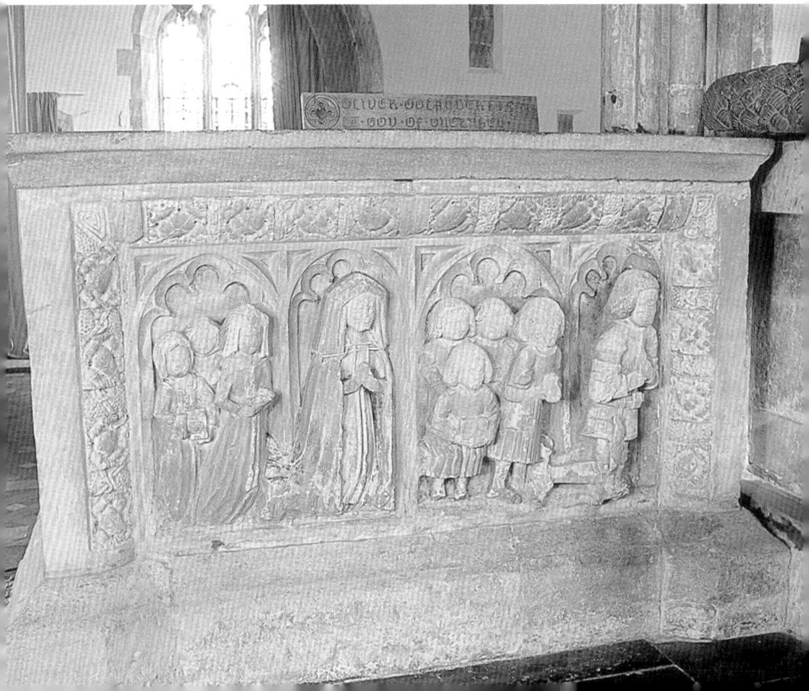

26. Shorwell, St Peter, north arcade, probably *c.* 1615–30; pulpit with tester dated 1620 (p. 272)
27. Yarmouth Castle, 1545–7 and later (p. 305)
28. Shorwell, North Court, *c.* 1615, east front (p. 274)
29. Arreton Manor, 1637–9, south front; extension of 1812, left (p. 76)

26 | 27
28
29

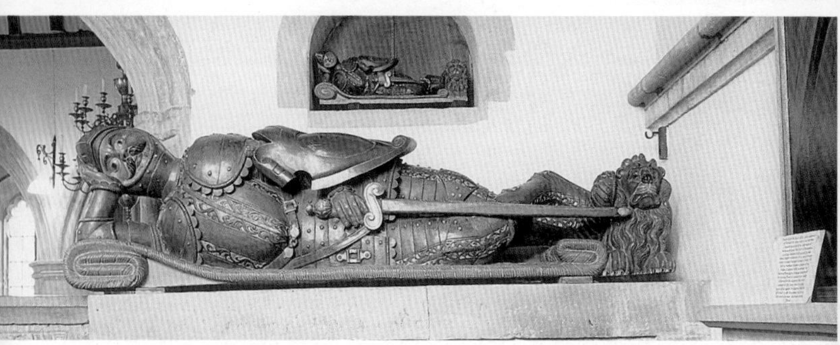

30. Godshill, All Saints, monument of Richard Worsley †1565 (p. 155)
31. Brading, St Mary, effigies of Sir John Oglander and George Oglander (above), *c.* 1649 (p. 94)
32. Wootton, St Edmund, pulpit, early C17 (p. 302)
33. Newport, St Thomas, pulpit, 1631 (p. 174)
34. Carisbrooke Castle, well-house, 1587 (p. 111)

VOICE LIKE A TRUMPET
ISAIAH 58

35. Newtown, town hall, *c.* 1699, altered 1813 (p. 190)
36. Newport, God's Providence House, 1701 (p. 179)
37. Appuldurcombe, by John James, begun 1701, aerial view from the east (p. 67)
38. Appuldurcombe, east entrance, probably as altered 1713 (p. 67)

35 | 37
36 | 38

39. Shorwell, North Court, staircase, early C18 (p. 275)
40. Shorwell, Wolverton Manor, staircase, mid- to late C18 (p. 277)
41. Newtown, C18 cottages (p. 190)
42. Newport, former House of Industry (now St Mary's Hospital), 1771–4 (p. 187)

39	41
40	42

43. Cowes (West Cowes), the Round House, *c.* 1800, attributed to the office of John Nash (p. 133)
44. Niton, Puckaster, after 1812 and later, after Robert Lugar (p. 194)
45. Shanklin, Vernon Cottage, 1817 and later (p. 267)
46. Ryde, The Swan's Nest, *c.* 1830 and later (p. 241)

43 | 45
44 | 46

Vernon Cottage
FOSTER'S

WEDDINGS &
FUNCTIONS

47. Ryde, Westmont House (Ryde School), 1819–21, entrance hall (p. 245)
48. Cowes (West Cowes), Northwood House, by George J.J. Mair, *c.* 1836–7 and later, Egypt Corner (p. 131)

47 | 48

49. Cowes (West Cowes), Church Lodge, by John Nash, early C19 (p. 129)
50. Cowes (West Cowes), Northwood House, by George J.J. Mair, *c.* 1836–7 and later (p. 129)
51. Newport, No. 54 Pyle Street, right, and corner of St James Square, early C19 (p. 126)
52. Cowes (West Cowes), Birmingham Road, Blenheim House, 1835 (p. 124)

CAPITAL
JEWELLERS
DECORATORS 
PHARMACY

53. Ryde, Pelhamfield, No. 60 Spencer Road, 1829 (p. 233)
54. Ryde, Brigstocke Terrace, by James Sanderson, 1826–9, south elevation (p. 232)
55. Ryde, Royal Victoria Arcade, by William Westmacott, 1835–6, interior (p. 230)
56. Cowes (West Cowes) St Thomas of Canterbury (R.C.), 1796–7, probably by the Rev. Thomas Gabb, interior (p. 123)

53	55
54	56

URIAH'S HEAP

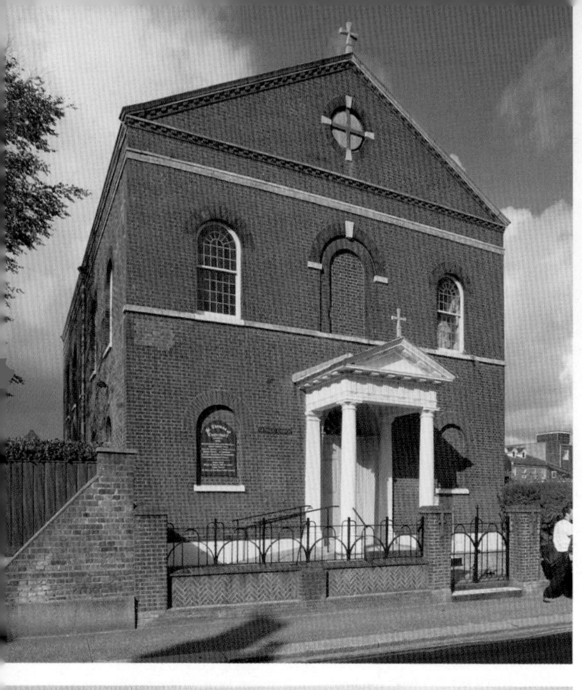

57. Newport, St Thomas of Canterbury (R.C.), 1791 (p. 176)
58. Cowes (West Cowes), St Mary, tower by John Nash, 1816 (p. 121)
59. Ryde, Town Hall, by James Sanderson, 1829–31, altered and extended by F. Newman, right, 1867–8, tower by Thomas Dashwood, 1867–8 (p. 228)
60. Newport, former Guildhall, by John Nash, 1814–16, tower added 1887 (p. 177)

57	59
58	60

VICTORIA
TOURIST
INFORMATION

61. Ryde, Holy Trinity, by Thomas Hellyer, 1841 and later (p. 222)
62. Whippingham, St Mildred, by A.J. Humbert, in association with Prince Albert, 1854–62 (p. 293)
63. Newport, Baptist Church, front of 1872 (p. 176)

61 | 62
63

64. Ryde (Swanmore), St Michael, nave interior, 1861–3 by the Rev. William Grey with R.J. Jones (p. 224)
65. Ryde, St Mary (R.C.), by Joseph Hansom, 1846–8, interior (p. 226)
66. Brighstone, St Mary, stained glass, by William White, c. 1900 (p. 99)

64 | 65 66

67. Osborne House, by Prince Albert and Thomas Cubitt, 1845–51 and later, aerial view from the north-west (p. 200)
68. Osborne House, view from the east showing terraces of 1847–54 (p. 209)
69. Osborne House, view from the west showing the pavilion and Flag Tower, centre (pp. 202, 204)

67 | 69
68

70. Osborne House, by Prince Albert and Thomas Cubitt, 1845–51 and later, Drawing Room, with decoration by Ludwig Grüner (p. 207)
71. Osborne House, Dining Room (p. 207)
72. Osborne House, Durbar Room, by John Lockwood Kipling with Bhai Ram Singh, 1891, detail of minstrels' gallery (p. 209)

70 | 72
71

73. Ryde, No. 2 John Street, 1840s (p. 239)
74. St Lawrence, Lisle Combe, 1839 and later, from the south-east (p. 250)
75. Shanklin, Rylstone Gardens, The Chalet, *c.* 1880 (p. 269)
76. Whippingham, Coburg, 1870–2 (p. 297)

73	75
74	76

77. Quarr Abbey, by Dom Paul Bellot, 1907–14 (p. 215)
78. Quarr Abbey, brick arches within the eastern tower, 1911–12 (p. 217)
79. Shanklin, St Saviour, stained glass by Christopher Whall, *c.* 1913 (p. 265)
80. Binstead, Holy Cross, stained glass by Gabriel Loire, 1971 (p. 85)

77	79
78	80

81. Cowes (East Cowes), former Frank James Hospital, by Somers Clarke & Micklethwaite, 1893 (p. 135)

82. Cowes (West Cowes), Shooters Hill, Jolliffe's, *c.* 1917 (p. 125)

83. Freshwater (Totland), St Saviour (R.C.), by W.C. Mangan, 1923 (p. 145)

84. Bembridge, K1 telephone box, 1929 (p. 80)

85. Shanklin, Eastcliff Promenade, lift, 1956 (p. 266)
86. Ventnor, Chert, by Gilbert & Hobson, 1969–70 (p. 291)
87. Wroxall, County Primary School, by Michael Rainey, County Architect (project architect J. Petrie), 1986 (p. 303)

85 | 86
87

88. Newport, St Mary's Hospital, by Ahrends, Burton & Koralek, 1985–91, entrance block (p. 188)
89. Sandown, Dinosaur Isle, by Rainey Petrie Johns, 2000–1 (p. 255)

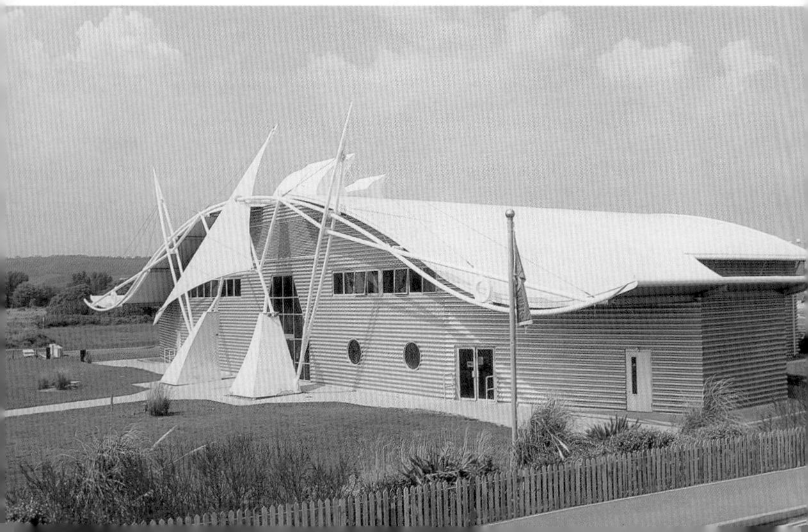

ing Sir Galahad's face on the horseback figure was based on that of Ellen Terry, sometime wife of Watts, while the head of an angel above Sir Galahad in armour was inspired by Emily Tennyson, the poet's wife.)

MONUMENTS. On the N chapel wall a late C14 BRASS to a knight. The figure is 34 in. (86 cm.) long. – In the S chapel, INDENTS of three lost C14 brasses with their canopies. The outlines are clear, especially those of the ogee-topped canopies with crockets. – TABLET to Anne Toppe, †1648, nave N wall, W end. In dark marble with white outlines; topped by a rounded pediment containing the representation of a ship. – BUST of Tennyson by *Mignon Morrisot Jones*, 1992, within the medieval tomb recess in the S chapel. Strongly realistic.

ST AGNES, Bedbury Lane, W of Freshwater Bay. By *Isaac Jones*, 1908, in rough stone. Thatched, with a wooden W bell-turret and an apse. Simple W elevation with two small lancets flanked by buttresses, contrasting with the contrivedly picturesque N frontage. Inside there is a broad space with rough walls and roof with braced tie-beams. The dominating feature is the three-arched, thinly constructed SCREEN of *c.* 1943–6. The detailed carving, including vines and foliage, was by the curate, *T.G. Devitt*. The CHOIR STALLS have panels densely carved in geometric patterns.

The buildings in the area are covered in an irregular itinerary which begins at All Saints church (*see* above), in the original settlement W of the head of the estuary of the River Yar. The route first goes generally S to the coast at Freshwater Bay, then W to Farringford (Lord Tennyson's house), and finally inland towards the present–day centre of Freshwater.

THE CAUSEWAY descends SE from All Saints and crosses the end of the estuary with a fine view back to the church on its bluff. On the r., in extensive grounds, is AFTON MANOR; early C18, sensitively restored in the C20. It is two-storeyed, of rubble stone with ashlar dressings and a hipped tiled roof. The main (W) elevation is of seven bays, the S of five. The Tuscan porch is early C20 (as is the main staircase). The Causeway meets East Afton Road leading to the W, where, on the N side, are the C18 GATEPIERS to the grounds of Afton Manor. They are low, with semi-spherical tops. Taller outside piers are linked by curved walls.

Westward is FRESHWATER BAY, the focal point of seaside activities in the area. It is a rounded cove, breaking into the range of cliffs which abut its entrance, with lower-lying land on its inward side. There were very few buildings around the bay before the C19, and none of those now facing it call for comment. The most distinguished building in the vicinity is RUSHWORTH HOUSE in Greystone Lane, which leads

N off Military Road immediately E of the bay. It is an early work of *John Seely* (for whom *see* Mottistone), *c.* 1924; Neo-Georgian, two-storeyed, white-rendered, with a hipped tiled roof. The garden (E) front is straightforward, of four bays with tall sashes on the ground floor. The W front, facing the lane, is more complicated. It has five sashes on the first floor, the central three grouped closely (the middle one narrower than the others). The simple rounded entrance, flanked by small windows, has a flat canopy suspended from diagonal iron brackets – almost a Voysey touch. The frontage extends into single-storey wings with small windows, and urns at the corners. (The tall ground-floor windows at either end of the main part of the W elevation are later additions, making the overall design somewhat confusing.) The house used to stand out in its whiteness when seen from the W, but trees have reduced the effect.

GATE LANE leads NW from Freshwater Bay into an area which developed intermittently from the 1850s, when Tennyson moved into nearby Farringford (*see* below). In Terrace Lane, to the l. is DIMBOLA LODGE, the home from 1860 to 1875 of Julia Margaret Cameron, pioneer photographer and friend of Tennyson. In 1860 she bought two identical two-gabled, bargeboarded villas, which must have been recently built, and linked them with a three-storey castellated tower. Much of her work, very important in the early history of photography, was based here, and the house was the scene of gatherings including artistic and literary people. It is now open to the public, with examples of her work. Past St Agnes (q.v.), VICTORIA ROAD forks to the r. It has a mixture of buildings which reflect the spasmodic growth of Freshwater. There are C18 thatched cottages, varied Victorian villas and too much C20 infill. TOWER HOUSE on the W side is a fantasy of *c.* 1865–70, with a stumpy spire, bargeboarded gable, and a pair of rounded windows under a pediment. Nearby WHITECLIFFE HOUSE, a more conventional stuccoed villa, was a childhood home of the model for Lewis Carroll's Alice. In the angle of Victoria Road and Bedbury Lane (which continues Gate Lane) is ORCHARD BROTHERS, occupying a building of *c.* 1865 in buff brick with red dressings. The shopfront facing the corner is original, with two windows under wide pointed arches and a central arched doorway flanked by spiked columns.

Bedbury Lane leads W past FARRINGFORD, the medium-sized country house which Alfred Tennyson leased in 1853 and bought in 1856; now a hotel. It lies in grounds to the S; on the r., opposite the entrance, is a LODGE of 1860, like a small-scale villa with gable-end and canted windows. Farringford is eclectic and irregular. Its principal (N) frontage, largely in buff brick, has 'Gothick' details as well as debased classical features, with elementary castellation at different levels. The first house, fairly modest and essentially classical, was built *c.* 1806; this, much modified, forms the basis of the present E wing. In or before 1825 the house was bought by John Hambrough, who extended it westwards, creating most of the present frontage. In 1833 Hambrough started to build Steephill Castle, Ventnor, to which he moved in 1835 (*see* p. 289). The frontage must therefore date largely from *c.* 1825–33. The first-floor windows are irregularly spaced; most have four-centred arches in squared frames, with geometrically shaped glazing bars; a pair projects as an oriel. Much of the ground floor is fronted by a veranda with five depressed arches, including keystones. To the E of this is a strangely designed porch, projecting slightly with canted ends; it has columns with bunched shafts supporting a frieze with oddly patterned details. Further E is the wing based on the older house, to which Hambrough gave a new elevation. This has, on both storeys, two pairs of 'Gothick' windows, each pair contained in a four-centred arched opening. Attached to the E side of the wing is a tall one-storey extension, gabled and battlemented, with a prominent bay window. This was built as a drawing room and is now the hotel lounge. The S frontage is confused, owing partly to accretions since *c.* 1960. In 1871 Tennyson added a wing at the SW corner. Its ground floor is obscured by a single-storey range. The upper floor is in somewhat gaunt buff brick, with simple battlements to match the earlier parts.

The former DRAWING ROOM has the finest interior in the part which existed before Tennyson's residence. A four-centred doorway in a squared frame, with Gothic panelling, opens from an internal passageway. A wooden FIREPLACE with four-centred arch, and flanking octagonal columns ending like turrets above the mantelshelf, has more Gothic panel decoration. Opposite is a tall square-headed bay window of three main lights. The cornices in the room itself and the adjoining passageway have simple Gothic details. One might assume that this room was added by Hambrough, but stylistically the details seem later than those on the N front. Tennyson's SW wing includes his STUDY on the upper floor. It has an elaborate wooden fireplace, in no orthodox style. Its mantelshelf is supported by corbels with figures, small-scale panelling on the frieze, and geometrical patterns on the flanks. Around the iron hearth are bands of tiles with strident quatrefoils set against a red background. There is an interesting internal view towards the E, where, beyond a wide low-pitch pointed arch spanning the room, is a three-light Gothic window with cusped upper tracery. Tennyson would have enjoyed an extensive vista, now partly obscured by the growth of greenery.

Further to the S is a very interesting cluster of buildings added to the hotel by *Clough Williams-Ellis* and *Lionel Brett* (information from Rodney Hubbuck). These include six single-storey COTTAGES grouped round a small green. Each has shuttered casement windows under tiled roofs.

To the S is TENNYSON DOWN (originally High Down), a long chalk ridge with sheer cliffs on its S side. On the down is the TENNYSON MEMORIAL, a late work by *J.L. Pearson*, 1897. It is a Celtic cross with a tapering stem on a stepped base, executed by *Farmer & Brindley*. From here are superb views over land and sea.

W of Farringford, Bedbury Lane turns l. into MOONS HILL. THE BRIARY is set back to the W beyond the turn. The present house is a replacement, in a different style, of the one built in 1873 by *Philip Webb* for G.F. Watts's friends Mr and Mrs Prinsep, which Watts visited frequently. It was destroyed by fire in 1934. Further along Moons Hill on the SE side are MIDDLETON FARM COTTAGES, Farringford Estate cottages mainly in rough stone with terracotta dressings, with '1554 restored 1884 by AET' (Alfred and Emily Tennyson) on a lintel. The SW end, with ashlar quoins, may be of the former date. Back to Bedbury Lane, from which a turning leads N to the old hamlet of POUND GREEN. There is indeed a former POUND, a circular stone enclosure of *c.* 1800, beside the picturesque green which has varied houses around it. LITTLE HOLT, of rough stone and thatched, C18 or earlier, has peculiar early C19 casements with glazing bars forming triangular patterns. KIPPAX, on the corner of Camp Road, has similar windows with diamond patterns. Camp Road leads NE to Stroud Road where STROUD COTTAGES are Farringford Estate housing dated 1850 (i.e. pre-Tennyson), built of rough near-local limestone. Originally there were four cottages, in pairs set back-to-back as if they were in an industrial town, with double gables at the end. They were embellished later in the C19 with decorative terracotta chimneystacks, and also with framing in the same material round the windows (cf. Middleton Farm Cottages, above). Some of the frames have the initial T (for Tennyson). Another cottage was added on each side to the E during the C20, making two terraces of three, still back-to-back.

From the crossroads at the N end of Stroud Road, SCHOOL GREEN ROAD leads W into the present-day centre of Freshwater, which developed informally during the later C19 and C20 alongside the irregular green of the old hamlet of School Green. To the NE, HOOKE HILL leads up to the small original village centre of Freshwater, with All Saints. (The spelling was changed from Hook Hill to commemorate Robert Hooke, the distinguished scientist and architect, closely associated with Sir Christopher Wren. He was born locally in 1635, the son of the curate of All Saints.)

TOTLAND BAY

Totland Bay started to develop *c.* 1870 when an estate company was formed. In 1880 a large hotel (now demolished) and a small simple PIER were opened. Villas were built, often on hilly, wooded sites with seaward views, e.g. in CLIFF ROAD where they show typical half-timbering, gabled projections and, in places, tile-hanging. SENTRY MEAD in Madeira Road, now a hotel, is larger than most of the others, with a corner tower topped by a tiled spire. A new village centre developed a little inland, along THE BROADWAY, giving informal, almost picturesque effects which must have been largely contrived. Two- and three-storey buildings, often multi-gabled, are set along a slightly curving, gently sloping street which opens at the S end into a small green where the WAR MEMORIAL, an obelisk on a tall base, is the focal feature. To the S was the older hamlet of WESTON. In Weston Road is a small BARN, perhaps late C17, with a colourful amalgam of varied stones, both as rubble and in blocks of different sizes.

CHRIST CHURCH, New Road and York Road. Originally built 83
1875 by *Habershon & Pite*; the nave, with two-light Geometrical windows, dates from then. S aisle 1905–6; chancel rebuilt 1910, both by *Percy Stone*. The oddest feature is an octagonal N annexe to the chancel, to which a wooden upper storey with conical roof was added in 1936 to form a belfry. Inside, the three-bay arcade has slender piers of grey stone. – STAINED GLASS. Two W windows, and one to the N in the nave are by *Lavers & Westlake*. – E window by *Jones & Willis*, 1910. Figures with a deep blue background, and Gothic tracery in the glazing above. – LYCHGATE by *Percy Stone*, 1908.

ST SAVIOUR (R.C.), Weston Lane, to the SE of the main part of Totland Bay. By *W.C. Mangan*, 1923. A strange building to find in a largely rural setting, very different from the chapel of Weston Manor a short distance away (*see* below). Of red brick, patterned in places. Perhaps the form was based on that of a Romanesque basilica, but with overtones of Art Deco and strident individualism. The low-pitched roof has boldly projecting eaves; the S aisle continues round the corner as a narthex with five arches; an octagonal projection at the NW angle has broad eaves to its lid-like roof, as has the slender tower which rises beside it.

Spacious interior; largely of red brick like the exterior. Arcades with segmental arches on square pillars, and herringbone patterns in the spandrels; clerestory with round-headed windows. The simple round chancel arch, the short chancel with semicircular clerestory windows, and the apsidal sanctuary with three small round-headed lights, are now painted white, setting off the colourful STAINED GLASS figures in the windows.

WESTON MANOR, off Weston Lane, to the S of St Saviour. A house of 1869–70 by *George Goldie* for W.G. Ward, a Catholic convert (*see* Northwood House, Cowes, p. 129). Rambling and incoherent, in rough stone with fine dressings, under slate roofs of varied heights and shapes; polygonal hips, spired turrets and gabled dormers. The elevational details are equally eclectic: cross-windows on the first floors; flat-arched openings with small ogees on the ground storeys; a two-bay High Gothic porch entrance with a similar composition on the balcony above. The CHAPEL is prominent in the NE corner, with broad cusped lancets, paired in the polygonal apse. Its interior, furnished and redecorated *c.* 1898 following the precepts of A.W.N. Pugin's *Glossary of Ecclesiastical Ornament*, is the *tour de force* of Weston. The elaborate SCREEN of 1895, with figures, is by *Peter Paul Pugin*; the ALTAR with carved representations of the Entombment, and the REREDOS are by Goldie (presumably *Edward Goldie*). The walls are treated in patterns predominantly in deep reds, with intricate friezes in buff and brown containing family heraldry. The climax is the series of figure paintings on patterned backgrounds in the compartments of the wood-vaulted apse, focusing on the Risen Christ in a vesica over the altar.

NORTON

The N part of Freshwater parish has loosely scattered buildings. NORTON GREEN is the most coherent cluster. Modest houses in stone and brick face a tapering green which narrows at its W end into a grass-bordered street. HILL LODGE, on Copse Lane NE of the green, is late C18, of stone with brick-framed windows and doorcase with open pediment. KING'S MANOR to the E, close to the estuary, is a larger early C18 house with four-bay main (S) front; it was enlarged to the NE in matching style *c.* 1970, with an open-pediment doorcase. There are substantial former STABLES, mainly early C19, on the S side of the house. BUDDLE'S BUTT, off Hallett Shute, ⅔ m. W of Yarmouth, is a late C18 house altered in the C20; its N front has a bold two-storey bow, and is topped by a circular belvedere (early C20) with Tuscan columns and conical roof.

In the mid C19 substantial defensive works were built on the NW coast – Fort Victoria in 1852–4 and Fort Albert in

1854–6 – to protect the W approach to the Solent against a possible French attack. FORT ALBERT is not prominent on the landward side, but very visible from the sea. It had four storeys of casemates (gun chambers). It became obsolete for defence quite early, and was adapted as a torpedo base, 1885–1906. Since the 1970s it has been divided into apartments. FORT VICTORIA, 1 m. W of Yarmouth town centre, is on a very different, low coastal site and is accessible to the public. It was a triangular fort with one storey of casemates on two sides; the other (landward) side was taken by defended barracks, now demolished. Today one sees two ranges of brick arches, originally the backs of the casemates, many of which are now infilled for different uses. Guns were positioned on the tops of these ranges as well as in the casemates.

The two main coastal forts were supplemented by batteries along the coast between the Needles and Fort Victoria. In 1863–7 GOLDEN HILL FORT was built as a principal base for the garrison covering these defences. It was a massive defended barracks, on a high inland site W of Norton Green, with views over the coast. One enters through a brick arch in an outer earthen rampart, and then through another arch into the hexagonal courtyard of the two-storey, brick-built barrack ranges. Three sides have sash windows facing the courtyard; the other sides have balconies with slender ironwork. At the time of visiting, repairs and alterations were taking place for a variety of new uses.

HEADON WARREN, an area of gravel heathland NE of the Needles in National Trust ownership, is the site of a very large Bronze Age round barrow which lies at the top of Headon Hill. It is one of the relatively few surviving examples away from the chalk downs. 81 ft (25 metres) in diameter, 7 ft (2.7 metres) high.

AFTON DOWN, to the E of Freshwater, contains a Bronze Age round barrow cemetery and a single Neolithic long barrow, sited in the middle of a golf course but visible from the Tennyson Trail. The long barrow is located at the western end of the round barrow cemetery, 76 yds (70 metres) S of the golf clubhouse. Oriented ENE–WSW and irregularly tapering in plan, with the broader end to the ENE, the mound is 140 ft (43 metres) long and 4 ft (1.2 metres) high. The top of the mound was flattened during construction of the golf course, when the ditches were presumably levelled. Trenches cut in the mound by the Rev. J. Skinner in 1817 produced no information, the central disturbance being of earlier date. The round barrow cemetery extends eastwards from the long barrow for *c.* 380 yards (350 metres), only one round barrow being sited W of the long barrow. Eighteen round barrows have been identified, some very small and not readily discernible, although the larger mounds reach up to *c.* 8 ft (2.5 metres) in height. The majority are bowl barrows, the commonest type of round barrow, comprising a simple mound with or without a ditch. There is one definite bell barrow and three possible examples; this barrow type having a berm between the central mound and the surrounding ditch. Most of the barrows were opened by Skinner at the same time as the long barrow. Three contained primary interments (the first burial in a barrow) by cremation without urns, and also had secondary cremations in urns near the top. One contained a primary cremation beneath an inverted urn, and in a further barrow only a secondary cremation in an urn was located.

4580 GATCOMBE

A very small village delectably set in a fold of the chalk and sandstone hills in the centre of the Island. Chillerton, a bigger village, straggles along the Newport–Chale road to the S.

ST OLAVE. A Norse saint – a strange dedication in such a place. Small; aisle-less nave, Victorian chancel, relatively grand W tower. Of at least C13 origin, on the evidence of a lancet in the S wall, and the chancel arch. (A small round-headed doorway in the N nave wall is unlikely to be Norman; it may be C17.) Two nave windows on the S side and one on the N are handsome Perp of *c.* 1500; of two lights with quadruple upper lights under segmental arches. The tower, *c.* 1500, is a smaller version of that of Carisbrooke. String courses have grotesque carvings underneath, and diagonal buttresses end with the stumps of pinnacles; there are intermediate stumps of other lost pinnacles on the sides of the parapet. The S porch dates from 1910, including the carving of a monster head on the apex of the gable (which Pevsner said 'might give some people a real fright').

Inside, the C13 chancel arch frames a vista to the E window with its Pre-Raphaelite glass (the church's finest possession); the arch has two orders of roll mouldings and curiously tall squared plinths. Smaller flanking arches date from 1917. The chancel was rebuilt in 1864–5 in Geometrical Gothic by *R.J. Jones* at the expense of the non-resident rector John Branthwaite, who was Principal of St Edmund Hall, Oxford; Branthwaite also commissioned the E window. The church was restored by *W.D. Caröe* from *c.* 1920; his are the organ chamber and vestry N of the chancel. He also designed the tierceron-star vault under the tower, with an open circle for bell ropes. The springings for the ribs already existed, intended for a vault which was not constructed when the tower was first built. It is similar to the late medieval example at Carisbrooke, and also to that at Shorwell (qq.v.). The CHOIR STALLS are likely to be *Caröe*'s; individualistically carved with patterned panels and scroll-shaped ends. The FONT is probably early C13; octagonal bowl of Purbeck marble with the usual two plain flat pointed arches on each side.

The church is mainly memorable for its STAINED GLASS, not only Victorian work but also the only medieval glass surviving in an Island church. This is in the four upper lights of the window E of the porch, and probably dates likewise from *c.* 1500. It depicted angels with elaborately feathered bodies and wings, tinted in pale yellow, under human-looking heads surrounded by circular haloes. The angels' feet stood on small wheels above chequered boards. These features do not all survive intact, but those in the second light from the E are well preserved. The windows in the chancel are of 1864–5 by *Morris, Marshall, Faulkner & Co.*, and include work by five designers associated with the firm at its inception – *William Morris* himself, *Dante Gabriel Rossetti, Edward Burne-Jones, Ford Madox Brown* and *Philip Webb.** The E window is of three lights with tracery. In the centre light is the Crucifixion by *Rossetti*, with pale colours against a dark background, the figure of Mary standing out in blue clothing and that of John in a partly yellow robe. To the l. is the Last Supper by *Morris*, with tightly crowded figures, and on the r. the Entombment, by *Ford Madox Brown*, with particularly expressive faces and robes with sinuous folds. Above and below these three scenes are patterns of small circles in pale shades of red, blue and yellow, the different colours informally arranged. These, together with the borders with emblematic roses, were designed by *Philip Webb*. Set within Webb's patterns of circles are five diamond-shaped panels with angels playing music – by *Morris* himself. In the three circular tracery lights are the Lamb of God and choirs of angels, by *Burne-Jones*. The chancel side windows are small single lights. In the westernmost on the S side is the Ascension, in that to its E the Three Maries, both by *Morris*; intensely portrayed in the tiny spaces. One window on the N side – the Baptism of Christ – by *Burne-Jones*. Another by him was lost when part of the chancel wall was demolished for the organ chamber and vestry.

MONUMENTS. In a recess in the chancel is a strange wooden effigy of a knight with crossed legs and a dog at his feet, in the C14 manner. However, as Percy Stone pointed out, some of the stylistic details are related to later periods. He suggested that the effigy was self-consciously antiquarian work of the C17 (cf. the wooden effigy of Sir

*There is contemporary glass by *Morris & Co.* in the chapel of St Edmund Hall, Oxford, also commissioned by Branthwaite.

Gatcombe church, effigy of a knight, aquatint by Charles Tomkins. From Tomkins, *A Tour to the Isle of Wight*, 1796

John Oglander in Brading church, q.v.). The knight's face and an angel by his pillow have been relatively recently re-cut. – In the nave, a white marble effigy of Charles Grant Seely, a young soldier, †1917, by *Sir Thomas Brock*, on a brown marble tomb-chest by *Caröe*, with panels containing shields and scenes in relief.

GATCOMBE PARK, SSE of the church. The house was rebuilt in 1751 by Sir Edward Worsley, of a junior branch of the family – perhaps in an attempt to rival Appuldurcombe.* Three-storeyed, almost a cube. The main (E) façade, in ashlar with rusticated quoins, is of seven bays, the centre three brought forward slightly under a pediment. The windows have raised surrounds with keystones (the three central ones on the first floor replaced a Venetian window at some time in the early C20). The porch, projecting slightly with simple cornice and rustication, is unpretentious. At the centre of the top floor is a round-headed niche. The sides are of six bays, with no significant features except the windows, which have raised surrounds. The W frontage is irregular; it is very much a back-side except that a Venetian window (lighting the staircase) is the centrepiece in the recessed middle part. Further W, a separate wall between two chimneystacks is curved downwards, to strange effect,

*The estate was owned by a branch of the Seely family from the late C19 into the C20.

Gatcombe, Sheat Manor, drawing by Reginald Blomfield. From Percy Stone, *The Architectural Antiquities of the Isle of Wight*, 1891

so as not to obscure the view from this window. Internally there is fine ceiling plasterwork, probably contemporary with the house. A very ornate Rococo fireplace was presumably brought from elsewhere. The stair hall, at the W end of the house, is reached axially from the entrance. It has round archways to l. and r. between large fluted pilasters rising to entablatures with triglyphs. The STAIRCASE is particularly fine; it is of well form with slender turned balusters and scroll carvings on the treads. The landing is lit by the Venetian window described above.

The STABLE BLOCK to the SE has a two-storey façade of stone with a dentilled cornice; the central part is brought forward with a pediment over two wide arched recesses.

SHEAT MANOR, ½m. SSE. A moderate-sized manor house built by the Urry family *c.* 1605.* It is little-altered on its principal (S) frontage, of two main storeys in coursed sandstone. The gabled wings have four-light mullioned windows on each main floor, and small three-light windows in the attics. There is a single-storey porch of lighter stone with an embattled parapet. Its outer doorway has a moulded arch topped by a keystone with triple fluting, resting on prominent imposts, to quite sophisticated effect. The inner doorway has a depressed arch and jambs similarly moulded, with the original studded door. The N elevation is greatly altered, but retains small mullioned windows on the first floor and a gabled porch with rounded archway. The house had been reduced in status and subdivided by the C19; a

* In 1605 Sir William Oglander of Nunwell gave oak trees towards building 'the new house at Gatcombe' when his relative married Thomas Urry.

splendid wooden overmantel with symbolic grotesque figures and the Urry arms was removed *c.* 1930. A smaller CHIMNEYPIECE remains in the hall, with fluted pilasters, caryatids and carved heads round a simple moulded stone fireplace with a nearly flat arch. Four standing wooden figures in the same tradition, probably brought from elsewhere, are set around another fireplace.

THE DAIRY COTTAGE is a converted building separate from, but originally related to, the house. Its date and original use are uncertain, but the S gabled elevation appears to be mid- to late C17. It is built of rough stone with large ashlar blocks as quoins. The gable has kneelers but no coping, and its slopes are edged by the angles of triangular blocks of ashlar whose vertical and horizontal sides are embedded in the stonework – a variation, in stone, of the effect of tumbling-in brickwork. The most distinctive features are two blocked windows in the gable, each a broad oval slightly taller than it is wide, in a raised frame. Such a feature suggests a date of *c.* 1675.

CHILLERTON FARMHOUSE, to the E of the road S of Chillerton village. Two-storey stuccoed house of *c.* 1820, with hipped roof and three widely spaced sashes on the first floor. Long veranda on main (W) front with single-pitch glazed roof on iron supports with delicate openwork patterns. The veranda extends along the short S frontage.

CHILLERTON HILL-FORT. On Chillerton Down, to the SW of Chillerton village, ½ m. NE of the TV Station. Called Five Barrows on old maps. Despite this appellation the monument is thought to be an Iron Age promontory fort cutting off a steep-sided spur of the chalk down, about half a mile long, near the centre of the Island. The top of the spur is almost level, rising gradually to 494 ft (152 metres) at the NE end. At the SW end the ridge narrows to a neck, and here the defences cross the summit, cutting off the spur from higher ground further to the SW. The rampart is 268 ft (82.5 metres) long, *c.* 10 ft (3 metres) high and 58–68 ft (18–21 metres) wide. It takes the form of five mounds in a line, the material being thrown up from a ditch on the SW side. The curious form of the earthwork, which gave rise to the name Five Barrows, suggests that it was thrown up by five parties or gangs working in sections. Possibly the work was not completed, or it may have been thought unnecessary to level the crest. No excavation has taken place and accurate dating is therefore impossible.

5080

GODSHILL

A village for long popular with visitors, because of its picturesque qualities. The main street now has less appeal than formerly, partly because of traffic, but the charm survives around the hilltop church. The row of stone-built thatched cottages in front of the church tower has been reproduced on innumerable postcards. The parish is large, including Appuldurcombe (q.v.) – hence the memorable monuments in the church.

ALL SAINTS. The view S over swelling countryside is marvellous. The church has an unusual plan: a double nave and chancel of roughly equal width, small transepts, porch and NW tower; generally in coursed sandstone. Its building history defies easy interpretation. The two lower stages of the tower are probably C14; the top stage is late Perp with small belfry lights and pinnacles, including intermediate ones – restored more than once after lightning damage. The E end is C14 with different tracery in its two three-light windows. That to the S is reticulated, while the one to the N has an intersecting pattern with daggers and trefoils. There is comparable Y-tracery in the two-light side windows on the S chancel.

Inside is a six-bay arcade without any break between naves and chancels. It has octagonal piers, capitals with hollow undersides, and plain arches of two chamfered orders and piers on tall plinths, suggesting that the arcade was built to accommodate pews. There is evidence, on each of the side walls, of the presence of a former rood screen. Such a feature could hardly have been related to the present arcade, which may be part of a post-Reformation reconstruction (cf. Shorwell). There is C17 work elsewhere in the church – see the W window of the S nave with its strange

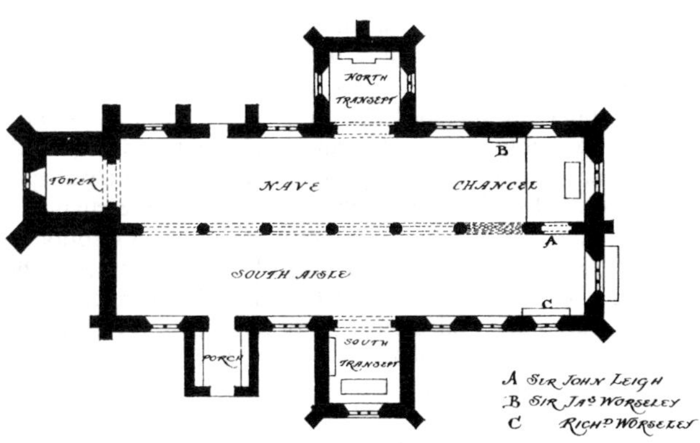

Godshill church, plan.
From Percy Stone, *The Architectural Antiquities of the Isle of Wight*, 1891

adaptation of the Perp style, and a simpler three-light window in the S wall.

The small S transept is late C15 or early C16. In 1520 Sir John Leigh of Appuldurcombe (whose monument is in the church) obtained a licence to set up a chantry in the church. Although no location was specified, it is likely to have been in this transept. The S window is normal three-light Perp. The roof is remarkable, with moulded arch-braces and horizontal beams forming a panel pattern, in the West Country tradition. The braces at the centre and S end of the transept rise from stone corbels with carved angels and have what amount to false hammerbeams with wooden figures. On the E wall is the wall painting described below. In the external gable of the transept is a restored arched canopy on stone figure corbels, with a sanctus bell. The arch from transept into nave has two broad chamfers and no capitals. There is a comparable arch into the N transept, which was rebuilt to contain the Worsley monument of *c.* 1747 (*see* below) with round-headed keystoned windows to E and W.

FURNISHINGS. ROOD and BEAM in front of S chancel, 1948. – COMMUNION RAILS with turned balusters in the N chancel, C17. – Former ALTAR TABLE in the N chancel 1631, with ring-moulded legs, and inscribed names of churchwardens. – WALL PAINTINGS.* On the E wall of the S
22 transept a most unusual altar painting of the Crucifixion, contemporary with or perhaps very slightly later than the construction of the transept itself. Christ is shown crucified on a cross of three branches, each branch dividing at the top into a further three, and flanked by fictive textiles which clearly acted as backdrops to sculpted figures now lost. Stencilled motifs ornament the background, and a curious shield-like motif attached to a fleur-de-lys is crossed by the branch below Christ's r. arm. Two scroll-bearing angels fly down from above, while a further four inscribed scrolls flank the crucified Christ. Their inscriptions are now hard to decipher, but one includes the words 'ora pro nobis', and all are probably invocatory prayers. These would be particularly appropriate if the transept served as a chantry chapel established by Sir John Leigh in 1520.** On the chancel S wall, a consecration cross and remains of an inscription. – PAINTING. In the N nave a copy of Rubens's Daniel in the Lions' Den, given by the 2nd Earl of Yarborough from his Appuldurcombe collection (the original is in the National Gallery of Art, Washington). – ROYAL ARMS. Queen Anne, 1707, over the S door.

* Descriptions contributed by David Park.

** The painting might then be compared with the Crucifixion imagery on the E wall of other chantry chapels, such as that of Sir Henry Vernon (†1515) at Tong in Shropshire, where the subject is accompanied by an inscription requesting prayers for members of the Vernon family.

MONUMENTS. An outstanding series. Sir John Leigh, 23
†1529, and his wife Agnes, ancestors of the Worsleys of
Appuldurcombe; a canopied tomb between the two sanc-
tuaries; the E respond of the arcade abuts on it. A richly
detailed work in Caen stone. Moulded four-centred arch,
elaborately cusped and sub-cusped; traceried panels on the
underside with painted roses and other devices; traceried
circles and daggers in the spandrels; frieze with quatrefoils
including roses and shields; crest with busts of angels
carrying shields; panelled tomb-chest. The effigies, of
alabaster, have long-drawn faces showing little expression.
She has a finely folded headpiece and gown; his feet rest on
a boar (reputedly the cause of his death in an accident),
with two small figures of hooded bedesmen beside them.
The tomb is sumptuous but many of the details are repetitive.* – Sir James Worsley, Sir John Leigh's son-in-law, *p. 156*
†1538 (he was closely associated with Henry VIII), and his
wife Anne, †1557, N chancel. A world away in architectural
terms. Two kneeling figures in a shallow recess with fluted
Ionic pilasters. The broad entablature has an elegant frieze
with scrolled stems and foliage, brought out in green paint-
work. Putti with shields stand above and beside a tall pediment. The figures, painted, kneel with realistic expressions
at desks, both facing E. – Richard Worsley, †1565 (he was 30
Captain of the Island and organized the building of the
Solent forts), S chancel. No figure, only a long inscription
in a canopy which is typically Early Elizabethan, with free-
standing fluted columns on either side; modillion cornice,
and enriched Vitruvian scroll frieze, repeated in outline on
the base of the canopy.** Large heraldic achievement above
the entablature, in a round-topped canopy with ball finials
and scrolled sides; urns with grotesque heads at the ends of
the canopy. – Sir Robert Worsley, builder of the present
Appuldurcombe, †1747, and his brother Henry, N transept.
Unsigned, but in the style of *Scheemakers*. A grand piece in
mottled marble with pink columns and pilasters against a
grey background; central part projecting with triglyph
frieze, pediment and trophy above. Two busts with Roman
drapery (Henry was a classical traveller and collector) on
the sarcophagus; large mourning putti on either side. – Sir
Richard Worsley, †1805. A monster monument to the traveller, collector and last of the Worsleys, erected by Lord
Yarborough well after his death. Sarcophagus with rounded
ends resting on lions' claws; side panels with foliage; tall
plain base. It has been moved around the church and now

*There are affinities with the tomb of Lady Wadham at St Mary, Carisbrooke (*see* p. 114), suggesting work by the same craftsman.

**The scroll friezes are similar to those on the tomb of Bishop Gardiner (†1555) in Winchester Cathedral.

Godshill church, monument to Sir James Worsley (†1538), elevation. From Percy Stone, *The Architectural Antiquities of the Isle of Wight*, 1891

stands, partly screened, in the S nave. On a smaller scale, James Worsley (of Stenbury, *see* Whitwell), †1787, by *Bingley* of London. Wall monument with a mourning woman by an urn in front of an obelisk.

In the main street, the METHODIST CHURCH, 1838, of minimal form; ashlar front, low gable and Y-traceried windows. By contrast, the GRIFFIN to the E, built by the Appuldurcombe Estate *c.* 1840, is a stone-built pub with bargeboards and bulgy chimneystacks. Eastward along the

Shanklin road is the beginning of the best approach (on foot) to Appuldurcombe, 1½ m. to the S. Back in the village, the way to the church is up Church Hill or a path that branches off; in the fork is THE BAT'S WING, humble and thatched but with a Late Georgian double shopfront, each side bowed with thin glazing bars. At the W end of the village GODSHILL PRIMARY SCHOOL includes the buildings of a school rebuilt 1826 by Lord Yarborough; long ashlar frontage of one storey; central gable over round entrance arch; broad windows with keystones. The former SCHOOL HOUSE has a dormered upper storey, gabled porch and windows with Neo-Tudor hoodmoulds.

BRIDGE COURT, ¾ m. SW. Stone farmhouse with two-storey gabled porch; 1688 on plaque. C19 sashes on the main front, replacing mullioned windows of which parts of the hood-moulds remain; tall brick chimneystacks.

GREAT BUDBRIDGE MANOR, 1½ m. N in Arreton parish. Early C17 stone-built house with brick chimneystacks; slightly off-centre porch dated 1688, of two storeys with gable containing an attic window and four-centred doorway in square frame; original mullioned windows on the first floor.

STENBURY. *See* Whitwell.

GOTTEN MANOR *see* CHALE

GURNARD 4595

A coastal village which developed casually from the mid C19 and has acquired a haphazard charm, with buildings of different shapes and styles, including beach huts, set against the shoreside slopes. Hardly any are architecturally notable. Among the few is the GURNARD SAILING CLUB by *Rainey Petrie Design*, 1997. This looks quite modest from the NE, with white walls, low-pitched roof and porthole openings, but has a two-deck sea frontage with a bridge-like structure above, reached by a ramp and spiral stairway at the side. Among the bungalows and houses to its NE, No. 9 Princes Esplanade stands out as a small piece of romantic Modernism by *Colin Graham*, 2000. It has white walls, irregular massing beneath a flat roof-line, and a metal balcony on the first floor backed by glazing and a short veranda. The coastline was affected in the past by erosion; the remains of a shore-side Roman building were lost in 1864. Offshore deposits of limestone exposed by tides were once quarried for local use.

ALL SAINTS. 1892–3 by *E.P. Loftus Brock*; on the inland edge of the village. Simple nave and chancel in local buff brick with red variegation, lit by lancets except for the three-light E window. Spired turret over the nave E gable. Inside, the brick polychromy comes into its own, especially the red and black pattern round the chancel arch. – STAINED GLASS. E window by *A.L. Moore & Son*, 1911. Figures against intricate background in diffuse colours.

REW STREET FARMHOUSE, 1 m. SW. The house is on the E side of the road facing N. The further part, *c.* 1810, has a stark three-storey, three-bay façade in ashlar under a rudimentary gable pediment. To the W is a lower, older part of rougher stone with C20 windows. (Inside are the remains of two CRUCKS, possibly of *c.* 1400; one is largely intact though affected by internal subdivision; little is visible of the other. They probably defined the central hall of a small three-bay farmhouse.) A late C19 photograph indicates that the older part of the house was then thatched; very interestingly it shows an exposed cruck frame on the W gable wall bordering the road. This wall is now faced in stone with no outward trace of the cruck.

HAMSTEAD *see* SHALFLEET

HASELEY *see* ARRETON

5590

HAVENSTREET

Ryde

A village of mainly C19 and later growth, with a few older buildings. In 1882 John Rylands, a Lancashire industrialist, bought and enlarged a local house (renamed Longford House after his property in Lancashire; it later became a hospital and has been much altered). He was a benefactor to the village, which he provided with a large community building, the Longford Institute. He died in 1888; his wife Enriqueta founded in his memory the John Rylands Library, Manchester.

ST PETER. 1852 by *Thomas Hellyer*. Small, of rough local limestone with an open W bellcote. The windows are thin lancets as in many of Hellyer's early churches. The grand REREDOS, almost blocking the triple-lancet E window, was set up during the incumbency of the Rev. H.N. Thompson (1897–1909). Of triptych form; the main part has a wide panel under a coved canopy, painted with an Ascension scene and flanked by narrower panels depicting saints; the angled ends have similar painted panels. The paintings have been attributed to the monks from France who were at Appuldurcombe from 1901 until 1908, when they moved to Quarr Abbey (q.v.). The ROOD SCREEN with open tracery was set up in Thompson's memory.

The former LONGFORD INSTITUTE of 1885–6, by *Josiah Cutler* of Ryde, rears above the houses of the village street. It is in red brick patterned in buff, with tall round-arched windows; the entrance, under a pediment, is in a set-back part of the frontage. Rylands provided a library, recreation rooms and a large hall, but the public uses did not last and the building has been converted successively for several other purposes. The RAILWAY STATION is now the base for the Isle of Wight Steam Railway which runs over part of the former Ryde to Newport line, opened in 1875; the present station building is a replacement of 1926.

On a small hilltop N of the village, difficult of access, is a WAR MEMORIAL commemorating R.T.C. Willis-Fleming, †1916, and others. Open-fronted limestone structure under a hipped stone slate roof, from the crest of which rise two tapering iron turrets, ending in diagonal crosses. (Inscription carved by *Eric Gill*.)

KINGSTON *4580*

Shorwell

A manor house and former church with a few scattered houses; it was a civil parish until the 1930s.

ST JAMES. Redundant as a church in 1985 and since converted to a house. A small rectangle, basically C13 (cf. the lancets on both sides at the E end). Restored 1872 by *R.J. Jones*, usually an interesting architect. He added the S porch and relatively large vestry to its E, and renewed several windows in E.E. style – but the two-light E window dates from an earlier restoration. Above it is a re-set medieval carved head. Another head is carved on a kneeler at the SE angle. The open-arched W bellcote is probably early C19. Prominent inside is a small two-bay arcade by *Jones*, with moulded arches and slender pier, opening into the vestry. To its E is a surprising feature, a large trefoiled recess – a sedile? – with a roll-moulded frame shaped as a gable above. The recess looks medieval; can the frame be? – STAINED GLASS. E window, *c.* 1851. W window, *c.* 1872 by *Lavers & Barraud*.

KINGSTON MANOR. The main part is a long rectangle built of sandstone, basically mid to late C17, with a lower C19 service wing to the E. Of its two special features, one compels attention as we approach the N side: a large stone chimney-breast ending in a rectangular brick upper stage, with five blank arches on the long side and one at each end. This is topped by octagonal stacks. The arch decoration made Pevsner think of Vanbrugh, although he suggested that it might be earlier, e.g. *c.* 1675. The principal front of the house is to the S – but it is deceptive. It has cross-windows and a gabled two-storey porch, but Stone in his drawings of 1892 shows a plain front with sash windows on the upper storey, and no porch. Clearly this part was restored *c.* 1900, although an old three-light mullioned window survives on the ground floor. In the main room is a fireplace (connected with the chimney-breast) with a plain, slightly arched stone bressumer; this could be *c.* 1675,

Kingston Manor, chimneypiece, elevation.
From Percy Stone, *The Architectural Antiquities of the Isle of Wight*, 1891

but hardly of the time of Vanbrugh. The second major feature of the house is the richly detailed C17 wooden overmantel in the middle room (over a fireplace of *c.* 1900); probably later than most of the Island series of chimneypieces, but continuing their tradition. The central panel has a coat-of-arms in a squared frame. Narrower side panels are carved with arabesque decoration related to arched shapes which have an affinity with those on the brick chimneystack. Flanking the panels are free-standing Composite columns; above are grotesque beasts and heads. On either side of the fireplace are thin pilasters coeval with the overmantel, with arrays of military motifs.

KNIGHTON GORGES *see* NEWCHURCH

LAKE 5580

A built-up area between Sandown and Shanklin. The best topographical feature is the clifftop path, with fine views over Sandown Bay.

GOOD SHEPHERD, by *Temple Moore*, 1892–4. A very unusual church with twin naves opening into one chancel. This provides an odd effect when the roof-lines are seen from the E, but on the W front (facing the main street) the dual pattern is unified by a central timber-framed porch, which contrasts with the smooth though irregular stonework of the church itself. The arches of the three-bay central nave arcade are simply moulded, and merge, without capitals, into diagonally set piers – an up-to-date stylism for *c.* 1892. There are two chancel arches, one on each side of the arcade – but this strange arrangement emphasizes the quality of the chancel with its intricate five-light E window, in an individualistic version of the Dec style. – STAINED GLASS. Windows by *Francis Skeat* – including the E window?

BROADLEA PRIMARY SCHOOL, Berry Hill, on the NW outskirts of Lake. By *Rainey Petrie Design*, 1993. Two ranges of one main storey, forming an L-shape. The main visual emphasis is provided by the sweeping tiled roofs, continuous on each range. The tiling is accentuated by a continuous inverted-V pattern of darker tiles along the upper parts of the roof slopes – an inventive and effective form of decoration. Entrance porch with small glazed gabled roof, under the main gable at the S end.

LUCCOMBE *see* SHANKLIN

5080

MERSTONE

Arreton

A small village in the central vale. Its special building is at the end of a lane leading W off the short main street.

MERSTON MANOR. Built *c.* 1615 by Edward Cheke, younger son of Thomas Cheke of Mottistone Manor (q.v.). Unusual for an Island house of the period in being mainly of brick, although the side and back elevations are partly of stone. It passed from the Cheke family in the 1660s, and by the C19 was in decline, until restored in 1895. Percy Stone recorded the house just before then in his *Architectural Antiquities of the Isle of Wight*, when it was 'in a deplorable state of dilapidation'. The main (W) frontage is in E-form with fairly deep gabled wings and two-storey porch with gable pediment; the entrance is a simple doorway with a nearly flat arch under a squared hood. The windows in the central recessed part of the elevation and on the porch are of four lights, stone-mullioned and transomed. The wings have heavy canted bay windows inserted in 1895, when ball finials were also added to the stone kneelers and apexes of the gables.

Stone's drawings show that there was a screens passage within the hall to the S. Two upstairs rooms had elaborate early C17 chimneypieces and panelling. At the restoration the screen was removed and the passage space added to the hall. The upstairs OVERMANTELS were re-erected on the E and N sides of the enlarged hall, and another from elsewhere was introduced on the S side. That on the E side is placed over the pre-existing low-arched stone fireplace. It has two main panels with rectilinear panelling, flanked by short pilasters topped by male torsos. In the centre is a female standing figure, and above are panels with winged and tailed creatures, bordered by grotesque heads. Fluted Ionic half-columns flank the fireplace. The overmantel now at the N end of the hall is fairly similar, though coarser; its main panels have lion's-head masks. But there is no fireplace here, nor at the S end of the hall – the re-set chimneypieces in these positions are merely ornamental. That to the S was not recorded by Stone. Its two main panels have simple diagonal patterning with embossed Tudor roses on the centres; the flanking pilasters have garlands but no figures. On the frieze are a cartouche with Cheke heraldry, and military accoutrements including a musket. The hall has panelling, including fluted Ionic pilasters with Tudor roses above them, and strapwork decoration; all or some of this was probably moved from the upper rooms at the house's restoration.* Altogether the woodwork at Merston, although not in its original locations, forms an impressive ensemble in the early C17 tradition.

MOTTISTONE 4080

Brighstone

Mottistone looks a set piece with its sloping village green, the church on a hillock to the W, and, to the N, the long, low L-shaped Manor, backed by a wooded hill-fold rising a little higher. The Chekes owned the estate up to *c.* 1620; the family reached its peak socially in the mid C16 when members of it (though not of the Island branch) had important connections at Court.** In 1861 Charles Seely, then living at Brook House, Brook (q.v.), bought the estate. In 1925 his grandson General Jack Seely, later the 1st Lord Mottistone, commissioned his architect son *John Seely*, of the newly formed partnership *Seely & Paget*, to restore Mottistone Manor, then used as a farmhouse. John Seely inherited the house as 2nd Lord Mottistone in 1947, carried out further alterations, and left it, with the estate, to the National Trust in 1963.

ST PETER AND ST PAUL. An enigmatic building, picturesquely set in a churchyard sloping up from the E and S. Double-gabled E end with chancel and N chapel. Short nave with aisles, under a catslide roof. At the W end, a curious tower, built, like the rest of the church, of a mixture of local sandstones with ashlar dressings. The top storey projects a few inches on a corbel course on three sides; it has small round-headed belfry lights. The battlemented parapet and short spire date from 1863 when the church was restored by *Willoughby Mullins* (cf. Brook). Before then there was a broach spire, presumably of wood. The tower has no openings below the belfry except a thin W lancet, suggesting a possible origin as a defensive structure (cf. Shalfleet). Mullins is reputed to have replaced a Norman archway between tower and nave with the present Gothic arch, but no representation of the old arch exists. The body of the church, where not restored, is C15 or later. The two-bay nave arcades are double-chamfered with octagonal piers; the capitals and responds, now colourfully painted, are unconventional, with two tiers of mouldings and hollow under-

* The Tudor roses probably refer to the earlier connections of the Cheke family with Henry VIII and Edward VI (*see* Mottistone).

** The most famous family member was Sir John Cheke, tutor to Edward VI, Greek scholar and politician.

sides; the larger chancel arch is similar.* The square-headed side windows of the aisles are restored, but the four-centred S aisle E window has old stonework. The chancel is large in comparison with the nave; the three-light Neo-Dec E window is a renewal by *Mullins*. Old illustrations show a square-headed window of four lights. The N (Cheke) chapel is wider than the N aisle and has a quite elaborate three-bay arcade of four-centred arches with several orders of moulding and capitals fairly similar to those of the nave. The piers are remarkable, with thick shafts and hollows between, giving an almost quatrefoil section. The chapel E window is of three lights with half-lights above, all uncusped. The external label stops of this window have the Cheke arms to the N and a Tudor rose to the S; a string course close to ground level has a range of grotesque heads. The chapel roof has a boarded waggon ceiling, slightly pointed, with thin ribs in a rectangular pattern.

FURNISHINGS. Largely of 1863. – PULPIT. Octagonal, early C17; two tiers of panels with circle and diamond patterns; repeated rose motifs (which presumably refer to the Cheke family's past connections with the Tudor dynasty). – FONT. Square with angle columns, Norman in style. It may in part be original late C12. – The N CHAPEL was refurbished in memory of the 1st Lord Mottistone, †1947, by his son *John Seely*. Three moulded beams, supported by slender columns which rise from wooden partitions forming parts of the structure of pews, enclose an unusual and elegant 'chapel within a chapel'; the beams carry a continuous Latin inscription. – STAINED GLASS. The E chapel window, by *Reginald & Michael Farrar Bell*, 1948, is largely semi-opaque, but includes a kneeling angel, in pale yellows and browns, holding the end of an inscribed scroll. They also designed the E window with a strongly coloured Ascension and pale figures of angels, again with an opaque background. – MONUMENT. Table tomb in E bay of chapel arcade. Two arches on its S face with keystones and decoration in the spandrels, including a coat-of-arms. It is reputedly that of Jane Freke, †1674, wife of Sir John Dillington, the owner of the Manor, but she is also commemorated at Newchurch (q.v.).

p. 27 MOTTISTONE MANOR. A mainly C16–C17 house set against a hill-slope to its E and NE, with a long wing running roughly N–S and a shorter, taller main part aligned westward at slightly more than a right angle. A porch in the angle is a focal feature. Dating of different parts of the house presents

* The bases of some of the piers and responds have angle spurs; this has led to the dating of the bases as *c.* 1200, but this seems unlikely. Could the arcades date, with other parts of the church, from late C16 or early C17 reconstruction – cf. Shorwell, Godshill?

problems. The main part is built of large squared blocks of sandstone, the wing is partly in rougher stone; the roofs are of stone slate for about half their pitch while the upper parts are tiled – a striking example of the use of stone slate for the lower courses of otherwise tiled roofs. When *Seely & Paget* were commissioned to restore the building in 1925 the main part was a farmhouse, but most of the wing was uninhabitable because there had been a landslip in the early C18, half-burying much of its E side.* Part of the restored wing became, at first, the service quarter of the re-created house, but when *Seely* altered the house again after 1947 he divided off most of the wing as separate accommodation.

On the porch (described below) is an inscription 'T Anno Domine 1567 C', usually taken to indicate when Thomas Cheke completed the main part of the house. This has two four-light transomed windows to each of the two floors on its principal, S, elevation, and a gabled dormer over the centre. The W end is plain, with a small window in the gable; the N side is irregular. (Without the evidence on the porch, one might have dated the main part of the house a few decades later in the Island context.) The porch is curious; it is built of the same stone as the main part of the house, and has a gable on its S side (although the entrance faces W). The doorway has a nearly flat arch with moulding. Above is a wide panel in a moulded frame, containing a smaller heraldic panel and the inscription already mentioned. On either side of the smaller panel are two terminal figures on pedestals, of uncertain origin (they were inserted here by Seely in his second restoration).

It is sometimes stated that the S wing is older than the main part of the house, but the long W front of the wing suggests a late C16 to early C17 date, with three-light mullioned windows on each floor, and two doorways with nearly flat arches. Some of the windows, however, were inserted or rearranged by *Seely*; previously the fenestration had been more irregular. Internal features, including ground-floor roof beams and a fireplace, support a late C16–early C17 date for most of the wing. (However, the DCMS list indicates the remains of an arch-braced roof with collar truss at the N end of the wing, suggesting that something does survive from a late medieval house. The roof at this end rises less high externally than that of the rest.)

The porch opens into the entrance hall, which was formed by *Seely* through internal rearrangement; it has a simple marble fireplace with *cyma recta* frame brought from

*General Seely knew *Lutyens* and showed him the manor as a partly ruined farmhouse; Lutyens persuaded him to restore it and live there.

Appuldurcombe.* A doorway leads l. into the principal room of the house, which has a stone fireplace with a nearly flat arch, in the style of the porch doorway and of other fireplaces and internal stone doorways in the main part. The walls are covered with painted hangings by *Brian Thomas*, showing vibrant scenes from the *Pilgrim's Progress*, commissioned by Seely *c.* 1947. *Seely* inserted a wide screen at the E end, incorporating bookshelves and topped by thin turned balusters. On the wall behind this screen part of an early C17 overmantel was re-set. It has four caryatid figures on pedestals and a strapwork frieze.[2] The main upstairs room has the remains of mural paintings in black and yellow, with a frieze originally inscribed with texts from a 1538 translation of the Bible; the one text that survives runs: 'If a man saye I love God and hateth his brother he is a liar.' The staircase – unusually of stone around a square stone well – is in a small N wing.

Finally, the former BARN to the W of the house was skilfully altered by *Seely* after 1925. He created an entrance passage through the centre, with low-pitch arches, to provide the main approach to the house – first seen, through the inner arch, across the lower part of the GARDEN which, created in stages over the last few decades, rises up the fairly steep slope to the N.

PREHISTORIC REMAINS

7 The LONGSTONE lies on Mottistone Common, aligned along the edge of a narrow ridge of Lower Greensand 455 yds (420 metres) N of Mottistone Manor. The monument is a badly damaged earthen long barrow with a free-standing stone upright and fallen stone constituting the remains of an entrance façade. The recumbent stone was moved slightly during an unproductive C19 excavation. A small excavation by Jacquetta Hawkes and J.D. Jones in 1956 revealed traces of a stone kerb surrounding part of the barrow. The standing stone is 13 ft (4 metres) high, 7 ft (2.1 metres) wide and 4 ft (1.2 metres) deep, the recumbent stone 9 ft 6 in. (2.9 metres) long, 4 ft (1.2 metres) wide and 2 ft 6 in. (0.8 metres) deep. The mound is low and vague, lying ESE–WNW. It has been so greatly disturbed by sand digging and erosion that the original shape and dimensions cannot be determined, but the present length is *c.* 98 ft (30 metres) and the maximum height is 6 ft (1.8 metres).

* Date uncertain; it could be early or late C18.

** In his first restoration Seely placed this overmantel above the fireplace in the main room. He moved it again in his second restoration. It is not clear where it came from.

CASTLE HILL is an enclosure of probable Late Prehistoric date situated on higher ground to the E of the Longstone. The earthwork is sub-rectangular and aligned approximately ESE–WNW. Its maximum dimensions are 231 ft (71 metres) N–S and 221 ft (68 metres) E–W including external ditches. The west bank is the best-preserved and is highest at the N end where it reaches 6 ft (1.8 metres) high and 29 ft (9 metres) wide. There are slight traces of a ditch on the W and S sides, between 13 and 23 ft (4 metres and 7 metres) wide and up to 2 ft (0.6 metres) deep. Parallels with similar earthwork types on the mainland suggest that it may be a stock enclosure. A survey published in 2003 states that, on balance, the most likely date for the earthwork is Iron Age or Romano-British.

On MOTTISTONE COMMON to the W of the Longstone is a large Bronze Age ROUND BARROW about 110 yds (100 metres) N of the path. This is one of only a few extant round barrows away from the chalk downs. 59 ft (18 metres) diameter, 9 ft (2.8 metres) high.

At the summit of MOTTISTONE DOWN ¾ m. N of the Manor, four Bronze Age ROUND BARROWS are clearly visible. The name HARBORO is attached to the largest barrow. This may be derived from the Old English word for earthwork. French attacks on the Isle of Wight took place in the C14, C15 and C16 and a beacon network was set up to provide early warning of foreign raids. 'Hauedburghe' was included in a list of beacon sites dated 1324 and may equate with 'Harberoe Down' included in a similar list of 1638. The Mottistone Down barrows were the subject of an early C19 excavation by the Rev. John Skinner, a Somerset clergyman and antiquary. A collared urn covering a cremation was found and is now in the County Archaeological Collection. The Harboro barrow is 104 ft (32 metres) in diameter and 10 ft (3 metres) high. The remaining barrows vary in height from 9 ft 6 in. to 3 ft (2.9 to 0.5 metres).

Near the foot of Mottistone Down, close to the National Trust car park, two smaller Bronze Age ROUND BARROWS, badly damaged by rabbits, can be seen to the N of the Tennyson Trail. One is 49 ft (15 metres) across and 4 ft 6 in. (1.4 metres) high, the other 46 ft (14 metres) across and 4 ft (1.2 metres) high.

The much larger BLACK BARROW can be made out to the S on the edge of Grammar's Common. It has been suggested that this feature could be a natural rise but it is now thought to be a Bronze Age barrow occupying a rise, and therefore appearing unusually large.

NETTLESTONE *see* SEAVIEW

5585
NEWCHURCH

The name is deceptive; a church existed by early Norman times. The parish extended across the Island from the site of Ryde to that of Ventnor, and was reduced only when those towns developed in the C19. The village is well inland, on the edge of the east-central vale, much of which is devoted to special crops with extensive greenhouses. To the N and NE is hillier country, first Upper Greensand, then chalk.

ALL SAINTS. Stands prominently at the N end of the village street, picturesque with its red-tiled roofs, rough sandstone walls and weatherboarded tower over a S porch, capped by a short spire. The road descends steeply on the W side of the church, so that from the opposite direction it appears to be on a bluff, the catslide roof of the nave and N aisle giving a barn-like effect. The church is cruciform, with a long chancel whose N wall has three widely spaced lancets; there are smaller lancets at the W ends of both aisles, and one pair in the N aisle side wall. All this suggests that the present building is substantially early C13 – an impression confirmed inside. The interior is surprisingly grand, because of the apparent scale of the crossing arches to E, N and S (there is none to the W). These are of three chamfered orders on the sides facing the central space. Similar mouldings continue below the thin responds, interrupted only by thin abaci. A small lancet in the gable over the E arch opens into the chancel roof-space (what was its purpose?). In a corresponding position in the W wall is a small eight-cusped circular window. There were considerable changes in the Late Middle Ages or after. The E and S walls of the chancel were rebuilt with three-light windows, square-headed outside but with four-centred rere-arches. There is a similar S window in the S transept (above this is the date 1725, when the transept may have been lengthened and the window perhaps re-set). The nave arcades are enigmatic. They have double-chamfered arches and octagonal piers, with curiously elongated hollow-sided capitals which do not look convincingly medieval. They may perhaps be replacements of the late C16 or early C17 (cf. Shorwell, Godshill). The S porch, stone-built, is of uncertain date; the wooden belfry above, *c.* 1800, with its weatherboarding (rare on the Island), quatrefoil openings and outline of battlements, is absurd but appealing. The church was restored by *A.R. Barker*, 1883.

FURNISHINGS. PULPIT, 1725. Part-octagonal with plain panels in two tiers; of wood on later stone base. It had a

Newchurch, All Saints, crossing, drawing by Percy Stone. From Stone, *The Architectural Antiquities of the Isle of Wight*, 1891

huge hexagonal canopy of inlaid wood which has been taken down and used as a table. – LECTERN, incorporating a splendid gilt pelican with three young: C17–C18? It came from the parish church at Frome, Somerset, where it is said to have topped the pulpit. – ROYAL ARMS, 1700. – CREED AND COMMANDMENT BOARDS in cusped Gothic frames, *c.* 1800, moved from chancel to W wall. – STAINED GLASS. E window by *Kempe*, *c.* 1909. – MONUMENTS. N transept, Jane Dillington of Knighton Gorges, †1674. Small cartouche with shield; plaque with attractive lower-case lettering. – S transept, Maurice Bocland, †1765. Tall tablet with broken pediment and shield; foliage below. – Chancel,

William Bowles, †1749. Cartouche with scrolled Rococo surround.

The large CHURCHYARD has, sadly, been cleared of tombstones. N of the church a former SUNDIAL of 1678 survives, made for Knighton Gorges (*see* below), and given to the church after the house's demolition. It is shaped like a thick baluster, broadening in the middle, with round moulded top (the actual dial has gone) and a stepped base.

WACKLAND, 1m. SW. Medium-sized house of 1736 with five-bay two-storey elevation faced in mathematical tiles. Wooden keystones to ground-floor windows and simple pedimented doorcase.

p. 24 KNIGHTON GORGES, 1½m. N. About 50yds (46metres) E of Knighton Shute (a road leading from Newchurch towards the chalk ridge) is the site of one of the grandest mansions on the Island, demolished in 1821. Held by the Morvilles until 1256, it passed to Ralph de Gorges, whose descendants held it for two centuries or more; in 1563 the estate was bought by Andrew Dillington, whose family was in occupation until the mid C18. The owner into the C19 was George Maurice Bisset, who demolished the house in his old age following a family dispute, ensuring that his daughter and heir never lived there.

The house is illustrated and briefly described in Sir Henry Englefield's *Description . . . of the Isle of Wight* (1816). Many of the details depicted must have dated from the later C16 to mid C17, but because of its irregularity the house cannot have been built from the start during the period. It was presumably a substantial medieval house to which piecemeal additions and alterations were made. The principal elevation, to the N, was not illustrated by Englefield. According to his description, 'At the north-east angle of the house [was] a plain square tower of great strength and antiquity . . . Near this tower part of a very handsome pointed window remains, similar to windows in Arreton Church and the chapel at Swainston.' This window would have dated from around the time of Ralph de Gorges.

(To the W and SW, between the house site and the road, are the sites of domestic GARDENS, investigated in 1989 by Frank and Vicky Basford. They were partly surrounded by banks and by walls of Greensand and brick, probably C18. An ALCOVE in the E wall of the main part of the garden, backing on to the house site, has a brick-arched entrance with keystone, leading into a brick-vaulted space. The gardens continued to be maintained for some time after the demolition.)

The one fairly conspicuous survival from Knighton Gorges is a pair of C18 GATEPIERS to the E of the road, S of the house site. Square, rusticated, about 10ft (3 metres) high; with thin cornices and rounded caps.

NEWPORT 5085

Newport was founded *c.* 1180 by Richard de Redvers, the lord
of Carisbrooke Castle (q.v.). The castle was the feudal centre
of the Island, but the village of Carisbrooke could not be easily
expanded and did not have immediate access to navigable
water. The site of Newport about 1¼ m. away, reasonably flat
and focused on the head of the Medina estuary, was much
better suited to urban development. So a town was laid out,
largely to a grid pattern of streets – reminiscent of that in
larger medieval planned towns such as Bury St Edmunds or p. 25
Salisbury, though without the great churches of either of
these. The town was sacked by the French in the C14, like
Yarmouth and nearby Newtown, but unlike the latter it eventually recovered. By the early C17 it was prosperous as a place
of trade, and in Georgian times was the commercial and social
centre of the Island. The development of Ryde and other
towns in the C19 challenged its status in these respects; it 6
remained essentially a market town. Today it is the Island's
main shopping and administrative centre.

Although its central street pattern is medieval, Newport has no buildings of earlier date than the C17 and few from before the C18. There is no visible early timber framing. Stone was used in some C17 buildings (notably the Old Grammar School of 1614), but by the early C18 brick from varied nearby sources became the essential local material. As in southern England generally the combination of red and grey bricks was common until the early C19 – either in chequer patterns or, more frequently, with red bricks used for quoins and dressings in walls otherwise of grey brick. From *c.* 1800 national trends in the use of buff or 'white' bricks were influential. Bay windows, either rounded or canted, were prominent from the mid C18. Generally the old streets display a typical market-town variety of C18 or C19 frontages, from the moderately grand with sophisticated details to the simple vernacular. Through the Georgian period local builders displayed versatility in their use of the classical vocabulary. There are some fairly recent bad intrusions, but, except on parts of its fringes, the centre of Newport escaped large-scale C20 redevelopment. As in other market towns, long stretches of street frontage have lost most of the original ground-storey elevations to shopping development, but some streets, such as Quay Street, retain many old frontages intact. There was evident decline in some parts around the mid C20, but there have since been notable examples of rehabilitation and restoration of streets and buildings. Much of this process is indicated in the Perambulations, e.g. in and around Crocker Street and Lugley Street, and in parts of Pyle Street.

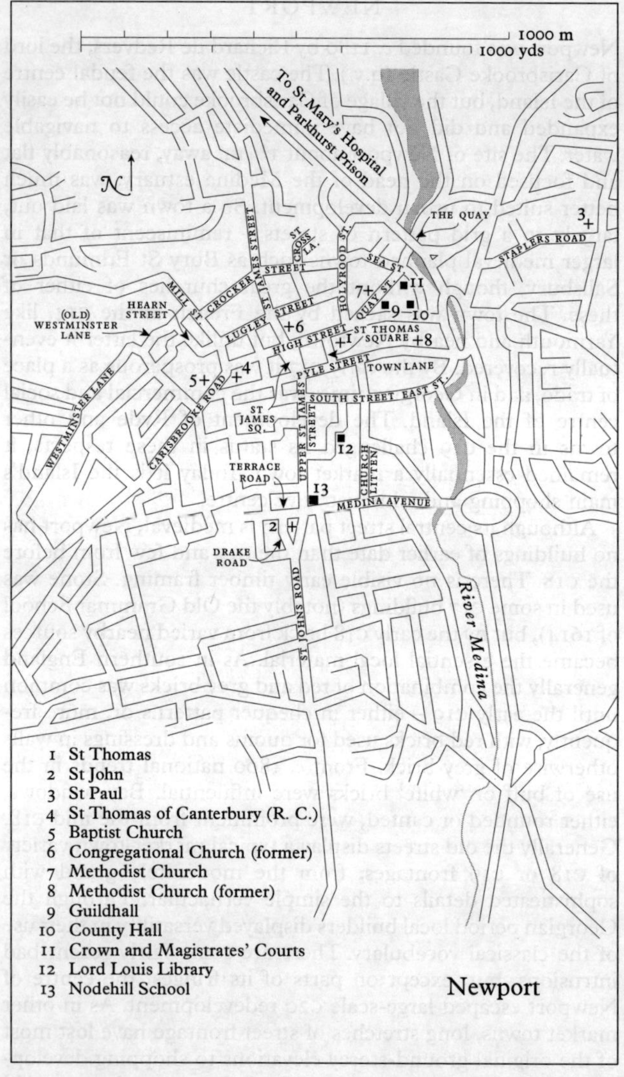

CHURCHES

Newport was in the ancient parish of Carisbrooke; the medieval St Thomas remained officially a chapelry until replaced by the present parish church in the 1850s – when there were already two other Anglican churches on the out-

Newport, old church.
Engraving by P. Brannon, early C19

skirts of the town. The Roman Catholics, remarkably, had their own church in 1791; the Nonconformists are represented by an interesting series of chapels.

ST THOMAS, St Thomas Square. The first chapel was built *c.* 1180 in the marketplace here, and like churches in other towns founded about this time (for instance Portsmouth and Lymington in Hampshire; Salisbury a little later) was dedicated to Thomas Becket.* It survived with alterations until replaced in 1854–6 by the present building on the same site designed by *S. W. Daukes*. Although only a chapelry, the medieval building was substantial; early C19 views show Transitional arcades with round piers, scalloped capitals and pointed, well-moulded arches. It was partly reconstructed in the early to mid C17; the aisles were heightened with upper tiers of windows, square-headed and mullioned, which lit galleries. There were important C17 furnishings including a five-bay chancel screen with segmental arches, and the surviving pulpit.

Daukes (who was originally based in Gloucester but moved to London in 1848) won a competition for the design of the church, of which Prince Albert laid the foundation

*The dedication was changed to St Thomas the Apostle after the Reformation. It was altered again after the Victorian rebuilding to St Thomas of Canterbury and St Thomas the Apostle. (Confusingly, the R.C. church was at that time already dedicated to St Thomas of Canterbury.)

stone. It is built of roughly textured stone with ashlar dressings, and has a dominant W tower, separately gabled aisles and windows with elaborate Geometrical, not quite Curvilinear, tracery. The tower has a powerful upper storey with large paired belfry lights, open traceried parapets and prominent NE turret with spirelet; it punctuates many street scenes and views of the town from outside.

Inside the church there is an emphasis on height. The four-bay nave arcades have tall piers, alternately round and octagonal, with simply moulded arches. The chancel arch is more elaborate, with an inner order rising from short marble shafts, their capitals and corbels carved intricately with foliage – as are the corbels supporting the nave roof. The clerestory (not evident outside because of the aisle roofs) has small traceried lights; one on each side is circular with tracery infill.

33 FURNISHINGS. The PULPIT of 1631 is the church's *tour de force*; one of the most richly detailed of its period in England. It was given by Stephen March, merchant and mayor. The craftsman was *Thomas Caper* of Salisbury, said to have had Flemish associations.* It is polygonal, with elaborate canopy, broad angled reading shelf, and two tiers of panels with carvings in intricate relief. Those in the top tier represent Remembrance, Fortitude, Charity, Faith, Justice, Meekness and Hope; the lower ones have scrolls inscribed Grammatica, Dialectica, Rhetorica, Musica, Arithmetica, Geometria and Astrologia. Under the reading shelf are angels, a pelican, and human figures above scrolled brackets. The crest of the sumptuous canopy has figures representing Peace and Justice and angels blowing trumpets; a gilded inscription runs round the frieze; the canopy is edged with paired open-arch patterns; a dove hovers underneath. – The curious READING DESK was formed from unspecified parts of the C17 furnishings in the old church. Two sides have segmental arches containing narrow rounded openings with thin twisted columns, carvings of angels and humans, and an incomplete inscription; a third side has linenfold panelling. – The CORPORATION PEWS would in a different setting seem remarkable. Made in the 1840s for the Mayor and Corporation at formal services, and reinstated in the chancel of the rebuilt church, they have poppyheads and traceried backs. – The sanctuary has a REREDOS with five traceried blank arches, matching SEDILIA, and a low brass SCREEN with delicate open decoration on the N side. –

* Charles Tracy, *Continental Church Furniture in England* (2001), cites the pulpit as a rare example of a piece of English church furniture for which a craftsman of foreign origin had been named: '. . . the artistic level of the figure style is only provincial. It is difficult to point to a Flemish prototype, yet the carving is certainly not English.'

ORGAN GALLERY at the W end, supported on wooden pillars with, on its E side, ornate iron tracery and one of two ROYAL ARMS of Queen Victoria (the other, larger example is over the chancel arch). – Two FONTS; one, contemporary with the church, is octagonal with thin marble columns. A C17 font has been returned to the church; it has an octagonal convex bowl and a stem which used to have four handle-like attachments with volutes, but two have been broken off; there is a small wooden cover with carved panels and frieze. – STAINED GLASS. E window by *William Holland* of Warwick, *c.* 1857, variedly colourful with biblical scenes (the central one renewed after war damage). – N chapel E window, Wise and Foolish Virgins, by *Lavers & Barraud*.

MONUMENTS. Sir Edward Horsey, †1582 (he was a nautical adventurer before becoming Captain of the Island in *p. 32* 1565, and lived at Haseley Manor, Arreton). Dark marble and alabaster; Composite capitals supporting a canopy with strapwork background and three achievements above; stiff effigy in armour, originally with a sword; his head rests on the rolled end of a mat. – Princess Elizabeth, daughter of Charles I, †1650 aged fourteen when imprisoned in Carisbrooke Castle; she was buried in the chancel. Commissioned by Queen Victoria at the rebuilding of the church, with *Baron Marochetti* as sculptor. White marble effigy in a segmental recess; long robed figure asleep with her head resting on a Bible. Also by *Marochetti* a medallion portrait in profile of Prince Albert, on the N chapel wall.

ST JOHN, St John's Road and Drake Road. By *R.G. Wetten*, 1835–7, in pre-Ecclesiological Gothic. A rectangle with tall lancets between prominent buttresses. The central part of the W end projects between two octagonal turrets. Walls of rough stone; turrets and buttresses of ashlar. Spacious interior; the nave roof is supported by iron girders of flat profile, ending in curved brackets on corbels (explaining the massiveness of the buttresses). Small polygonal chancel with tall lancets rising higher than the well-moulded chancel arch. Large W gallery containing the organ. – PULPIT, 1896, unusually set against the E wall to the N of the chancel arch; polygonal front, canopy with angled corners; Gothic details. – MONUMENT. Rev. William Carus Wilson, †1861, by *S. Westmacott* (presumably a little-known later member of the family of sculptors). A soldier with a Bible in his hand and a gun at his feet.

ST PAUL, Staplers Road, Barton, on the E side of the town. Built in 1844, by *J. W. Wild*, best known for his ambitious Neo-Romanesque Christ Church, Streatham, London, of 1840–2. St Paul is also Romanesque in its details (though far more modest than Christ Church). Built of rough coursed limestone, with aisled nave, apsidal chancel and SW tower with short spire. The windows, including a trio at the w end, are like large round-headed lancets. The tower has paired rounded belfry lights, but with its slender outline and spire is Gothic rather than Romanesque in character. The nave arcades are rounded and roll-moulded, on slender circular piers with square abaci; the apse has a plaster semi-dome and a thinly detailed blind arcade below the windows. – STAINED GLASS. In the three apse windows are figures derived from those by Sir Joshua Reynolds in the chapel of New College, Oxford, in strident colours; *c.* 1844–50. Triple w windows by *Kempe*, 1899. – MONUMENT. Rev. W.H. Nutter, †1909. Elaborate wall monument in veined marble with heavy scrolled broken pediment and fluted Ionic pilasters.

ST THOMAS OF CANTERBURY (R.C.), Pyle Street (w end),
57 1791. Of outstanding interest because it is claimed to be the first purpose-built Roman Catholic church for ordinary congregations (i.e. not for private use or for important foreigners) erected in England since the Reformation; the Catholic Emancipation Act of the same year made this possible. The patron was Mrs Elizabeth Heneage, who five years later founded a similar church in Cowes (q.v.). A simple rectangle in red brick with two tiers of round-headed windows. Street (ritual w) elevation with circular window in the pediment, string courses, and w porch of stone with Tuscan columns, triglyph frieze and pediment with dentils. Charming interior, sympathetically restored. A gallery runs round the church except to the E, with fluted Composite columns; at the w end it curves slightly forward. The simple altar is set in a coved apse (there was never an impressive E termination, as in the church's counterpart at Cowes). Parts of the former ALTAR RAILS, relatively tall, with slender turned balusters, have been re-erected against the wall at the w end; their design has been adapted for the renewed balustrades to the gallery. The adjoining PRESBYTERY (No. 96 Pyle Street, originally a private house) is mid C18. Seven-bay brick frontage, its windows irregularly disposed. It has a STAIRCASE in the Chinese Chippendale style with open square-patterned balustrade, and two fine C18 fireplaces with scroll and garland patterns on the friezes.

BAPTIST CHURCH, High Street (w end). Built 1812, but the
63 front is of 1872 – a bold Corinthian composition, conservative for its date. Its main part is brought forward with giant columns under a pediment with prominent dentil decoration. The rounded windows at first-floor level have balustrades below their sills; there are three arched doorways with keystones. Nice railings on the pavement frontage.

Former CONGREGATIONAL CHURCH, St James Street (N part), 1848 by *Francis Pouget*. Walls of rough stone; Gothic details. Tripartite street front, of which the centre part is taller and rises to a gable, with pinnacles; gabled turrets like large pinnacles at the corners.

METHODIST CHURCH, Quay Street, built as the Bible Christian church 1879–80, by *Frederick Mew*. Wildly Gothic front with gables and asymmetrical pointed turret – in great contrast to the Baptist church frontage of seven years earlier. Acceptably incongruous in this varied street.

Former METHODIST CHURCH (now APOLLO THEATRE), Pyle Street (near the E end). Built 1804, enlarged 1833. Uncommonly fine façade, presumably of the latter date, of three bays in plum-coloured brick, with a broken pediment into which a giant arch reaches up, containing a lunette window. Doorway with thin Doric columns. The chapel had a notable interior with side galleries, and a coved apse containing the pulpit behind a balustrade at elevated level. Little of this remains.

UNITARIAN MEETING HOUSE, High Street (E end). Built 1775 but enlarged, including the present front, in 1825. This is in red brick, of two storeys; windows with Y-tracery; above is a late C19 frieze of geometrically patterned tiling. Simple slate-hung back elevation.

PUBLIC BUILDINGS

GUILDHALL, High Street and Quay Street, by *John Nash*, 60
1814–16. Now the Isle of Wight Museum. It originally contained a courtroom and council chamber on the first floor, with market space at ground level.* A grand Neoclassical composition in stucco, to which the tower at the SW corner was added in 1887 for the Queen's Golden Jubilee. The W elevation has a tetrastyle portico with tall unfluted Ionic columns and plain pediment, rising from a ground storey with open arches. Behind the portico three windows light the former courtroom. The S elevation to High Street has an engaged Ionic colonnade. The tower ruins the symmetry of the building but is an admirable feature in the townscape. It is plain up to cornice level, with three slightly diminishing stages above; the uppermost stage contains a clock, and is topped by a cupola with open colonnade.

COUNTY HALL, High Street. The Isle of Wight obtained a county council in 1890, but County Hall was built in 1938. By *Gutteridge & Gutteridge* of Southampton; extended 1969 and later. The original building is moderately civic-monumental, in simplified Neo-Georgian with a dash of 1920s Swedish. The ground floor is faced in stone, the rest in brick. The centre bay has a window rising through two

*Before the C20 the Guildhall was usually called the Town Hall. It is sometimes confused with the County Club (*see* p. 181).

storeys above the entrance; other first-floor windows have balconies with iron railings. The 1969 extension has curtain walling with blue-and-white chequer pattern.

CROWN AND MAGISTRATES' COURTS, Quay Street. By *Rainey Petrie Design*, 1993–4. It faces NW, on a site which rises slightly to the SW, in a street with varied, low-key, largely Georgian buildings – *see* Perambulation 2, p. 182 – into which it fits reasonably well. Mainly of red brick; two-storeyed with even roof-line, but with a three-storey entrance bay under a gable pediment towards the upper end. There is a similar entrance of lower profile further down the street. Some of the windows, on the upper floors and over the entrances, jut out like arrowheads.

LORD LOUIS LIBRARY. *See* Perambulation 3.

NODEHILL SCHOOL (former Seely Library and Technical Institute). *See* Perambulation 3.

ST MARY'S HOSPITAL. *See* Outer Newport.

PARKHURST PRISON. *See* Outer Newport.

MEDINA SCHOOL AND LEISURE CENTRE, *see* Outer Newport.

PERAMBULATIONS

Newport's late C12 street pattern, basically a grid, survives nearly intact. There are two long E–W thoroughfares, High Street and Pyle Street, with the shorter Lugley Street and Crocker Street to the N. Other streets cross from N to S, and Quay Street runs diagonally NE to the quay at the head of the estuary. There were two marketplaces: St James Square, a widening of the main cross-street, and St Thomas Square, originally rectangular.

Three Perambulations cover the central area: 1 includes St Thomas Square, High Street and St James Square, going W to Carisbrooke Road; 2 goes to the Quay, Crocker Street and Lugley Street; and 3 reaches the southern fringe.

1. St Thomas Square, High Street, Pyle Street and St James Square to Carisbrooke Road

ST THOMAS SQUARE began as a rectangular space between High Street and Pyle Street. St Thomas's chapel, forerunner of the parish church, was built in the middle, splitting the square into two connected parts. Both parts were encroached on later by islanded blocks, on the sites of original market stalls which eventually became permanent – as happened in so many marketplaces across England. So there is now a sequence of spaces of different shapes around the church, creating varied and fascinating townscape effects. The church has no churchyard of its own; paved sur-

faces come up to its walls on every side. The buildings which surround the assertive Victorian church contrast with it and are characteristic of central Newport: generally C18 to mid-C19, modestly classical with many variations, of two or three storeys, faced in differing local bricks or stucco, usually with shops on the ground floors. The best is GOD'S PROVIDENCE HOUSE (No. 12) at the SE corner. Its 36
entrance, in an alley leading S, has a splendid shell-hood on large spiral brackets, with a plaque above dated 1701. The elevation to the alley is in red brick with rubbed brick lintels. The upper part of the frontage to the square is painted, and there are two fine Late Georgian bowed shop windows under a continuous fascia. The modillion cornice is characteristic of the date of the building. Inside is an original staircase with turned balusters. No. 14 is part of the same structure, with continuing roof-line, but altered. Nos. 8 and 10, on the adjoining E side of the square, have differing upper-floor bay windows, each locally characteristic. That on No. 8, early C19, is segmental, with a central sash four panes wide and narrower flanking sashes, all following the curve. The window on No. 10, mid C19, is flat-fronted with curved ends.

The SW corner of St Thomas Square forms an attractive small *place* (the term seems apt, as the townscape has a decided French feel), dominated by the church tower. It contains the WAR MEMORIAL, *c.* 1920, a tall Celtic cross on a tapering base and, to the E, a nicely incongruous building of *c.* 1900 in red brick with a Flemish skyline (it was once a mineral-water factory). On the W side No. 18, Late Georgian, has a staircase with a squared Chinese Chippendale pattern in the balustrade. To the N a roughly triangular block lies between the church and High Street. This was partly redeveloped *c.* 1990, but it preserves the earlier ground plan with the rounded eastern angle of the block forming one side of the exit from St Thomas Square – to good visual effect, especially when one looks back towards the church from the N.

HIGH STREET runs for about ½ m. E–W on a slightly sinuous course. We enter it opposite the Guildhall (*see* above), which contrasts in its relative grandeur with the casual irregularity of the frontages around it. Going E, No. 19 on the S side is now a pub; mid C18 in grey and red brick. The central upper window is brick-arched with white keystone and imposts. No. 147 on the opposite side is of *c.* 1800; in chequer brick, of five bays, of which the end ones are brought slightly forward. It retains its whole façade (without a shopfront), including a Tuscan doorcase. Beyond this, the long frontage of County Hall (*see* above) takes over on the N side, but facing it are interestingly varied buildings. No. 15 is curious; it is of grey brick with elliptical arches on the ground floor and, above, two straight-ended bay windows with slightly curved main sashes – perhaps *c.* 1830. Past the set-back Unitarian Meeting House (*see* above), No. 9 has a pair of two-storey canted bay windows, a dentilled cornice which continues round them, and a small central upper window with radiating stones on the lintel. These varying façades show how versatile, and sometimes unorthodox, were the local C18 and early C19 builders in their use of the classical vocabulary.

High Street ends at a traffic gyratory system. We walk r. and r. again into parallel PYLE STREET, which begins unpromisingly but soon asserts itself as a street – curving slightly to the l. with the church tower rising beyond the rooftops on the r. A tendency for it to feel like a back street has been partly offset by the sensitive repair of several buildings – e.g. No. 137 on the N side, grey and red brick with fluted pilasters to the doorcase and a fine panelled room inside. Beyond is the former Methodist church (*see* above), and opposite are Nos. 26–27, early C18 with small casement windows. Then, on the same side, CHANTRY HOUSE, a well-restored early C18 seven-bay range in chequer brick, with leaded-light casements under rubbed lintels, of which three on the upper floor are wavy-edged. Further on the N side is an alley leading to St Thomas Square past God's Providence House (*see* above). On the E corner of the alley is a building probably of the same date as the latter (*c.* 1700), though altered. It has a similar cornice and a small original oval window on the upper floor. On the SE corner of Pyle Street and TOWN LANE is a complex redevelopment of *c.* 1990, including a furniture shop (DABELLS) and offices. A flat-topped four-storey corner block in warm buff brick has square-sided bay windows on the W frontage; the ground floor is set behind segmental concrete beams on pillars. The flanking façades are, by contrast, in dark red brick with round-arched ground storeys and steep-pitched roofs with dormers. The differing treatment of each part works successfully on this prominent site. Less successful was the rebuilding, *c.* 1970, of Nos. 46–47 Pyle Street, opposite the opening to St Thomas Square. This was a late C18 buff brick house of seven bays with an applied pediment. Its façade was reproduced supposedly in replica but the effect is not satisfactory, partly because of the brickwork.

We continue along Pyle Street until it meets ST JAMES SQUARE. This was part of the main N–S thoroughfare of the medieval grid, which widened northwards between Pyle Street and High Street to form one of the town's market-
51 places. No. 54 Pyle Street at the SW corner of the intersection, early C19, has a striking first-floor bay window with three curved sashes, and a triglyph frieze which passes over this window. Otherwise the Square is lined with C18–C20

frontages – impressive, on the whole, as informal townscape, and culminating on the E side in the COUNTY CLUB at the corner with High Street, built in 1810–11 in Portland 6
stone as the Isle of Wight Institution, by *William Mortimer*. It is of five bays, of which three project slightly with Doric pilasters under a pediment. The ground floor is rusticated, with three segmental arches flanked by smaller ones. In front is the QUEEN VICTORIA MEMORIAL by *Percy Stone*, unveiled in 1903 – suitably elaborate to commemorate the locally resident monarch, and eclectic in its details. Its triangular base with concave sides stands on a stepped plinth, with three bronze lions crouching at the corners. Above them are angels, also in bronze, standing at the foot of a column which rises to a capital with Art-Nouveauish stiff-leaf foliage. At the top is a Gothic tabernacle with narrow gabled niches, crowned by a spirelet. To the S is another MONUMENT with a bust of Earl Mountbatten on a tall tapering base, unveiled in 1982 (he was the Governor of the Isle of Wight). Looking eastward along High Street (from a position further W) the County Club is a focal feature on the r., and the street continues on a slightly wavy alignment to the fairly distant Guildhall – a notable informal townscape punctuated by formal buildings. No. 117 (the former Bugle Hotel) lies across High Street to the N of the Club, to which it acts as a foil, with its austere upper storeys in dark grey brick (the ground floor has been altered). Further E, No. 43 on the S side of High Street has impressive bow windows on two floors.

To the W along High Street, the POST OFFICE (No. 99 on the N side) has early C19 upper storeys with red dressings, and a ground-floor frontage of 1903 with a pediment-hood on ogee brackets. Then THE RED HOUSE (Nos. 97–98), Early Georgian, of five bays and two storeys in chequer brick. The end bays are brought forward slightly, with moulded pediments over the ground-floor windows, and the parapet has short ranges of open balusters. A porch with Ionic columns has gone. Further on the same side, the CASTLE INN has a brick front reconstructed in the early C20. A plaque is inscribed 1684; the gabled end elevation round the corner in Mill Street could date from then – one of the few examples of early stone building in the town. The small HOLYROOD HALL opposite, stuccoed with Gothick windows, was once a Quaker meeting house. High Street bends to the l., passes the Baptist church (*see* above), and merges with Pyle Street, with the Catholic church of St Thomas of Canterbury a short way along the latter.

CARISBROOKE ROAD leads SW from the town centre – a fine exit indeed, with a long terrace of the 1860s on the NW side; three-storeyed and mostly stuccoed. Each house is two bays wide, but the first-floor frontages alternate between having two windows and iron balconies, and single canted bay windows, creating an impressive rhythmic effect.

2. The Quay, Crocker Street and Lugley Street

QUAY STREET runs NE beside the Guildhall towards the estuary. It begins narrowly, then bends r. to become a broad thoroughfare. On the outside of the bend, Nos. 28–30 are early C19 in buff brick; No. 30 has a tiled frieze of 1880, with leaves and berries, on the ground floor. Then, past the Methodist church (*see* p. 177), the street descends gradually, with mainly Georgian buildings on both sides. Materials vary; No. 21 on the r., *c.* 1800, is in buff brick, the earlier Nos. 19–20 are chequered. The doorcase to No. 20 has a pediment on convex brackets, and that to No. 19 has a thin moulded cornice and fluted pilasters. The most prominent building on the l. is No. 38, built *c.* 1820 for the Literary Society; three-storeyed, stuccoed, with tall *piano nobile* and rusticated ground floor. Alas, features which were there *c.* 1980 have gone – a first-floor iron balcony, the original cornice, and a parapet with a taller central part. Cornice and parapet ought to be restored. The main part of No. 39 is mid-C18, of chequered brick; a slightly later extension to the r. is in lighter grey with round-headed ground-floor windows framed in red. No. 41, early to mid C18 with segmental-headed windows and keystones, is painted over. Across the street the succession of older façades is broken by the Crown and Magistrates' Courts (*see* p. 178). Looking back, there is a fine vista up Quay Street as it narrows towards the Guildhall, with the top of St Thomas's tower in the distance.

THE QUAY is at the head of the Medina estuary, where contributory streams flow in: the upper Medina itself from the SE, and the Lukely Brook from the W. SEA STREET took a curving course on the town side of the two streams. Until *c.* 1970 there was a range of C18–C19 warehouses and granaries between it and the upper Medina, built of brick with some rubble, many with round-headed iron-grilled openings, but these have been swept away, together with a railway viaduct. A concrete road viaduct now crosses the estuary further N. On the W side of the estuary head, around the confluence of the Lukely Brook, another group of commercial buildings has been successfully converted into the QUAY ARTS CENTRE by *Tony Fretton Architects*, 1997–8. Several former warehouses, late C18 to early C19, back on to the S side of the tidal water. They are of red brick, to different widths and gable heights, and retain round-arched, iron-grilled apertures, interspersed with windows which were inserted (or converted from old openings) in the remodelling. These are linked to a plainer, later, three-gabled brick building on the W side of the water, which now contains a theatre and restaurant. To the N, connected by a canopy, is a three-storey former rope store, early C19 in red brick with slate roof abutting the road viaduct. Here is a special example of conversion and partial remodelling of a group of interesting buildings into an ensemble which exploits, and enlarges on, their inherent qualities and those of their surroundings.

Only one section of Sea Street, whose quarter-circular course looks so distinctive on old maps, is now recognizable as a street – the part just W of The Quay, with the entrance to the Arts Centre on the r. Opposite is SEAL HOUSE, early C18 in red brick with a modillion cornice; the windows have segmental heads and flush frames, but the doorcase is later. Sea Street joins HOLYROOD STREET, one of the N–S streets of the medieval grid. (This street led to the small priory of St Cross or the Holy Rood further NW, founded on a then isolated site as a cell to the French abbey of Tiron *c.* 1135 – i.e. before the establishment of the town of Newport. The priory was closed by the 1380s; nothing survives.) Buildings at the S end of Holyrood Street are described later in the Perambulation.

CROCKER STREET, leading W, is the northernmost of the parallel medieval streets. It was for long dominated at its E end by a brewery, and became shabby and partly derelict after this closed. With conversion and repair of older buildings and partial redevelopment, it has become an attractive street. Nos. 73–74 at the N corner with Holyrood Street are Late Georgian with a mansard roof; No. 70, in grey and red brick, was the brewer's house.

Nos. 66–69 formed the MALTHOUSE, converted in 1984 for residential use. The main part is Late Georgian with a splendid façade, mostly of dark grey brick with nine large recesses framed in red brick, the central one being wider. These recesses now contain domestic windows, and some of the original grilled openings have been retained and adapted. The malthouse was extended E in a different style fairly soon after it was built. The extension (also converted) is in buff brick with cornice and parapet instead of eaves, and narrow round-headed recesses rising through both storeys. The site of the brewery itself, behind the malthouse, was redeveloped for housing *c.* 1985–90, partly round a small green. A restored two-storey N projection of the malthouse, faced in weatherboarding and topped by a large cowl, is a notable feature. W of the brewery site, St Cross Lane leads N to the former ST CROSS MILL, C18 and later, one of several watermills which once stood on the edges of the town. No. 7 Crocker Street on the S side is early C17 – the oldest house in Newport in recognizable form. It has a

Newport, houses in Crocker Street, drawing by A.L. Collins. From *The Victoria County History, Hampshire and the Isle of Wight* vol. 5, 1912

roughcast street front, brick gabled end elevations and bracketed eaves. On the upper floor are two wooden oriels of three main lights with canted ends and brackets under the sills; the casements retain their original iron frames. The ground-floor windows are similar but restored. Nos. 12–19 are modest but varied late C18 to mid-C19 houses with an interesting range of brickwork; harsh grey to warm red, some in chequer pattern. No. 62 on the N side, 1761, is in brown-grey brick with red brick lintels. In a round-headed niche is the figure of a girl (a charity school, founded elsewhere in the C18, moved here in 1877). Crocker Street crosses ST JAMES STREET, part of the main N–S thoroughfare of the medieval grid. Nos. 120–123 on the E side, just S of the crossroads, form a prominent mid-C19 three-storey terrace of buff-grey brick, with plain round-headed doorways and, on the first floor, locally typical flat-fronted bay windows, curved at their ends.

The W part of Crocker Street is less consistently interesting than the rest, and readers may wish to shorten the Perambulation by turning S along St James Street, reaching Lugley Street beside the Old Grammar School (*see* below). The full Perambulation continues along Crocker Street past the WORSLEY ALMSHOUSES, a single-storey range originally built in 1618 with a street frontage of brick, wood-framed casement windows and gabled end elevation partly of stone. It was elaborated in 1879 when three porches were added with conspicuous half-timbering, and fretted tiled cresting was provided on the angles of the roofs. Crocker Street meets Mill Street, and OLD WESTMINSTER LANE continues W to CROCKER'S MILL of 1773. This, converted to residential use, is the finest of the town's remaining former watermills, three-storeyed in dark red brick with bands of grey; a weatherboarded gantry projects on the top floor. HEARN STREET leads uphill S. Early Victorian terrace houses of two or three storeys make handsome groups; some have rounded entrances, others simple bracketed door hoods.

The street turns E at its upper end and continues into LUGLEY STREET. LUGLEY HOUSE, set back on the N side, is three-storeyed, mid-Georgian in red brick with grey bands with a pedimented doorcase. It lost its chimneystacks in a fairly recent renovation, and their absence is noticeable. Opposite, No. 33 has a huge segmental bay window on the first floor containing three separate sashes; the wall surfaces between and below the sashes are faced in wood grooved to imitate stonework – an oddity indeed. Then the MASONIC HALL, 1892, in deep red brick and terracotta. On the ground floor are arches with rugged rustication and a circular plaque showing a ship. The first floor has brick pilasters under a vigorous cornice, and an axial chimneystack on a concave-sided base provides a skyline feature. At the crossing with St James Street is the OLD GRAMMAR SCHOOL of 1614 which, with its roughly textured walls, looks like a small manor house in town, with gables fronting both streets, and a chimney shaft on the Lugley Street frontage. Details are plain; restored wood-mullioned and transomed windows and a simple doorway with squared hood. (The fine chimneypiece illustrated in Percy Stone's *Architectural Antiquities* does not survive.) The E part of Lugley Street has buildings varied in styles and roof-lines, many repaired and improved in recent years. Among the best is No. 8 on the N side, mid C18 in red brick with segment-headed windows. Lugley Street enters HOLYROOD STREET (*see* above); No. 20 in the E side is early C19 in grey brick with windows framed in red. Nos. 24–26 opposite has a carriage entrance with a painted board referring to a posting establishment; the upper floor, with tall windows, may have been an Assembly Room. The street is narrowed at its S end by an islanded block adjoining an alley to the E, clearly the result of early encroachment. It enters High Street close to the Guildhall.

3. *South of the Town Centre*

This is a short Perambulation, beginning at Lord Louis Library (the Island's chief public library) in Orchard Street, and passing the earlier Seely Library, now a school.

LORD LOUIS LIBRARY, by the County Architect *R. Smith* (project architect *Michael Rainey*), was opened in 1981. It is an axial building with three main components, each under broad slated roofs rising above single-storey walls of brick. A wide pillared porch opens at the E end into the main octagonal space. Beyond are the smaller, more complex, children's library and, finally, the reference section in the form of an elongated octagon. The composite massing with the low-pitched polygonal roofs, punctuated by roof-lights, is particularly effective when seen from the adjoining CHURCH LITTEN PARK. This was formed from a cemetery established in 1583 and entered through a stone GATEWAY of that date, E of the Library. It has a four-centred arch under an ogee-shaped gable ending in a flattened point. One MONUMENT remains, to Valentine Grey (a chimney-sweep aged ten), †1822; an obelisk topped by an urn, with an inscription condemning his treatment. We turn r. from the park into MEDINA AVENUE with Late Victorian villas, past St John's Lodge, originally *c.* 1837 (the date 1868 on the house refers to alterations), to the crossroads with ST JOHN'S ROAD.

NE of the crossroads is NODEHILL SCHOOL, which occupies the buildings of the Seely Library and Technical Institute opened in 1904. By *W.V. Gough* of Bristol; red brick with profuse stone dressings. The main part of the complex has semicircular windows on the upper storey; a small gable with panels and finials rises above the centre, and an ornate porch with Ionic columns projects below; the gabled wings are topped by small white cupolas. It is a relief to look at Nos. 2–6 St John's Place opposite, a simple three-storey stuccoed terrace of *c.* 1835 with rusticated ground floor. The group is completed by the present SCHOOLS AND CHILDREN'S LIBRARY SERVICE office S of Nodehill School, built as a Board School *c.* 1895: a nice composition of brick and stone and slate roofs with a central spirelet.

To the S is St John's church (*see* above), surrounded by varied Victorian houses. Nos. 5–6 TERRACE ROAD, SE of the church, are the most distinctive; a three-storey pair of *c.* 1850 in rough stone, with bargeboarded gables and squared bay windows on the two lower floors. ST JOHN'S ROAD leads S; Nos. 19–31 on rising ground to the E form a nice two-storey mid-Victorian terrace; the central and end houses have gabled attics with decorative bargeboards. Return to the town centre is along UPPER ST JAMES STREET, past a succession of C18–C19 frontages.

OUTER NEWPORT

ST MARY'S HOSPITAL, about 1 m. N of the town centre. The modern hospital is part of a complex of buildings of which

the oldest is the former HOUSE OF INDUSTRY, 1771–4. This 42
was one of the first examples nationally of a workhouse (or institution for the destitute) which served a considerable area – in this case the whole Island – rather than a single community or parish. Some of the original buildings partly survive. The austere main block, aligned E–W, is two-storeyed and of nineteen bays on its main (S) elevation, which faces a garden courtyard. It is mostly in red brick, but the central five bays are faced in grey headers with red surrounds to the windows, and the round-arched doorway has a rusticated frame – all under an exceptionally wide pediment-gable containing a lunette. This block included common rooms, with a (former) chapel projecting axially on the N side. At right angles to the E is a range nearly as long but without a centrepiece, which contained servicing facilities. These ranges formed two sides of a not very regular courtyard, of which the S side (with schoolrooms and the main entrance), and the original W side (including wards) have disappeared. Later C19 to C20 buildings were provided to the W and N.

The main HOSPITAL is by *Ahrends, Burton & Koralek*; 88
planned from 1985 and opened 1991. Energy efficiency was a prime consideration; to achieve this, stainless steel with high insulating qualities was used as cladding on external walls and roofs. However, problems arose relating to corrosion, and large-scale remedial work, using zinc sheeting, began in 1997.

As seen from the A3020 (Newport–Cowes) road to the W, the hospital forms a large and very complicated composition, with almost infinite variations of massing, height, roof-line, fenestration and alignment, set on a site gently sloping up to the N. The layout (though this not apparent at first sight) is based on four blocks of cruciform shape, arranged radially in a quarter-circle curving from W to N, connected by an internal passageway through their converging ends. Outpatients' and daytime services are sited on the ground floors; wards are generally in the upper storeys. Medical and servicing facilities are focused in the area at the hub of the quadrant. The structure is basically a concrete framework with steel roof trusses. The cladding was, at the start, applied uniformly over most of the external walls and roofs. The original steel sheeting was ribbed, giving linear effects (usually horizontal but sometimes vertical), which are perpetuated in slightly different ways with the zinc. However, bases of walls are of pale brick, and there are bands of white aluminium between windows.

As we approach from the road, the dominant feature is a rectangular block, aligned at right angles from the main mass of the building at the top of the slope, with a long straight roof-line and uniform cladding above ground-floor level; the name 'St Mary's' is proclaimed in large letters near 88 the top on both sides. The entrance to the hospital, however, is some way down the slope, marked by a conspicuous canopy with a multi-curved fabric roof rising to two concave-sided points. This shelters the porch itself, with its glazing and slender framework painted boldly red and white. The main circulation, within and beyond the irregular lobby (with its well-proportioned staircase), is designed to be friendly and welcoming. Artworks, including murals, are set in conspicuous places. Because of the diagonal placing of some of the principal blocks, there are small internal courtyards of irregular shapes, which have been landscaped. Larger-scale informal landscaping, including a sheet of water, extends up to the main buildings on the SE side. Finally, in a conspicuous position on the W side of the hospital, is a free-standing conical feature, painted in layers of bright and varied colours, by *Liliane Lijn*, 1997.

(PARKHURST PRISON, together with Albany Prison and Camp Hill Prison, lies to the W of the Newport-Cowes road about 1¼ m. N of the town centre. The first substantial buildings in the area were the Albany Barracks (which do not survive), built in the 1790s. A hospital related to the barracks was built in 1799 to the design of *James Johnson* and *John Sanders*, architects to the Barrack Department of the War Office. From 1838 the hospital buildings were used as a prison for juveniles, for which purpose they were converted and enlarged in 1843–4 by *Joshua Jebb*, an army engineer and prison specialist who became Surveyor-General of

Newport, Parkhurst Prison.
Mid-C19 engraving

Prisons in 1844. In 1863–9 they were used as a women's prison. Since 1869 Parkhurst has been a men's prison, continually adapted, enlarged and partly rebuilt.

The oldest building in the prison, which became the Administrative Offices and was latterly called the White House, was part of the hospital of 1799. It is timber-framed, faced with mathematical tiles and partly stuccoed, with a central cupola containing a clock. Another remarkable feature is the Cloverleaf Building of 1843–4 sw of the White House, part of *Jebb*'s enlargement. It is two-storeyed, of trefoil shape; the upper storey contained the chapel and the ground floor included schoolrooms. There is internal iron framing, with cast-iron columns on the ground floor supporting concealed beams at first-floor level.

Albany Prison, on the site of the first barracks, dates from 1963–7. Camp Hill Prison was built in 1909–15 to an open plan, with a central building in Neo-Georgian style. At first it housed inmates undergoing preventive detention, a form of sentence since discontinued, rather than penal servitude. It was extended in 1976.)

Newport Roman Villa is located in Cypress Road about a mile s of the town centre. From St Thomas's Square the villa can be reached via Town Lane, Church Litten, and Medina Avenue. The villa, under a modern cover building and open to visitors seasonally, is of 'winged corridor' type, dating from the c3. It contains one of the best-preserved bath ranges in Britain. The bath suite comprises a frigidarium (cold room) with cold plunge bath, tepidarium (warm room), caldarium (hot room) with a semicircular hot bath, and sudatorium (sweat room). All the warm rooms in the bath suite were heated by an underfloor hypocaust which 8
can still be seen. The main wing of the building includes a dining room with a tessellated floor of chequerboard design and a fireplace.

Medina High School and Leisure Centre, off Fairlee Road, ¾ m. ne of the town centre; on the edge of a country park. Built 1975–80 by the County Architects' Department; project architects *M. Rainey* and *D. Hosking*; Leisure Centre extended 1995–7 by *Rainey Petrie Design*. The school has a low profile to fit a gently sloping site, higher to the e; there is a central n–s spine, and two large blocks on each side with low single-pitch roofs and walls mainly of brick. A theatre of similar profile abuts on the s side. The Leisure Centre is to the sw; the swimming pools and smaller gymnasium were completed in 1980, with their main roof supported on laminated timber beams. The adjoining large sports hall was opened in 1997 – again internally impressive but plain outside. The most interesting part of the composition is where the theatre is connected with the

Leisure Centre by a bridging upper storey, part of the 1995–7 additions.

BELLCROFT, No. 79 Staplers Road; ¾ m. E. A fine house of buff brick, *c.* 1800; of two storeys and four bays, the centre two brought forward under a gable-pediment containing a large lunette with fluted fan decoration. The side elevation has a bold two-storey bow containing a round-headed window on each floor. The house has been altered and extended to form flats.

4090

NEWTOWN

Calbourne

The ghost of a medieval town, founded in 1256 by Bishop Aymer of Winchester in his manor of Swainston (q.v.).
2 Streets were laid out in a grid beside a navigable creek, with over seventy burgage plots; for a time it was a significant port (*see* Introduction, p. 25). In 1285 it came into possession of the king, but in 1377 was devastated by a French raid. It may already have started to decline by then; it never recovered, and by the C16 there were few houses. Yet in 1585 it was granted the right to send two Members to Parliament, the votes going to the owners of identifiable burgage plots, not many of whom lived locally. The electors formed a corporation, the existence of which led to the building of
35 the TOWN HALL *c.* 1699; it was altered in 1813. Of red brick with banded stone quoins under a hipped roof, on a tall base of ashlar blocks – apart from the S end which has buff mathematical tiles and a stone doorway reached by a double flight of steps. There are four big round-headed windows with keystones on the E side, and smaller rounded windows at the N end above a four-columned porch. The building could be in a respectable market town, but it stands in a grassy space which was once a wide street. A narrow thor-
41 oughfare leads W past a few C18–C19 stone cottages to the CHURCH OF THE HOLY SPIRIT, built in 1835 on the site of a ruined medieval chapel. By *A.F. Livesay* of Portsmouth – an architect often interesting and surprising.* What he designed suits Bishop Aymer in style: E.E., small and rectangular but relatively tall, with gabled W bellcote. Inside it is a satisfying early work of the serious Gothic Revival; plaster-vaulted with stiff-leaf bosses, moulded ribs and correctly E.E. shafts; two-light Geometrical E window with sexfoil upper circle.

*Livesay's *tour de force* is Andover church, Hants; he also restored Calbourne church (q.v.).

The church is evocatively placed on the NE corner of what was a central crossroads of the medieval town. Grassy lanes, once streets, lead S and W towards the creek, where there must have been quays. On the S side of the western lane is CAUSEWAY COTTAGE, 1973–4 by *Raymond Erith*; three-storeyed, three-bay vernacular Georgian with hipped slate roof. The windows are slightly unevenly spaced, reflecting the irregular internal planning which was influenced by views and sunlight penetration. From near the church one looks N along another grassy thoroughfare to the former VICARAGE, of dressed stone with decorative bargeboards and oriels; is it by *Livesay*?

NINGWOOD MANOR *see* SHALFLEET

NITON 5075

Niton and Whitwell

The most southerly parish on the Island, with the wildest coastal scenery – resulting from successive landslips of which the most dramatic in modern times was in 1928. This severed the original main road near the coast, and destroyed much of the formerly gorge-like Blackgang Chine (*see* Chale). The village proper is about ¾ m. inland; its S extension Niton Undercliff has a scatter of mainly C19 houses, placed where practicable in the tumbled landscape.

Niton church, engraving, before 1854.
From J.L. Whitehead, *The Undercliff of the Isle of Wight*, 1911

ST JOHN THE BAPTIST. Set in a pretty churchyard sloping up to the W, with walls of rough sandstone, and a castellated W tower capped by a stumpy spire. Inside, the architecture is pleasantly jumbled. The three-bay N arcade is late C12, its two main arches slightly pointed with rounded chamfers, the western arch smaller and simpler. The E pier is round with a square abacus, characteristic of the Island; the W pier (and both responds) are square-shaped with chamfered angles, and with curious capitals moulded in two tiers. The S arcade is a little later, with round piers and capitals. The W window of the S aisle looks late C13 with a quatrefoil in a circle. The simpler E window of the S chapel and N window of the chancel, both two-light, are of the same period, but the main E window, with three trefoiled lancets, dates from the restoration of 1864 by *R.J. Jones*. Also by *Jones* is the N aisle with simple lancets. The S porch is tunnel-vaulted, with pointed transverse arches (cf. Arreton, Whitwell) – late C15, C16 or early C17? The tower, with diagonal buttresses, broad flat S stair-turret ending below the parapet, small square-headed openings and low spire, may be C17.

FURNISHINGS. REREDOS by *Percy Stone*, 1930. Painted wood with ogee panels, elaborate cornice, and figures under canted canopies to the sides. – PULPIT. Presumably by *Jones*, showing his characteristic originality. Octagonal, in wood, with open trefoiled panels between slender balusters with shaft-rings. – FONT. Norman, of cauldron type, with a rope moulding at the top. – STAINED GLASS. The main E window and that of the S chapel, both mid-Victorian, are notable; who were the designers? In the S aisle a two-light window shows six scenes from the life of St John, by *Geoffrey Webb* in association with *Ernest Heasman*, 1917. – MONUMENT. George Arnold of Mirables (*see* St Lawrence), †1806, signed *H. Rouw*. A female figure, with a pelican, leans on a tall oval pedestal with a relief portrait of the deceased. Surprisingly, it is in a Gothic surround with a four-centred arch.

In the CHURCHYARD, several table tombs, and the massive four-stepped base of a medieval CROSS, surmounted by a war memorial of Celtic form by *Joseph Clarke*, *c.* 1920. – Striking LYCHGATE by *J. Bevir* of Lymington, 1920; arches of stone, slightly pointed but without moulding or capitals; flint patterning in the outside gable.

The village proper is fairly compact, with several thatched stone-built houses interspersed with other buildings. The former SCHOOL SE of the church, 1905–6, is many-gabled with mullioned windows and a small turret. The present VILLAGE HALL, long and single-storeyed with sash windows, began *c.* 1760 as a malthouse, became a Baptist chapel in 1823, and was later a school. MELLBURY in

Niton, engraving of 1840 showing the Sandrock Hotel.
From George Brannon, *Brannon's Picture of the Isle of Wight*, *c.* 1844

Newport Road to the N has a pleasant stuccoed front of *c.* 1840 with squared and rounded openings. The BAPTIST CHURCH was built in 1849 using stone from the site; simple lancets and gabled porch. ST CATHERINE'S HALL, on the E side of Barrack Shute S of the village centre, is a notable stone-built house of *c.* 1850 with different-sized gables, lacy bargeboards and first-floor jetties brought out in stone to strange effects.

NITON UNDERCLIFF attracted visitors in the early C19. A house enlarged in 1812 as the Sandrock Hotel, where Princess Victoria stayed with her mother, helped to set the pace; it was burnt down *c.* 1990. MOUNT CLEVES, to the W of its site off Sandrock Road, has a stuccoed exterior of 1829 round an older core, with giant Ionic pilasters and a Tuscan porch. The stump of the old narrow coastal road leads to where it was cut off by the 1928 landslip, with spectacular views over the chaotic scenery. The BUDDLE INN on St Catherine's Road further S retains a C17 fireplace under a massive bressumer beam. ST CATHERINE'S HOUSE opposite is a two-gabled mid-Victorian villa with laced bargeboards, and an odd open-pedimented porch. St Catherine's Terrace nearby is built on a site sloping down steeply; only gabled upper storeys with openwork bargeboards are seen from the road, to odd effect. A private road leads SW to ST CATHERINE'S LIGHTHOUSE, built in 1838–40, reduced in height in 1875 and added to in 1932 – the ultimate successor to the medieval lighthouse 1 m. NW (*see* Chale). On the way to the lighthouse a weathered pair of square GATEPIERS, *c.* 1838, marks the entrance to an intended house which was built instead on a less exposed site. Another pair of gatepiers now forms the entrance to Reeth Lodge in CASTLE HAVEN LANE further E; they are similar but have plain cornices and massive finials. These were built *c.* 1810 as the entry to a building beside the beach, for some time a hotel, but eroded away in the late C19. THE WELL HOUSE stands at the turning to Niton Undercliff from the A3055, a fantasy of *c.* 1870.* From the front it is like a miniature château crowded with detail; mansard roof with ironwork and tapering central turret; portico with rounded open pediment and balustraded wings; urns on the corners. But the back, bordering another road, is plain.

44 PUCKASTER, in a rugged tree-grown setting above the coast to the E of Niton Undercliff, was built between 1812 and 1824 as a *cottage orné* for James Vine, a dilettante with a merchant background, to a design of *Robert Lugar*. It was later enlarged, combining picturesque effects from the Regency and Victorian periods.** The form of Lugar's 'cottage' is still clear: rectangular, with a rounded S end; of one main storey under sweeping roofs with dormers, but with what amounts to a shallow two-storey transept on the E side. The rounded southern end formed an open veranda supported by rough tree trunks. The original thatch was replaced by tiles before 1849, and additions were made after *c.* 1862, particularly on the W side, including gables of varied sizes with elaborate bargeboards. The interior was refurbished at some time *c.* 1903–39, when wooden fittings were brought in from elsewhere, including panelled doors (not all used as such), which appear to be of C16–C17 date and foreign origin; the panel carvings are mostly arabesque or grotesque but include scenes of the Nativity. There are also friezes of classical figures in white against blue (which may have been associated with Vine, who was acquainted with Josiah Wedgwood). The early C20 alterations – for which no further information has been obtained – included the insertion of a bay window within the rounded S veranda, reducing its openness but retaining the immediate setting of the free-standing tree trunks.

* It was built for Frederic Vilmet, son of George IV's French chef.

** *Robert Lugar* designed, and published books illustrating, houses and cottages in the early C19 Romantic manner. James Vine based his *cottage orné* at Puckaster on one of Lugar's published designs; Lugar himself visited it when work was in progress and suggested modifications. A house with similar characteristics is Swan's Nest, Ryde (*see* p. 241).

Norris Castle, engraving, 1844.
From George Brannon, *Brannon's Picture of the Isle of Wight*, *c.* 1844

NORRIS CASTLE 5095

East Cowes

Built from *c.* 1799 by *James Wyatt* for Lord Henry Seymour, on a hill-brow E of Cowes, making a splendid sight from the Solent – a Romantic neo-medieval castle, not archaeologically correct, but hard to match as a piece of theatrical setting, with grassland plunging down to the water in front.* Work was completed by 1805. If seen from the sea it is a long composition aligned SE–NW; the dominating feature – at the SE (l.) end – is a big round tower with taller stair-turret. Then, to the r., is a fairly short stretch of frontage up to a much smaller square tower, then a lower service range, and finally a large stable block, taller than the service range – all under castellated roof-lines at varied levels.

(However, the impression is different on the landward approach, from New Barn Road in East Cowes. The landscape was probably designed by *Humphry Repton* (he was consulted, though no Red Book survives). The drive sweeps past a castellated farmyard (*see* below), then curves to arrive near the round tower, with the two-storey entrance range on the inland side. The tower – built like the rest of the castle in rough coursed local limestone, with fragments of flint in the mortar as galleting – has three main storeys lit by sash windows with rounded tops, and an attic storey with small circular windows just under the castellation. The entrance front has similar round-topped windows and a

*The castle is not visible from the sea on the present ferry routes to Cowes.

simple porch with a four-centred arch; at the l. end is a small squared tower (matching that in a similar position on the Solent frontage). Beyond is the service range, set back; beyond that, projecting well forward, is the massive stable block, two-storeyed over a basement, with the corners and central entrance slightly higher to appear as low towers. (The stable had a central courtyard, now roofed over.) Finally, at the NW end, a rounded platform projects boldly at basement level.)

(Internally the castle has few elaborate details. The rooms inside the main tower are circular, with splendid views over the Solent. The library, within the entrance range, has curving bookcases to *Wyatt*'s design; there are cupboards of similar form in the adjoining circular drawing room. A hall-passage is divided by transverse arches and each section is vaulted.)

(The FARMYARD, about 300 yds (275 metres) S of the main building, is like a castle in itself when seen from a distance, but the frontage to the drive is symmetrical and fairly domestic, with a central two-storey bailiff's house and flanking entrance arches (all under embattled roofs). However, a castle-like curtain wall encloses a very large adjoining area, including the kitchen garden.)

(LODGE at the end of New Barn Road, Cowes. Two-storeyed. Attributed to *James Wyatt*.)

Princess Victoria stayed at Norris Castle with her mother, the Duchess of Kent, in 1831 and 1833 as guests of Lord George Seymour. It was then that she became familiar with this part of the Isle of Wight, with its picturesque scenery and views over the Solent. This led her later to choose the area for her new private residence, eventually buying Osborne (q.v.).

NORTH COURT *see* SHORWELL

4590 NORTHWOOD

Cowes

Northwood was the northern, well-wooded part of the original parish of Carisbrooke. It became a separate parish in 1545, extending from near the edge of Newport to include the site of Cowes. Cowes started to develop soon after this, and became a distinct administrative entity by the C19. Northwood is now a S appendage to Cowes, still part-rural, especially around the secluded church which lies down a lane leading E from the A3020, close to the Medina estuary.

St John the Baptist. Built in the late C12 as a quite substantial aisled building (although until 1545 it was only a chapelry of Carisbrooke). The first impression externally is deceptive, with the small W tower and spire of 1864, and a catslide roof over nave and aisles. The S doorway, set in a Victorian porch, indicates the true quality of the building; it is late Norman with three orders of zigzag and a label patterned with diamond shapes; the jambs have shafts with scalloped capitals. The four-bay arcades have the characteristic *c.* 1200 Island form: circular piers, square chamfered abaci, pointed arches with a slight chamfer. The N arcade is the earlier of the two by a little. Later medieval half-arches span the narrow aisles to curious effect, two to the S and one to the N; they were presumably inserted as buttresses against thrust from the roof structure. – PULPIT. Mid C17, octagonal, with plain panels. The high canopy is the best feature, edged by segmental arches with intermediate bosses, and rounded pendants at the angles. – MONUMENTS. Three cartouches in the chancel. Samuel Smith, †1689, and wife †1681, with jolly-looking representations of Death: grinning skull with projecting bones at the bottom, faces looking outward amid contorted foliage, and an angel at the top. – Ann Chobbery Christian, wife of a rear-admiral, †1799. A Rococo design with scrolled frame and an angel below. – Rev. Thomas Troughear, vicar, †1761, his wife, née Holmes, †1788, and five children; the cartouche is bordered by drapery. (One son inherited the fortune and title of the Holmes family formerly of Yarmouth, q.v.) – Attractive well-grown CHURCHYARD, not over-tidied.

Northwood House. *See* Cowes, p. 129.

NORTON *see* FRESHWATER AND TOTLAND

NUNWELL 5585

Brading

A medium-sized country house in a splendid situation ¾ m. W of Brading, with the chalk ridge rising to the S, and an expansive view E towards the sea. The Oglander family were manorial lords from at least the C12 (tombs in Brading church, q.v.). Their best-known member was the diarist Sir John, †1652. His writings provide vivid evidence of Island life and topography, and of society at local and national levels, in a turbulent period.

The original manor house (of which nothing survives) was to the W. There was a fairly substantial house on the present site in the C16, which Sir John Oglander rebuilt (or greatly remodelled) from *c.* 1607. It was altered and enlarged several times from the mid C18 to the early C20. The result is a building of strangely varying character when seen from different directions.*

It is best to start with the S and W sides. The C17 house, the plan of which is recorded in a drawing dated 1735, had a main S frontage with short wings. Of this the W wing is recognizable. Its eastern wall is of brick (an early example on the Island), with stone quoins and a four-light stone-mullioned window on the ground floor. The S wall of the wing is of later brick, but round the corner the W frontage is all built of rough stone with ashlar quoins. This elevation is in two sections – the S part, extending over two bays, is double-storeyed; the remainder, of three bays, is a storey higher. The quoins on the two sections abut, indicating that each part was built separately during the C17, the S presumably first. The windows on this frontage, which are either of cross form or casements, are partly framed in brick and are of uncertain date.

The present form of the S frontage between the wings dates from the mid C18. It is of five bays, faced in red mathematical tiles. The windows have stone surrounds with keystones; those in the upper floor are taller and contain sashes, while the lower windows have wooden cross-frames of relatively recent date. The dominant feature is a remarkable doorway, in stone, with rusticated pilasters flanking an arch which is also rusticated and has a keystone. Above is a shallow hood with dentils. Although this is the main entrance to the house, there is no porch. There are clues and limitations to the possible dating of the frontage in its current form. A plan dated 1735 shows the main entrance in its present position, but with a porch. An outline of the house on an estate map of 1748 also indicates a porch. So the present arrangement cannot predate 1748. The use of mathematical tiles was well established by then. The curious design of the doorway is paralleled in two earlier buildings in Berkshire (now Oxfordshire), both with no known connection with Nunwell: Radley House of 1721–7, and Kingston House, Kingston Bagpuize, probably *c.* 1720. Possibly the doorway was brought from elsewhere when the S front was remodelled.

The plan of 1735 shows that the E wing then extended no further S than the W wing (though it was wider), and that the house had a relatively short E elevation. An inscription on the plan indicates that it was intended to rebuild the E

*Much information about the house was obtained from 'Nunwell House: Documented History of the Landscape'; report by Fanny Oglander, 1996.

side, including the wing. The outline on the estate map of 1748 shows that this had been accomplished. The new frontage was a little further E than before, and was inclined slightly NE of the previous alignment. This arrangement did not last for long, since in 1767–8 Sir William Oglander, the 5th baronet, altered the house again. He enlarged the E wing southwards, and provided a new E façade. This overlies the one which was new in 1748 and continues over the extended wing. It makes an impressive frontage overlooking the garden; three-storeyed, of seven bays, the three central bays brought forward in a canted composition which rises to full height. It is of grey brick in header bond with thin red brick dressings (quite different from the S frontage with its red mathematical tiles). Two single-storey additions have been made to the N end of this elevation, neither of them intrusive when seen from the garden. The first, of 1896, has a Venetian window; the second, of 1905–6 by *Percy Stone*, has a doorway within an arched surround on the N side.

Another single-storey addition was made in the late C19 at the S end of the E frontage, originally as a conservatory (with brick flanking walls; there was glazing in the roof). It was converted *c.* 1920–30 by *John Seely* (cf. Mottistone) into a loggia with an open three-columned S front, under a stone parapet with ball finials.

The S frontage has been asymmetrical since the E wing was extended, with three storeys instead of the previous two, in 1767–8. There were further alterations to the W side of this wing, including the insertion of bay windows, in the early C20.

The house is centred on the HALL, which partly retains its C17 dimensions. It is set behind the E part of the main S façade, with the entrance doorway opening into its SW corner. The stone fireplace, on the N side, is original, with a slightly cambered lintel and a torus frieze under the mantelshelf. The hall ceiling, with a pattern of writhing lines in relief, is probably early C19. The finest room is the present LIBRARY, originally the drawing room, formed by Sir William Oglander in 1767–8 within the extended E wing. Its ceiling is delicately detailed with floral garlands, acanthus and circular patterns; the bold cornices have triglyphs and paterae, and a marble fireplace has a garlanded frieze. The present DRAWING ROOM is the main room on the E side, focused on the canted bay window. The main STAIRCASE, NE of the hall, formed part of the alterations completed by 1748. It is of well shape, with slender turned balusters and Tuscan columns at the angles; the handrail ends in an elegant scroll. In the W part of the house is a C17 SECONDARY STAIRCASE with square newel posts and flat shaped balusters. There are notable C17 to early C19 features, including panelling and cornices, in some upstairs rooms. Especially remarkable is a CORNICE around a room in the NW part of the house, which is likely be of the early to mid-C17 date when this part was built. It is wooden, of *cyma* or ogee form, carved in a rustic foliage and palmette pattern, with brackets at intervals carved with heraldic cartouches.

In 1807 *John Nash* prepared a plan for rebuilding Nunwell. It would have been a remarkable house, with curved corners to many of the rooms, an oval staircase, and a semicircular portico – but it was not built; Nash carried out only repairs and redecoration.

The former STABLES (now residential), SW of the house, are mid to late C18. Of red brick, with pediments in the centre and on the wings, each containing lunettes; windows in recessed arched frames, and blank circular panels on the upper façades round the courtyard. There was probably once a cupola. Early formal GARDENS disappeared when the park was landscaped *c.* 1770. The present gardens, with many interesting features, were designed by stages in the late C19 and C20.

The EAST LODGE, by *Stephen Salter*, *c.* 1900, is like a small villa with gabled roughcast upper storey, patches of tile-hanging, and triple chimneystack. The GATEPIERS are of rusticated brick with ball finials.

5090 ## OSBORNE HOUSE

East Cowes

THE OSBORNE ESTATE

67 Victoria stayed, as Princess, at Norris Castle (q.v.) in 1831 and 1833. The locality left a deep impression on her, and in 1845 she and Prince Albert bought the nearby Osborne Estate as the site for a new private retreat, secluded yet within fairly easy reach of London (following the opening of railways on the nearby mainland). The existing house was a big plain late C18 mansion in grounds which extended to the shore, with splendid views over the Solent. The present Osborne House was built mainly in 1845–51, adjoining and overlapping the site of the older house.

Osborne is special in many ways. It is a House, not a Palace; the Queen and Prince built it privately for themselves, independent of the body – the Commission for Woods and Forests – which then controlled Crown properties. No architect, formally recognized as such, was employed; the design and layout were undertaken by *Prince Albert* in association with *Thomas Cubitt*, then at the height of his reputation as a builder and developer in Belgravia and other fashionable parts of London. Albert had many talents;

Osborne House, engraving.
From W.H.D. Adams, *Nelson's Handbook to the Isle of Wight*, 1866

he wrote poetry, composed music, painted pictures, was fascinated by science and technology and was deeply interested in architecture, gardening and landscape. He particularly admired the art and architecture of the Italian Renaissance. The house itself is a major example of the British Italianate style, which was essentially introduced by Charles Barry *c.* 1830–40 – e.g. at the Travellers' and Reform clubs in London, at Walton House (later Mount Felix, now demolished) in Surrey, and at Trentham Hall (largely demolished) in Staffordshire, where Victoria had stayed.*

Thomas Cubitt came to Osborne intermittently from 1845; he lived during his visits at Victoria Cottage, East Cowes (p. 136).** His last visit was early in 1851, when the House was almost complete. Cubitt's London houses were essentially Italianate in their details, and were usually built of brick faced with stucco. Osborne was constructed in a similar way, even though the use of stucco to imitate stone was at that time going out of fashion with the growing emphasis on the honest use of materials. Internally, iron girders supporting brick vaulting were used at the main floor levels, according to the principles of 'fireproof' con-

*Pevsner in 1967 noted the popularity in Germany of asymmetrical Italianate compositions, e.g. the Pfingstberg at Dresden, 1849. He might have added that German architects active during Albert's youth, especially Leo von Klenze and Friedrich von Gärtner in Munich, rivalled England in the Italianate revival – albeit without the asymmetry.

**Information about Cubitt's work is largely from Hermione Hobhouse, *Thomas Cubitt: Master Builder* (1971, new edn, 1995). Otherwise English Heritage's successive guidebooks to the house, by Michael Turner, are invaluable.

struction which were then well established for industrial buildings (although at Osborne this is, of course, concealed by the internal decorative treatment).

John Blandford, Cubitt's Clerk of Works, continued in that post after 1851, and took over responsibility, in association with *Prince Albert*, for building and maintenance until his death in 1857. The Prince remained in touch with Cubitt, and when he asked the latter to suggest a professional designer to work with him on the reconstruction of the parish church at Whippingham (q.v.), Cubitt recommended the little-known architect *Albert Jenkins Humbert.** Humbert proved to be a very interesting and inventive architect. Following his work at Whippingham, he was probably responsible for several of the more fanciful houses in the S part of the Osborne Estate (see Whippingham). He designed Osborne Cottage, East Cowes (*see* p. 136). His *tour de force* was the Royal Mausoleum at Windsor (1862–71) where he worked with *Ludwig Grüner* (*see* below, p. 207). He also designed part of Sandringham House, Norfolk for the Prince of Wales, from 1870.

After Blandford's death, *John Randall Mann* became Clerk of Works, a post he held until 1892. He too was responsible for Estate buildings, although it is not always clear how this responsibility was divided between him and Humbert. Mann's most considerable works included the new stable block of 1859–60, later converted to the Royal Naval College (*see* p. 212), and the exterior of the Durbar Wing, 1890–1.

Following the Queen's death in 1901, the house became a national, rather then royal, possession. The Main and Household wings were adapted as a convalescent home for officers of the armed services (this use continued until 2000), while the main reception rooms on the ground floor of the Pavilion, together with the Durbar Room, were first opened to the public in 1904. The Queen's private apartments were opened by 1955. English Heritage assumed responsibility for the House and its surroundings in 1984, and has since restored the buildings and gardens very thoroughly.

COMPOSITION AND SETTING

As an architectural composition Osborne has several compo-
69 nents. The first part to be built (1845–6) was the PAVIL-

*Cubitt may have known Humbert through the latter's partnership with C.F. Reeks, who had been a pupil of his brother Lewis Cubitt.

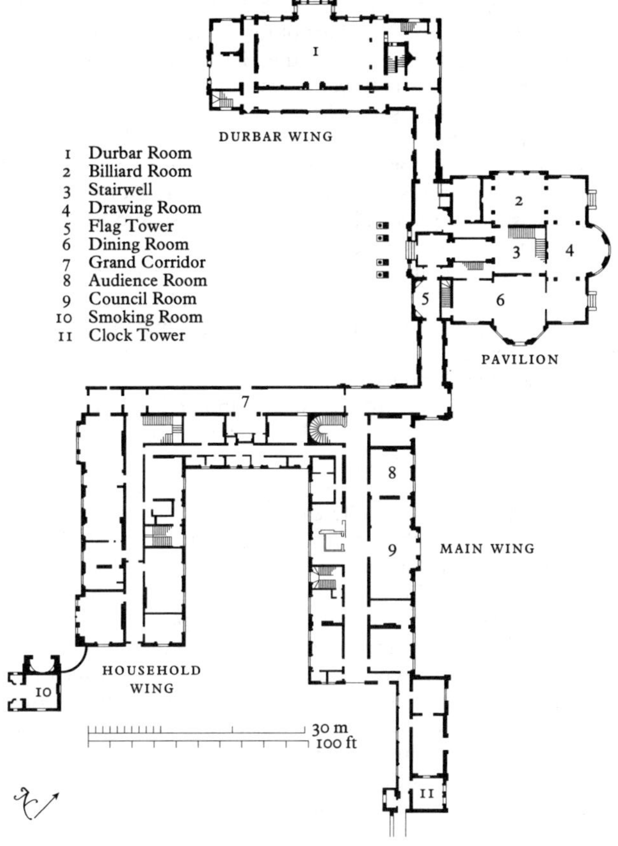

Osborne House, plan.
Courtesy of English Heritage

ION, the Queen's domestic accommodation, relatively modest by royal standards. It is square on plan and three-storeyed, and stands at the NE corner. Provision had to be made to accommodate the Royal Household and guests, and for the conduct of affairs of state when the Queen was in residence. For these a larger complex was erected SW of the Pavilion. This consists of three long ranges, which face W, N and E and back onto a rectangular area open to the S.

(Further S are simpler structures with service accommodation, which do not form part of the main composition.) The ranges facing W and N form the HOUSEHOLD WING built in 1846–7, where the Royal Household was accommodated. The other range is the MAIN WING of 1848–51, facing towards the Solent; it contained the Council Room, and accommodation for important guests. This wing was built over much of the site of the older Osborne House (mainly demolished 1847–8). The Main and Household wings have three main storeys, below which is an extensive service and storage basement, connected with the service facilities in the buildings further S. The angle formed by the Main Wing and the N part of the Household Wing is linked, by a short
69 two-storey range, to one of Osborne's two towers, the FLAG TOWER, which abuts the SW corner of the Pavilion. This is balanced by the CLOCK TOWER standing beyond the S end of the Main Wing, to which it is linked by an externally similar two-storey range.

The House was built on the brow of an irregular slope which descends generally eastward to the Solent, and also less markedly to the NE. The upper parts of this slope were
68 transformed in 1847–54 into a complex series of TERRACES on two levels, with elaborate walling, fountains and statuary. Although each section is formally planned, the variations in the slope means that the collective effect of the Terraces, as the foreground of the House on its eastern side, is irregular. There is a certain ambiguity about the composition of the House itself on this side. The principal part, including the Main Wing and the links with the two towers, is symmetrical, but the Pavilion makes the whole ensemble markedly asymmetrical – an effect emphasized by the form of the Terraces.

The western side of the House never made a dramatic composition comparable to that on the E, partly because of the absence of a notable foreground. The original, fairly effective relationship between Pavilion and Household Wing, at right angles to each other, was transformed by the building in 1890–1 of the DURBAR WING to the NW of the Pavilion. There were now three elements forming an irregular open-ended courtyard. The Durbar Wing was the only substantial addition to the House after *c.* 1851. It was built to contain a room suitable for banquets and similar occasions – embellished inside with Indian references, to commemorate the Queen's title of Empress of India, adopted in 1876.

EXTERIOR

The Queen reached Osborne through the Royal Entrance to the N (*see* Cowes, p. 136), and along an avenue for over ¼ m.

Modern visitors use the side entrance at the junction of York Avenue and Whippingham Road, to the W of the House. The approach from here is fairly long and informal, and initial impressions of Osborne can be confusing. The first part of the House to be seen is the W range of the HOUSEHOLD WING. This has a regular, three-storey, seven-bay main façade where the five central bays are closely grouped, but the two end bays are more widely spaced outward, each with a tripartite window on the ground floor. At the N end of this frontage is a two-storey extension of one bay, slightly set back, with a round-arched doorway which now forms the visitors' entrance.

To reach the original main entrance – in the W front of
the PAVILION – one goes into the open courtyard with the 69
Pavilion at the far end, and the long N range of the Household Wing on the r. These formed an L-shaped composition until the building of the DURBAR WING on the l. in 1890–1. The Pavilion frontage has a central four-columned Tuscan porch of Portland stone, but is otherwise markedly asymmetrical. To the r. of the porch is the Flag Tower (*see* below), and beyond that is the short link to the E end of the Household Wing with a 'Venetian' opening on the upper floor. On the l. of the courtyard a two-storey range, with windows of similar design, links the Durbar Wing with the Pavilion.

The N side of the Household Wing provides the most impressive frontage to the courtyard. Its nine-bay upper storey is set well back from the boldly projecting fronts of the two lower floors. Along the first floor is an eleven-bay loggia fronted by 'Venetian' openings, modelled (like their counterparts flanking the Pavilion entrance) on Palladio's Basilica at Vicenza. On the ground floor are round-arched windows with diamond-cut pilasters; these light the Grand Corridor (*see* Interior).

The Durbar Wing has two-storey elevations by *J.R. Mann*, Clerk of Works to the Estate, in keeping with the rest of the House. There are cornice-like string courses, pilasters between the windows, and a W entrance with a rusticated arch flanked by pairs of columns. This restrained classicism contrasts with the exuberance of the interior.

To see the E frontage of Osborne one has to walk past the N side of the Durbar Wing and then round the NE corner of the Pavilion. This frontage forms a grand ensemble with differing elements. The Pavilion projects at the N end, the long Main Wing provides the central component, and the towers give powerful punctuation. The ground falls in front, its natural contours hugely modified to create the Terraces.

The PAVILION is square in plan, its roof-line emphasized 68
by a bold cornice. With three storeys but only five bays on each side, it is relatively tall for its width. The central part of its E elevation comes out in a bold bow, with a tent-roofed

veranda opening from the Queen's sitting room on the first floor. From here she enjoyed splendid vistas of the Solent. The S elevation has a canted central projection, giving a view over the Terraces from each floor. The Flag Tower abuts the SW corner of the Pavilion, and a short two-storey range (already described from the courtyard side) links it to the Main Wing. This linking range has first-floor openings to the same 'Venetian' design used around the courtyard.

The façade of the MAIN WING is set back from that of the linking range. It is of nine bays, restrained as a whole but varied in details. The ground floor has round-headed windows, rusticated in the Florentine manner. The central window on each floor is tripartite – 'Venetian' on the top storey, pedimented on the storey below, arched and rusticated like the others on the ground floor (where the central window lights the Council Room). At the S end another two-storey range, matching that further N, projects forward and links with the Clock Tower. As already emphasized, the Main Wing, its flanking ranges, and the culminating towers form a bold balanced group to which the Pavilion is strikingly asymmetrical.

The TOWERS are similar to each other but differ in detail and in height. The Clock Tower, 90 ft (28 metres) high, has six unequal stages, all except the penultimate (which contains the clock) with paired round-headed windows. The Flag Tower rises 107 ft (33 metres), and is seen for its full height only on its W side facing the entrance courtyard, where it projects from the frontage of the Pavilion. It is five storeys high, the three lower ones with windows related to those on the Pavilion. The two top storeys rise above the Pavilion roof level; the topmost has three prominent round-arched windows on each side. On both towers are low-pitched pyramid roofs ending in broad eaves with dentils. The bold outlines of these eaves, together with the rounded openings at the tops of the towers, provide the strongest elements in the Osborne skyline.

The E frontage is continued, on a smaller scale, a little way beyond the Clock Tower. A wall with three arched recesses under a balustrade is set back from the alignment of the tower; it conceals a service block behind (*see* below). At its further end is a small square projection with open rounded arches to its N and E. This was Queen Victoria's ALCOVE, where she sat to read or write, or take informal meals, enjoying the sights and scents of the grounds and gardens.

(The SERVICE BUILDINGS to the S, hidden from the E and NE by the wall and Alcove, have a complicated history. The stables of the 1770s belonging to the old house were at first retained, with additions made for kitchen and other purposes under *Cubitt.* They were reconstructed in 1861, mainly for kitchen use, after new stables were built elsewhere (*see* below). The present building is an austere, classically proportioned block in yellow brick round a courtyard open to the W. It is three-storeyed, the lowest storey being at the level of the basement of the Household Wing. Further S is a simple three-storey stuccoed building by *Cubitt*, 1849–50, originally called the Servants' Barracks.)

Finally – to return to the W side of the House – an interesting feature at the SW corner of the Household Wing remains to be mentioned. This is the SMOKING ROOM, a small rectangular structure built in 1866, with an arched entrance facing W. The Queen would not permit smoking anywhere in the House itself; members of the household and even of the royal family who wanted to smoke had to retire here.

INTERIOR

The visitor enters at the NW corner of the Household Wing, passing into the GRAND CORRIDOR which runs along the N side of the wing. It is essentially a gallery of sculptures, many of them set on plinths, under a succession of coffered ceiling panels with intricately detailed cornices and mouldings. These are generally, as elsewhere in the House, in the Regency–Early Victorian manner favoured by *Cubitt* in his grander London houses. The decoration was carried out with the advice of *Ludwig Grüner* in association with *Prince Albert.* Grüner, who came from Dresden, was appointed adviser on art to the Queen in 1845. He designed the interior of a garden pavilion at Buckingham Palace (now destroyed) before working at Osborne and Windsor. At Osborne, contrastingly coloured details on and around the cornices of the Grand Corridor are set off by pale shaded treatment of the coffers and walls. Notably, the Greek key pattern is painted in strong red on the undersides of the beams between the ceiling panels. The effect was completed by elaborately patterned *Minton* floor tiles, now largely protected by carpeting.

Another corridor leads to the r. into the Main Wing, past the COUNCIL ROOM in the centre of its E side. Here the Privy Council met when the Queen was in residence, and important visitors were received. The decoration of the ceiling, together with that in the adjoining AUDIENCE ROOM, was enriched by *Grüner* in 1859.

Back to the Grand Corridor, which turns l., to reach the Pavilion. Visitors are directed into the main reception rooms – the Dining Room and Drawing Room, followed by the

Billiard Room. These are respectively on the S, E and N sides of the ground floor, enclosing a square central stairwell. The Dining Room is set behind the large canted bay window
70 which faces the Terraces. The DRAWING ROOM (the principal room in the house) occupies the whole E frontage of the Pavilion, and is focused on the big rounded bow giving views over the Solent. Its ceiling is divided into three by cross-beams, each supported by two scagliola columns with Corinthian capitals. The ceilings in all the reception rooms are richly detailed in versions of the style of Cubitt's London houses; the broad cavetto bands above the Drawing Room cornices have freely flowing spiral and foliate patterns. The plasterwork was repainted by *Grüner* in 1857; before then the effects may have been less intense. Surprisingly, the fireplaces are relatively simple; they may have come from Cubitt's basic stock. The way in which the reception rooms are aligned at right angles to each other was
71 practical and convenient. The DINING ROOM is partitioned from the Drawing Room with double doors, but the BILLIARD ROOM opens off the Drawing Room with no structural partition other than two scagliola columns, making it in effect an extension of the Drawing Room. It was possible for members of the household, or others, to be in the Billiard Room but out of sight of most of the Drawing Room, so that they were not necessarily required to stand when the Queen was present, as etiquette would normally have demanded. The decoration on the side panels and legs of the billiard table was designed by *Prince Albert.*

The Queen's and Prince's PRIVATE APARTMENTS are on the first floor. Her sitting room is on the E side, with the bow window and veranda. On the top floor is the NURSERY SUITE. The central STAIRWELL is lit from above; its walls have arabesque decoration by *Anthony Muller*, 1861–2, with foliage and figures. A life-size STATUE of Prince Albert by the German sculptor *Emil Wolff*, 1842–4, stands in a round-arched recess at the head of the staircase. The STAIRCASE itself has iron balusters with crowded decoration. The outstanding feature of the stairwell is a FRESCO of 1847 by *William Dyce*, which depicts Neptune resigning the Empire of the Seas to Britannia. (Prince Albert was particularly interested in fresco painting; Dyce was one the artists commissioned for major works, including frescoes, in the rebuilt Houses of Parliament, by a Select Committee set up in 1841 with the Prince as chairman.)

A corridor on the W side of the Pavilion leads past a lift inserted in 1893, and turns into the Durbar Wing, opened
72 in 1891, with its fantastic DURBAR ROOM, used as a banqueting hall. Although the exterior is soberly classical, the main room is lavishly treated in ways which commemorated the Indian empire. *John Lockwood Kipling*, father of

Rudyard Kipling and head of the School of Art in Lahore, directed the internal work in collaboration with *Bhai Ram Singh*, who was on the staff at Kipling's art school and who supervised most of the detailed execution. (Bhai Ram Singh had previously carried out work for the Duke of Connaught at Bagshot Park, Surrey.) *Princess Louise*, Queen Victoria's daughter who had a reputation as a sculptor, also contributed. Intense decoration in traditional Indian styles was applied to the coffered ceiling, including rounded pendants and large flower-shaped panels overlaid with dove-like figures. There is Gothic-seeming decoration in the wide coved cornices. The walls are faced with intricate decoration in plaster and *carton pierre* (a form of papier mâché). The doors and the lower parts of the walls are framed in teak, with plaster panels in intricate relief. There is a so-called MINSTRELS' GALLERY with three richly detailed 72
Moorish-looking arches, the centre one wider and taller. The dominant feature is a sumptuous FIREPLACE on the S side, with an arched overmantel containing a huge representation of an outstretched peacock, designed by *Princess Louise* to represent the Peacock Throne of the former Mogul rulers. The arch is four-centred, at first sight more Gothic-looking than oriental; it rises from imposts supported by triple clusters of columns. The Durbar Room, which provides the climax to tours of the interior, was restored by English Heritage in 2000–1.

THE TERRACES

The Upper and Lower TERRACES provide the foreground on 68
the eastern side. They were formed through excavating the brow and upper part of the declivity towards the Solent; their construction, including retaining walls, was one of the most substantial operations related to the creation of Osborne. *Prince Albert* worked on their layout from 1847, in collaboration with *Cubitt* and *Grüner*; the whole was completed in 1854. Most of the drawings for the retaining walls, stairways and other architectural features – largely finished in cement or stucco – were from Cubitt's office, though some of the more detailed ones are signed by Grüner. Many of the lesser sculptural details in the Terraces – some in cement, others in zinc coated in bronze, a few in granite – were obtained commercially; several are based on classical or Renaissance models.

The Terraces have been thoroughly, and admirably, restored by English Heritage over several years. Because of tree growth, the views from them are not as extensive as in the Queen's time, when they must have contained a very wide stretch of the Solent with its ever-varying vistas of vessels.

The Upper Terrace is in two parts. One part fronts the Main Wing; the other extends E in front of the Pavilion; these are described below. The LOWER TERRACE is in the angle between the upper parts, with a retaining wall topped by balustrades on each side. The W side forms a very Italian composition, with three arched recesses in the centre of the retaining wall, flanked by two-flight stairways, with balustrades, vases and urns. The focal feature of the Lower Terrace is a FOUNTAIN in a circular pool, designed by *Grüner* and surmounted by a statue of Andromeda by *John Bell*, which came from the Great Exhibition. A short flight of steps descends, from each cardinal direction, to the low-lying path which surrounds the pool, and on the platforms bordering the flights are small SCULPTURES representing sea allegories, by *William Theed*, 1858–60. The axis of the Lower Terrace is continued, down steps, as a path across open land to the E. To the S is a PERGOLA of 1855.

The southern part of the UPPER TERRACE, in front of the Main Wing, has a three-tier FOUNTAIN in a circular pool, by *Grüner*. It is the centrepiece of a series of parterres of varying shapes, some circular, others concave-angled, all re-created as part of the restoration scheme. (They had been lost when the terrace was largely grassed over in the early C20.) The section of the Upper Terrace E of the Pavilion has another series of parterres, generally smaller than those of the other part of the terrace, and similarly restored. In the centre is a large vase-like feature by *Grüner*, 1849, with four winged sphinx-like figures around it, all set on a circular base.

Returning to the front of the Main Wing, the Upper Terrace ends southward above a retaining wall. Below this is another formal garden, relatively simply treated. It is reached down the curving HORSESHOE STEPS and through an impressive archway, flanked by pairs of Tuscan pilasters. The garden provides the foreground to a mainly single-storey range to the W. The N part of this range contained the ORANGERY. In 1884 the Queen built a PRIVATE CHAPEL which formed the S part of the range – behind a screen wall previously built to mask the service buildings behind. The whole range was converted into the Terrace Restaurant in 2004.

OUTLYING BUILDINGS

The SWISS COTTAGE, ½m. E of the house, was built in 1853–4 in imitation of an Alpine farmhouse, with broad eaves and first-floor balcony. It was formerly thought to have been prefabricated in Switzerland, but investigation has revealed that the parts were constructed in Britain,

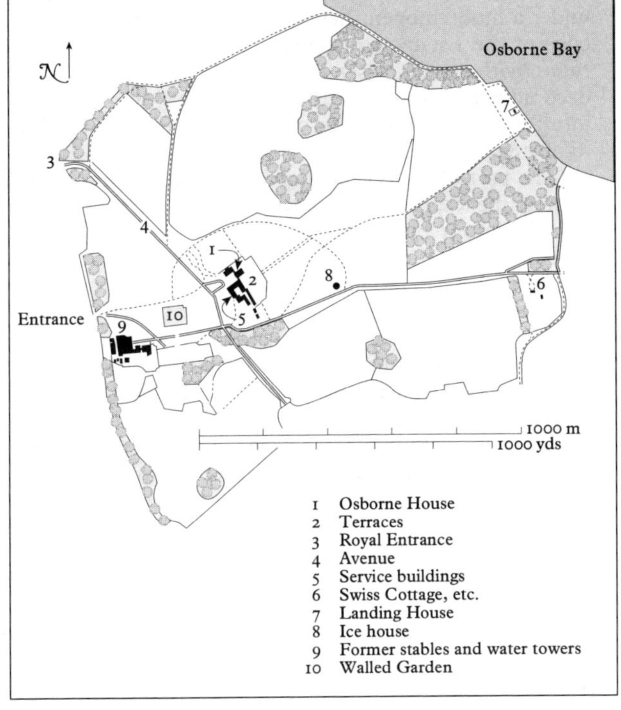

Osborne House.
Estate map

probably on the Osborne Estate, using North American pine. *Prince Albert* intended it to be a place of instruction and recreation for the royal children, where they could learn the rudiments of housekeeping. At first it also accommodated items intended to form a historical collection, but for these a smaller building in similar style was built nearby in 1862 as a MUSEUM. This adjoins a miniature FORT constructed in 1856, in brick with related earthworks – in the manner of the forts built then and later around Portsmouth and Gosport on the Hampshire mainland. To this a model BARRACKS was added in brick in 1860. (The miniature fort and barracks were built of small bricks specially made in the Estate brickworks.) All these features are set in and around a domestic garden (recently restored), which was established in 1850 for use by the royal children, enabling them to learn the principles of productive as well as ornamental gardening.

The Queen's BATHING MACHINE is preserved nearby under a modern open shelter. It stood on the beach at the edge of the Estate (*see* below), and contained a changing room (with a water closet fed by a tank), and a balcony with decorative iron supports. It ran on wheels over stone rails into the sea. The Queen recorded her first use of the facility in 1847.

(The part of the Solent shore nearest to the house, over ½ m. to the NE, is reached down a wooded valley. There are two significant buildings. The Queen's Alcove is a small semicircular, half-domed structure facing the sea, colourful inside. Nearby is the more substantial LANDING HOUSE of 1855–6, which stood at the landward end of a former jetty used by vessels bringing the Queen and others to and from Osborne. It was designed by *John Blandford*, Clerk of Works to the Estate. Pevsner considered it very original in its form and wrote: 'The centre is an Italianate tower with far-projecting eaves, with two bays to the l. and two to the r., and a top terrace. A curved outer staircase in two flights leads up to the house.' The Landing House is not in the area owned by English Heritage; it is a private house, not easily seen except from the Solent.)

Between the main house and the Swiss Cottage is a former ICE HOUSE constructed by *Cubitt* in 1845. It is a domed brick structure, to which a Classical entrance feature with rusticated arch was added in 1853.

(Just inside the present entrance to the grounds from York Avenue/Whippingham Road, S of the approach to Osborne House, is a group of buildings which began as the STABLE BLOCK in 1859–60, was adapted for the Royal Naval College which operated 1903–21, and has since been put to varied uses. The block of 1859–60, designed by *J.R. Mann* (*see* p. 202) in association with *Prince Albert*, consisted of four ranges in rendered brick around a courtyard. The new buildings and alterations for the college were mainly designed by *H.N. Hawks* of the Office of Works, who died in 1911. In the Second World War the buildings were leased by Saunders-Roe, the aircraft and marine firm. Most of the wartime and later structures have now been demolished. Parts of the buildings can be seen from the approach road. The exterior of the EASTERN RANGE of the stable block substantially remains, altered and enlarged. As *Mann* designed it, the range had a gabled centrepiece with a round-arched entrance, above which was a Venetian window on each frontage. The flanking parts, at first single-storeyed, were made two-storey for the college under *Hawks*, who replaced the Venetian window on the E side by a tripartite window. Hawks also designed the single-storey COCHRANE BUILDING of 1905, SE of the eastern range, which has features related to Edwardian 'Old English', including pebbledashed walls and gables with half-timbering.)

WATER TOWERS. The most conspicuous buildings on the former Royal Naval College site, visible from Whippingham Road. They date from 1903 and 1913, but are very similar; the earlier is by *Hawks*, the other by the *Naval Architects' Department*. Each has two lower storeys of pebbledashed brick, and an upper storey, containing the tank, which has applied half-timbering and is jettied (this seems an appropriate term), with corbels underneath. The towers are topped by domestic-looking roofs with tiling and hips.

THE WALLED GARDEN

The Walled Garden, W of the main house, was the KITCHEN GARDEN of the older Osborne House. Later in Victoria's reign the emphasis was more on growing flowers for use in the house. The C18 brick walls were heightened in 1848 under *Cubitt*, including a stuccoed dentilled cornice with rusticated pilasters, topped by ball finials. A substantial porch with open pediment was added, containing a wide arch with alternating stonework, re-set from the old house. Within the porch is an entrance feature also from the old house: a tripartite composition with pilasters flanked by narrow lights, and a fanlight above.

(The walled area has been restored, including two lean-to GLASSHOUSES of 1854. A new area of GARDEN was added in 2000 to the design of *Rupert Goldby*, in which fruit and flowers favoured in Victorian times are grown.)

PARKHURST *see* NEWPORT

QUARR ABBEY *5590*

Ryde

The ancient Quarr Abbey was founded in 1132 by Baldwin de Redvers, lord of the Island, for monks from Savigny in France – of an order which became part of the Cistercian Order in 1147. It took its name from long-established quarries nearby (*see* Binstead). The abbey passed in 1536 to John Mill, a Southampton merchant; the buildings were nearly all demolished, some of the stone being used for fortifications elsewhere. The site has since been largely vacant. Excavations in the 1890s established most of the plan and recovered many fragments. The modern Quarr Abbey, on a site slightly to the NW of the ancient abbey, dates from the years before the First World War.

The remains of the medieval abbey are described first, followed by an account of the truly remarkable buildings of the modern monastery.

THE MEDIEVAL ABBEY

What survives indicates a set of buildings of early to mid-C13 date, suggesting reconstruction a century or so after the abbey was founded, with few later alterations. The CHURCH had a typical Cistercian plan: nave with narrow aisles, transepts each with three E chapels, and a short presbytery to which side chapels were added later. Almost nothing of the church remains above ground; the lane from the N part of Binstead towards the modern abbey runs over the site of the S arcade and aisle. The CLOISTER and MONASTIC BUILDINGS were to the N of the church, contrary to usual practice; this arrangement was probably related to water supplies.

Fronting the lane on the N side, just W of the church site, is a small early to mid-C19 former FARMHOUSE with sets of triple lancet windows and a wide Gothic arch in the centre of its façade; these are partly imitation features but may include re-set medieval details. The house backs on to a building aligned N–S, for long used as a barn. This is basically the range which abutted the cloister on its W side, although the upper parts have been reconstructed. There are blocked doors and other openings and, on the E side, an addition containing the entrance to the barn. This has in its gable a genuine, but re-set, triple lancet window with tall central member – one the few aesthetically rewarding details on the site.

Otherwise the site contains a few irregular pieces of WALLING. One fragment survives between the site of the refectory, on the N side of the cloister, and the small kitchen to its W, including a hatch with a moulded segmental arch. Fairly substantial walling at the N end of the site may relate to the abbot's lodging. Towards the E is a section of the N wall of a building which may have been the infirmary chapel, with the fairly well-preserved ribbed internal frame of a rounded window. Percy Stone, who excavated the site, included in his *Architectural Antiquities* imaginative reconstructions of parts of the abbey based on the ground plan and surviving fragments.

The precinct was surrounded by a DEFENSIVE WALL after licence to crenellate was given in 1365, in the period of French attacks. Parts of this survive.

THE MODERN ABBEY

The modern abbey was begotten by Benedictine monks from 77
Solesmes, near Le Mans, who came to England in 1901 as a result of anti-clerical legislation in France. They settled temporarily in the mansion at Appuldurcombe (q.v.). In 1907 they bought QUARR HOUSE, a rambling, largely Victorian house W of the old abbey site, and new buildings soon rose beside the house. They were designed by *Dom Paul Bellot* (1876–1944), whose father was the French equivalent of a surveyor, and who studied architecture at the École des Beaux Arts in Paris. He took his diploma in 1900, but decided for a monastic life. In 1902 he became a novice in the community of monks at Appuldurcombe; he took his vows in 1904. However, the Order directed him back to architecture; he was commissioned in 1906 to design a new church at Oosterhout, Holland, where other monks from Solesmes had settled. Shortly afterwards he was called back to the Isle of Wight to design the first new monastic buildings at Quarr, including the present cloister, refectory and chapter house, together with dormitory accommodation. These were started in 1907, and were sufficiently complete for the monks to move to Quarr in mid 1908 (using at first a temporary wooden church moved from Appuldurcombe).*

The ABBEY CHURCH was built to *Bellot*'s design during p. 216
1911–12 – a remarkably short time considering its size and complexity, and the fact that it was fully completed. Bellot's last work at Quarr was the ENTRANCE BLOCK, including guest accommodation, S and SW of the cloister, finished in 1914. After the First World War he worked in Holland, France and Canada, where he died. His later monastic buildings developed his style and methods of construction with great inventiveness, but Quarr, in Pevsner's words, 'is his outstanding achievement'. The abbey church has, without any doubt, the finest interior of any building on the Island.

Bellot's style was related to Expressionism, the artistic and architectural movement which developed in northern Europe before the First World War, and became most influential around 1920. Expressionism emphasized importance of form rather than indication of function in the design of buildings, and encouraged the creation of impressive, sometimes dramatic, effects through sculptural shapes and conspicuous features. Holland and Germany were the main early centres; the Dutch architects Berlage and de Klerk

*The main body of monks returned to Solesmes in 1922, but some remained to form the basis for the present community, to which separate status was granted in 1937.

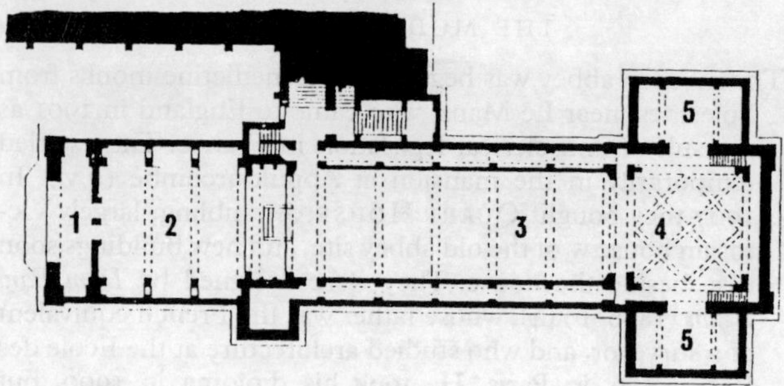

key
1. porch
2. congregation
3. monks' choir
4. sanctuary
5. chapel

Quarr Abbey, plan of the church.
From *Architectural Review* vol. 141, 1967

were influential. There were also indirect relationships with the works of Gaudí in Barcelona. But Expressionism declined in importance as the Modern Movement, with its emphases on function and structure, developed.

In its heyday Expressionism made little obvious impact in England. When Pevsner visited Quarr Abbey in the mid 1960s he was therefore astonished by the architecture of the abbey church, of which he wrote: 'It is built of Belgian bricks, rough, unattractive bricks, bricks others would have tried to hide. It is high and long and high again, and its plan is wholly original. It consists of a short and low nave, then, a few steps up, a long choir with bare side walls, very narrow side passages (like Gaudí's corridors at the college of St Teresa at Barcelona), and ampler galleries above, and then an altar space under a high square tower. Everything is of the same brick, externally and internally. Externally the low nave looks like a Cluniac ante-church or a narthex; for it is followed by the high S tower, the low N tower, and much high bare wall between. The square tower at the E end is not as high as the S tower but mighty in its square volume and overwhelmingly blunt in its marking the E end of the whole building.

'Paul Bellot was a virtuoso in brick. All is brick and all has to be done angularly; for such is the brick's nature. Instead of pointed arches triangular heads. Stepped gables for the low façade of the church and for the entrance to the abbey, cut-back friezes and stepped patterns of all kinds. They are again curiously reminiscent of Gaudí. Inside the church, and also the chapter house and the refectory, Paul Bellot repeats one powerful motif: transverse pointed brick

arches carrying the roofs, and that is a Catalan motif as well, used in religious and secular architecture and especially similar to Quarr in the Cistercian abbey of Poblet. But it is also present in such South French Cistercian buildings as Le Thoronet. But Spain altogether must have impressed
Paul Bellot most; for the tremendous arches inside the E 78
tower of the church, dazzling with the arched openings pierced in the spandrels, are inspired in their crossing – two diagonal ribs and four running from the middle of one side to the middle of the next – by the Mosque at Cordova. The way in which the four immensely high narrow windows in the E wall are cut into by the ribs in the tower and the series of open arches in the spandrels is brilliant indeed and establishes Dom Paul Bellot beyond doubt as one of the pioneers of C20 Expressionism.'

Pevsner's concise and pungent account deserves elaboration and further comment. Although the nave is relatively low and short it has a dramatic W elevation with a broad pointed arch, moulded and without capitals, opening into a shallow porch-like space. Above the arch a series of inset panels, stepped at their tops, rises into the boldly stepped gable. The southern tower (in fact at the SW corner of the boldly massed choir) is a dominant feature, with long inset panels on its exposed sides; it is surmounted by a circular, columned bell-turret ending in a cone, the tallest feature of the composition. The E tower is not so high as the S tower, but seen from the E (not a usual viewpoint for visitors) it is a tremendous composition, with massive squared corner turrets, machicolated parapet and four very tall thin windows in the E wall, square at their tops but set within broader arched panels.

Inside, the nave is more complex than its exterior suggests. There are transverse arches at close intervals, and narrow flanking arches to every bay, each in triple recession. A few steps lead up to the choir with its stark lower walls (concealing the narrow passages which Pevsner mentioned). The sanctuary has a cruciform internal shape with four great arches within the space of the E tower; they rise from respond capitals made of concrete. The spandrels and wall spaces above the arches are pierced by lancet-shaped openings. These contribute to the effect of the axial vista where the E crossing arch, with the pierced wall above it, cuts into the view of the high narrow windows beyond. But Bellot's ultimate *tour de force*, the view up into the tower space above the sanctuary, with its fantastic interplay of arches supporting the roof, cannot be appreciated until one is right at the E end.*

*Visitors to the church normally enter the nave, and see the sanctuary only from a distance. The eastern part is not generally accessible.

The ENTRANCE BLOCK of 1913–14, including guest accommodation, has a stepped gable with square-topped panels – a development of the pattern over the W church entrance (to which it stands at a right angle). Otherwise the cloister and related accommodation are as *Bellot* finished them *c.* 1908, with the refectory to the W, the old adapted Quarr House at the NW corner, and three-storeyed residential blocks on the E side and the E part of the N side. The CLOISTER has plain external arches on three elevations, in a not entirely regular pattern, and transverse arches within; the range to the S (which is related to the entrance block) has strange three-light ground-floor openings with diamond-shaped upper tracery. The REFECTORY has transverse arches brought out in alternating patterns with slightly lighter and darker bricks; the capitals and corbels are in concrete, as is a single free-standing shaft. The CHAPTER HOUSE, on the E side behind the residential block, has simpler transverse arches.

5080 ROOKLEY

A C19–C20 village. The brickworks, closed *c.* 1974, were the last to operate on the Island. Former SCHOOL and school house on the NE side of the A3020, *c.* 1846 – ambitious for what was then a very small place (formerly in Arreton parish). In rough stone with red brick dressings; mainly one-storeyed, but with a two-storeyed gabled centre containing a Tuscan columned porch. PIDFORD MANOR, W of the main road to the N, has a five-bay mid- to late C18 front in red brick. Doorcase with open pediment over an arched doorway. (Inside is a Chinese Chippendale well staircase; there is a similar staircase in CHAMPION FARMHOUSE, ⅔ m. NW of the village: DCMS list.)

5590 RYDE

Ryde is a 'period' town of the Regency–Victorian overlap. There were originally two small villages; Lower Ryde by the seashore, and Upper Ryde which straggled along the line of the present High Street about ½ m. inland. Fashionable villas with seaward views began to be built in the surrounding area before 1800. In 1780 William Player, the main landowner, laid out what is now Union Street linking the two villages, but little was built along it until 1810 when restrictions against long-term leases were ended. The foreshore at Lower Ryde had for long been the landing place for small boats from Portsmouth. In 1814 the first pier was built, hugely improving access.

Ryde, view from the sea, engraving of 1840.
From George Brannon, *Brannon's Picture of the Isle of Wight*, *c.* 1844

Regular steam ferries to Portsmouth operated from 1825. Population grew from *c.* 600 in 1801 to nearly 3,000 in 1821 and *c.* 9,300 in 1861. New streets were laid out, forming a not wholly regular grid on the slopes and over the plateau above. They were built up piecemeal on leasehold plots. The Player Estate was split, and by the mid C19 two families, the Linds and the Brigstockes, owned much of the town between them.

Two London-based architects contributed to Ryde's early development. *William Westmacott*, of the family famous for
sculpture, designed the internally superb Royal Victoria 55
Arcade of 1835–6, and *James Sanderson* (†1835) the original
Town Hall, the monumental Brigstocke Terrace, and the 59, 54
church of St Thomas (and St Clare, a castellated mansion E of the town now demolished). There were no architects based in the town with known works of before *c.* 1840. A distinctive early to mid-C19 local tradition developed for simple, basically classical frontages, often with plain pilasters. Tripartite windows became common, as did bay windows with flat fronts and curved glazing at the ends. Some houses have bold bows rising through two floors. Iron balconies and verandas were common, as elsewhere; in Ryde a fairly high proportion have survived, including several two-storey examples. The universal buff brick and stucco are varied in places by rough local limestone. But by the mid C19 the design of houses in Ryde generally followed national rather than specifically local traditions. Osborne, however, had its influence, especially in the fashion for Italianate prospect towers attached to houses.

Few Victorian designers of national importance are represented: *Sir George Gilbert Scott* (All Saints' church), *Joseph
Hansom* (St Mary, R.C.) and *S.S. Teulon* (Woodlands Vale on 65

the E outskirts). But two very individualistic architects, *Thomas Hellyer* and *R.J. Jones*, practised from the town.
61 Hellyer's delicate spire of Holy Trinity and Scott's grander steeple of All Saints are important features in the skyline. A contrasting landmark is the cupola added to the Town Hall in 1868 by another local architect, *Thomas Dashwood.*

Resort development slowed down for a time after the mid 1860s, when the railway opened linking Ryde with Sandown, Shanklin and Ventnor, where subsequent seaside growth was faster. By *c.* 1970 much of the town was in a shabby state, with two of its finest buildings, the Royal Victoria Arcade and Brigstocke Terrace, in a deplorable condition. Since then, Ryde has visibly smartened, and these buildings have been restored. Walks along the many streets built up piecemeal during the early years now provide pleasurable experiences for those who appreciate good architecture and townscape.*

CHURCHES

The church history of Ryde is curious. The town was at the N end of the very long parish of Newchurch which stretched across the Island, with its church about 5m. away. In 1719 Thomas Player built the first, rural, St Thomas as a privately owned Anglican chapel to serve the then small villages. It was rebuilt in 1827 when the town was fast developing. In the same year St James, also a private chapel, opened. The first regular Anglican churches were Holy Trinity and St John in the 1840s, followed by St Michael in the 1860s. In 1872 All Saints was consecrated as the new main parish church – a sign of the prosperity and pride of what had become a considerable town. The Roman Catholics built the remarkable St Mary from the 1840s. Two substantial Victorian Nonconformist churches, Baptist and Methodist, remain in the centre (a third, originally Congregational, was demolished in 1974).

ALL SAINTS, prominent at the junction of Queen's Road and West Street. By *Sir George Gilbert Scott*, 1869–72; tower and spire 1881–2 by *J. Oldrid Scott.* Large, conventional High Victorian in rough Swanage stone. Aisled nave with three-gabled W front; chancel with shorter chapel (and later accretions) to the S. The steeple, on the N side of the chancel, has a complicated outline, with two tiers of pinnacles, and sharply gabled lucarnes on the spire. The window tracery is elaborately Geometrical; an intended clerestory was never built. The N porch is lavish, with large pinnacles, statues in niches and a deeply moulded doorway. This specially rich treatment is explained by the fact that the Royal Victoria

*I owe a great deal to Mr Roy Brinton, who has studied the town over many years, and has provided a huge amount of detailed information.

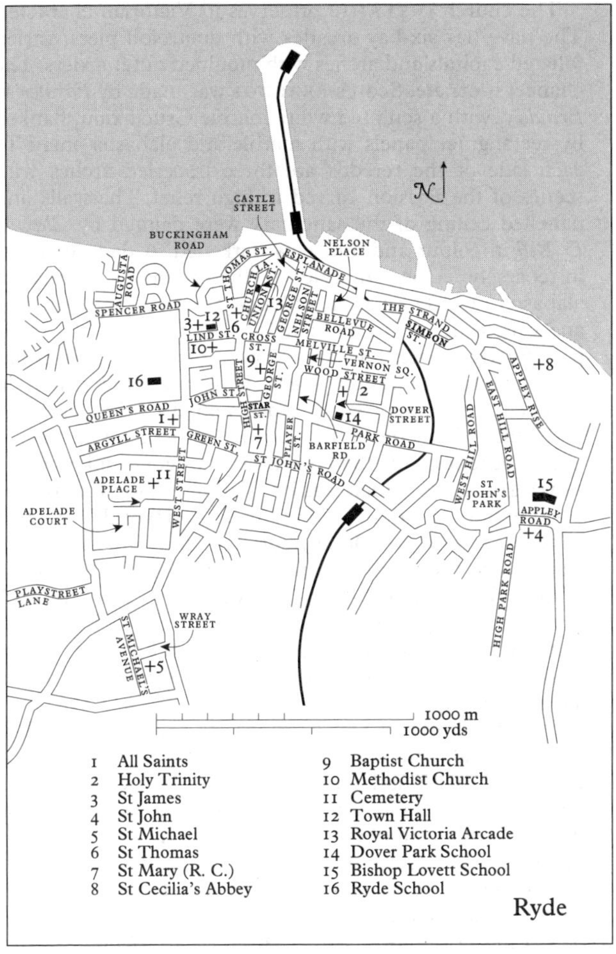

Yacht Club paid towards its building, in memory of Prince Albert.

A fairly substantial VESTRY was added to the SE in 1892 by *C. Pemberton Leach.* It is an elongated octagon with three-light windows, parapet and steeply sloping roofs, linked to the S chapel by a short covered way; it accords well with the church when seen from the SE. An early and successful example of the kind of accretion which has frequently, and often inappropriately, been made to older churches in more recent times.

The church INTERIOR preserves its Victorian character. The nave has six-bay arcades with quatrefoil piers, varied foliated capitals and arches with moulded outer orders. The chancel is ornate. Scott's REREDOS was made by *Farmer & Brindley*, with a sculpted white marble Crucifixion, flanked by rectangular panels with marble and alabaster inlay. To each side of the reredos are three traceried arches with scenes of the Passion carved in high relief. The walls and panelled ceiling of the sanctuary were painted by *Clayton & Bell* in colour and gilt, now darkened. A dado of 1905, in coarsely veined marble, is discordant. – Octagonal alabaster PULPIT by *Scott*, with black marble angle columns and carved figures in the panels. – *Scott*'s FONT of 1872 is particularly ornate. The circular bowl of white alabaster has four sculpted figures of angels with quatrefoil panels in between; it is supported by black veined marble columns. Ogee-shaped wooden FONT COVER with elaborate tracery and crocketing, of 1886 or after; designer unknown. – STAINED GLASS. Much was by *Clayton & Bell*; that on the S and W sides was destroyed in the Second World War. Their large E window (Te Deum) survives, and three four-light windows in the N aisle are probably by them. – Window E of the N door by *Ion Pace*, 1913; a Nativity, with limited dark shades against a generally paler background. – Five-light W window by *Lawrence Lee*, 1951, a lively and colourful composition depicting Christ in Glory amid smaller figures set against plain glass.

W of the church is *Scott*'s former VICARAGE of 1871. It is asymmetrical, with two uneven gables facing N and two E; in red brick with dark bands and diagonal brick pattern on part of the N side. Windows plain and square-topped, doorway with a simple wooden porch with Gothic arch. NE of the church, close to the road intersection, is the WAR MEMORIAL of 1921, with a tapering stem topped by a short shaft containing a crucifix under a small gable.

61 HOLY TRINITY, Dover Street. By *Thomas Hellyer.* Started 1841, but mainly built 1844–6, with aisled nave, W tower and broach spire, and chancel with polygonal apse. S transept added 1848, N transept 1860. Paired lancets in the aisles; single lancets in the apse. The steeple is a masterpiece, because of its general proportions and the relationship of detailed features to the whole. The spire, unusually, has tall pinnacles rising from the broaches at the angles. It also has sharply gabled lucarnes – one to each of the eight sides of the spire, and not, as normal, on the cardinal sides only. The set-back buttresses of the tower are well-proportioned. All these features give the steeple a specially distinctive outline.*

*The pinnacles were removed during repairs of 1963, but when the tower was again restored in 1968 under *John F. Ford* new pinnacles were erected to the old design.

Internally the church is more ordinary. The arcades have slender quatrefoil piers and moulded arches, all now painted. Thin roof timbers. – FONT. Octagonal, with a triangular panel and dense carving in the spandrels on each side. – HIGH ALTAR by *Jones & Willis*, 1894; of wood with traceried panels. – REREDOS by *Cox, Buckley & Co.*, 1898. Three panels with painted scenes, smaller side panels, and pinnacles. – Another REREDOS in S chapel by *F.E. Howard* of Oxford, 1922. Five panels with carved scenes under traceried canopies. – STAINED GLASS. Lancets in apse by *Powell's*, 1913. S chapel E window by *Francis Skeat*, 1916.

ST JAMES, Lind Street, W of the Town Hall. Opened 1827 as p. 44 a proprietary chapel – which it still is. By *Greenway Robins* of Walworth, London. His was a gimcrack design, more sugary than nearby St Thomas, with an embattled S elevation, aisle windows in two tiers under external four-centred arches, and an elaborate W front with prominent doorway under a gabled pinnacled turret. The church was restored by *R.P. Thomas* in 1968–9, when it was stripped of external details and decorative features, apart from the turret. This was later removed, leaving the church looking like a simple hall with low-pitched roof and, under the W gable, a feature with intersecting curves, supposed to represent a fish. But the interior is a surprise – it is still that of a pre-Ecclesiological church, with side GALLERIES supported on piers which continue up more thinly to four-centred arches. The W gallery contains the organ. The BOX PEWS have triangular-headed end panels and simple finials, which together just suggest Gothic. The E end has a simple wooden TRIPTYCH with cusped central panel inscribed 'Till He Come' in Gothic lettering. The PULPIT, to the S, is square with canted angles; and panels with triangular motifs reminiscent of the pews.

Attached to the E end, a CHURCH HALL, with gabled end projecting towards the street. It is stuccoed with a three-light window, approximately Perp, and a small porch with four-centred doorway. This must have been added soon after the church was finished; the exterior survived the alterations of 1968–9.

ST JOHN, Appley Road and High Park Road, in the outer E part of the town. The first church of 1843, by *Hellyer*, was aisle-less and cruciform, with lancets and W bellcote. The W front and most of the large transepts survive from then. The former has a triple window with taller central lancet, and the bellcote has two arches under a steep gable. The S aisle was added in 1864 and the N aisle in 1879, still by *Hellyer*, with small two-light W windows. The most interesting parts are to the E. The S chapel, with lower vestries abutting to E and S, was built in 1914 by *W.D. Caröe*. It has simple three-light windows over the roof-lines of the vestries, and a finely moulded two-bay arcade opening into the chancel, with no intermediate capital. The chancel was extended E in 1953–4; Hellyer's triple E lancets were re-set. Above them is a strange wheel window with thin tapering spokes and a hollow hub, which existed by 1914 in the original wall – was this also by Hellyer? Tall pointed niches on either side of the window. – Wooden COMMUNION RAILS with band of open quatrefoils. – STAINED GLASS. Two two-light windows, N aisle, by *Lavers & Westlake*, 1903.

ST MICHAEL, Wray Street and St Michael's Avenue, Swanmore, S of the town centre. The main part 1861–3 and later by the *Rev. William Grey* in conjunction with *R.J. Jones*; E end by *Jones* alone, 1873–4.* Big and serious; cruciform with a flat-topped tower (a spire was intended), aisles, and polygonal apse; lancets throughout. The exterior is in rough
64 Swanage stone with ashlar dressings; the interior is very different, with its varied materials. The nave and aisle walls have brick patterns in yellow, red, blue and black, with circular panels in the spandrels containing crosses in different forms. The nave arches are of stone, with thin chamfers and no proper capitals; the piers are octagonal, their diagonal faces making the transitions with the square-section arches by means of hollowed trefoils. The crossing arches are more ornate, with foliage capitals, carved by *Farmer & Brindley*, on short marble shafts resting on corbels. The crossing space acts as the chancel, with the sanctuary in the apse. This is faced in stone and vaulted with thin marble shafts in the angles. Triple sedilia with marble columns form a fourfold composition with an adjoining arched opening. – Low stone SCREEN across the W crossing arch, with colour-painted figures in trefoil niches between marble shafts; the polygonal stone PULPIT to the N has similar niches and figures. – Suspended ROOD by *F.E. Howard*, 1930. – STAINED GLASS. Most of the C19 windows were destroyed in the Second World War, but three figures by *Lavers & Westlake*, 1884–6, remain in the apse.

The former CLERGY HOUSE of 1862 by *Grey* and *Jones* is to the ENE of the church. From the garden on the S side, a mainly two-storey composition of six bays in Swanage stone with brick bands (an unusual combination). But the third bay from the W rises by an extra storey, under a short-hipped roof. The first-floor windows are low casements, except that of the taller bay, which is a pair under round brick arches – as is the ground-floor window underneath. A substantial canted bay window on the ground floor at the W end completes the irregular composition. The N elevation, facing Wray Street, looks more awkward; it is set back

*The Rev. William Gray was an amateur architect; he designed Rownhams church near Southampton.

Ryde, St Thomas, with Brigstocke Terrace behind.
Engraving by George Brannon, 1828

behind a wall of stone and brick. A porch contains two entrances, each under a gable.

ST THOMAS, off the S end of St Thomas Street. Restored and adapted as a public hall. The first chapel of 1719 was simple and rural; *James Sanderson*'s replacement of 1827–8 is pre-Ecclesiological Gothic. Of local limestone (unusually with yellow brick dressings), with castellated roof-lines, tall two-light nave windows (transomed because of the galleries within), and a rectangular W tower, wider from N to S, which lost its spire in 1951. The W front is complex; the tower is flanked by low-gabled projections ending slightly in front of it. Three W doors, each four-centred, the outer ones originally to gallery stairs. Over the central door, a plaque with the Player coat of arms – they and their successors, the Brigstockes, were proprietors of the church into the C20.

Remarkable interior of one broad span with low-pitch open-panelled trusses. The GALLERIES have simple patterned fronts on thin iron columns. BOX PEWS survive under the galleries, but the central space (which had later C19 pews) has been cleared. The E end is a strange mixture. Under the triple-lancet E window, with STAINED GLASS of 1888 by *Alexander Booker*, are three panels in memory of Mary Harriette Player Brigstocke, †1894, owner of the chapel, with texts below of the Creed, Commandments and Lord's Prayer, characteristic of early C19 Anglican churches. – MONUMENT to Vice-Admiral Locke, †1835, with the stern of a warship in a turbulent sea. – ROYAL ARMS, W gallery, of William III (i.e. from before the first chapel was built).

In the former CHURCHYARD are C18 and early C19 TOMBSTONES, some with shaped tops and intricate stem and scroll patterns.

ST MARY (R.C.), High Street (towards the S end). By *Joseph Hansom*, 1846–8; a 'rogue' Gothic design from one of the most versatile C19 architects; founded and well endowed by the Countess of Clare. The W frontage to the narrow street is a wild composition. The central part has three sharp lancets in densely moulded frames, a vesica above, and a deeply recessed doorway; the S aisle has a triangular window in its gable. The tower is *sui generis*, rising from the street front N of the doorway, and diminishing to a slender upper stage with a short stone spire. The N aisle originally ended a few feet back, but was brought forward to the street in the 1880s, with a range of seven tightly spaced lancets and a porch further N.

65 The interior is also individualistic. The arcades have slender round piers, and depressed arches which spring from short vertical pieces above the capitals, but these are contained within arched recesses which rise much higher and include quatrefoiled circles. The chancel arch is tall and thickly moulded; the chancel roof has transverse arched braces, brought out in paint and gilt, and the high E window is a trefoiled circle. The High Altar is a 1970s replacement, but behind it is a wall arcade with eight triangular panels, each with a pair of trefoiled arches below. The S chapel (LADY CHAPEL), added in 1893, has an ALTAR with carved panels, attributed to Pugin – presumably *P.P. Pugin*, although possibly based on A.W.N. Pugin's drawings. The chapel walls and roof have elaborate PAINTINGS, including narrative scenes, by *Nathaniel Westlake,* carried out in 1894. The chapel roof is extraordinary: it is pitched; each side is divided by wooden ribs into twelve panels in three tiers; the lower two tiers have painted scenes; the upper tier on each side is glazed. Much of the painted decoration was restored by *Marianne Rodrigues c.* 1993. She also repainted the Stations of the Cross in the N aisle, originally by *Westlake*. The CHAPEL OF THE SACRED HEART, 1898, with a five-sided apse, ribbed vault and lancets, opens at a right angle from the N aisle through a moulded arch with marble columns.

STAINED GLASS. Many windows of *c.* 1880–5 by *Westlake*, including the lancets of the S aisle, variedly colourful, culminating in an Assumption in the SE aisle window based on a painting by Murillo. The E window commemorates the Countess of Clare, †1879; the Sacred Heart, and the Countess's coat-of-arms held by an angel. The sevenfold window at the W end of the N aisle depicts the Sacraments.

The PRESBYTERY, 1863, is built against the E end of the church on descending ground; another wild composition, partly of three storeys plus attic, with an asymmetrical assortment of windows including a two-sided bay.

ST CECILIA'S ABBEY, Appley Rise, near the E end of the seafront. Developed from APPLEY HOUSE, erected in 1726 and altered in the early C19 (not generally accessible; it has a stuccoed garden front with central canted bay). This was enlarged in 1878–9 for a boarding school. In 1906 the buildings were taken by nuns who, like the monks at Quarr (q.v.), had been exiled from Solesmes, and who returned to France in 1922. They were succeeded by a community of nuns established on the Island in 1882. The CHURCH of 1906–7 was designed by *Edward Goldie* in a very conservative style, with tall lancets and a W tower topped by a wooden louvred belfry under a pyramid roof. The walls are of buff brick, externally and internally. A short nave with transverse segmental ribs opens into a central space with a free-standing altar of 1970; the E end is polygonal. A large S transept, lit by paired Geometrical windows, contains the nuns' stalls, with gallery and organ at the far end.

BAPTIST CHURCH, near the S end of George Street. By *Francis Newman*, 1862. Tall Gothic street front in buff brick with red trimmings; five-light window with Geometrical tracery; corner turret rising in two stages to a spirelet.

METHODIST CHURCH, Garfield Road. By *Charles Bell*, 1883. Striking main front facing S; the central window, set within a semicircular arch, has elaborate wheel tracery above round-topped lower lights. Below is a pair of doorways inside another arch, also rounded, all under a low gable. Low wings with sloping roofs flank either side. A smaller church hall in the same manner is attached to the E.

CEMETERY. *See* Outer Ryde: West, p. 245.

PUBLIC BUILDINGS

Described, as follows, in the Perambulations and in the accounts of Outer Ryde, East and West.

TOWN HALL. *See* Perambulation 1, p. 228.
ROYAL VICTORIA ARCADE. *See* Perambulation 1, p. 230.
FREE SCHOOL, Melville Street. *See* Perambulation 2, p. 235.
DOVER PARK SCHOOL. *See* Perambulation 2, p. 236.
PAVILION, Esplanade. *See* Perambulation 2, p. 238.
RYDE PIER. *See* Perambulation 2, p. 238.
ST JOHN'S ROAD SCHOOL. *See* Perambulation 3, p. 240.
BISHOP LOVETT SCHOOL. *See* Outer Ryde: East, p. 242.
RYDE SCHOOL. *See* Outer Ryde: West, p. 244.
Former NATIONAL SCHOOL, Green Street. *See* Outer Ryde: West, p. 245.

PERAMBULATIONS

Three Perambulations, each starting at or near the Town Hall. Perambulation 1 goes generally to the N and NW, Perambulation 2 to the E and NE, and Perambulation 3 to the S.

1. North and North-West: Lind Street, Union Street and Spencer Road

59 The TOWN HALL was built in 1829–31 by *James Sanderson* for the Improvement Commissioners, newly formed to manage the facilities of the growing town. In 1867–8 it was enlarged by *Francis Newman,* Town Surveyor, and a tower rising from roof level, with a tall cupola, was added at the same time to the design of *Thomas Dashwood.* The original part of the building has an impressive upper storey with a tetrastyle Ionic portico and pediment, standing on a basement which projects over the pavement. The portico was at first free-standing, spanning less than the width of the upper storey, but in the 1867–8 enlargement the flanking façades were brought forward, so that the portico now stands *in antis*. The basement was intended for markets; it has a short open frontage to the street with Doric columns. When first built, the town hall must have

Ryde, Town Hall, before enlargement.
Early C19 lithograph, after Whittock

seemed surprisingly grand for a town of still modest size and recent growth.

At first there were long single-storey wings bordering the street. In 1867–8 the E wing was reconstructed and heightened, with an upper storey as tall as that of the original building. The western part of this wing has five recessed arches, containing smaller windows, on the upper floor. The eastern end is brought forward slightly, with engaged Ionic columns, and there is a handsome E elevation, also with Ionic columns, facing St James Street (*see* below). Parts of the basement frontages, both in the original main part and in the E wing, have rusticated walling with open cambered arches. The W wing remains single-storeyed. The TOWER has a square base, an intermediate stage with a clock, and a tall columned cupola ending in a small dome. Part of the building is adapted as a theatre.

LIND STREET is handsome, with the Town Hall on its N side. To the E of the latter, ST JAMES STREET leads off N. No. 1, facing the side of the Town Hall, was built in 1834 as the Mechanics' Institute; it is one-storeyed, with Ionic columns flanking a single window. Further E is the handsome COLONNADE of 1835–6, possibly designed by *Sanderson* (†1835). Two plain upper storeys project across the pavement over eleven Tuscan columns supporting a long plain entablature.

The buildings on the S side of Lind Street are varied but generally consistent in style. No. 5 towards the E, later than the rest, was built in 1866–7 for the YMCA by *Thomas Dashwood.* The prominent E elevation has rusticated pilasters and rounded ground-floor windows. Nos. 6–9, of after 1845, form an elegant quartet; Nos. 7 and 9 project slightly, creating a rhythmic effect emphasized by the iron balconies fronting tripartite windows on the first floors. No. 10, built in 1853–4 as an assembly room axial to the Town Hall, is more grandiose, with giant pilasters and arched windows. Nos. 11–18 are similar to Nos. 6–9 with their rhythmic frontages, but vary in details. Nos. 19–22, set back, are earlier, with tripartite ground-floor windows and iron balconies above.* Opposite is St James (*see* p. 223); beyond, Lind Street leads into West Street (*see* Perambulation 3, p. 239).

At its E end Lind Street opens into ST THOMAS SQUARE. This is a shapeless, trafficked space at the meeting of important thoroughfares, including Cross Street leading E (*see* Perambulation 2, p. 234), and High Street to the S (for the further part of which *see* Perambulation 3, p. 240). On the corner of Lind Street is the NATIONAL WESTMINSTER BANK of 1966–7, in a style typical of its date. It looks best

* *William Westmacott* was asked to prepare plans for the S side of Lind Street in 1835; this could relate to Nos. 19–22, which are on a map of 1836.

from Lind Street, where the façade has three ranges of thinly mullioned windows, slightly projecting and rising through both storeys, and the roof-line is defined by a black fascia. On the site was a theatre of 1871, destroyed by fire in 1961. To its S is the CROWN HOTEL of 1830–1 which, architecturally, is quintessentially Ryde. Three-storeyed, with a Doric doorway between bold bows which rise through two floors, the upper range topped by iron-railed balconies.

UNION STREET leads downhill from the NE corner of St Thomas Square. Little was built along it between 1780, when it was laid out, and 1810, when restrictions affecting lengths of leases were removed. From then it developed steadily and piecemeal. There were shops and hotels by *c.* 1840; today it is almost entirely commercial. Roof-lines vary greatly, and although the predominant tone is still that of Regency to Early Victorian stucco, there are later styles and some flights of fancy. A little way down on the r., LLOYDS TSB (No. 35), *c.* 1830–40, shows well the local style of the period; it is three-storeyed with a strong cornice and suggestion of a pediment. The flat-fronted, round-ended bay windows on the first floor are of a type which recurs in the town. Across the street, No. 53 (N of Yelf's Road), is a little later. It has a balustraded parapet and an inset rounded corner (a fairly common feature in Ryde); a window with segmental pediment follows the curve.

The ROYAL VICTORIA ARCADE of 1835–6 by *William Westmacott*, on the W side, is one of the finest early arcades surviving in Britain (named after Victoria as Princess, after she stayed at Norris Castle). Unfortunately the street frontage was altered in 1856, when three arches were replaced by a single flat opening. The top of the façade is original, with serif lettering under a dentilled cornice and elaborate royal arms, between slightly projecting wings. The
55 superb Neoclassical interior is essentially intact. The central passageway, fronted by shops with upper storeys, separated by giant pilasters, leads to a saucer-domed space from which short transepts open; the main axis continues for one bay to a back entrance. The shopfronts are fairly simple; the upper floors have tripartite windows and shallow balconies with iron grilles. Light enters through a square-topped clerestory with almost continuous glazing. The main roof has a flat profile with large panels containing rosettes, and in the saucer dome is a fanlight with coloured glass, replaced in 1974. A showroom opening off the N transept is an original feature. The arcade narrowly escaped demolition *c.* 1970, but was preserved after an inquiry and restored.

Further down Union Street is REGINA HOUSE, a wildly designed building of 1865. Four life-like statues poise on the parapet, and a belvedere caps the northern end; an oriel

Ryde, Royal Victoria Arcade, interior.
Engraving after William Westmacott, *c.* 1840

topped by a spike brings a Gothic touch. Across the street, further N, No. 15 provides an antidote with its four-columned portico, pediment and balustrade in one tall storey; it was built for a wine merchant as late as 1869. Back on the W side is the ROYAL SQUADRON HOTEL, opened as the Kent Hotel in 1835, when the stuccoed front part was added to an older building. The two main upper storeys have pairs of giant fluted Corinthian pilasters under a strong cornice and tall attic. Further down, the corners with Church Lane (leading W) and Castle Street (E) are taken in interesting ways. There is an inset curve on the NE corner. The NW corner opposite is rounded at first-floor level, with a window and balcony following the curve.

Union Street reaches the Esplanade at its W end – *see* Perambulation 2, p. 237 – with the Pier to the NE. ST THOMAS STREET leads to the W, on the line of the original lane between Lower and Upper Ryde; its curving, casual course contrasts with the straightness of Union Street. PRINCE CONSORT BUILDINGS on the N side were built in 1846–7 as the ROYAL VICTORIA YACHT CLUB; the design is attributed to *W. Huntley* of Dover. Prince Albert laid the foundation stone. The main part is Italianate, of two storeys in stone and stucco with arched windows. On the street front is a heavily detailed one-storey forebuilding, probably added in 1864, with balustraded parapet and paired Corinthian columns flanking the entrance. The frontage to the Solent makes a finer show, with a Tuscan colonnade supporting a broad balcony, onto which opens an arcade of nine closely spaced windows. GLOUCESTER HOUSE to the W, mid C19, has a strange front with two stuccoed projections, one under an eaved roof, the other gabled. No. 18 beyond has boldly arched windows and broad angle pilasters. In contrast, Nos. 40–44 across the road, 1874, are Neo-Jacobean with shaped gables.

St Thomas Street turns and climbs S, between garden walls of rough local limestone (used also in some of the villas behind them), past RYDE COURT (formerly Sydney Terrace) on the r. and the spectacular BRIGSTOCKE
54 TERRACE on the l.; both are at right angles to the highway. The former is a four-bay terrace of 1853 with odd features: gabled dormers, and rounded pediments over the central parts of tripartite first-floor windows. Brigstocke Terrace, 1826–9 by *James Sanderson*, is the only grand classical urban terrace on the Island, restored in 1974. It is rendered, of five storeys including attics and basement, and the frontages on both sides extend for twenty-seven bays under a low-pitched roof with eaves. The N frontage is articulated, with the three bays at each end, together with the tenth and seventeenth bays, being brought forward slightly; there are first-floor iron balconies under veranda roofs at the centre and ends. The S elevation has a different rhythm, with the centre bays stepped forward in two stages, and small iron balconies to some, not all, of the first-floor windows. Because of the sloping site the basement is largely below ground level on the S side but not on the N, so the proportions of the two elevations are different. The street continues up to St Thomas Square, passing varied early C19 houses on the r. and St Thomas (*see* p. 225) set back on the l.

SPENCER ROAD leads off W. The RYDE CLUB on the l., early C20, has a crowded small-scale frontage in red brick with profuse stone dressings; shaped gables are faced with curly patterns; square turrets with panelled sides mark the corners and flank the central doorway – ending, like the gables, in bulbous pinnacles. Nos. 7 and 9 beyond, *c.* 1830–40, are both typical of early to mid-C19 Ryde. No. 7 has a broad canted bay for its whole height; the ground storey is rusticated, the upper two are in rough limestone with stucco quoins. No. 9 is all stuccoed, with cornices to the first and attic storeys and pilasters on the main floors; it is asymmetrical since the windows to the W are tripartite. BUCKINGHAM ROAD leads off N and curves back between stone walls – a relic of rural Ryde. MIMOSA LODGE facing the bend, *c.* 1800, has a front in grey brick headers with red dressings and side walls of stone. BUCKINGHAM VILLA, in a large garden to the W, was built by the 1st Marquess of

Buckingham in 1812–13; low and stuccoed (with right-angled bay windows facing the Solent). Further W is an area developed deplorably *c.* 1960, covering the grounds of WESTFIELD PARK HOUSE (formerly Westfield) – which survives, greatly altered. It was built in or before 1811 as a villa for the 2nd Earl Spencer, and enlarged in 1855 for Sir Augustus Clifford by *Thomas Hellyer*; his is the porch-tower with triple rounded windows at the top, evoking Osborne. A stone GATEWAY built by Clifford in 1864 remains by the road; it has an arch with keystone, dentilled cornice, and parapet with a motto, surmounted by a stag.

We leave this mainly C20 enclave and enter its contrasting C19 counterpart to the W. The area called PELHAMFIELD was developed *c.* 1820–60 with detached houses in mixed styles along the N side of Spencer Road, and down AUGUSTA ROAD which leads N to the Solent.* AUGUSTA LODGE on the E corner of the two roads, built 1838 and extended 1850, is of rough stone partly stuccoed, with many gables, twirly bargeboards, and brick chimneys with spiral decoration. No. 44 Spencer Road, W, of 1853, is square, rendered, with pillared porch and pediments over the ground-floor windows. No. 50 next door, 1854–5, is similar but with exposed stonework and no window pediments. No. 52, 1837–8, has an iron veranda. No. 54, *c.* 1840, is heavier; of three storeys plus a later wooden belvedere rising from the roof. Its gateway from the road has incised patterns on the piers and an urn on top. Nos. 58 and 60, both 1829, have 53
end pilasters showing sunk squared decoration in the Soane manner.

In Augusta Road BERWICK LODGE, 1850, has a tower of variegated stone with parapets stepped up at the angles. Beyond the end of the road a group of houses backs on to the Solent. ST ANNE'S and ST ANNE'S LODGE of 1843, divided from one house in 1864, are in rough stone with many gables, a turret and tall chimneys, YARBOROUGH HOUSE to the W, 1835, is stuccoed, with more end pilasters showing sunk decoration and a two-storey iron veranda on the seaward side. In contrast, the adjoining ASHBY of 1837 has a partly gabled and jettied first floor.

At the W end of Augusta Road is BELDORNIE TOWER, of 1835, altered (e.g. in 1880); the entrance gateway from the road has the date 1894. The main (S) elevation is mildly Neo-Jacobean, rendered and whitened; on the E wing is a first-floor oriel; the porch has a four-centred doorway, and the W wing a stepped gable. The N side facing the Solent is more complex; the main part is faced in coursed rubble, with a tall octagonal turret of brick (formerly topped by a

* Mr Roy Brinton has studied the Pelhamfield area, and I am particularly grateful to him for the detailed information.

short spire) at the NW corner. The interior was enriched in the late C19 when panelling, wooden chimneypieces and other features in early to mid-C17 style were brought in; some of these are, at least in part, imitation work. They show round arches, strapwork, square-pattern panels, fluted pilasters, caryatids and other details characteristic of the style, recalling C17 features in Island manor houses, but are more lavishly detailed than most of the comparable locally based work. The date 1660 is carved on one chimneypiece.

Back to Spencer Road. CONISTON (formerly Corstorphine Lodge) on the S side is a villa of 1835 with pediment-gables, windows in thick architraves and a two-storey bow. Spencer Road continues to Binstead Road (*see* Outer Ryde: West, p. 245).

2. East: George Street, Vernon Square and the Esplanade

From St Thomas Square (*see* Perambulation 1, p. 229), CROSS STREET leads E to an intersection with GEORGE STREET, which was laid out parallel to Union Street *c.* 1810. No. 12 Cross Street of 1837–8, on the NW corner of the intersection, has a specifically Ryde character: upper two storeys of buff brick with plain pilasters, first-floor bay windows with rounded ends. In total contrast was the Congregational church of 1870–2, by *R.J. Jones* on the SE corner of the crossing (Pevsner: 'an architectural nightmare', with a tower 'changing by exceedingly steep long slopes into an octagon and carrying a very steep spire'). Its demolition in 1974 was a serious loss to Ryde's townscape and skyline; its replacement is an insipid block, incongruously in red brick. But Nos. 73–77 George Street immediately S, *c.* 1835–40, are robustly in the Ryde tradition; stuccoed with pilasters, tripartite windows and curved-ended bays. Buildings further S up George Street are described in Perambulation 3, p. 241.

Going N from the crossroads, No. 69 on the r. corner is a stucco villa of *c.* 1825–30, swelling out at its N end in a two-storey bow with balcony and canopy; a trellis porch with tent-like top completes the picture. Just beyond is the ROYAL YORK HOTEL, 1937–8 by *J.B. Harrison & H.F. Gilkes*, one of the town's interwar landmarks. Modernistic, with white-painted walls, curved corners, even parapet, windows set in banded strips, and three tiers of round-ended balconies on the street frontage. The dominant element is an oval entrance tower set against the angled NW elevation, with staircase windows rising through three storeys. Inside, the stair is a dramatic spiral in concrete beneath a small round roof-light. The rest of the street has a mixture of scales, materials and dates, though the styles of *c.* 1820–45 prevail. No. 62 (W side, set back) is a villa in coursed stone with tall tripartite windows and a Tuscan porch. On the other side, No. 61, in rough stone, has a huge elliptical bow running through three storeys. Further down, Nos. 19–21 have square-ended bay windows and iron balconies.

George Street intersects CASTLE STREET, parallel with the shore; quite modest at this end. Going E, No. 16, formerly a pub, is an odd composition, higher than its neighbours, with prominent cornices to the first and attic floors and a broad ground-floor window with segmental arch. Nelson Street (*see* below) and Nelson Place lead S uphill. NELSON MANSIONS on the E corner of the latter was a substantial stuccoed villa, now subdivided, with a prominent cornice, tall attic, plain porch fronting Nelson Place and – its best feature – a tetrastyle Doric colonnade towards Castle Street. It is the first of a series of stuccoed villas of *c.* 1830–40 along the S side of Castle Street. Of these, No. 23 has a striking frontage with a tent-roofed iron-framed veranda, rising from a first-floor balcony with intricate balustrade and very thin columns – one of the best examples of house-frontage ironwork in Ryde.

Up NELSON PLACE, which has low-key houses framing a long view back across the Solent, and into BELLEVUE ROAD. This runs E–W and is partly bounded on its S side by stone garden walls overhung with trees, which belong to houses fronting the parallel Melville Street (*see* below). The W part of Bellevue Road is more built up; No. 7 is in chequered brick, rare in Ryde. Bellevue Road joins NELSON STREET, where varied C19 houses frame another seaward view. Turn l. here towards Melville Street. On the W side of Nelson Street is a former Wesleyan CHAPEL of 1844, in rough stone with ashlar dressings; a central arched recess is flanked by thin windows, with a (probably later) porch, also round-arched.

MELVILLE STREET runs W–E, continuing Cross Street. All the houses on the N side as far E as Dover Street were built by 1836. No. 10 (WYNDHAM HOUSE), on the W corner with Nelson Street, is the grandest; three bays wide on each elevation; the upper storeys in buff brick between Ionic pilasters; stuccoed ground floor; Tuscan porch. No. 9 is simpler, without the pilasters. To the W is the former FREE SCHOOL of 1812, a long building in rough stone with a hipped slate roof; single-storeyed except the W part which was a teacher's cottage under the same roof-line as the rest. Countess Spencer was the patron. In the centre an ashlar-framed doorway with triple keystone. The E part of Melville Street is described later in the Perambulation.

VERNON SQUARE, opening S off Melville Street, is the Island's only landscaped residential square. The central garden was first planted by 1836; the landscaping was well restored in 1988–9. Building round the square took place gradually, with single or paired villas. Nos. 4–5 at the SW corner, *c.* 1840–5, are semi-detached and stuccoed, with broad segmental bay windows rising into the attic. No. 3 on the SE corner, perhaps a little older, has a plain two-storey frontage under a broad-eaved roof. Its garden front facing E towards Wood Street is grander; a central elliptical bow rises through to an extra attic storey, with a fretted veranda round its base. VERNON HOUSE on the S side of the square, built by 1833, was rebuilt in 1989 with the frontage replaced supposedly in replica. This is an interesting design, of five bays with a first-floor bow resting on four Doric columns taken from the old building. WOOD STREET leads E from the square and crosses DOVER STREET, where No. 1 to the NW of the intersection, *c.* 1835–40, has a Tuscan porch, and a bold bow facing E. S of the crossroads, Dover Street is dominated by the impeccable spire of Holy Trinity (*see* p. 222), set among villas which mostly date from after 1850.

DOVER PARK SCHOOL, a little S of the church, was built in 1987–8 by the County Council (County Architect *Michael Rainey*). It is on a slope descending E, with walls of pale brick, and roofs of low pitch with broad eaves and end projections. The front (W) elevation rises from a level slightly below that of Dover Street; mainly single-storeyed with a long range of windows, but the N part two-storeyed, including a semi-basement. A porch, with low projecting gable, round arch and circular columns, projects over a platform which bridges the level of the semi-basement – an effective feature.

Returning to Wood Street and going E, GOTHIC COTTAGE and ORMONDE HOUSE are stuccoed Neo-Tudor villas, *c.* 1835–40. The first has a big canted bay under battlements and, to one side, a small first-floor oriel on a substantial sill with apron. Ormonde House is larger, with buttress-like projections ending in small caps above the parapet, and an assortment of windows – mainly square-headed but including one topped by an arched recess with Gothic tracery. A low wall, with open panels intersected by diagonals, borders the road.

Trinity Street leads N into the E end of MELVILLE STREET (*see also* above). No. 29 on the N side was built for himself in 1855 by *Thomas Hellyer*, the leading local architect. It is basically a mid-Victorian villa of three bays and two storeys in buff brick, but embellished in idiosyncratic ways. The porch has a flat-topped arch between columns with large vertically banded capitals, and a balustrade which continues over a projecting bay of the ground floor to the l., creating asymmetry. Band of red brick at the upper level of the first-floor windows, which are emphasized by segmental lintels; central dormer with a shaped top. Internal features

Ryde, The Strand, looking west.
Engraving, 1870

include decorative doorcases, plasterwork, chimneypieces, stair handrail and stained glass. The house is entered from the street through a stone gateway with red brick arch and table-like top. Further on, No. 32 at the corner of Monkton Street has a back elevation to Bellevue Road showing an impressive array of ironwork, with two tiers of balconies.

Monkton Street runs N to join The Strand. In SIMEON STREET, which leads E off Monkton Street, are altered semi-detached houses with bargeboarded gables, hood-moulded windows and tall single chimneys at the centre of each pair: interesting precursors of early C20 'semis'. THE STRAND, as its name implies, runs parallel to the coast; the houses on its N side back onto the seafront. Most of these were built *c.* 1845–55 in variants of the local domestic tradition; stuccoed, or faced in rough stone. Nos. 4–5 towards the W are grander, with balustrades and Ionic pilasters; Nos. 9–10, exceptionally, have gables, with round-headed windows underneath. No. 42 on the S side has a graceful bow and doorway with keystone. The nicest group includes Nos. 31–38, with a succession of bow windows, on the r. near the E end.

At this point the continuous pre-1855 town ends. Nearby is the E end of the ESPLANADE, which extends for over ½ m. W, to the pier and slightly beyond. In its virgin state this part of the coast had a low shoreline edged with sand and shingle, on which boats were beached. When the first pier was built in 1814, building had already started along the shoreline, but only in 1855–7 was the first part of a formal Esplanade laid out, mainly in front of already existing buildings. This extended for less than ¼ m. E from by the pier, reaching its present length later in the C19. The foreshore on the seaward side was developed piecemeal, with reclamation of parts of the beach, through the late C19 and C20. Now there is a hotchpotch of buildings and spaces between the Esplanade and the sea. One building is special: the former PAVILION of 1926–7, now part of a bowling centre; designed by *Vincent & West*, with cast-iron components from *Macfarlane's* of Glasgow. It has a large rectangular iron-framed hall with timber-panel cladding and two-tier roof with red tiles. The lower tier has convex slopes; above is a clerestory. At the corners are square turrets with concave roofs, also tiled, which end in needle finials. These turrets hold their own amid the seaside clutter. On the landward side is RYDE CASTLE HOTEL, built in 1833–4 as a large Tudor-Gothic villa, in rough stone with smooth dressings. The main part (without the present E extension) has an irregular skyline with battlemented parapets. Entrance in a tower, with chimneys at its corners appearing as pinnacles; a taller tower with thinner pinnacles rises behind. To the W, in the angle between the Esplanade and Castle Street (*see* above), are nondescript apartment blocks of 1996–7, partly retaining C19 buildings. This was an opportunity missed, on a site where there could have been a late C20 feature as remarkable as are Ryde Castle and the Pavilion of their particular periods.

Further W, the Esplanade is fronted by buildings which partly predate it – a locally typical mixture with many bow windows. Grander than the rest is the ESPLANADE HOTEL of 1866–7 by *Francis E. Drake* of Leicester, extended 1873: assertive High Victorian in brick now painted over, with an assemblage of iron balconies and busy skyline. No. 15 to the W, mid C19, has on the ground floor a range of round-arched windows and doors, curving round into George Street. Further W, No. 7 has a very different Late Victorian shopfront, with three arches formed in slender ironwork, densely patterned in the spandrels.

Finally, RYDE PIER. The first structure of 1813–14 was extended in 1824, and the pier reached its present length of nearly ½ m. by 1842. A parallel pier immediately to the E was built in 1864 for a horse-drawn tramway, electrified later and closed in 1969; remains of its substructure survive. A third parallel pier of 1880 carried steam trains to other parts of the Island – represented today by the electric train service to Shanklin. Architecturally there is hardly anything to note, apart from the repetitive heavy Victorian ironwork on the balustrades; the present buildings at either end are unremarkable. Visually, the best thing about Ryde Pier is the view from it of the town. Buildings climb the slope and the skyline, still Victorian, is punctuated by church spires and the Town Hall turret. Towards the W, and more distantly the E, the buildings are interspersed with greenery.

3. South: West Street, High Street and St John's Road

Most of this area is densely developed, but the buildings described are fairly scattered, apart from a concentration at the beginning. From the Town Hall, Lind Street leads into WEST STREET, which climbs steeply S. No. 77 (W side) was built for himself by *Thomas Dashwood* in 1865–6; it is fairly ordinary, in buff brick, but has an 'Osborne' tower with paired openings. Further up on the r., two former villas of *c.* 1835, both now related to Ryde School (*see* Outer Ryde: West, p. 244). WESTHILL HOUSE, No. 84, has a simple street frontage, but on the N side are engaged Ionic columns flanking the central upper window, and panelled angle pilasters. OXFORD LODGE, No. 83, has a bold semicircular bow of two storeys with three windows at each level.

West Street meets a fivefold road junction beside All Saints (*see* p. 220). N of the church, in the angle with QUEEN'S ROAD, is the best of a group of villas of *c.* 1860, of coursed local stone with stucco dressings. It has a varied outline with low-pitched roofs; canted bay windows and a Tuscan porch with a balustrade. West Street continues S, past WELBY on the l., full-blooded Gothic of *c.* 1874 with arched windows in alternating stones, with a belvedere capped by a sharp tiled roof. Opposite, the house on the corner of Argyle Street has an odd façade with heavy quoins and paired rounded windows under the gable. (Buildings along and off West Street further S are described under Outer Ryde: West, pp. 245–6.)

Back to the junction by All Saints. JOHN STREET, leading E with a gentle curve, was laid out in 1831 and retains several early villas. No. 1 faces the junction on the N side, with gable-pediment and round-arched doorway. No. 2, from the 1840s, is very distinctive: Anglo-Italian, in rough coursed 73
stone with stucco details. The *piano nobile* windows have round-arched frames of two orders, with balustrades to the sills; the porch has Tuscan columns, arched entrance, and balustrade with ball finials. No. 3, ANGLESEA LODGE, is much more modest; stuccoed with wide pilasters, the entrance between shallow wings, of which the W one projects more than the other. Nos. 4–5 are a pair of 'semis' with tripartite windows. Further along the N side, the FREEMASONS' HALL of 1848 has a busy elevation, with rounded first-floor arches between paired pilasters, and prominent pediment.

John Street leads into HIGH STREET, which represents the pre-C19 thoroughfare of the small straggling village of Upper Ryde. It is long and slightly winding, attractive as a whole and generally C19 above the shops. A few buildings call for comment. The CASTLE inn, *c.* 1850, takes the S corner with John Street elegantly with a rounded angle set slightly back, as elsewhere in the town. Before turning S, No. 174 High Street, a little way N on the l. side, should be noted: a former pub restored in the 1990s, partly faced in red mathematical tiles, with canted bays on the first floor. (The structure behind is basically timber-framed, possibly C17.) Back towards the S; the STAR inn of 1873 in the angle with Star Street, l., has a heavy balustrade and canted corner. Further S, St Mary (*see* p. 226) punctuates the street with its turret and lively façade. W of the church, No. 131, formerly a Temperance Hall, has an odd façade (1884 on plaque), with a circular upper window between blank arches, and segment-headed windows at ground level. Finally, THE OLD HOUSE, on the l. beyond St John's Road, is a surprise. Originally a box-framed structure, probably early C17, it was enlarged in the C19 and later. The exposed timber framing, with brick-nogging in diagonal patterns, is clearly visible at the N end.

Turn E along ST JOHN'S ROAD, a long, mainly Victorian thoroughfare, with a view along it of the distant trees and villas of St John's Park (*see* Outer Ryde: East, p. 241). The former ST JOHN'S ROAD SCHOOL on the l. is a somewhat grim, buff brick Board School of 1883 by *Hellyer*, with mullioned windows and two Norman-looking doorways. Then at the

Ryde, Swan's Nest.
Early C19 lithograph, after Whittock

corner of PLAYER STREET is another surprise – THE SWAN'S NEST, a *cottage orné* built *c.* 1830 and altered in the mid to late C19. The main part, aligned N–S, has one principal storey under a sweeping roof with dormers, originally thatched. Its S part is semicircular and open, forming a veranda under a roof supported by timber posts and irregular rustic braces. To W and E are gabled two-storey wings, taller on the E side. The W wing, facing Player Street, has a jettied upper floor with half-timbering under a decorative gable. These features may be later alterations, together with the prominent paired chimneys on the E side with a spiral red and buff pattern, and the roof tiling, which is deep red with horizontal black bands. The house has a marked similarity with Puckaster (*see* Niton), built about ten or fifteen years before, especially in the veranda. When built, it stood in open country. 46

Player Street leads N to Park Road and continues as BARFIELD ROAD, with C19 villas. BARFIELD HOUSE, r., built by 1836, has a set-back frontage, now roughcast, with taller central part under a pediment; a round archway opens into an elongated porch. Barfield Road continues into Vernon Square (*see* Perambulation 2, p. 235); instead, turn W to reach the S end of GEORGE STREET. Buildings here are very mixed. Nos. 103–105, r., are a stuccoed pair of *c.* 1840 with heavy rounded doorways under open pediments. No. 104 opposite has a nice canted bow rising two storeys; No. 100 has a bolder semicircular one with iron balconies. Then, on the E side, a High Victorian range. Nos. 85–87 are big 'rogue' villas of *c.* 1860–70 in buff brick with bracketed eaves, heavy bay windows and extraordinary doorways; No. 79 is smaller and more delicate with a pair of arched windows under an open gable-pediment. Then back to the earlier Ryde traditions with Nos. 73–75, etc. (*see* Perambulation 2, p. 234). Opposite, SUFFOLK TOWERS, adjoining the Baptist church (*see* p. 227), a villa of *c.* 1840 to which an Italianate porch-tower with arched top storey, recalling Osborne, was added *c.* 1870.

OUTER RYDE: EAST

Before the C20 a succession of houses in large grounds dotted the undulating country E of the town; some of these survive. Ryde itself expanded to the SE after *c.* 1850. The notable buildings here, too widespread for a normal Perambulation, are described in an itinerary which begins at the E end of the Esplanade, close to The Strand (*see* Perambulation 2, p. 237).

EAST HILL ROAD climbs gently from the seafront. On its W side an area of villas called ST JOHN'S PARK was developed from 1854, to an interesting layout by *Thomas Hellyer* with houses facing roads, and communal open space behind. They were built piecemeal in mainly Italianate styles; none is known to have been designed by *Hellyer* himself. The best series begins with ARGOSY on the W side of East Hill Road, just over ¼ m. from the seafront; buff brick, with red brick quoins and arched doorway to the porch. The next house S is much the same but with stucco dressings. Then a former service building with turret and cupola. VICTORIA LODGE to the S has a very odd porch. WEST HILL ROAD branches off and curves past NEW LODGE, the best house in the group. A heavy two-storey bay is topped by a balustrade, as is the porch; segmental pediments bracketed over the first-floor windows. Its balustraded boundary wall has ball finials on low piers at intervals.

Turning E into APPLEY ROAD beside St John's church (*see* p. 223), the wooded grounds on the l. are those of the former ST JOHN'S HOUSE, now BISHOP LOVETT SCHOOL. The house was built *c.* 1769 by William Amherst, and named after the capital of Newfoundland with which he was associated. It was bought in 1797 by Edward Simeon, who employed *Humphry Repton* to landscape the grounds down to the seashore. Little or nothing of his landscape is left, and his picturesque lodges and shoreside buildings have been demolished. The house survives, with a seven-bay S front in coursed local stone, the middle part brought forward under a pediment with a bullseye window. The E wing, since altered, was added in 1871, when the grounds were reduced and re-landscaped. The school started in 1947; of subsequent buildings the best is that to the W by *Robert Smith*, Deputy County Architect, *c.* 1969 – single-storeyed, with a very broad and low-pitched central gable, flanked by wings with monopitch roofs. The Lodge on Appley Road dates from *c.* 1871; single-storeyed with a canted bay. It adjoins the more elaborate APPLEY TOWERS LODGE to the E which belonged to a vanished house; Neo-Jacobean in brick with shaped gables, spiked finials and a canted bay with balustrade. Further E, APPLEY MANOR HOTEL (formerly Sturbridge House) was a villa of 1861–2 by *Hellyer*, with an 'Osborne' tower.

PUCKPOOL HOUSE, off Puckpool Hill, was enlarged from an older house in 1822–4 by *Lewis Wyatt* as his seaside retreat; he retired there in 1836 and extended it. It was altered and enlarged in the later C19 and C20; the sequence is not fully clear. Wyatt's retreat was a substantial *cottage orné*, as can be seen on the N frontage, which must have had spacious verandas on two floors. The upper floor, under a broad hipped gable, is still fronted by two rough tree trunks with diagonal braces, but immediately behind them is a C20 glazed partition. On the ground floor the wooden supports have been replaced by brick piers. An E wing, with jettied first floor on the N side, was added by 1838; this has on its SE corner a turret, octagonal at its top with a thin lancet on each face; it originally had a conical cap. (St Clare, just W of Puckpool House, demolished *c.* 1960, was an irregular castellated mansion of 1823 by *James Sanderson.*)

Puckpool Hill descends to the Solent shore at the W end of Spring Vale on the edge of Seaview (q.v.). From here a coastal path leads back to Ryde. About ¼ m. along it is PUCKPOOL LODGE, originally the seaward adjunct to St Clare, and perhaps, like that house, by *James Sanderson.* It has contrasting external effects; to the W is a plain half-octagonal frontage, but the S side is richly romantic – a gabled jettied projection has applied half-timbering and spiked pinnacles. The N side facing the sea is fairly similar but was largely hidden by foliage when visited.

Back along the coastal path towards Ryde, APPLEY TOWER is a seaside folly of *c.* 1875 which belonged, confusingly, to the vanished house called Appley Towers (*see* above). It is circular and castellated, with a tall rounded turret corbelled out on one side and, facing the sea, an oriel resting on a bracket.

WOODLANDS VALE, off Calthorpe Road on the SE outskirts of the town, is a house of *c.* 1860 enlarged in 1870–1 by *S.S. Teulon* for Col. Somerset John Gough-Calthorpe, who bought the property in 1869. He was the son of the 4th Lord Calthorpe (of Edgbaston, Birmingham), and inherited the title in 1910; there were several additions and alterations in the late C19 and early C20.

Teulon's entrance front (NW) is dominated by a three-storey stone tower derived distantly from French château precedent, with a steep-sided slated roof like the base of a pyramid, crowned with an iron weathervane. Attached on its S angle is a round stair-turret, rising higher to an embattled top. An amazingly incongruous half-timbered porte cochère was added in 1893 by *Stephen Salter*, with a round-fronted upper balcony. To the l. of the entrance is a small tower heightened in 1912 to contain a lift, with a low copper dome.

The long garden front (NE) is as eventful. Its basic structure is that of *c.* 1860, with shallow wings and a low-pitched roof, but *Teulon* added canted bay windows to the wings, rising to small shaped gables with finials. In between, a three-arched loggia was inserted in 1880 (by *Tarring & Wilkinson*), with a balustrade partly of terracotta. A two-bay iron veranda with intricate detailing extends across the bay window to the l. Further to the l. is a round tower under a conical roof, by *Teulon.* Finally, a billiard room was added at the SE end in 1894 by *Stephen Salter* (replacing a conservatory), which could hardly be more different from his porte cochère; it has a classical outline, canted on the E and SE corners, with pediments fronting NE and SE, and a copper-sheathed roof curving to a glazed roof-light.

The best feature by *Teulon* is a nine-bay round-arched SCREEN WALL which continues the line of the garden front to the NW. Arches are of red and buff brick, piers of stone; urns rise from the parapet. Further on is a SUMMERHOUSE (1874, also *Teulon*), in a weird style with Gothic-derived details. The spacious garden, now mostly grassed, has an axial vista NE to the sea; towards its far end is a TERRACE with low openwork brick walls, and tiled walkways flanking geometrically patterned pools.

The INTERIOR is confusing. Many features are from the house of *c.* 1860, including the well STAIRCASE with its iron balusters, panelled ceilings and fireplaces. *Teulon* remodelled some rooms, especially the ENTRANCE HALL, which has strident geometrical patterns in *Minton* tiles, on the floor and forming dados. Stained-glass windows depict various subjects including figures, birds, plants and fruit; one heraldic window by the staircase is dated 1873.

The former COACHHOUSE by *Stephen Salter*, 1894, has an Arts and Crafts feel; it is of buff brick, cruciform, with a copper-domed clock turret rising from a tile-hung base. Gabled dormers with red terracotta patterns under their sills, which continue down to the brick arches of ground-floor windows; a circular window under an end gable has similar embellishment. The LODGE on Calthorpe Road, also by *Salter*, 1900, is complex: gabled upper storey with a Venetian window over an arched entrance, to the l. an octagonal tower with onion dome.

OUTER RYDE: WEST

As with Outer Ryde: East, the buildings described are not close enough for Perambulations, but are included in two itineraries each beginning at All Saints church (*see* Churches and Perambulation 3, pp. 220, 239).

RYDE SCHOOL occupies WESTMONT HOUSE, off Queen's Road NW of the church. The house was built in 1819–21 for Dr John Lind. There have been additions to E and W, but the unusual five-bay S front, in coursed local limestone with ashlar dressings under a broad hipped roof, is intact. A portico of four Ionic columns under an elongated pediment is the dominant feature, with three closely spaced windows above it. Flanking parts are brought forward slightly, with arched windows on the ground floor. A central dormer with its own pediment is prominent. The N front, overlooking park-like grounds and, in glimpses, the Solent, has the same general shape, and is faced in ashlar. It has a segmental

portico with four Ionic columns, dentilled cornice and iron balcony, the spaces between the columns now glazed. Who was the architect? One asks this even more keenly in the entrance hall, with its complex shape and varied details. 47
The main part of the ceiling forms an oval saucer-dome with plaster fluting and a large central rosette. This dome is supported by elliptical arches with small rosettes in panels on their undersides. Little else survives of the original interior.

Queen's Road leads W, past C19 and later villas, into BINSTEAD ROAD, running NW. ST VINCENTS on the l. is a villa of 1871, now a retirement home, in rough stone with ashlar dressings. The S front has a gabled projection with a blank pointed arch over a square-headed window; the pattern is repeated on the E front. A Gothic S porch prepares one for the stair hall, with two tiers of paired pointed arches on marble piers with lush capitals. The staircase itself is wooden, with trefoil panels.

RYDE HOUSE, built by 1810 for George Player, now a private residential home, is set in a former park (partly a golf course) N of Binstead Road, ⅔ m. NW of All Saints. It is basically a simple rectangular house in local limestone, with accretions. On the garden front (NE), a stuccoed centrepiece is framed in giant pilasters with inset panels. Between these, windows open on to iron-framed balconies on both floors, above a semi-basement projection. On the entrance (SW) side is a broad porch with inset Doric columns.

Returning to All Saints, the itinerary leads S along WEST STREET, passing at first buildings described in Perambulation 3 (*see* p. 239). GREEN STREET leads E, past the former NATIONAL SCHOOL of 1856–7, probably by *Hellyer*; symmetrical, with tall central and smaller flanking gables, and mullioned windows.

Further S along West Street, on the r., is RYDE CEMETERY, established 1842. The strident Gothic entrance of 1861–3 has a main vehicular arch and a smaller one for pedestrians, both under gables. Its basic structure is of stone, but the arches are brought out in deep red brick with radiating wedges of black, and the stonework with red and black brick bands. Its architect was *Francis Newman*, like the coeval pair of CHAPELS, of stone with triple lancets arched in brick, linked by a timber arch with braces and brackets. Another, disused, chapel fronts the street N of the cemetery entrance. Its gabled W end, of limestone rubble, has a two-light Geometrical window over a moulded and shafted doorway, of weathered freestone which makes the chapel almost look medieval. It probably dates from the 1840s.

Further S, ADELAIDE COURT, off Adelaide Place, is an admirable scheme for old people's housing and day facilities; 1985–6 by *Michael Rainey* as County Architect. Of warm buff brick, with horizontal bands and rounded-arched frames in darker brick, providing effective contrasts. Subtle variations in alignment and slightly projecting features contribute to the effects. The main communal block has sweeping roofs and a central rectangular turret with rounded openings – a slight reminiscence of Osborne. (An earlier, adjoining nurses' home by *Seely & Paget* has been demolished.)

On the S side of PLAYSTREET LANE, further S, are two houses of the 1890s by the versatile *Stephen Salter.* One (formerly Perivale) is in a style distantly related to Old English and Queen Anne; red brick, with white mullioned windows, a cornice-like string course and a big porch with a sun-patterned tympanum in a semicircular hood. The centre is slightly recessed under a small pediment, with a wide dormer above. Set back further W is RYE HOUSE, formerly Horsenden, 1896; red brick with similarly bold string courses, an octagonal corner feature, and a festoon pattern on the main cornice.

ST CATHERINE'S HILL *see* CHALE

6085

ST HELENS

A village with a huge green, long and tapering towards the E. Most of the houses round the green are simple C19 or C20. The original focus was on the coast about ¾ m. E, where a small Cluniac priory was established in Norman times, possibly on the site of an earlier church or chapel. It was dissolved as an alien monastery in 1414; the church remained for a time but was ruinous by the C16. In 1717–19 a new church was built about ½ m. N of the village, near the centre of the extensive parish which included the sites of present-day Seaview and the E parts of Ryde. Part of the TOWER of the old church was kept as a seamark – oddly triangular since it was sliced diagonally, probably in the C18. This left the original W and S sides, with a brick NE wall, now painted white, which faces the sea and rises higher than the older part. The old fabric is early C13, of rough limestone with a plain W door and small lancets in what was the belfry.

St Helens lay N of the once extensive Brading Haven, of which the smaller Bembridge Harbour (p. 80) is the surviving part. Ships sometimes anchored offshore to take victuals and water before long voyages (cf. Cowes).

ST HELEN. The church of 1717–19 was rebuilt in 1830–3. Nave, transepts and W tower in basic pre-Victorian Gothic; Y-tracery; thin tower with a broad parapet with rudimentary castellation. Chancel of 1862. – STAINED GLASS. Three-light E window by *Wailes*, 1862; Nativity, Crucifixion, Ascension. Touches of deep colour; details show clearly against dark background. – S transept, Sermon on the Mount by *J.H. Dearle* of *Morris & Co.*, 1913; crowded scene with central figure in strong red robe beneath dark hills and deep blue sky. – ROYAL ARMS, W gallery; George I. – MONUMENTS. In the chancel, large tablets to Sir Nash Grosse, a judge, †1814, and Edward Grosse, †1815, both of The Priory; the latter signed *W. Pistall*, New Road, London. At the angles of the former are fasces; the latter has draped military trophies in the same positions. N nave wall, Ellen Ellison, †1857, elaborate open canopy with foliage carving and flanking angels. – LYCHGATE, wooden with Gothic tracery, by *E.J. Caws*, 1920.

THE PRIORY, now PRIORY BAY HOTEL, 1 m. N of the village, adjoins a former farmstead on a site originally belonging to the Cluniac priory (*see* above). The main house dated from 1799, but has been altered and enlarged, particularly in the 1930s when a C13 DOORWAY was brought from an unspecified location in France. It is more elaborate than anything which could have existed on the medieval Island, with triple shafts, stiff-leaf capitals, two orders of crowded figures round the arches, and a crocketed hood. In the tympanum is a carved representation of St George, of different provenance. Inside, a CHIMNEYPIECE from Arreton Manor (q.v.), also introduced in the 1930s. It is one of the most substantial works of the local early C17 school of woodcarvers, with strapwork, vine trails, grotesque heads and military insignia. The central panel has a carved relief showing the Sacrifice of Isaac.

Part of a small former FARMHOUSE of the late C16 or early C17, of rough stone with simple mullioned windows, forms a wing to the house. To the S is the former FARMYARD, including the shell of a once-impressive BARN of coursed limestone, with two regular tiers of small square-topped openings. It was reconstructed after a fire in 1727. Another fire in 1999 destroyed the queen-strut roof, which was thatched. Nearby, a rectangular DOVECOTE, probably of similar date; tall and gable-ended, in roughly coursed stone with tiled roof and wooden turret.

THE CASTLE, between the village and the old church tower, was a fairly simple stone-built house of 1842, to which additions were made in 1860. The E front has a recessed central part with broad arched entrance, and an attractive tent-roofed iron porch (1842), with open circular patterns in the supports. On each side of the frontage is a castellated turret of 1860. The W elevation is similar, with an iron-framed veranda, and a turret only to the S. The S end, with battlements and rounded corners, dates from 1860; it projects between the turrets. A large N wing was added at right angles to the W frontage in 1903. Inside, the main feature is the STAIRCASE, with an impressively long central flight axial to the entrance.

YAR QUAY and SELWYN COURT, off Latimer Road to the S of the village, form a range of flats built *c.* 1978–80. They are best seen from Bembridge Harbour to the SE, with their irregular skyline of monopitch roofs, sloping in opposite directions at different heights.

5075 ST LAWRENCE

Ventnor

The Undercliff W of Ventnor is dramatic. The huge landslips thousands of years ago left a strip of land up to half a mile wide between the Upper Greensand ridge and the present coastline, where much of the sandstone formation, with chalk above it, had 'slipped' down the sloping band of Gault clay below (*see* Introduction, p. 5). The resultant cliff faces are still conspicuous along parts of the inland ridge; other steep slopes on the face of the ridge are wooded. The present coastline has low cliffs, unstable in places towards the W. In between is a broken landscape, where stretches of farmland are interspersed with woodland and the grounds and gardens of scattered houses. Many substantial houses were built (or enlarged from smaller beginnings) during the C19, using the local stone; some are romantic and irregular, others solid and plain. C20 development is largely confined to the fringes of Ventnor on the E. Not a great deal of the landscape can be appreciated from the A3055 which threads the area; it is best seen from the lanes and paths leading off, or from places on top of the inland ridge.

Distances and directions are from the Victorian parish church on the S side of the main road.

OLD ST LAWRENCE. A minute church probably of C13 origin, on a hillside about 200 yds (185 metres) NW of its successor. It was a simple rectangle until a chancel was added in 1842. Gabled W bellcote of uncertain date; small irregular windows of different periods; blocked N doorway, simply moulded, within an internal frame with segmental top; coved ceiling to the nave. Restored and largely refurnished 1926–7 by *Percy Stone*. – ROYAL ARMS framed on the W wall; 1663, repainted 1926.

ST LAWRENCE. 1878 by *Sir George Gilbert Scott*, one of his last works. Nave, chancel, N aisle, with Geometrical

St Lawrence, Old Church, interior before restoration, drawing. From *The Victoria County History, Hampshire and the Isle of Wight* vol. 5, 1912

windows and gabled double bellcote, nicely integrated with the buttresses of the W front. Little-altered interior with wooden panelled REREDOS and octagonal stone PULPIT. The nave arcade is oddly formed: vertical members rise from the round capitals on their E and W sides to merge with the arches above. The church has STAINED GLASS mainly by *Morris & Co.*, *c.* 1873, originally in the chapel of the Royal National Hospital for Diseases of the Chest which stood a short distance to the NE in Ventnor (*see* p. 291). It was brought here in 1974 after the hospital's demolition. The glass was in a three-light window at the hospital, with figures and biblical scenes. The figures are now in the centre lights of three S nave windows; the W one is St John the Evangelist in a dark red robe, to a design by *Burne-Jones* originally intended for the Savoy Chapel, London; in the centre is St Luke in a brown cloak, by *Ford Madox Brown*; to the E is St Peter in a golden robe by *Burne-Jones*, first intended for Peterhouse, Cambridge. The biblical scenes are arranged in a box, with light switch, in the N aisle. On the l. is The Raising of Jairius's Daughter by *Morris* himself; in the centre Christ carries a woman with an issue of blood, by *Ford Madox Brown* (the only part of the original specially commissioned for the hospital); on the r. is the Raising of Lazarus, also by *Morris*. More telling than any of the Morris glass is that by *Reynolds-Stephens*, 1892, now in the three-light W window – where the tracery is different from that of the window in which it was set at Ventnor, so that the upper parts were modified. The main part cannot be better described than by Nicholas Taylor and A.C. Sewter in the

Architectural Review, March 1967: 'It has a liquid, luminous colour quite different from Morris's, although recognisably of the same school . . . The main subject is a row of angels . . . the one in the centre playing a lute, with a little boy and girl seated at her feet, and two on each side are singing from books of music. They have graceful flowing robes and "simple life" headdresses. Below, a man receives medicine and a doctor takes a woman's pulse.' The church already had its own glass: SE nave window by *Walter Tower*, 1897, a figure broadcasting seeds; E and S windows both by *Kempe*'s firm, *c.* 1919.

MARINE VILLA, ¼ m. E. In about 1791–4 Sir Richard Worsley of Appuldurcombe (q.v.) built a seaside retreat adjoining an old small house (it was originally called Sea Cottage, later St Lawrence Cottage). Lord Yarborough owned the villa from 1806; Princess Victoria and the Duchess of Kent visited from Norris Castle in 1832. It was altered and enlarged in 1838–9. It may originally have been classical, but the main exterior parts have Neo-Tudor features which are much more likely to date from *c.* 1838 than the 1790s (they are not quite in the spirit of an earlier *cottage orné*).* The principal (SW) front, of sandstone blocks, has a central gabled projection with a wavy bargeboard, first-floor oriel and flanking tripartite windows. The SE elevation has two gables of different heights with bargeboards, and a later gabled extension on the r. The house is now subdivided; the northern section, called The Old Cottage, incorporates parts of the original building. Worsley landscaped the surroundings and built temple-like structures, of which one survives in the garden of Lisle Combe (*see* below).

Near the entrance to Marine Villa is ST LAWRENCE WELL, an Early Victorian grotto-like structure with finely moulded, heavily hooded Gothic entrance to a rib-vaulted interior.

74 LISLE COMBE, ⅓ m. E.** A many-gabled house of sandstone, first built in 1839 for the second son of Lord Yarborough, owner of the adjoining Marine Villa. It was then rectangular, aligned roughly E–W; in 1843 a nearly separate wing was added to the SE with a single-storey link; after 1849 the link was replaced by an inner wing, projecting less far than the 1843 addition. The resulting romantic composition when seen from the S–SE has elaborately fretted bargeboards of different sizes, windows including square-sided bays and small oriels, a veranda with central wooden gable, and brick

*An undated early C19 elevation and plan in the Isle of Wight Record Office shows a purely classical building with projected extensions.

**This is not the original name. For long it was called Southwold.

chimneystacks with spiral patterns. The entrance front (N), with flattened-arched doorway under an oriel, is less frenetic. This is probably the best example, externally, of a romantic Early Victorian villa on the Island.

In the garden to the W is a SUMMERHOUSE designed to resemble a Doric temple, the survivor of three temple-like structures built by Sir Richard Worsley *c.* 1800 in what were then the grounds of the Marine Villa (*see* above). Only two sides are classical, with columns and triglyph frieze in wood; there is a tetrastyle end façade with pediment, and a side elevation with five columns and big sash windows between them.

OLD PARK, now a hotel, ¾ m. W. A farmhouse was transformed *c.* 1820–30 for a solicitor from London into a 'Gothick' villa. It is stone-fronted with Y-tracery windows, canted bay and low octagonal tower to the W; all two-storeyed under a many-angled slate roof; impressively set when seen from the S, against steep woodland with the cliff-edged escarpment in the background. It was bought in 1865 by General Sir John Cheape who added a wing to the E, with balustrade and shaped gables; he installed early central heating and air-conditioning systems. Inside the wing is an elaborate stair hall, the upper stage with flat fluted columns and patterned ceiling; the well staircase has ribbed iron balusters sprouting spiral decoration. On the S side of the hall is an ornate three-bay round-arched arcade (with landing above). Its square piers have strange geometrical decoration in relief; the spandrels and frieze are patterned in white against dark. The arcade is repeated to the S, forming a passageway between. There are tiled floors with geometric patterns. Who was the architect of this extravagant work?

In 1881 Wilhelm (William) Spindler, a German industrialist, bought the estate; he attempted to develop a small town with a promenade (which fortunately failed before much was done). He also provided a water supply in the surrounding area, *see* Whitwell.

CRAIGIE LODGE, in the angle between the A3055 and Old Park Road, ¾ m. W. Built 1889 by *T.R. Saunders* for William Spindler (*see* Old Park, above). Pleasant exterior with hipped gables, half-timbering on the first floor and pillared veranda to the W. Remodelled internally *c.* 1898 by *Walter Spindler*, William's son, artist (and friend of Sarah Bernhardt), for Pearl Craigie, writer and dramatist, who published under the name of John Oliver Hobbes. Good Arts and Crafts features including tiles with versatile patterns round the fireplaces, plasterwork, plaques, and *Morris* wallpapers. Much of the detailed work, notably the design of the tiles, is attributed without certainty to *Spindler*.

FAIRWAYS, a mid-Victorian house to the W, is very different; it has a two-storey iron veranda with arched openings facing Old Park Road.

N of Craigie Lodge, across the A3055, are three latter-day *cottages ornés* of 1936–7 by *M.H. Baillie Scott*. ST ANN'S with white walls, casement windows and thatched roof is almost convincingly vernacular; ST LAWRENCE COTTAGE, along Spindler's Road, is larger; FARTHINGS in between is also thatched, but less deliberately cottagey with its big-paned windows.

In the grounds of WOOLVERTON MANOR, ½m. SSW, is the ruin of a late C13 stone building, which consisted only of a rectangle 25 by 12ft (7.7 by 3.7 metres) and a wing about 13 by 7ft (4 by 2 metres). It had an undercroft with, presumably, hall and chamber above – a very small manorial house. One gable end partly survives, containing a tall, slender, trefoil-headed lancet with a wide internal splay.

MIRABLES, 1½m. W. Romantically set on high ground above the sea, backed by wooded slopes. It began by the C17 as a stone farmhouse, of which something remains in part of the E frontage, with a two-light mullioned window. In about 1791–4 a wing with half-octagonal end, originally with a veranda, was added at the SE corner. The W part of the house was rebuilt and extended, with plain gables and mullioned windows, *c.* 1865. The middle part was replaced *c.* 1895 on a larger scale – with, on the N side, a polygonal tower under a tall conical roof, capped by a spiked turret and, on the S, a two-storey wooden veranda with arches and openwork spandrels. Inside this section is a substantial STAIRCASE, of well type with turned balusters, said to be of mid-C18 date and to have come from a house in East Sheen, Surrey.

CHERT. *See* Ventnor.

6080

SANDOWN

A seaside resort in a splendid natural setting. The shoreline of Sandown Bay curves sweepingly NE to the chalk Culver Cliffs near Bembridge, and extends S with sandstone cliffs to Shanklin and beyond. Unlike Shanklin and Ventnor, where the town centres are a little inland, the main part of Sandown is closely related to its seafront. The Esplanade and sea wall were laid out in 1889; the High Street is roughly parallel, with some densely built streets behind.

Before the C19 there was a scattered hamlet. A coastal fort was built in the 1540s, succeeded, after erosion, by another in 1636 (*see* Introduction, p. 26). This was in turn superseded by a fort a little further N in 1866, of which parts of the stone-faced ramparts survive in the Isle of Wight Zoo. Barracks were

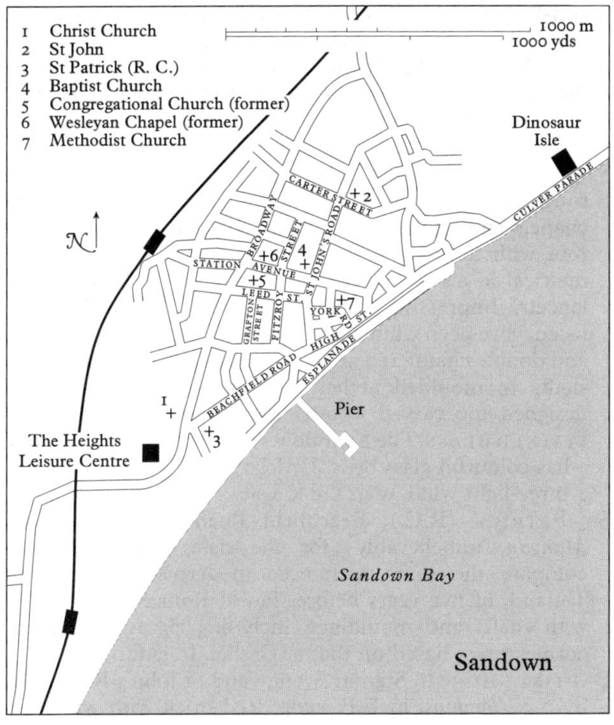

built in the Napoleonic Wars to the S of the original settlement (one block remains adjoining the Heights Leisure Centre). There was some seaside-related building before the railway from Ryde was opened in 1864, after which Sandown quickly grew into a town.

CHRIST CHURCH, Broadway (SW end). Built in 1845–7 to serve the developing village and the garrison, by *W.H. Woodman* of Reading, in Geometrical style. It first had a S aisle and S porch-tower, partly contained within the aisle, with stone spire; the N aisle was added 1863–4. The chancel was rebuilt 1874–6 by *S.E. Tomkins*, still in C13 style, with a S chapel and an organ and vestry space to the N. The W end was reconstructed 1876–8, with a deeply moulded W door and a rose window containing three cusped circles. The nave arcades differ: the piers on the S side are octagonal, those on the N round, with moulded capitals. The chancel has two-bay arcades on both sides with rich capitals, stiff-leaf and naturalistic. The S chapel was associated with the Crown Princess of Germany, Queen Victoria's daughter, who visited Sandown; she gave the STAINED GLASS in the SE window, 1875 by *Clayton & Bell* – who also designed the E chapel window. Also in the chapel, an elaborate C17 wooden ALTAR TABLE said to be of Austrian origin.

ST JOHN, Carter Street. 1880–1 by *C.L. Luck*. Big church in rough near-local stone, nearly rectangular with aisles and chapels ending just short of the chancel; continuous tiled roof with flèche towards the E. C13-style windows; Geometrical in aisles; paired trefoil lights in clerestory; tall W lancets. Impressive interior: the walls, originally brick-faced, have been whitened; arcades with slender round piers and double chamfered arches. – PULPIT. Octagonal; marble shafts to moulded arches. By *Jones & Willis*, who also designed the carved wooden REREDOS; both 1910–11. – STAINED GLASS. The E window – two tiers of cusped lancets – has colourful glass by *A.T. Moore*, 1910. He also designed a three-light window in the N aisle.

ST PATRICK (R.C.), Beachfield Road. 1928–9 by *W.C. Mangan*, unbelievably (for the date) Neo-Norman – compare the same architect's modernistic St Saviour, Totland, of five years before. Florid Romanesque W door with shafts and mouldings, including zigzag, and round corner turret based on that at Cashel, Ireland.

BAPTIST CHURCH, Station Avenue and St John's Road. 1882 by *S.E. Tomkins*, in E.E. style. Red brick with white and black brick decoration; high gabled street front with three lancets, and corner turrets with small pointed tops.

Other Nonconformist chapels are of rough stone with fine dressings, and have gabled street fronts with elaborate traceried windows. The former CONGREGATIONAL CHURCH, Leed Street (now a snooker club), 1872–3 by *Thomas Elworthy* of St Leonards, Sussex, is quite a landmark with its corner tower topped by a slender octagonal steeple and tall spirelet. The former WESLEYAN CHAPEL, Station Avenue (now a furniture store), 1865–6 by *W.W. Pocock*, has small corner turrets with pyramidal caps; the METHODIST CHURCH, York Road, built in 1882 as a Bible Christian chapel, has bands of darker stone on its street front.

GOOD SHEPHERD. *See* Lake.

Sandown retains its PIER, the only pleasure pier remaining on the Island (that at Ryde is for transit). Started in 1879, extended 1895, partly reconstructed *c.* 1970–3. The shore-end PAVILION, built in 1933–4 in modernistic style, was refurbished and extended in 1989–90. The present frontage does not call for architectural comment; the sides, with plain whitened walls rising to even roof-lines, still suggest the 1930s. The Esplanade runs mainly NE from the pier. In the opposite direction, it ends abruptly, and largely natural cliffs rise behind the beach, with a small promenade in front, for about 1 m. towards Shanklin. The transition is now marked, dramatically, by NAPOLEON'S LANDING of *c.* 2000–3, a range of apartments in sections of different heights from four to ten storeys with metal balconies.* Each section has a central rounded piece of roof-line.

To the NE of the Pier, a mixture of C19 and C20 buildings faces the ESPLANADE. The three-storey CARLTON HOTEL of *c.* 1990, on a slight curve, has a grid of balconies in a concrete framework. Further along, the buildings are set back at higher level. The oldest, two-storeyed and gabled, is part of the OCEAN HOTEL, built *c.* 1850 as the King's Head. It was extended in 1900 with a grand frontage to the parallel HIGH STREET, of nine bays, three-storeyed and stuccoed. The wider end bays have paired pilasters; the bay on the r. contains the arch of a former carriageway. High Street became densely built in the later C19, and part of the NW side has a succession of upper storeys with canted bay windows. On the opposite side, S of the Ocean Hotel, are two houses of *c.* 1850, in coursed stone with gabled two-storey porches and wide stuccoed frames to the windows – the latter suggesting a lingering local 'Georgian' tradition, indicated also on a humbler scale in some of the tight-knit streets to the NW, e.g. Fitzroy Street. In the otherwise obscure GRAFTON STREET is the TOWN HALL, built in 1868–9 as a privately owned place of assembly. Stylish and conservative, the main part of three bays with giant fluted pilasters under a pediment containing the Prince of Wales's feathers (why?). The windows have individual pediments, round except in the centre bay. To the l. is a lower wing, also pedimented; the corresponding r. wing has been separated and treated differently. Nearby in Leed Street is the former Congregational church (*see* above). In the parallel STATION AVENUE, next to the Baptist church (*see* above) is a former cinema, where a new front was added to an older building in 1921. Simple Art Deco with lines radiating on the upper part of the façade to a stepped roof-line.

Back to the Esplanade. The WAR MEMORIAL, a Celtic cross on a broadening base, is well placed on a platform above the beach. The Esplanade is continued NE along the seafront by Culver Parade; about ½ m. along is DINOSAUR ISLE, a museum of geology and prehistoric fauna, by *Rainey* 89
Petrie Johns, 2000–1. It is low, broad and jolly-looking as we approach; the roof has an undulating curve based on the shape of a prehistoric flying reptile, protruding as a canopy

*The name refers to landings, which did not take place, by either Napoleon I or III, against the possibility of which the C19 fortifications were built.

on the main front, with an external pattern of thin diagonal shafts and a triangular entrance feature like an open tent.

HEIGHTS LEISURE CENTRE, off Broadway on the S side of the town. On part of the site of the BARRACKS, first built during the Napoleonic Wars. The surviving thirteen-bay block, now Council Offices, is severe and simple, in grey brick with red dressings and low slate roof, the three bays at either end brought slightly forward. The main part of the Leisure Centre, opened 1982, has little architectural distinction, but additions of 1991–2 by *Jenkins Milton Partnership* are lively and conspicuous, set above grassy slopes well seen from the road. Of these, the square-shaped single-storey Health Suite has a slate pyramid roof rising to a glazed apex; its roof is broken by dormers and extends to form canopies; the set-back walls in pale brick are enlivened by bands of darker colour. A smaller wing on the S side is in a simpler version of the style.

6090 # SEAVIEW

Nettlestone and Seaview

A seaside and one-time maritime village on the NE coast. The main part developed after 1800 behind Nettlestone Point, a broad bulge on the shoreline, and at first was partly inhabited by pilots who guided ships in the Solent and Channel. To the

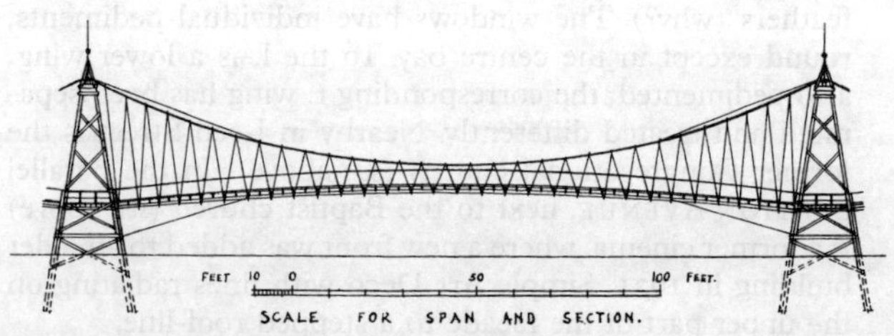

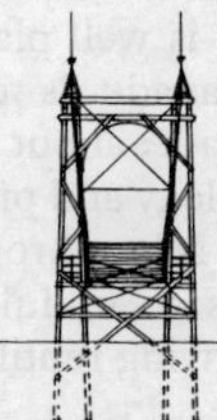

Seaview Pier, part-elevation and section.
Drawing by V. Launder, 1946

W was a former tidal inlet, later marshland, where salt was produced from *c.* 1790. By the 1840s the present name was adopted and Seaview grew as a small resort, with a strong fashionable element. Its outstanding feature, the Pier, was opened in 1881. It was the only one in Britain, apart from the original Palace Pier in Brighton built sixty years earlier, which was constructed as a series of suspension bridges; there were three main spans in this form. Unfortunately it was destroyed in a storm in 1951 – the worst architectural loss suffered by the Isle of Wight, apart from that of East Cowes Castle, during the C20.

ST PETER, Church Road. It stands out in its close-built setting, with triple end gables and walls of rough Swanage stone. First built 1859–62 by *Thomas Hellyer* with nave, N aisle and small chancel. Chancel enlarged and N vestry built *c.* 1871, with Geometrical E window to each. S chapel (with similar E window) and incomplete S aisle by *Stephen Salter*, 1920. The N arcade is remarkable, with short octagonal piers, complicated capitals and low-pitched arches bordered in red brick, but faced in yellow brick underneath. This design was copied by *Salter* in the two extant bays of the S nave arcade. The chancel arch (*c.* 1871) has short paired marble shafts with elaborately carved capitals and corbels. It contains the most memorable feature, the SCREEN of 1909 by *Jones & Willis* in thin ironwork, with gables, cusps and intricate patterns in panels and spandrels. The CHOIR STALLS with traceried panels, also 1909, are by the same firm. – STAINED GLASS. E window, St Peter with flanking figures, against a dense pattern of diagonals and rosettes; by whom?

The centre part of the village is close-knit, with domestic and commercial properties built and altered piecemeal through the C19 and since. The short informal ESPLANADE faces a rocky beach, with slipway and moorings. The lower part of HIGH STREET on the W side was one of the first areas to develop; JASMINE COTTAGE (until recently a bank but re-converted to a house) has bold two-storey bows of the early C19. The numerous mid-Victorian houses are mostly of buff brick, sometimes variegated – for instance in STEYNE ROAD, corner of Ryde Road, where red brick quoins make a zigzag pattern. The Arts and Crafts influence is seen in SANDLANDS of *c.* 1900, further up Steyne Road, in fanciful 'Old English' with timbered gables, tile-hanging, moulded chimneys, and a shaped gable pattern in brick on the side of the stack. Nearby Sandlands Cottage, an C18 survival, makes a nice contrast with its simple brick front and stone side wall. On the N side of RYDE ROAD (amid buildings of different character) is a pair of houses by *Stephen Salter*, *c.* 1910; roughcast, with end gables over lattice windows, and brick chimneys with thin cornices – a cluster of six rises at the centre of the composition. In SALTERNS ROAD to the W is a row of cottages which were occupied by salt workers in *c.* 1800 but which may go back earlier; Nos. 1–2 have single-storey rendered elevations with sweeping tiled roofs and dormers; the others are two-storeyed. The owner of the saltworks built SEAFIELD HOUSE *c.* 1815, now surrounded by early C20 houses on the S side of Bluett Avenue. Buff brick, with a large bowed centrepiece framed by a veranda with iron columns and broad openwork brackets. Externally this is one of the best of the many villas of the period in the Ryde area.

The Pier was to the SE of the main village. A Victorian hotel facing its site at the far end of Pier Road was replaced with a massive series of flats called SEAVIEW BAY by *Broadway Malyan, c.* 1988–90; of two to six storeys with stepped sloping roof-lines, white walls, diagonally projecting windows, and a scatter of porthole-like openings.

SPRING VALE developed as a separate settlement to the NW. Stuccoed villas of *c.* 1830 face the sea, two with bows. Among them is the SPRING VALE HOTEL of *c.* 1890, with Italianate corner towers, balustraded bay windows both bowed and square-ended, and iron portes cochères at either end.

NETTLESTONE is an older village to the SW, now joined to Seaview. NETTLESTONE MANOR, NW of the Green, was a manorial farmhouse of *c.* 1600 or a little before. The ground floor is of rubble with very large ashlar quoins; the first floor is of brick – an early use of the material on the Island. The windows are mostly renewed.

HORSTONE POINT off Gully Road, ¾ m. S of the centre of Seaview, was designed as a holiday home in 1928 by *Oliver Hill*, who combined elements of the Arts and Crafts tradition, the styles of Lutyens, Neo-Georgianism and interwar Modernism in compelling ways. It is basically a rectangle with roughly rendered walls and a sweeping roof of jade-green tiles. The main (garden) front faces SE, with three wide arched windows on the ground storey, and pairs of metal casements on the first floor, their transverse glazing bars tilted off the horizontal. The NE elevation has a big canted bow on both floors and a balcony to the r. The SW façade is striking, with a semicircular window over a broad short stem in the gable end, and jade-green shutters to the casement windows on the first floor, giving the effect of a chequered horizontal band. Much the same effect is achieved with shutters and windows on the entrance front, over a semicircular doorway. Inside there is one main room, with ample views through the rounded windows and a very distinctive fireplace. This has a wide frame faced in varied red-brown tiles, with short stretches of green tiles along the top, and concave walls of thin bricks flanking the hearth. Details including staircase balusters (almost bottle-like in the way they narrow upward), bookcases with splayed shelf-ends, and slender hinges to oak doors, are designed with a skill which makes such simple features seem special.

THE PRIORY (Priory Bay Hotel). *See* St Helens.

SHALFLEET *4085*

Shalfleet first grew at the head of a creek, from which the tidal water has receded; it is now a main-road village at the crossing of a stream. The parish is large, with several outlying estates. One, HAMSTEAD about 2 m. NW, was bought by *John Nash c.* 1802 as a retreat from his main Island home, East Cowes Castle. He built a romantic villa (of which nothing survives); it had a round tower with views over the Solent. His widow continued to live there, with members of the Pennethorne family who were her distant relatives (Sir James Pennethorne, an associate of Nash who became a distinguished architect in his own right, was not himself a resident but an occasional visitor). Pennethorne ownership lasted into the C20.

ST MICHAEL THE ARCHANGEL. One of the most interesting – indeed perplexing – churches on the Island, with notable Norman, High Gothic and post-Reformation work. The Early Norman W tower is like a small keep, broad and short, with clasping buttresses and billet moulding under a string course. Its only entry is from inside the church. The ground storey has small lights in the three external sides, in their present form Gothic, with cusps. The upper stage has only one small window, above the nave roof – this, of two *p. 19*

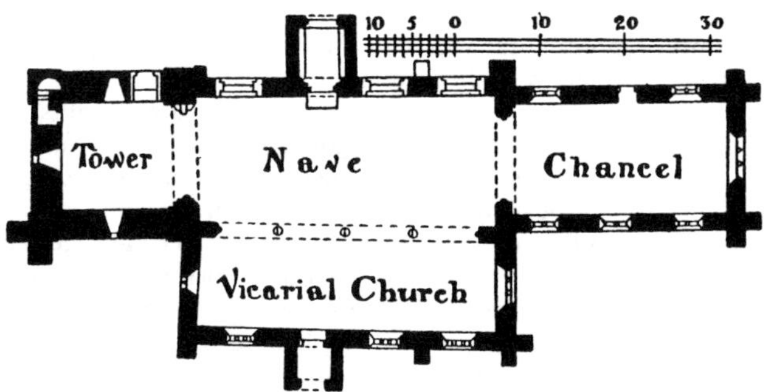

Shalfleet church, plan.
Adapted from *The Victoria County History, Hampshire and the Isle of Wight* vol. 5, 1912

pointed lights, must also be post-Norman. Clearly defence was a consideration when the tower was built. (A low broad spire was added *c.* 1800 but removed *c.* 1910; there is now a battlemented parapet.) The oldest feature in the body of
11 the church is the C12 N doorway (behind a simple porch of 1754). It is of three orders, the inner one roll-moulded on the arch but with squared jambs; the other two plain round the arch, but with shafts and decorated scallop capitals. There is a remarkable sculpted TYMPANUM; the significance of the scene portrayed is not obvious. In Pevsner's words, 'A bearded man in a lay robe grips by their heads two affronted lions, one of their heads in profile, the other frontal. But both have long tails sprouting out into ornamental forms almost as in Steinberg drawings.' In fact the lions' tails end in quite elaborate foliage, suggesting a relatively late date in the Norman period.

The church was remodelled in the mid to late C13, with details of high quality resembling contemporary work on the Island and in Hampshire (*see* pp. 20–1). A S aisle was added with a noble four-bay arcade, almost identical to the S chapel arcade at Arreton (q.v.), with high moulded bases, tall slender Purbeck marble piers, finely moulded bell capitals, and double-chamfered arches which rise from cylindrical springer blocks above the capitals. The chancel was rebuilt with delicately formed Geometrical windows; their slender mullions show half-round shafts internally, and also externally on the E and N sides, to pleasing effect. The upper tracery of the chancel side windows and the E window is in the form of circles with interlocked trefoil patterns (cf. Arreton again). The chancel arch has Purbeck-shafted responds; the plainer tower arch is probably a little later.

The S aisle, ending in a chapel, presents a puzzle. It has a simple two-light C13 window in an arched frame high in the W wall, where it looks re-set; the external stonework indicates that the aisle was widened at some time by 2 ft (65 cm.) or more. Three windows on the S side show highly odd tracery. Each has three main lights without cusps (the centre one wider and taller) and three oval upper lights, of which the side ones are set diagonally. However, the fourth window on the S side, lighting the chapel, is simpler – three-light, square-headed. To add to confusion there is a trefoil PISCINA in the adjoining S wall, obviously C13. A suggested building sequence, complicated but plausible, is that the C13 S aisle, narrower than the present one, opened into a chapel of the present width, explaining the piscina. Later the main part of the aisle was enlarged to the width of the chapel, as now. The date 1630 is inscribed on what appears to be a stone REREDOS in the chapel; this consists of two inset panels under depressed arches each containing a plain shield, with a cornice at sill level. Might this date also refer to the widening of the aisle, and could the aisle have included a gallery at such an early date – helping to explain the size and height of the three side windows, and the likely re-setting of the small window high in the W aisle wall? A further confusing feature is the E window of the aisle-chapel; it was altered and heightened in 1889, when new upper tracery was added, similar to that of the main S windows. (Previously this window had a squared head, like the S window of the chapel.)

The nave N wall was largely rebuilt in 1812; the windows have intersecting tracery in brick frames. The interior was scraped of plaster in 1889 to reveal rough stonework. Late Georgian BOX PEWS remain, with simple panelling, but they are less high than before the restoration. – PULPIT. Early C17, with a bookrest on brackets all round; the upper set of panels has arches in false perspective. – CHANCEL SCREEN, *c.* 1910, but with old linenfold panelling in its dado. – STAINED GLASS. S chancel window 1888 by *Ward & Hughes*, for the Pennethorne family. War memorial window, easternmost on N side of nave, by *Jones & Willis*, 1919. E window also by *Jones & Willis*, 1923.

SHALFLEET MANOR, N of the church across the road. Long low S façade of stone, with slightly taller one-bay E extension; near the centre is a gabled porch. Small mullioned windows on the upper floor – of two lights in the main part and three in the E extension – with tripartite sashes below. The porch has a mullioned window over a round-arched doorway; it has the date 1680. (A beam inside is also dated 1680.) Can this be the date for the main building – very conservative in style – with the taller part being slightly later?

NINGWOOD MANOR, 1¼ m. SSW. Bought by John Pinhorn, a London banker, and enlarged by him *c.* 1784 (date in roof structure). Handsome five-bay stone front with rusticated quoins, stone-framed sashes and a Tuscan-columned porch with dentilled cornice. Above the parapet is a tall balustrade; ranges of balusters alternate on each side with open diagonal Chinoiserie patterns. There are urns above the ends of the balustrade, and a larger one, draped, over the centre bay.

ARTIGIANO, Elm Lane, 1 m. SE. An outpost of a fashion firm, converted from two large agricultural sheds by *The Manser Practice*, 2000–1. The sheds, of different sizes with low-pitched roofs, have been refaced with rough-sawn planks rendered grey, and the space between filled by an entrance pavilion with glass front under a broad white fascia. The larger shed is roofed with ply panels forming a wide coved ceiling; the end wall of the smaller shed is entirely glazed with views over farmland. A supremely elegant adaptation of unpromising buildings in an unlikely setting.

5580 SHANKLIN

Shanklin was a small scattered place, mainly of stone-built and thatch-roofed cottages, which was 'discovered' around 1800 by adventurous travellers who were thrilled by its picturesque setting, cliff-bound coastline and gorge-like Chine with a
p. 7 waterfall. It developed first as a romantic rural-maritime retreat; what is now the Old Village evolved into a collection
4, p. 40 of *cottages ornés* with a few genuine older cottages. The first small hotels were opened in 1824 and 1833, and villas were

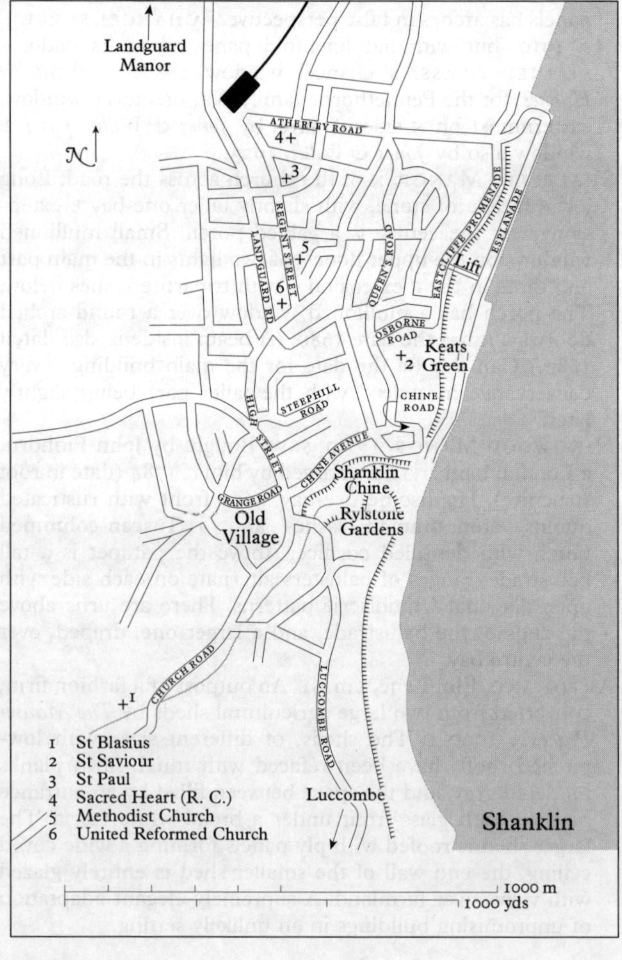

built increasingly on choice sites before the railway from Ryde arrived in 1864. After that Shanklin grew quickly into a town, mainly to the N of the Old Village – but much remains of the earlier rustic retreat. The seafront is in two tiers; quiet and grassy on the clifftop, crowded (in season) along the Esplanade below, which developed with buildings one deep against the cliff face. A lift has connected the two levels since 1892. Unfortunately the coastal centrepiece, the pier, has gone; it was damaged beyond repair in the storm of 1987.

CHURCHES

ST BLASIUS, Church Road, SW of the Old Village, and still on the edge of open country.* A simple rectangle till the C19. A N transept was added in 1853 and a S transept, short S aisle, and central turret in 1859, when the nave was extended W. The chancel remains basically C14. Attractive exterior of rough stone, with the entrance porch on the E side of the S transept. The octagonal wooden lantern turret rises from a tapering tiled base at the crossing, and is crowned by a spirelet. The character of the interior is diverse; the crossing, with its intersecting beams and view up into the turret, recalls the work of the Victorian architect E.B. Lamb. Around the sanctuary is traceried panelling of *c.* 1914, with gaps to reveal the sharply trefoiled C14 SEDILE and PISCINA. – The C19 PULPIT has four panel carvings of the Apostles and the Virgin, probably Flemish of *c.* 1520–30. – A very remarkable CHEST evidently came from Winchester Cathedral; it has a profusely carved front containing the name of Thomas Silkstead, Prior (of the cathedral monastery), and the date 1512; his initials are entwined on panels with arabesque decoration. It may have been brought to the Island before the Civil War. – ROYAL ARMS of William III, painted board on the S nave wall. Also two small boards of the 1630s on the S transept walls, one with a royal rose and CR, the other with the Prince of Wales's feathers and CP. – STAINED GLASS. Two single-light windows in S transept, both 1861, with scenes in Gothic canopies; by whom? – MONUMENTS. Sarah Popham, †1808 aged twelve, with a relief of her rising to Heaven (chancel S wall). Two black marble FLOOR SLABS in the chancel, one for Grace Broad-Popham, †1773, with particularly good Roman and script lettering. – LYCHGATE by *Sir Arthur Blomfield*, 1894. *p. 264*

ST SAVIOUR, Queen's Road, the church of seaside Shanklin, with a spire rising behind the clifftop buildings. The oldest

*The dedication was to St John until *c.* 1900; it was changed on the strength of a reference to a medieval altar of St Blasius in the church.

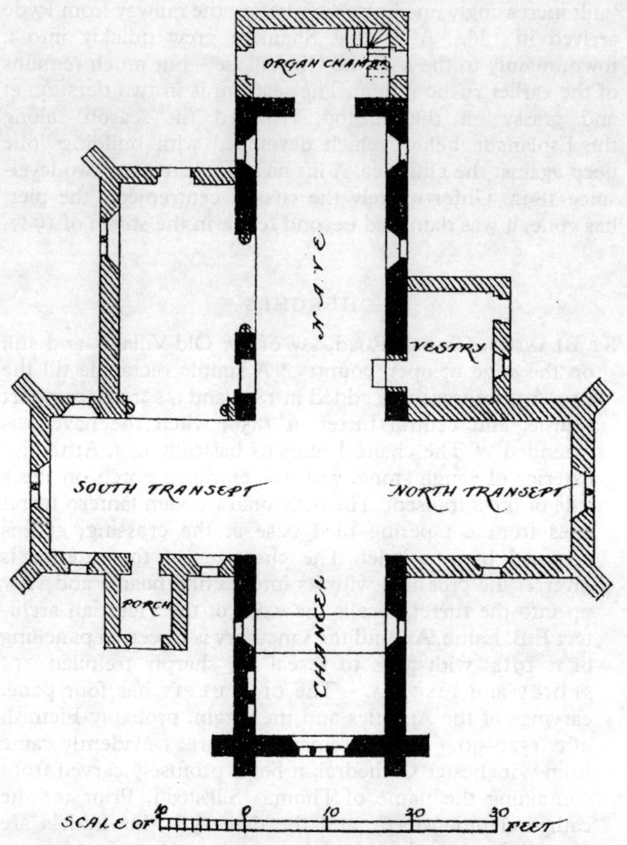

Shanklin, St Blasius, plan.
From Percy Stone, *The Architectural Antiquities of the Isle of Wight*, 1891

parts by *Thomas Hellyer*: nave and chancel 1867–9 and S aisle 1871. N aisle 1875–6 by *T.E.C. Streatfield*; NW tower and spire 1885–7 by *W.O. Milne*; W extensions by *Milne*, 1903–5, including galilee porch and round-ended SW baptistery. Above the galilee, *Hellyer*'s W front has two Geometrical windows and a sexfoil circle above. His clerestory is odd, with cusped circular lights flanked by small lancets. The E window, a triple lancet, is an alteration of 1875 by Streatfield. The tower and spire are complex. The basic shape changes from square to octagonal at the belfry stage, but this is partly concealed by buttresses which rise to the

parapet; continuing pinnacles which used to cluster round the spire have been removed. But the upward thrust is still emphasized by sharply gabled spire lights. Inside, the arcades have thin round piers and moulded capitals, suggesting local C13 work. – Main REREDOS, 1876. Three cusped panels with coloured and gilt mosaic showing the Ascension with animated spectators – who was the artist? It holds its own against marble and mosaic WALL DECORATION on either side by *Powell*, 1914, with figures and dense details. – PULPIT. 1903, of wood; dense Gothic details; panels with circular motifs and entwined floral patterns. By *Editha Plowden* (church guide). – REREDOS in Lady Chapel (N aisle) by *Sir Charles Nicholson*, 1948, classical. – STAINED GLASS. SE chancel window by *Joseph Bell*, *c.* 1902, of two lights with large sexfoil circle; lively colourful details. – SW chancel window by *Powell*. – S aisle, two-light E and three-light SE windows by *E.R. Frampton*. – The next window to the W, also three-light, is by *Christopher* 79
Whall, *c.* 1913, depicting the Nativity; the figures and robes are largely in white, with strong patches of red and other colours; in the background is the outline of a town. – To its W, window commemorating a Boy Scout in uniform, †1926. By *Morris & Co.*, executed by *W.H. Knight*. – Windows by *Kempe*, *c.* 1905 or later, in baptistery and galilee, and N of the altar in the Lady Chapel.

Interesting CHURCH HALL to the NE, 1876 by *Streatfield*, with dormer windows over a lean-to roof supported by stone half-arches, providing a curious open-sided passage; a short wing links with the church. To the E, the former VICARAGE, 1870–1 by *Henry Woodyer*, his only building on the Island. Ground floor of stone with four narrow arches on slender piers facing the church, the two l. ones blind (except for small windows), the others opening into the porch. Upper storey with tile-hanging, scalloped in alternate courses; transomed window with trefoil lights over the porch, and a two-tier canted bay on the S front.

ST PAUL, Regent Street, by *C.L. Luck* (cf. St John, Sandown). Started 1875–6, completed by 1890; externally of ashlar. Damaged by a bomb 1943. The nave, and chancel with polygonal apse, have a continuous clerestory under an unbroken tiled roof; the aisles continue round the apse by what amounts to an ambulatory. Slender NW tower with rustically open wooden top stage. On the N side a parish room of 1897 with mullioned windows; W porch by *Percy Stone*, 1911. Inside, the arcades have moulded arches on round piers. A triforium-like range of blind two-light openings runs round the apse below the clerestory.

SACRED HEART (R.C.), Atherley Road, 1956–7 by *Gilbert & Hobson* of Ventnor. Brick, with N porch-tower containing a rounded doorway under a parabolic hoodmould. The side windows have backward-angled glazing, echoing the effect of the Coventry Cathedral windows on a small scale. Rectangular interior with wide-panelled, slightly cambered ceiling and canted W gallery. CRUCIFIX over the altar by *Henry Farmer*, *c.* 1949; commissioned for a temporary church built then to replace the earlier building, bombed in the war.

METHODIST CHURCH, Regent Street, 1883. Street front with unorthodox four-light Geometrical window; flanking turrets with spirelets.

p. 55 UNITED REFORMED CHURCH (formerly Congregational), prominent in the angle between High Street and Landguard Road. By *John Sulman*, 1888; E.E. style. The upper part of the tall tower was rebuilt by *Basil L. Phelps* in 1954 after war damage. The top storey has square corner buttresses ending with small pinnacles.

PERAMBULATION

The Perambulation begins outside the W end of St Saviour's church (*see* p. 264) in QUEEN'S ROAD, then proceeds to the clifftop with views over the coast, turns inland to the Old Village, and ends in the heart of the town. St Saviour was started (1867) soon after the railway reached Shanklin, and many houses to the S in Queen's Road pre-date it; the area to the N was developed – piecemeal – after the railway came. BELMONT HOTEL facing the church, *c.* 1875, has an irregular gabled front and wooden veranda with thin bracketed posts. Nearby Osborne Road leads E to KEATS GREEN, a grassy clifftop space from which one can appreciate Shanklin's setting.* To the r. the coastal vista ends with a tree-grown ridge which sweeps down to a rugged sandstone promontory over ½ m. away. In front, below the cliff, is the Esplanade, described on p. 268. To the l., EASTCLIFF
85 PROMENADE leads along the clifftop past the LIFT, one of Shanklin's chief landmarks, giving access to the Esplanade and beach; opened in 1892 and rebuilt in 1956. Externally it is a sensible concrete structure; a shaft of slender square section in front of the cliff face, with a glass-walled and glass-roofed passageway linking it with the clifftop. Across Eastcliff Promenade is the OCEAN VIEW HOTEL, *c.* 1960–70, in three white flat-roofed ranges, the centre range projecting slightly. The frontage of the upper storeys is open-framed, forming continuous balconies with slender vertical supports. The site is on a gentle slope, which adds to the effect. In partial contrast is a many-gabled building

*The Green itself has no connection with the poet. Keats stayed in the village in 1817 and 1819.

in the angle of Keats Green and Osborne Road, built in 1885 as the SHANKLIN CLUB; later it became the Keats Inn and it is now residential. The gables have fretted bargeboards; below are two tiers of iron-framed verandas with thin columns branching into traceried brackets. Further S is the back of *Woodyer*'s former vicarage (*see* St Saviour, p. 263).

The Perambulation turns W along Chine Road and CHINE AVENUE; Shanklin Chine is hidden to the S, giving no inkling of its gorge-like grandeur. On the corner of Queen's Road is BURLINGTON, an Italianate villa with heavy canted bays, notable for low boundary walls pierced with traceried diagonal patterns. Chine Avenue leads to the OLD VILLAGE, where C19 *cottages ornés* and older genuine cot- *p. 40*
tages cluster tightly along the winding CHURCH ROAD – all too busy with traffic. Most are in rough local stone and thatched, but the CRAB INN, an C18 survival, is surprisingly of brick; an *orné* S wing in stone with decorative bargeboards was added *c.* 1865. Then on the E side PENCIL COTTAGE and THE OLD THATCH form a self-consciously picturesque group with scrolly bargeboards, followed by the larger GLENBROOK HOTEL with similar gable treatment; the last three all existed by 1842 (the date 1882 on Glenbrook relates to an alteration). Across the road HOLLIERS HOTEL, originally built in 1824 (as a hotel) with a thatched roof, was enlarged by 1870 and now looks urban, not cottagey, but C18 cottages adjoin.* Church Road continues SW to St Blasius church (*see* p. 263), while to the E and SE are the upper entrance to the Chine and also Rylstone Gardens (*see* below).

The Perambulation turns N up HIGH STREET. A short way along Grange Road, leading W, is the former OLD CHURCH PARISH ROOM (now a school of dancing) of *c.* 1860, surprisingly classical with stuccoed temple front; paired Tuscan pilasters flank the entrance. VERNON COTTAGE on the E side of High Street is the best *cottage* 45
orné in Shanklin, built in 1817 with a thatched roof and many gables with bargeboards similar to those in the centre of the Old Village. It has been little altered externally except for a mid-Victorian NW wing in keeping, although half-timbering has been added to the jettied end elevation of the original part. DAISH'S HOTEL, nearly opposite, expanded *p. 268*
with the growth of the resort. The original part was built as a hotel in 1833; its main (E) and S elevations are of stone with plain gables, mildly Picturesque but not *orné*. There is a very different N extension, perhaps *c.* 1870; stuccoed

*Longfellow stayed in the old hotel in 1868 and called the village 'one of the quietest and loveliest places in the kingdom'.

Shanklin, Daish's Hotel, engraving by A. Brannon.
From George Brannon, *The Pleasure Visitor's Companion in Making the Tour of the Isle of Wight*, 1850

Italianate with round-arched ground floor. Different again is a taller late C19 stone-built wing to the SW, with a gabled skyline.

Northward is the Victorian town centre; the High Street follows the twisting line of a previous country lane. STEEPHILL ROAD leads r. On the corners are assertive buildings of buff brick with stuccoed ground floors and pointed angle turrets; the one to the N, *c.* 1890, was a bank and the other, 1899, the Post Office, with keystoned round-arched windows on the first floor. These buildings frame the view E to the SHANKLIN THEATRE, on the site of a Literary and Scientific Institute of 1879, which became the Town Hall in 1913 and, after a fire, was reconstructed in 1933–4 as a theatre by *Cooper & Corbett*. The ambitious façade dates from then; in a French Classical style, its upper portico with attached columns and plaques, ribbons and other French C17 and C18 motifs. The S part has an irregular frontage with short spire; this must survive from the original Literary Institute.

THE ESPLANADE

Before 1800 Shanklin foreshore was simply beach backed by sandstone cliffs, with Shanklin Chine opening off towards the S, and the lesser Small Hope Chine ½ m. to the N. By the time of the Tithe Map of 1842 plots for buildings had been laid out on reclaimed land in front of the cliff, with a footway and sea wall in front, for about 400 yds (370 metres) N of Shanklin Chine; by 1862 most of the plots were filled with houses. In 1873–6 an ESPLANADE of the present width was laid out on reclaimed beach further N, together with building plots against the cliff and a connecting road in what had been Small Hope Chine. In the 1880s the Esplanade was extended S towards Shanklin Chine, in front of the older development. Victorian and later buildings of little distinction (most of the earlier ones altered) now front the cliffs one deep. The Pier was built in 1888–91; following its loss (*see* above) there is no focal point on the seafront other than the modest CLOCK TOWER of 1897, square with slightly broader clock stage, topped by a slender spirelet. Small beach-side SHELTERS at intervals; those towards the S, probably *c.* 1890, are elegant with hollow broad-eaved roofs and ironwork cresting. But the greatest landmark on the seafront is the Lift (*see* p. 266), its shaft soaring in front of the clifftop – all the more conspicuous since buildings to its SE have been demolished.

OUTLYING BUILDINGS

In RYLSTONE GARDENS, a public park S of Shanklin Chine, is RYLSTONE HOUSE, *c.* 1860, now a hotel, stone-built with jettied half-timbered projection. More remarkable is the nearby CHALET of *c.* 1880, which has a two-storey wooden 75
veranda with slender columns and openwork balustrade running round three sides; the low-pitched roof extends continuously over the upper storey. It is related stylistically to the former Shanklin Club on Keats Green (*see* p. 267).

In LITTLESTAIRS ROAD, off Sandown Road to the N, GREEN TILES (No. 33) is a house of 1929 with white walls, mullioned windows, a simple pedimented door hood and the roof treatment which gives it its name; the date is on a plaque.

LANDGUARD MANOR, off Landguard Manor Road, about ⅔ m. N of the town centre. A modest mid- to late C18 house, facing S, was extended N by a large range in 1878; the whole was remodelled in 1906. The original C18 front is of five bays in brick with stone quoins. The present main frontage is the E side of the 1878 range; it is irregular, stone-built, mainly Neo-Jacobean, but with a sumptuous balustraded porch, round-arched in front and at the sides, which was probably added in 1906. (Internally there is a two-tiered colonnaded hall, with a well staircase, of 1906. Wing with arched loggia to W.)

To the S of Shanklin is the beginning of the Undercliff (*see* p. 6), with a dramatic coastline of cliffs and precipitous slopes, subject to landslips. LUCCOMBE has scattered houses; NEW HOUSE in Bracken Dell Road, facing the cliff path, was built as a small seaside retreat by *F. R. S. Yorke* with

Penelope Whiting. Designed 1946, completed 1951. Single storey; the main part of the façade is a veranda under the flat roof, with casement windows behind; the exposed walls are of rough local stone. It remains essentially as built externally, although windows may have been altered in detail. DUNNOSE COTTAGE, about ½ m. inland near the head of Luccombe Chine, is a thatched *cottage orné*. It is a rectangle with wings making it a cruciform shape, the S wing providing the centre of the frontage; an uncannily symmetrical arrangement for a building of this type.

SHEAT MANOR *see* GATCOMBE

4580

SHORWELL

One of the most picturesque Island villages, set in Greensand undulations S of the chalk hills, with buildings in different varieties of stone. There are three manor houses, mainly C16 or early C17. North Court and West Court were associated with the Leigh family and Wolverton Manor with the Dingleys.

ST PETER has a complicated history. There was a chapel soon after 1200, dependent on Carisbrooke church; it was extended in stages and became a parish church later in the Middle Ages. Alterations were made, and furnishings introduced, by Sir John Leigh of North Court, *c*. 1615–30; the full extent of his work is debatable. The oldest visible features are two blocked lancets in the N chapel wall, and the S doorway which must be re-set – an elegant piece, early C13, with a band of nailhead decoration round the arch and Purbeck marble jamb shafts. It is contained within a porch of 1772. The windows are mostly Perp, those at the three-gabled E end showing an interesting variety of tracery. The main E window, under a four-centred arch, is of four lights, the centre two having ogee tracery; a window in the S wall of the aisle is of a similar design but set within a rectangular frame, with cusped circles in the spandrels.

A W tower projects beyond the ends of the aisles; it has small square belfry lights, battlements and a short spire. Tower and spire are built of squared stone blocks (most of the rest is externally of rubble). The S aisle extends further W than the N aisle; it was lengthened *c*. 1620–30 to store a gun, part of the precautions against invasion that required every parish on the Island to have one (cf. Brading, p. 94). A blocked W doorway gave access for the gun.

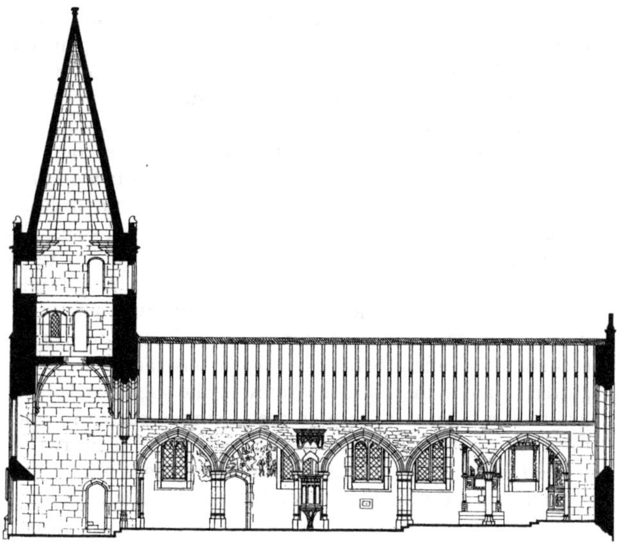

Shorwell church, section.
From Percy Stone, *The Architectural Antiquities of the Isle of Wight*, 1891

The W end poses problems of dating: how far is it pre- or post-Reformation? The two-light W windows to tower and aisles – the stonework of which was accurately renewed in the 1990s – are nearly identical, with curious cusped upper lights of dagger form. The date 1623 was inscribed over the N aisle window before the stonework was renewed, and the corresponding S window must have been of similar date because of the aisle's extension. The tower and spire as well as the W windows could be examples of C17 'Gothic Survival'. Similar questions are posed in respect of internal features.

In describing the interior, many of the FURNISHINGS must be considered in relation to the structure. Apart from the W end the church is rectangular, with continuous five-
bay arcades and no internal divisions between nave and 26
chancel (except at roof level), or between aisles and chapels. The PISCINA in the S chapel, with four-centred arch and prominent drain, indicates that this part of the fabric is medieval. The three bays forming the nave arcades have octagonal piers, hollowed capitals with thick plain abaci, and four-centred arches of two orders, the inner ones chamfered, the outer ones simply moulded. But the arches in the two bays adjoining the chancel are of one order only (the walls above them being thinner), and the piers are round

and more slender. Many descriptions of the church state that the arcades are C15, but their style is hardly plausible Perp of medieval date. They are surely C17 Gothic (as indeed the *Victoria Country History* suggests); if so, the
26 remarkable stone PULPIT must be of that period too. It is fixed against a short length of wall between the second and third bays (from the W) of the N arcade, with a stepped approach from behind. It is half-octagonal with trefoiled panels, rising from a concave stem with panelled sides. The design could just pass as C15, but this would be a strange location for a pulpit in a small medieval church. A fine semi-octagonal wooden canopy is fixed to the wall above the pulpit, with the date 1620; typically Jacobean with round-arched edges, angle pendants, and panels carved with vine patterns under the cornice. Many of the PEWS are placed lengthwise from W to E; they are of simple early C17 open form with panelled backs, and originally had plain round-topped ends. Unfortunately trefoil poppyheads were added to many in the C19. The FONT has a bowl shaped like the nave arcade capitals, on an octagonal stem. The small FONT COVER has tapering panels with circle and dagger patterns, a text around the rim and the figure of a dove at the top – quintessentially early C17. If the arcades and pulpit are of the date suggested, together with the older pews and font, this is a substantially preserved Anglican interior from the period after the Elizabethan settlement but just before that of Laud, focused on the pulpit. However, no furnishings survive to indicate what the E end was like in the C17.

OTHER FURNISHINGS. WALL PAINTING, above the N door.* An exceptionally elaborate depiction of St Christopher, shown as usual bearing the Christ Child across the river, but here flanked by two episodes from his legend: at l., standing beside a wayside cross, and bidding farewell to the devil he had previously served; at r., the attempted martyrdom of the saint with arrows, one of which flies back to pierce the King of Lycia in the eye. The large central figure of Christopher is accompanied by the lantern-bearing hermit standing before his cell at top r., and by charming depictions of ships and of a boat with oarsmen, as well as by various fishes naturalistically depicted, one of them being caught by a fisherman seated on the bank. The whole is somewhat repainted, but datable to *c.* 1470. A painting of the Last Judgment formerly existed over the opposite doorway. – BEAM AND CROSS spanning the entrance to the chancel, by *Percy Stone*, 1904. Christ in Majesty in front of a cross (i.e. not a rood), with archangels kneeling on either side, set on a beam with inscription. – MONUMENTS.

*Description contributed by David Park.

Shorwell church, monument to Elizabeth Leigh (†1619), elevation. From Percy Stone, *The Architectural Antiquities of the Isle of Wight*, 1891

Richard Bethell, vicar, †1518, chancel floor. Brass figure in gown, 20 in. (50 cm.) long. – Brass plate to the two wives of Barnabas Leigh of West Court, †1615 and †1619, E end of N chapel. They face each other holding a large ring containing a heart shape. – In the N chapel tombs of the Leighs. Sir John, †1629, of white stone. Small figure within a large wall canopy with Corinthian columns; he kneels at a desk, with the baby figure of his great-grandson, fully dressed, behind him. – Elizabeth his wife, †1619 (a Dingley from Wolverton); in the same general form but without a figure, and more accomplished in its details; within the canopy are strapwork and spiral patterns with a head in relief; at the top two standing putti with instruments of Death, and coat of arms amid strapwork. – John Leigh, †1688, between the earlier monuments and very different. Massive marble wall slab inscribed in fine writing with initial flourishes; garlanded borders and shaped top with coat of arms. – In the spandrels of the arcades is a series of circular tablets, in white marble with black borders, to members of the Bull family and others, *c.* 1790–1810, with fine lettering. That to Catherine Bull, †1795, is by *Flaxman.*

The varied old buildings of the village are strung along three roads that converge near the church. STONE PLACE, on the E side of the road leading S, is of chequered rubble with mullioned windows; early C17. Opposite the church is a pair of thatched cottages in a patchwork of sandstones. Further N, on the l. side, the POST OFFICE is unexpectedly urban (in the best sense) and in brick; early C19 with two bowed shop fronts and smaller bow windows above, the r. one under a gable containing a tiny segmental window. More stone-built thatched cottages to the N, opposite the entrance to North Court.

28 NORTH COURT, built *c.* 1615 by Sir John Leigh, is NNW of the church (but not visible from the village because of planting). Outwardly, when seen from the E and SE, it is the grandest surviving C16–C17 house on the Island, built of brownish sandstone and set in gently undulating landscaped grounds. Both house and grounds were rescued from dereliction in the 1960s and later. The house was greatly altered internally in the C18 and subdivided in the C20, but retains its fine original E frontage. This is symmetrical except for a N wing, and has tall ranges of mullioned-and-transomed windows on both its main floors – beginning on the l. with simple cross-windows, followed by five-light canted bays under obelisk-shaped pinnacles, then by cross-windows again, with a central four-light window over the porch; the pattern continues in reverse. Above are three gables, with more obelisk-pinnacles at their apexes and on the parapets between. The single-storey porch has an ogee-shaped gable with smaller pinnacles, containing a

plaque with the family arms and the date 1615 – but the doorway is square-headed with a keystone, an early C18 alteration. The short S elevation has a two-storey bay window, matching the ones on the main front but added *c.* 1840–4. The fairly shallow N wing conforms in structure and details with the rest of the frontage and appears to be part of the original build, but it creates an asymmetry which at the time of building was untypical of substantial houses. The N frontage is a jumble. It too seems to date from the same time (old string courses suggest this), but new windows were inserted in the C18 with raised surrounds and keystones; their sashes were later replaced by transoms and mullions. The N porch was built in the 1830s in front of an older side entrance. It is generally a copy of the E porch of 1615, with an ogee gable. The N frontage was extended W, partly by *Percy Stone* in 1905, to link with an earlier outbuilding.

The main rooms behind the E front date from the internal remodelling of the early C18. The ENTRANCE HALL has modillion cornices, and two arches with keystones and panelled undersides at the far end. The l. one opens on to the STAIRCASE – among the finest of the period on the Island. 39
It is of well type, with intricate scroll patterns in the treads, plain and twisted balusters, fluted newel posts, and a richly moulded scroll end to the handrail. Behind is a Venetian window. In an upstairs room is a C17 wooden overmantel, *ex situ* and painted over; it has arched panels, elaborated pilasters and stylized figures and masks. The N part of the house is now separate – approached through the N porch. The ceiling in an upper room has delicate plaster decoration which looks mid C18.

The GARDENS have an interesting history. Terracing on the hillside to the S of the house may date from Sir John Leigh's time. Richard Bull, who bought the house *c.* 1795, and his daughter Elizabeth landscaped the grounds and built a temple, mausoleum, rustic summerhouse, conservatory and Alpine bridge. None of these survives; the bridge, crossing the road to Newport, was replaced *c.* 1970. A small BATH HOUSE remains in front of the house, of rough stone, beehive-shaped with a rounded doorway. A KNOT GARDEN just S of the house dates from *c.* 1840–4. The gardens have been splendidly re-created since the 1960s. The former STABLES AND COACHHOUSE to the NW, early C19, have a central range with three big four-centred arches in brown stone, and lower wings of lighter stone with square-headed Tudor-style windows.

WEST COURT, ½ m. WSW. The smallest of the three Shorwell p. 276
manor houses. A composite building of rough stone and some ashlar. The range running N–S at the eastern end is said to date from the early C16, but nothing obviously

Shorwell, West Court, drawing by Percy Stone.
From Stone, *The Architectural Antiquities of the Isle of Wight*, 1891

indicates this. The E–W range of *c.* 1600 is more telling. Its N side is the main frontage, partly symmetrical with two gables and mullioned windows; a short wing projects to the E. In the angle between this and the main N elevation is an attractive two-storey porch of ashlar, with flat roof-line and a small lozenge-shaped panel over the W-facing doorway – which is four-centred in a squared frame. The S side is irregular, with a small gabled wing at the W end. The roofs are mostly tiled but the lower courses are partly in stone slates (cf. Mottistone Manor). There are two sets of brick chimneys, diagonally placed on stone bases (cf. Wolverton Manor).

WOLVERTON MANOR, ½ m. SSW, looks enthralling when first seen, facing E, from a footpath leading S from the village. Built by John Dingley, who died in 1596, and completed under his grandson Sir John, it has an impressive front on the E-plan, with gabled wings and two-storey porch with a flat roof-line; the walls are in dark brownish stone with details in lighter stone. The r. part of the façade is unaltered; l. of the porch are C18 sashes in raised surrounds. The unaltered part has three-light windows with transoms and mullions; on the ground floor of the wing is a panel of lozenge shape with raised moulded edges. The porch has a four-centred doorway in a square frame and a lozenge panel on the upper floor (a simpler version of that on the wing); both storeys of the porch have finely moulded cornices and octagonal, hollow-sided flanking shafts. The side and back

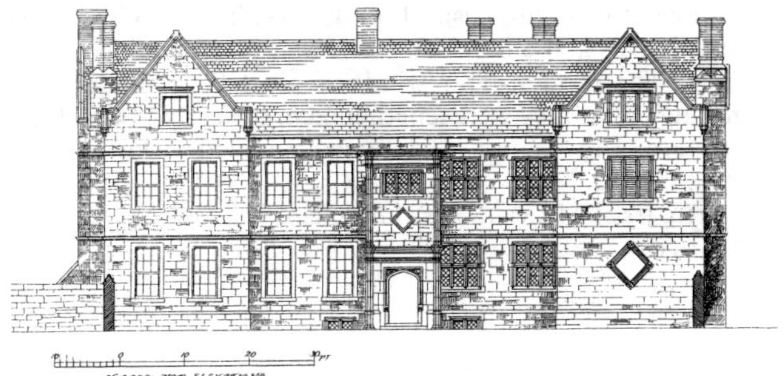

Shorwell, Wolverton Manor, elevation.
From Percy Stone, *The Architectural Antiquities of the Isle of Wight*, 1891

elevations are irregular. At the back is a projection with a blocked Venetian window, probably built to accommodate a staircase which was never constructed (cf. North Court, and also Gatcombe House). The chimney tops are of brick; some are set diagonally on stone bases (cf. West Court).

Wolverton was derelict in the 1960s but has since been carefully repaired. In the hall is a fireplace with a low Tudor arch, well-moulded stone frame and mantelshelf. Two similar fireplaces have restored wooden chimneypieces in the early C17 Island tradition. One, on the ground floor of the N wing, has arched panels and pilasters with torso figures of both sexes, supporting clusters of fruit and foliage in place of capitals. The other, upstairs, is grander. A coat *p. 29*
of arms is flanked by panels with spiral decoration; the pilasters on the mantelpiece and alongside the fireplace have female figures supporting Ionic capitals. Finally, and unexpectedly, there is a delightful mid to late C18 Chinese Chippendale STAIRCASE in the S wing, with square-pat- 40
terned fretwork balustrading, tread ends with scroll patterns and cusping on the angled beams under the flights.

Impressive group of subsidiary buildings to the SE. Long BARN, probably C17; thatched; rough stone walls with triangular ventilation openings. Adjoining brick GRANARY, *c.* 1800. Former STABLES (sometimes miscalled a chapel), probably early C17 with some C19 alterations. A long building of rough ironstone (darker than the stone of which the nearby barn is built), under a corrugated iron roof, with two- and three-light mullioned windows, some blocked, and a plain low-arched doorway. To the N of the house is a MOAT enclosing a fairly small area; no evidence has been found of any substantial building within it.

YAFFORD HOUSE, 1 m. SSW. Austere mid-C18 ashlar front of five bays and three storeys, the windows in moulded frames with keystones, emphasized on the first floor by Gibbs surrounds – as is the handsome doorway with moulded pediment. The ground-floor windows are taller, with thinner glazing bars – they were lengthened in the early C19. Behind the façade the house is quite shallow, with a lower, later wing behind.

BILLINGHAM MANOR. *See* Billingham.

KINGSTON, q.v.

STANDEN HOUSE *see* ARRETON

STENBURY MANOR, STRATHWELL MANOR *see* WHITWELL

4585 ## SWAINSTON

Calbourne

Swainston was a manor held by the early medieval bishops of Winchester, and included their only residence (used occasionally) on the Island; of this there are remarkable remains. The manor included Calbourne village and the port of Newtown (qq.v.). In 1283 the king took possession of the manor. From *c.* 1600 it was held by the Barrington family, who rebuilt the main part of the house *c.* 1750 and enlarged it in 1798. In 1833 it passed through marriage to the Simeons.* There were alterations to the C18 part of the house in the mid or late C19. In 1941 the whole house was gutted through an incendiary bomb, and was restored in 1951–4 by *Stratton & Millgate* of Newport, retaining the outside walls of both the medieval and Georgian parts. It is now a hotel.

The surviving parts of the MEDIEVAL MANOR HOUSE, which lie E of the C18 mansion, are puzzling. They include a rectangular block of about 50 ft by 15 ft (15 metres by 4.5 metres), largely of C13 date, aligned E–W, with a main storey above an undercroft. The walls are of rough limestone (which of course would originally have been rendered) with ashlar dressings. Attached to the N side is a smaller range, also aligned E–W. This was altered in the C18, but its E wall (about 15 ft back from that of the main block) dates from the late C12 – as shown by a window on the upper storey, of two rounded lights separated by an octagonal shaft with

*The Simeon family lived at St John's, Ryde (*see* Outer Ryde: East) from 1797.

Swainston manor house, drawings by Percy Stone.
From Stone, *The Architectural Antiquities of the Isle of Wight*, 1891

moulded capital and base. Such an early feature in an essentially domestic building is a rare survival.

The mid-C13 date for the main medieval block is attested by windows. There is a fairly large E window of three lights without cusps, above which are three circles, also uncusped (this may not have been its original design, for an early C19 engraving shows a large trefoil in the arch of the window, occupying the space of the three existing circles. Possibly the tracery was altered in a C19 restoration.) There are lancets in the side walls of the main storey. Two of these are on the N side, to the E of the abutting block, while the S wall has two remaining lancets, together with three later two-light windows with four-centred heads. Entrance to the main storey from outside is up a wooden stairway and through a four-centred doorway (but Percy Stone's *Architectural Antiquities of the Isle of Wight*, 1891, shows that this doorway was then blocked, and that the stairway did not exist). The undercroft has an irregular series of openings on the S side.

Internally, the main storey of the medieval block forms a single room. The lancet windows have deep splays, and the eastern one on the S side has a small drain in its sill, which suggests use as a piscina in connection with worship. The whole room could have been a chapel, but it is unlikely that an episcopal manor house, used only occasionally by the bishop, would have had a chapel as large as this. More probably the room was a domestic chamber, with an oratory altar at the E end. The roof is remarkable. It was wholly renewed after destruction in the Second World War, but Percy Stone's drawing shows that it is a close copy. There are slightly cambered collar-beams from which rise concave braces supporting the principal rafters. Under the collar-beams are arch braces which form wide semi-ellipses. The room probably formed, with the C12 adjunct, a solar wing to a former hall which may have stood on the site of the C18 part of the present house (the cellars of which retain stone structural work, perhaps of medieval origin).

The part of the house rebuilt *c.* 1750 was mainly a two-storey rectangular block with plain parapets. It was widened to the S in 1798 by *William Porden*, providing an impressive new GARDEN FRONT faced in ashlar. This is of nine bays; the three bays at either end are brought forward as shallow wings with pediments. The wings have bold segmental bows on the lower storey, each with three separate windows. Between the wings is a portico forming a porch, with two Tuscan columns and a central pediment. The doorway behind is arched, and is flanked by large arched windows. Balustrades were added over the portico and bows in the C19.

The W ELEVATION has an upper storey of five bays, representing the end frontage of the house of *c.* 1750, with a wider bay to the S indicating the 1798 extension. The ground floor of the older part was widened westward, probably in the mid or late C19, with tall windows above a low basement.

The ENTRANCE FRONT, on the N side, is somewhat awkward. The main section is basically of seven bays with a parapet, but the bays are unevenly spaced, particularly at the W end. The central bay, wider than the others, is emphasized by a balustraded parapet and plain pilasters on the first floor. Below is a portico forming a porch, with two Tuscan columns, rounded arches at the sides, and a balustrade.

The restoration of 1951–4 was thorough and painstaking. The main parts of the C18 interior were reconstructed largely to the old plan, with reinstatement of important features. Two Georgian fireplaces were brought in from elsewhere. Among the most striking features of the renewed interior are columns; two pairs in the hall have Ionic volutes, and four impressive Corinthian columns separate the five-bay extension on the W side from the main part of the adjoining room. If the latter columns are based on what existed before, the originals presumably dated from the mid or late C19.

Humphry Repton was consulted about the landscape *c.* 1811. This may have related to an area of former parkland S of the house, extending to the Newport–Calbourne road about ½ m. away. Mid-C19 maps indicate irregular clusters of trees on the W and S sides of this area, and scattered trees within it. Some of these remain. To the SE of the house is a small LAKE of an irregular wedge shape pointing S (no lake is marked on a detailed Island map of 1791). The lake is crossed near its N end by a stone BRIDGE with a single segmental arch, low rusticated piers at either end and a balustrade in between. The bridge, carrying the drive from the road to the house, is approached at each end by a short stone-banked causeway. Can the lake and the bridge have been parts of a scheme associated with Repton?

(In a secluded situation S of the Newport–Calbourne road is a TEMPLE, built as an estate feature in the 1790s. After dereliction it was restored *c.* 1990 as a house. It has a fine portico with six Doric columns supporting a triglyph frieze and pediment.)

THORLEY 3585

Yarmouth

The original Thorley includes a manor house, farm buildings and the remains of a medieval church, ½ m. from the coast. The present village, strictly Thorley Street, is a straggle of houses further SE.

ST SWITHIN, Thorley Street. 1871 by *W. T. Stratton,* a work of originality from an Island architect. Aisle-less nave and small transepts with lancets; chancel with Geometrical E window. Its special feature is a bell-turret between the S porch and transept, which begins as an oblong buttressed on three sides, develops into an elongated hexagon with four trefoiled openings, and ends with a spirelet. The church is of rough stone outside (some of it reused from the old church), but internally the walls and arches are faced in light buff brick with lively linear decorations in dark red. The sanctuary has WALL TILING with diagonal and linear patterns, stridently coloured in reds, browns and blue. – STAINED GLASS. E window, 1897 by *Powell's*. – FONT. From the old church. Plain octagon on a round stem and square base; said to be C17.

OLD CHURCH. Demolished 1871, except the gabled two-storey porch-belfry, which was on its S side. A two-light C13 window was re-set in the infilled N wall, between two buttresses protruding into the area of the former nave which were added after the demolition. (Inside are a cinquefoil niche, and small C17 and later MONUMENTS.) The churchyard has several TABLE TOMBS of near-identical design, with oval side panels and reeded pilasters at the corners.

THORLEY MANOR, adjoining the old church site. Built in 1712 by Henry Holmes, nephew of Sir Robert Holmes (*see* Yarmouth). It seems at first sight an excellent, if belated, example of the William and Mary style – of five bays in rough stone with ashlar dressings, deep modillion cornice, hipped roof; and tall end chimneys of brick. But the wooden mullions and transoms of the cross-shaped windows date from the C19. Flanking the main door, with its bracketed hood, are vertical oval openings. (Fine staircase with turned balusters.)

TOTLAND BAY *see* FRESHWATER AND TOTLAND

5575 VENTNOR

Ventnor is disappointing architecturally but its site is dramatic. It is built on a very irregular part of the Undercliff, where steep hillsides alternate with shallow hollows, legacies of the cataclysmic landslides of several thousand years ago (*see* p. 5). In the background are the steep slopes which characterize the inland side of the Undercliff and which, especially towards the NE, are partly tree-grown.* Before the early C19 it was only a hamlet, where a mill stood above a waterfall which tumbled to the shore; otherwise there were a few fish-

* Before the C20 many of the steep slopes behind Ventnor, especially to the E, were largely bare.

Ventnor, showing St Catherine's church, engraving of 1837.
From George Brannon, *Brannon's Picture of the Isle of Wight*, *c.* 1844

ermen's and quarrymen's cottages, a tavern and a farmhouse. Adventurous visitors reached the area by *c.* 1800, but development on a town scale started in the 1830s and increased in the 1840s, when the Undercliff gained a reputation for its soothing climate due to the sheltering effect of its protective hills. Like other resorts at the time it attracted retired or financially independent residents as well as those seeking recreation. The town was already fairly substantial, though loose-built, when the railway came in 1866.

The site could have offered great opportunities for sensitively designed layouts relating buildings to rugged landscapes, but this happened only in a few places. Most of the town was developed piecemeal, providing accidental relationships between buildings and broken land-form which are sometimes striking but too often seem simply awkward. Demolitions and replacements over the last eighty years (there was some wartime bombing) have added to the disjointed effects. The pier, which originated in the mid C19, was finally removed (after damage) in 1993, depriving the seafront of its main focus. The waterfall below the site of the pre-urban mill has become the Cascade, set within a public garden.

The early villas are built of the local sandstone, sometimes stuccoed, with either gables or eaves in the conventional styles of the period. Verandas and iron balconies were once common; there are a few attractive survivals. Some buildings mentioned would probably not seem important enough in more ordinary locations, but are included because of their relationship to their settings.

This entry deals with Ventnor proper. Bonchurch to the E and St Lawrence to the W are treated separately.

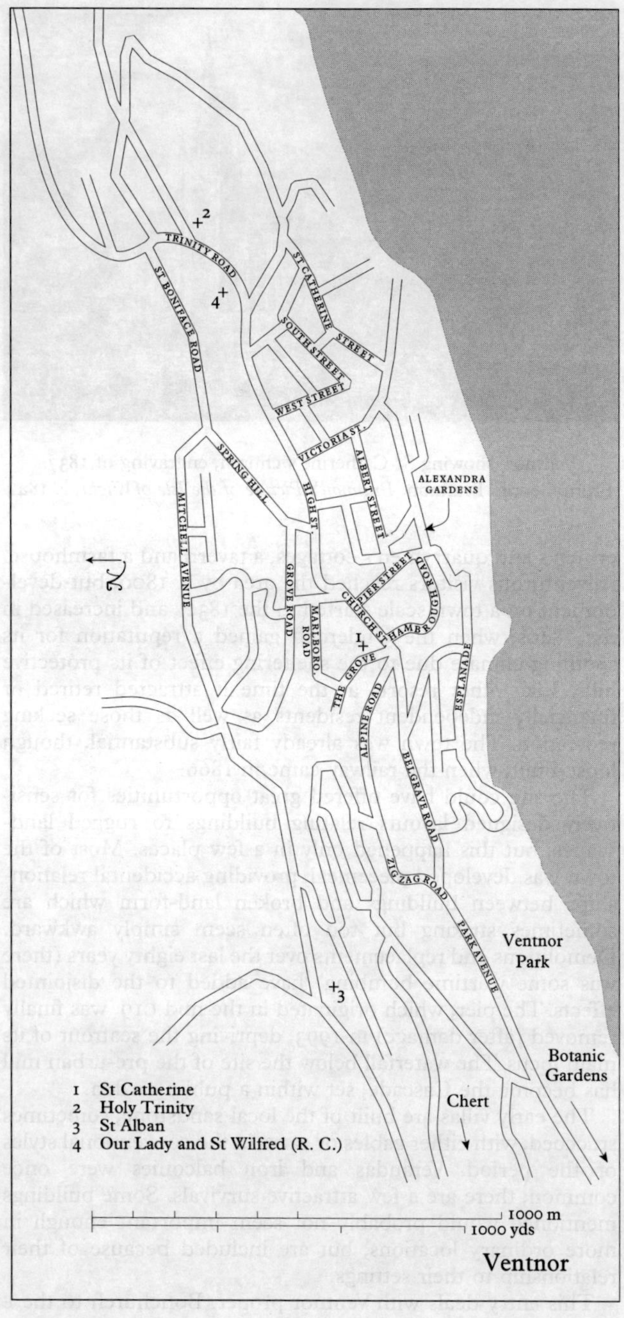
TRINITY ROAD
ST BONIFACE ROAD
ST CATHERINE STREET
SOUTH STREET
WEST STREET
VICTORIA ST.
ALBERT STREET
SPRING HILL
HIGH ST.
MITCHELL AVENUE
GROVE ROAD
MARLBORO. ROAD
PIER STREET
CHURCH ST.
HAMBROUGH ROAD
THE GROVE
ALPINE ROAD
ESPLANADE
BELGRAVE ROAD
ZIG ZAG ROAD
PARK AVENUE
ALEXANDRA GARDENS
Ventnor Park
Botanic Gardens
Chert
1 St Catherine
2 Holy Trinity
3 St Alban
4 Our Lady and St Wilfred (R. C.)
1000 m
1000 yds
Ventnor

CHURCHES

Ventnor was at the S end of the very long parish of Newchurch, which extended across the Island from Ryde (p. 168). It had no church of its own until 1837.

ST CATHERINE. 1836–7 by *Robert Ebbels*, of stone quarried nearby. It stands well when seen from the SW, with wooded slopes behind. The W tower is effective, with angle buttresses subtly diminishing to the castellated, corner-turreted top; it had a spire, demolished in 1921. After this the interior is disappointing. The nave is a simple space with tall lancets on the N side, low-pitched ceiled roof with open triangular spandrels in the trusses, and on the S side a blocked five-bay arcade with finely moulded arches. This opened into an aisle added in 1897–9; the blocking occurred in the late C20 to provide separate accommodation in the aisle. The chancel dates from 1849–50; the E window has triple lancets, flanked by other lancets a little distance away. Notable wooden WEST GALLERY with canted ends, supported on cantilevered brackets supplemented by very slender piers. *p. 283*

HOLY TRINITY, Trinity Road. 1861–2 by *C.E. Giles* of Taunton; of sandstone rubble. Elegant NW steeple, rising from a slender base with corner stair-turret, turning at the belfry stage into an octagon with shafted lancets, and ending with a needle-like shingled spire. Otherwise the church is in freely interpreted C13 style. Three-light aisle windows with big cinquefoil circles, paired lancets in the clerestory, and tall W window with Geometrical tracery. Impressive interior with diverse details; the piers of the arcades vary between round and quatrefoil. The dominant feature is the wooden CHANCEL SCREEN with delicate open tracery, one of several furnishings introduced from 1891 by *Charles Barker King*. It has a wide cusped archway contained within a gabled frame, from the apex of which rises the rood. The screen has a stone base with circular panel patterns, and iron gates. The two-bay S chancel arcade, opening into an organ chamber, is unusual. It has deeply moulded arches, and a central pier with a big square abacus supported by four marble shafts, each with a scrolled capital. The REREDOS by *Barker King*, a wooden triptych with painted and gilt figures and open cresting, slightly obscures very fine STAINED GLASS of *c.* 1862 by *Clayton & Bell* in the five-light Geometrical E window, with scenes related to the Apostles' Creed in a dense pattern of colours including strong blues and reds. The same firm designed the side windows of the aisles, also coeval with the church, but the four-light W window is later (*c.* 1900). – PULPIT. Octagonal, of stone with marble shafts at the angles. On one side is a figure in relief; on other sides are panels with stem and leaf patterns. It predates Barker King's work.

ST ALBAN, St Albans Road, in the NW part of the town. 1922–3 by *F. M. Coley*. On a difficult, steep site; built of coursed sandstone with shallow buttresses, in a simple Romanesque style with low-pitched tiled roofs. Continuous nave and apsed chancel; shorter S aisle also with apse; paired rounded windows to the aisle and square-topped clerestory lights. There is an impressive view of the building with its two apses from the lower ground to the SE. The W front is gabled with a five-arched porch spanning its width; the centre arch is segment-headed. An intended SW tower was never built.

Inside there is an undivided main space, ending with the apse. Three-bay S arcade with rounded arches and slender marble piers. On the N side of the nave is a low wall arcade. The E end is an anti-climax, with no windows or applied decoration in the apse, and a fairly simple altar and reredos. The W end is more distinctive, with three stone segmental arches, the centre one narrower, supporting a gallery containing the organ. – PULPIT. A surprising design, in wood. Two sides of a square with a canted angle. On each side, and at the angle, are open rounded arches flanked by bulbous balusters; within each arch is a shaped vertical feature. – STAINED GLASS. Two-light S aisle window by *Comper*, 1931.

OUR LADY AND ST WILFRID (R.C.), Trinity Road. 1871 by *J. Clarke*; early C20 N aisle. (The church is oriented S–N; this description assumes normal liturgical directions.) W front with triple lancets and gabled bellcote. N arcade with octagonal piers. The chancel has curious features. There are five circular windows high in the S wall, three tall traceried niches behind the sanctuary, and a high round E window with strong and colourful STAINED GLASS – which is matched by that in the triple W window. The latter, and probably the former, are by *O'Connor*.

PERAMBULATIONS

There are three Perambulations, each beginning at St Catherine's Church. Perambulation 1 covers the heart of the town, Perambulation 2 goes to the W, and Perambulation 3 climbs the slopes to the N and continues E.

1. The Heart of the Town

The setting of St Catherine's church summarizes much of Ventnor. Tree-covered slopes, partly dotted with houses, form the background. To the E, Church Street, busy and urban, leads into the town centre. To the SW open land drops steeply, with a view over jumbled seafront buildings towards a wooded promontory. Across the street, immediately S of the church, is KINGSVIEW, an apartment complex of 2003–5; concept architect *Christopher Dodd*; built on what had for several years been a vacant site. The street frontage is four-storeyed with flat roof-lines; pale buff brick with continuous balconies, that on the first floor acting as an entrance canopy. The windows on the upper floors are relatively small; metal-framed with horizontal panes. At the NW corner is a tower, slightly higher than the rest, continuously glazed on its polygonal W side. (The main part extends S over the steeply sloping site, including two more lower storeys because of the slope. Seen from the SW, Kingsview has a distinctive outline with its six floors, all with balconies, boldly stepped back.)

HAMBROUGH ROAD leads S off Church Street to the E of Kingsview. On the l. is a rather muddled terrace of the 1860s, three-storeyed with intermittent canted bay windows. The road turns E above the top of the CASCADE – the waterfall which descended from the mill which existed when Ventnor was a hamlet. (The mill, demolished in the mid C19, stood near the junction of Hambrough Road and Pier Street.) The Cascade is now the centrepiece of an ornamental public garden.

On high ground to the SE is the former WINTER GARDENS PAVILION of 1935 by *A.D. Clare*, a smaller-scale reverberation from the then new Bexhill Pavilion in Sussex. It has been altered, but the original form is recognizable: two-storeyed, white-rendered, with flat roofs of different heights and planes; angled entrance towards the town, and focal tower feature with glazed rounded front. Nearby are good viewpoints over the seafront to the SW.

As there is little of architectural note on the seafront itself, the Perambulation does not descend, and the following comments are based on views from near the Pavilion. The loss of the Pier as a focal feature has been partly compensated by the building of a substantial SHELTER above a (partly hidden) shoreside Pumping Station by *Rainey Petrie Design*, 1999–2000. It has a circular canopy with slender supports, topped by a rounded turret, and is a prominent and elegant landmark. The fairly short ESPLANADE, leading W, was formed within the natural Ventnor Cove in 1847–8. By the later C19 it was largely fronted by buildings with balconies and verandas, but few of these remain. It ends below a tree-topped promontory. Beyond are low rugged cliffs which continue W towards St Lawrence (q.v.).

ALEXANDRA GARDENS, N of the Winter Gardens Pavilion, is a terrace of houses, *c.* 1880 by *T.R. Saunders*, with canted bay windows and irregular slated roofs which break erratically into pyramid shapes – an odd composition, but effective on this prominent site. Narrow PIER STREET leads N into the close-built town centre which started to develop *c.* 1835–50. Nos. 10–16 on the W side are almost Regency in their upper floors, with Ionic pilasters. Pier Street meets High Street (r.) and Church Street (l.). This end of HIGH STREET has an odd and very Ventnorish quality. Nos. 1–9 on the NW side form a single varied composition in two styles. Nos. 1 and 9 are two-storeyed in rough stone with large quoins, each with a Gothic openwork bargeboard. The taller range between is built of the same materials but is basically classical on the upper floors. The view ENE from here along High Street is topped above the roof-lines by the wooded hillside behind. On the SE side, HURSTS is a Late Victorian shop with thin iron columns between plate-glass windows, and elaborate cresting above. The first floor has glazed round-headed openings. (The further part of High Street is described in Perambulation 3.)

CHURCH STREET, leading W, has a proper urban quality. Nos. 7–9 on the l., *c.* 1840, have paired Ionic pilasters and a prominent cornice. The POST OFFICE further W, 1901, is heavier in style, with round-arched rusticated ground floor, elaborate bay windows above, and rounded openings in the top storey. Beyond are Kingsview and St Catherine's Church.

2. *To the West*

BELGRAVE ROAD leads W from St Catherine's church along the side of a slope – beginning with a big rock outcrop on the r., and a view down to the seafront on the l. It has a mixture of C19 houses, few of them special. WESTHILL on the r. is a survivor of the Victorian type once common near the seafront, plain in itself but with verandas on two floors. ST ANDREWS on the l. is early C20, stone-built with an odd arrangement of windows including a circular one, in a kind of awkward vernacular Baroque. Opposite, COVE COTTAGE makes a contrast: simple basic classical of 1828, built for his own occupation by a mason employed at neighbouring Steephill Castle (*see* below). The ROYAL HOTEL opened as the Ventnor Hotel in 1838. Additions and alterations have resulted in a complex building of which the main part, to the W, is plain classical; other parts are more irregular.

Belgrave Road continues into PARK AVENUE, bordering VENTNOR PARK, laid out in informal municipal style in the 1880s; it extends S, over a ridge, to the coast. A small BANDSTAND, moved from elsewhere in 1903, has slender iron columns and a hat-like roof with domed top. Facing the Park on the N side of Park Avenue is a notable collection of Late Victorian villas, variedly with bargeboards, heavy bay windows and verandas. Several were designed by the local architect *T.R. Saunders*. (The architectural climax in this

Ventnor, Steephill Castle, engraving.
From George Brannon, *Brannon's Picture of the Isle of Wight*, *c.* 1844

direction was Steephill Castle of 1833–5, demolished in 1963, which stood on the hillside a little to the W. It was mainly two- or three-storeyed with battlemented parapets and a tall tower with projecting corner stair-turret. It was designed by *James Sanderson*, best known on the Island for his mainly classical buildings in Ryde (q.v.). The site and grounds have been developed for housing, though retaining many trees. Beyond are the Botanic Gardens, *see* below.)

Return can be made via ZIGZAG ROAD, which leads steeply N beside the Royal Hotel; it justifies its name. No. 15, facing S above the first bend, *c.* 1840–5, is stuccoed with eaves, and has a concave-roofed veranda. By contrast Nos. 14–16, standing above a higher bend, are of stone and were built about twenty years later, with florid bargeboards and a striking gabled greenhouse to the r. ALPINE ROAD leads to the r. back to St Catherine's, past *c.* 1860s villas.

3. *To the North and East*

THE GROVE leads N from St Catherine's Church, and MARLBOROUGH ROAD branches uphill to the NE, past the town's most picturesque building: the OLD MANOR HOUSE (formerly Ventnor Farm), possibly dating from the C17, and embellished as a *cottage orné* *c.* 1830. Thatched, with two wide gables facing S, the E one larger; each with an elaborate bargeboard. The house is built against a steep slope on the N side; Marlborough Road turns and passes it almost at roof level. The road continues E to join HIGH STREET (the W part of which was described in Perambulation 1). This section of High Street is narrow and slightly twisting, with varied upper storeys typical of a prosperous Victorian and early C20 town. Nos. 40–42 on the S side are stuccoed with plain pilasters; the first-floor windows have lacy iron balconies, and the central window to No. 40 is blind, with a decorative keystoned arch. No. 44, in similar style, breaks forward with the frontage line. SPRING HILL branches to the NE. On its broad W angle with High Street is an irregular range with a succession of curves. (Beyond here High Street has, in its next stretch, lost its coherence and character because of clearance and partial redevelopment. Buildings further E are described opposite.)

Past the Heritage Centre on Spring Hill is a sharp turning l. into GROVE ROAD, which climbs steadily to the W. On the N side is KING CHARLES COURT, a former hotel of *c.* 1860–70 in stone and yellow brick, slightly Italianate. A small building of rough stone attached to the E, possibly C18 or earlier but altered, was the original tavern of pre-urban Ventnor. ST CATHERINE'S SCHOOL on the l., beyond Tulse Hill, has an irregular Late Victorian, largely Gothic range including an upper-floor chapel of 1895, and a prominent saddleback tower with circular windows in the gables and lancets below. Opposite is a series of villas of *c.* 1840–50. ST ANN'S is of ashlar with a bowed trellis veranda in front of the entrance. PRIMROSE BANK is simpler, with a gabled porch; YARBOROUGH VILLA is grander, with central two-storey bow and a trellis veranda with tent roof. The road entrance has stone piers with ball finials and delicate iron gates.

Grove Road turns N and climbs very steeply to MITCHELL AVENUE, opposite the site of the railway station, which was opened in 1866 and closed a century later. Trains reached it through a tunnel behind. The TERMINUS inn, with decorative brick details, is a reminder. Further E is a former PUMPING STATION of 1885 by *J. G. Livesay*; small and elaborate, with two-tiered turret ending in a spirelet; it has fretted bargeboards, round-headed windows and red brick dressings to rubble walls. Beyond is an early, small ELECTRICITY WORKS, *c.* 1898, also in stone and brick, with blocked rounded openings and decorative porch. The tree-covered slopes of St Boniface Down rise immediately behind. Further on is HUISH TERRACE, a long, partly gabled range built *c.* 1860–70 as a holiday home for mission workers from London. It is faced in flint (with buff brick dressings), quarried from the down at a time when the local sandstone was in short supply. The road descends and turns S. Above the bend is the HILLSIDE HOTEL which began soon after 1800 as an inn accommodating visitors, but was enlarged as a private house *c.* 1843 when a third storey was added with a thatched roof. It is set idyllically against the slope of the down.

Mitchell Avenue joins the top of Spring Hill, which leads down to High Street (*see* above). But it is worth going a little further E along St Boniface Road, where Nos. 1–8 on the N side were built as pairs of gabled houses, *c.* 1850. Nos. 1–2 are quite elegant, with small rounded windows in the upper storeys, canted bays, and a porch of three flat arches with balustrade. The others are variants, with faintly Neo-Jacobean or Italianate features.

OTHER BUILDINGS

Finally (not part of the Perambulation), a few words about the E part of High Street and its vicinity. Beyond the Spring Hill turning (*see* opposite), the views across the partly open land to the N are at least redeemed by the down rising behind. Victoria Street leads S from High Street, and off it in Albert Street was the Town Hall built in 1878 as a private venture. It was replaced by apartments in the 1990s, but the stuccoed main façade was retained. This is heavy, busy Italianate with Ionic columns on the ground floor, Composite ones above, and dentilled cornice at each level. It stands out in what is otherwise an architecturally nondescript setting.

High Street regains coherence further E with assorted 1840s–60s houses, many converted to commerce. Past Our Lady and St Wilfrid (*see* p. 286), the spire of Holy Trinity beckons, and beyond it is Bonchurch (q.v.). In West Street, S of High Street, is a row of stuccoed cottages built *c.* 1840 for coastguards, in simplest classical style. From South Street (leading off West Street), a stepped pathway descends to St Catherine Street – interesting as small-scale townscape, and characteristic of the town. It bends slightly along the side of a steep slope, bordered by varied small houses and occasional larger ones. Odd groups of buildings stand out awkwardly on the higher ground. The street leads back to the town centre.

Botanic Garden, Steephill Road, 1 m. W. Opened 1972; occupying the grounds and site of the Royal National Hospital for Diseases of the Chest, built from 1868 and demolished in 1969. (The buildings were by *Thomas Hellyer*; stained glass from the chapel is now in the church at St Lawrence, q.v.) The Temperate House of 1986–7 is by *Lawrence Jay*. Two-tiered, with low-pitched roofs; light steel framing with polycarbonate sheeting, which curves in profile from roofs to walls, and is rounded at the corners.

Chert, on a steep and rugged site in Castle Court to the W 86
of the town, was built in 1969–70 as retirement accommodation for two people, to a straightforward design by the locally based architects *Gilbert & Hobson*. The living space

is on the upper floor, in separate units with a slender spiral staircase in between – all behind continuous glazing. The lower floor is used for servicing, garages and access; the central part projects with three wide openings, providing a balcony. A remarkable piece of Modern architecture on a small scale, which passed to the National Trust in 1993 and is now holiday accommodation.

WEST COURT *see* SHORWELL

WESTON MANOR *see* FRESHWATER AND TOTLAND

WESTOVER *see* CALBOURNE

5090

WHIPPINGHAM

East Cowes

A small village, formerly the centre of a large parish which included Osborne House (and, in earlier times, the site of what is now East Cowes). At about the same time as Queen Victoria bought Osborne, she and Prince Albert took possession of Barton Manor immediately to the S, together with its lands (*see* below). As a result of this and other acquisitions, the royal estate extended for a considerable distance to the S and SE of Whippingham village. Numerous farmhouses, cottages and lodges were built, initially under the impetus of *Prince Albert*. Some, especially the earlier ones, have Italianate references, but many are in fanciful styles – carrying on the traditions of *cottages ornés* and romantic Victorian villas. It is not always possible to establish the contributions of particular designers, either in collaboration with the Prince, or after his death in 1861. *John Blandford*, †1867, Clerk of Works for the royal estate, was closely associated with earlier estate housing. He was succeeded by *J.R. Mann* (who was responsible for the Durbar Wing of Osborne House, p. 202), but the extent of Mann's direct influence on design is not clear. The architect *A.J. Humbert*, who first became associated with the Prince in connection with the rebuilding of Whippingham church, was probably responsible for several estate buildings, especially some of the more fanciful ones. He continued to work for the royal family, at Windsor and Sandringham as well as Osborne, until his death in 1877 (*see also* Osborne).

ST MILDRED. A small medieval church with a saddleback tower was altered by *Nash* in 1804–6. In 1854–5 the chancel was rebuilt, with S and N chapels to accommodate the Royal Family and Royal Household respectively. The rest was rebuilt in 1860–2, with a massive central tower, transepts and aisle-less nave. The architect on both occasions was *A.J. Humbert* (*see* above) but *Prince Albert* played a major part. It is a weird design, especially the tower, in a mixture of Romanesque and Early Gothic. One approaches from the E. The chancel with its triple-lancet E window is flanked by the smaller gabled chapels, with a columned Italian Romanesque porch on the S side marking the royal entrance. But the dominating feature is the tower: square and big, with a row of six blank arches on each side containing thin lancets; square corner pinnacles end in spikes. At the top is a kind of truncated pyramid from which rises an eight-sided lantern turret with a short spire. The nave and transepts are Neo-Norman, though the transepts have rose windows, and at the W end is a wooden bell-turret ending with a flèche. In the W wall of the main porch a piece of SCULPTURE, probably from a Norman tympanum or lintel, with a Tree of Life and two affronted animals (with men riding on them?). 62

The interior is described from W to E, including furnishings (apart from stained glass and monuments). The FONT of 1861 (installed 1864) was designed by *Princess Louise*, Queen Victoria's daughter. Square bowl with three medallions on each side; marble columns with foliate capitals. The old font nearby makes a telling contrast; it is a Greek Doric column supporting a small square bowl. Was it designed by Nash? The wooden PULPIT, with carved scenes in the panels, is by *R.L. Boulton* of Cheltenham, *c.* 1902. It stands under the tower, which is dramatically open to the lantern. The crossing arches are Transitional in style, with flat sides and heavy mouldings; their spandrels, and the friezes under the tower windows, are painted in buff and brown to geometric patterns. The chapels are separated from the chancel by six-bay arcades with narrow, richly moulded arches on slender columns which stand on low walls. The N arcade is filled with bronze SCREENS of 1897 by *Sir Alfred Gilbert*, splendidly Art Nouveau with slender shafts and turbulent tracery – artistically the finest features in the church. They were inserted when the chapel, built to accommodate the Royal Household at services, became the Battenberg chapel (*see* below). A bronze SCULPTURE of an angel with long wings and flowing drapery, above the chapel altar, is by *Princess Louise*. The main REREDOS, with a carved Last Supper, was designed by *A.Y. Nutt* and presented by Edward VII *c.* 1903 in memory of Queen Victoria. He also replaced the pews in the S chapel, but they are not specially notable. – STAINED

Whippingham church, Prince Albert monument, engraving.
From *The Builder* vol. 22, 1864

GLASS. Much by *Hardman* and very good, e.g. the E window, and the patterned windows in the transepts. Those in the N chapel and two near the font are by *Ion Pace*. – MONUMENTS. N chapel. Prince Louis of Battenberg, †1896 by *A. Y. Nutt*. Large white tomb-chest with a sword on top; columns with triple grey marble shafts on the sides. In the S chapel are several wall monuments to royal relatives, all in arched recesses. – Prince Albert, by *A. J. Humbert* and *W. Theed*, 1864. White marble medallion portrait between two angels, on a darker marble base with trefoil panels and black flanking columns. – Princess Alice, Grand Duchess of Hesse, †1878, by *Frank Theed*, 1879. Garlanded portrait between kneeling angels. – Prince Leopold, Duke of Albany, †1884, by *F. J. Williamson*. Profile head in a wreath. – N transept. Lord Henry Seymour, †1828; kneeling figure in arched recess. – Sir Henry Ponsonby, †1898, by *Countess Feodora Gleichen*. Black, with medallion portrait between standing figures under a broken round pediment.

WAR MEMORIAL in churchyard NW of church. Openwork iron cross with trefoiled ends, on stone base.

CHURCH HOUSE, the former Rectory, S of the church. Reconstructed in 1859–61, presumably by *Humbert*. But a simple early C19 wing remains on the E side, and the internal shapes of some of the rooms may reflect work done in *Nash*'s office *c.* 1805. (Drawings for this work are in one of the notebooks of G.S. Repton, compiled when he was in the office.). The S and W elevations are rumbustious (like much of Humbert's work). Buff brick with strips and patterns in red brick; heavy tiled roof with hips and diagonal slopes; big mullioned bay windows.

PADMORE, 300 yds (280 metres) SE, is of C17 origin, altered in the C18, and again for S.E. Saunders of the Cowes aviation and maritime firm, who lived here 1920–33. The main, (SE) front is essentially mid to late C18. Stuccoed over stone; windows with stone frames and modillion cornice; C20 porch with paired columns. The NW elevation is early to mid C17 in rough stone with C18 windows on the first floor; the central gable with wavy outline is presumably C20. To the NE is a stone water tower built for Saunders, with balustraded top and pinnacles, linked to the main part by a slightly later wing. The strangest features are the windows on the short SW elevation, which are triangular bays, two on each floor, with sashes facing diagonally – an arrangement with few parallels. They must have been added by Saunders. He also laid out an elaborate GARDEN, including a complex series of pergolas with concrete pillars of alternating round and square section, and thin iron spans.

The buildings connected with Osborne are described topographically, going generally S and SE.

BARTON MANOR, ¾ m. NE of Whippingham church, is a partly C17 house, on the site of a small Augustinian oratory founded in 1275 but suppressed in 1439. It was leased by the Queen and Prince Albert when they first occupied Osborne, and bought by them in 1853. The house was remodelled as an annexe to Osborne in 1845–6 under *Thomas Cubitt*, in association with *Prince Albert*. Cubitt retained the early C17 E and S frontages, built of roughly coursed limestone, but reconstructed the interior entirely, as well as providing new N and W sides – unusually for him (perhaps uniquely) in the same essentially Jacobean style as the retained parts. The main (E) frontage is one of the most impressive of the period among Island houses, although straightforward in its elements. It is E-shaped; the deep wings are gabled on their front and side elevations, with simple mullioned windows. The porch is tall and gabled, with a three-centred doorway. Unexpectedly the ground floor of the N wall of the S wing has three lancets, which must remain from the C13 oratory (they appear on a drawing predating the 1845–6 alterations).* The S façade of the house is of six bays under three gables, with windows of classical shape with crossed mullions and transoms (they too appear on a pre-1845 drawing). All the gables have small finials at their tops and bases, restored in 1845–6. The older house had a notable set of brick chimneys with ribbed sides and massive tops; one, at the back of the SE wing, was retained as a model for others formed in the reconstruction.

The house itself was reduced in size, and a model farmstead was built to the W and SW. The former FARMHOUSE is an almost convincing version of an early C17 one in stone, with varied gables, small mullioned windows and brick chimneys like those on the Manor itself. The FARM BUILDINGS, completed in 1852, include a range partly of stone but with a brick front to a courtyard, converted in 1987–8 as a restaurant and display centre for visitors (this use is discontinued).** In it there were, at the time of visiting, the dismantled parts of a wooden CHIMNEYPIECE from the house, in characteristic early C17 style, with the date 1624 and the initials N and P. It was more substantial than other surviving chimneypieces of the period on the Island (*see* Introduction, p. 29) and may not be the work of the local school of woodcarvers; it could have been made elsewhere for the house in the C17, or brought in during the C19 or later. The overmantel has three recessed panels with rectangular patterns decorated with strapwork, flanked by pairs of short columns on tall panelled bases, under a heavy frieze and modular cornice; there are two-tier pilasters with arabesque decoration which adjoined the fireplace.

Finally, two LODGES on Whippingham Road (A3021), of stone with simple gables and, again, brick chimneys resembling those on the manor house. *Prince Albert* produced a preliminary design for one of the lodges. The S lodge dates from 1848, the N one from 1850.

WHIPPINGHAM SCHOOL (Primary), ¼ m. SE of the church. Built in 1863–4. The architect was *A.J. Humbert*, who had collaborated with *Prince Albert* in the early stages of the design. Main (SE) elevation of one storey and five bays with shallow wings, in buff brick with red bands; needle turret; big porch with stone doorway including inscription com-

*There is a single lancet similarly placed on the opposite wing, but its stonework is restored and it may not be in its original position.

***George Devey* designed, and made a model for, farm buildings at Barton Manor but they were not built.

memorating the Prince. Well restored 1983, with N extension, by *Michael Rainey*, County Architect.

ALVERSTONE ROAD leads SE from the A3021 near the school. Past C20 housing on the r. are six royal ESTATE COTTAGES of 1859, in an Italianate-influenced style. Red brick, with buff brick arches to the lower windows and buff string course. But the upper-storey windows are slightly pointed semi-dormers under small gables. Further on, MOUNT ROAD (formerly an approach to Barton Manor) leads N. To its E is ALVERSTONE LODGE of 1858, fully in the romantic style which was then becoming characteristic of Osborne estate buildings. It is in red brick with buff brick patterns, including diamonds and diagonals; under the W gable are square-ended bay windows, the upper ones jettied over brackets. A fine fourfold chimney cluster has been demolished, leaving only the stump. DALLIMORES (formerly Keeper's Cottage), to the E of Alverstone Cottage, has been altered, but retains a central wooden balcony over an open three-arched porch of curious design, all under a broad gable projecting from the eaves, supported by slender posts.

COBURG, a short distance N along Mount Road (and about 76
¾ m. ESE of Whippingham church) is by far the most fantastic building in the S part of the former Osborne Estate. It was built as a pair of cottages in 1870–2, supposedly in imitation of traditional buildings in Albert's princedom – ten years after his death. The roof is pantiled with concave slopes; chimneystacks have gabled Gothic-arched tops; the upper storeys and gable ends are slate-hung; a three-bay balcony dominates the front. Festoons, hangings and other devices are painted in white over the slates and on the balcony.

ALVERSTONE ROAD continues S. Nos. 1 and 2, just round the bend on the r., formed the original Alverstone Farmhouse. The exterior is much as built in 1716 when it was part of the Worsley Estate. Dark red brick with stone quoins and plinth. On either side of the upper window are diamond patterns in darker brick (a foretaste of the elaborate Victorian examples). This house was superseded in 1855 by the present ALVERSTONE FARMHOUSE further along the road (near the junction with the A3021), a solid piece of early Osborne Estate housing with classical proportions, in red brick with some buff dressings; substantial porch with keystone.

We are back with the full-blooded Osborne Estate style in HEATHFIELD FARM of 1869, a short distance away on the W side of the A3021 – again of red brick patterned in buff, but with wavy-edged bargeboards and red-tiled roofs which are punctuated by bands and spot patterns in black.

(BRICKFIELD COTTAGES, in East Cowes Road to the SW, were built in 1853 to house workers in an adjoining estate brickyard. *Prince Albert* drew a preliminary sketch, *John Blandford* provided the detailed design. Three gabled cottages to an H-plan, the central cottage broader than those forming the wings. In red brick with some stone dressings. Fretted bargeboards; gabled dormers; chimneystacks set diagonally in pairs. A central lean-to veranda has wooden supports and elaborated curved braces. An early example of a romantic style in an Osborne Estate building.)

Finally (but this summary of notable Osborne housing is not exhaustive), there is PALMER'S LODGE of 1864 on the N side of the A3054, E of its junction with the A3021. A rather confused example of the Osborne style with brick patterning, gables, bay windows like those on Alverstone Lodge, and a crowning cluster of four round chimneys, their tops embattled.

The VICTORIA AND ALBERT ALMSHOUSES, NE of the church, were built for retired royal staff in 1875–6. They have some of the characteristics of the more elaborate estate housing, but there is an Arts and Crafts feel. Very attractive single-storey ranges in warm red brick, with gables and variedly pitched roofs arranged with general symmetry, but giving picturesque effects. Wood-framed windows with small hexagonal panes, some in square-ended bays; hipped-roofed porches to three different designs; terracotta plaques including one with the name in Gothic-lettered scrolls.

WHITECROFT HOSPITAL *see* CARISBROOKE

5075

WHITWELL

Niton and Whitwell

A village in a broad valley backed by bold rounded hills, especially to the S and E. The older houses are of stone; some were built in red brick after a branch railway (now closed) was opened in 1897.

ST MARY AND ST RHADEGUND. This was really two chapels side by side, each related to a different manor and parish. The earlier was St Rhadegund, built in the C12; the smaller St Mary was added to the S by *c.* 1200.* The two naves are separated by an arcade. St Mary and part of St Rhadegund were reconstructed in the early C16 to form a single church, including a SW tower. There was a restoration in 1868 by *R.J. Jones*.

* St R(h)adegund, a C6 German princess, was the patron saint of a nunnery in Cambridge of which the C13 church partly survives as Jesus College chapel.

It is best to look inside first, where the oldest evidence is in the N side of the chancel arch of St Rhadegund. Parts of the respond and springing of the late C12 arch were retained when the rest of the arch was reconstructed in the early C16, but were concealed then under added stonework. They were revealed in the 1868 restoration. There is scalloped decoration on the remains of the respond, and the surviving fragment of the springing of the outer order has a zigzag pattern, with angles facing outwards. The arcade separating the two parts of the church, originally of three bays, is in the late C12 Island tradition; with round piers, square abaci with chamfered corners, and single-chamfered arches.

In the C16 the chapel of St Mary was widened as an aisle to the newly combined church, and extended to align with the E end of St Rhadegund. An arch was opened between the old chancels, forming a further bay to the arcade, with a strange pier between the new arch and the easternmost older one. This pier must have come from elsewhere; it is of Purbeck marble, octagonal, with a simply moulded capital. But it was too short, and a second, larger capital was superimposed, which also acts as the respond to each of the arches into the original chancels.

Even more curious is the treatment of the SW corner of the church, where the tower was built over the W end of the site of St Mary. The tower is less wide than the W bay of the arcade, so that a narrower arch, simple and chamfered, was inserted within the older one A similar arch opens E from the tower space into the aisle replacing St Mary.

The S side of the church, as reconstructed in the early C16, is of large coursed sandstone blocks, as is the tower with its simple castellation and small squared belfry lights.* The two S windows are plain square-headed Perp. The E window of the S chapel is unusual: of two lights with a transom (but its present form dates from 1868); the main E window is a smaller version without a transom. The N and W windows were restored in 1868.

The S PORCH is one of a distinctive trio on the Island (the others are at Arreton and Niton) with vaulted interior and stone-slated roof. The walls are of sandstone blocks, and it looks as if they date from the reconstruction of the S side of the church. The vault has two transverse chamfered arches, and the door into the church is very simple, four-centred without capitals. Above the door is a cusped image niche, indicating a pre-Reformation date.

FURNISHINGS. Octagonal PULPIT, early to mid-C17; one of the most notable of the period on the Island. Three tiers

* One of the stone blocks in the S wall has the date 1589 crudely carved under initials. This cannot relate to a building operation but is clearly graffito.

Whitwell church, pulpit, elevation.
From Percy Stone, *The Architectural Antiquities of the Isle of Wight*, 1891

of decoration; small panels with arabesques at the top; prominent arches in the middle with cusps, shafts and foliage patterns in the spandrels. These arches enclose vertical embossed panels of curious geometric form. At the bottom are moulded panels containing diamond shapes, fretted at the edges. – In the S chapel is an ALTAR TABLE of the same period, with bulbous legs and 'I will take the cup of salvation', with the representation of a chalice. – ROOD SCREEN, erected in the early 1920s as a war memorial. Elaborate open tracery and substantial coved loft. A fine piece of latter-day Gothic; designer not known. – Smaller

SCREEN in the same style across the arch to the S chapel. – STATUES. Virgin and Child by *Miss Dowson*, early C20. Another of Joan of Arc. – STAINED GLASS. Windows by *Lavers & Barraud* and *Lavers & Westlake*, especially the eastern one in the N nave wall, 1913.*

The former VICARAGE S of the church was built in 1867 for the Rev. R. Oliver, the first vicar of Whitwell as a separate parish. Irregular, in stone, with two large gables, Gothic porch, and informally placed mullioned windows. Probably by *R.J. Jones*.

HIGH STREET runs N from the church, with the looser-built KEMMING ROAD leading W. Along both at intervals are metal HYDRANTS painted red, about 3 ft (0.9 metres) high; rounded, fluted and dome-topped. They were provided in 1887 by William Spindler of Old Park, St Lawrence (q.v.) as a public water supply, and designed by *T.R. Saunders* of Ventnor. The former METHODIST CHURCH, 1884, faces S at the far end of High Street – in low-key but assertive E.E. style, with four lancets above the gabled S porch; the middle two are higher and topped by an arch pattern in pale brick against the generally darker red brick of the façade. On the N side of Kemming Road are ALMSHOUSES, probably *c.* 1870 and possibly by *Jones*, with brick patterns in relief on the string course and in Gothic arch form above the ground-floor windows.

STRATHWELL MANOR, ½ m. W (to which the Rev. Oliver moved after retirement) is a rambling stone-built mansion of the mid to late C19 with many gables, chimneys and Gothic details, now subdivided – possibly, at least in part, by *R.J. Jones.* (Fine oak OVERMANTEL in the lounge dated 1545, with four profile portrait heads, fielded panels, vine-leaf tendrils and carvings of grotesque boars in Flemish or North German style. DCMS.)

STENBURY MANOR, 1 m. NNE (in Godshill parish), is delectably set against downland slopes. T-shaped house mainly of early C17 origin, built of sandstone in roughly coursed blocks. It retains small mullioned windows, two- to four-light, on the long S front, but the windows on the N side are plain C19. The entrance, on the N side, is early to mid C18 with a simple moulded architrave and keystone. C17–C19 BARNS nearby.

*A copy is displayed in the church of an exceptionally interesting WALL PAINTING lost soon after its discovery in 1868. It was a gruesome late medieval depiction of St Erasmus being disembowelled with a windlass, an appropriate subject here since the saint was the patron of sailors. The copy shows interesting costume details, and an elaborate landscape setting (David Park).

WOLVERTON MANOR *see* SHORWELL

5090

WOOTTON

Wootton Bridge

Wootton began as a small settlement adjoining the site of a once important manor house, to which the medieval church was related. Wootton Bridge first developed as a group of buildings adjoining a crossing of the tidal Wootton Creek, ½ m. SE of the original settlement. Following extensive development in the C19 and, particularly, the C20 there is now a large village extending W from the creek, with the old church on its N edge.

ST EDMUND, Church Lane. A small but relatively long building of rough local stone, with nave and chancel under a continuous roof. The nave is of Norman origin, with a mid to late C12 S doorway – the finest feature of the church. It is of two orders of which the inner is quite plain, without imposts. The main arch has three tiers of zigzag, facing outwards, and there is a hoodmould with billet decoration. The doorway is flanked by shafts with single-scalloped capitals; the shafts rest on moulded bases raised above ground level on short pedestals.

A chapel was added *c.* 1200 on the N side of the nave, entered through a wide arch. This chapel was demolished after the Reformation and the arch blocked. When a new structure was built on the site in the late C19 (*see* below), the arch was unblocked and restored. It is Transitional; pointed, of two chamfered orders, with semi-cylindrical responds and multi-scalloped capitals. The chancel was lengthened in the C13 and has two lancets on each side. From the C14 are the W window of two tall ogee-headed lights, and a similar but smaller window in the S nave wall.

The church was restored in 1883 by *J. Middleton*. In 1893 an organ chamber, later vestry, and now Lady Chapel was built on the site of the N chapel by *T. Chatfeild Clarke* (*see* Oakfield, below). In the same year Chatfeild Clarke designed the gabled W bellcote (it replaced a small wooden belfry of the type common in Hampshire and Sussex). *Percy Stone* restored the church again *c.* 1908.

FURNISHINGS. Unusual FONT, C17 or C18. Concave bowl with pattern of leaves pointed upwards in flat relief, and rim with leaf pattern, on baluster-shaped stem which
32 broadens boldly. – Early C17 PULPIT; octagonal, with arched panels and diamond patterns below. The finest feature is the canopy, with fretted arches and angle pendants. The pulpit was restored by *Percy Stone*, 1912. – STAINED GLASS. E window by *Kempe*, 1894. – SCULPTURE.

Wooden figure of Christ on a plain cross-beam; tapering, with arms outstretched and slightly raised; by *Jack Whitehead*, 1975. – MONUMENT, N wall. Mary Rochfort, †1819, by *Coade & Sealy*. Woman weeping over an urn with a cherub's head below.

ST MARK, Station Road. By *Percy Stone*, 1910; an exercise in red brick with stone details. The street front contains the E window, divided by two mullions of brick alternating with stone, and arched with a similar alternation. It has thin tracery with a vertical emphasis. (The interior is striking. Nave with brick and stone piers of rectangular section, which rise to the roof without connecting arches. Triple chancel screen, with main and subsidiary arches in similar brick and stone. A remarkably original design from this usually conservative architect.)

OAKFIELD, off Station Road on the SW outskirts. Built *c.* 1880 for himself by *T. Chatfeild Clarke*, an Island-born architect who practised extensively in central London. A large house, now subdivided, showing Arts and Crafts influence. It has tall oriel windows rising like dormers, with tile-hung gablets, on two sides. At one end is a big gabled wing with applied half-timbering on the first floor.

WROXALL 5075

A village amid the hills behind Ventnor, adjoining Appuldurcombe (q.v.). It was very small before a railway was built in 1866, passing through a tunnel to Ventnor (the line is now closed). There are a few older stone-built houses, some Victorian villas, and much C20 development. Fortunately the village is still relatively compact and its setting largely unimpaired.

ST JOHN THE EVANGELIST. By *T.R. Saunders* of Ventnor, 1876–7. Nave and chancel in rough stone, with triple W lancets facing the street. The SW tower is unorthodox Gothic of 1911 with lancets halfway up, a big clock above and a steep pyramidal top with white-painted lucarnes. – Wooden REREDOS of 1911, with trefoiled painted panels. – STAINED GLASS of 1911 in the triple-lancet E window; clear and colourful – by whom? (Two side windows by *Heaton, Butler & Bayne*. – Window at W end by *Lawrence Lee*, 1952.)

METHODIST CHURCH, further down the village street. In unconventional E.E. style. Gabled street front with spiked turrets flanking a four-light window of which the centre two lights are taller and paired; single lancets under the lower slopes of the gable on either side.

COUNTY PRIMARY SCHOOL, Station Road, E of the church. 87
Of 1986; by *Michael Rainey*, County Architect; *J. Petrie*,

Project Architect. On a corner site with fine views. Buff brick with sparse red dressings; low-pitch roofs. The entrance is in the canted angle between two ranges; it has glazing in square panes, fronted by a hood supported on two slender columns.

YAFFORD HOUSE *see* SHORWELL

3585

YARMOUTH

Yarmouth was founded as a town *c.* 1170 by Richard de Redvers (cf. Newport and Lymington, which he also founded); for a time it flourished as a port. It lay on the E side of the entrance to a wide estuary and also (unlike other early Island ports) adjoined the open sea. It suffered French raids in 1377 and later, and declined in importance, although unlike Newtown (q.v.) it remained a small port, with a castle built by Henry VIII and connections to Lymington on the mainland. There was some recovery by the early C17 – several fairly substantial houses date in part from then – but the town had shrunk from its full medieval extent. Later growth was limited; Yarmouth's present importance is as a ferry port and yachting centre.

Sir Robert Holmes, an adventurer with a record of overseas exploits, was a prominent local figure; he became Captain (Governor) of the Island in 1668, and is commemorated in the church. The present George Hotel was probably his house at the time of his death in 1692.

ST JAMES. Consecrated in 1626 (Yarmouth had two earlier churches which suffered from enemy attacks and decay). It is mostly straightforward 'Gothic Survival', with aisled nave and W tower. Mainly in rough stone except for the upper part of the tower, which is in ashlar and was added in 1831 by *D.A. Alexander*, who lived locally. This, with its tall lancet belfry lights and battlemented top, is a landmark in the streets as well as from the sea. Inside, the arcades have octagonal piers and double-chamfered arches. There was a restoration in 1873, and in 1889 the chancel was lengthened by *John Colson & Son*, when the C17 E window was re-inserted in the new position. It is of six lights with four-centred arches in a rectangular frame, characteristics of domestic buildings of the period. The C17 aisle windows and the C19 side windows of the chancel are of two lights in the same style.

FURNISHINGS. FONT. 1873. Octagonal bowl of complex form; marble colonnettes with elaborate capitals. – PULPIT.

Also 1873. Stone, circular, with open trefoil arches. Who was the restorer of that date? – REREDOS in the Lady Chapel (E part of N aisle) by *Sir Charles Nicholson*, 1947; classical. – Ceramic PLAQUE on N nave wall, depicting the Virgin under a colourful flowered canopy; *c.* 1966; in the manner of Della Robbia. – ROYAL ARMS, 1715; above N door. – WEST GALLERY. 1832–3, extending over W bays of nave and aisles, probably by *Alexander*. Balustraded front with thin pointed panels; round wooden piers facing the nave. – STAINED GLASS. E window by *C.A. Gibbs*, 1867 (moved when the window itself was re-set), Christ with children in the centre four lights; scrolls and emblems at the ends. Strong colours and details; the background is blue, with flower and stem patterns at the top. – Side windows in aisles and chancel by *Powell's*.

MONUMENTS. The small Holmes chapel, externally in *p. 306*
brick with ashlar quoins, was added to the S of the chancel to house the monument of Sir Robert Holmes, †1692. It opens from the chancel through a grille in an elaborate doorcase with a broad bolection moulding and scrolled broken pediment. The monument itself is, apart from the head, an accomplished piece. A standing, over-life-size figure in white marble, dressed in Roman costume, leans against a cannon and holds a rolled document. The statue, headless, was captured from a French ship (according to an inscription); the head, different in style and of poorer quality, was added when the sculpture was used to commemorate Sir Robert. It is set in a clumsily executed canopy of brown marble. Also in the chapel, on the r., a tall marble tablet to Henry Holmes, †1751, and Thomas Lord Holmes, †1764, with thick foliage borders and a coat of arms. John Urry, †1802, by *Nollekens*; sarcophagus-shaped tablet with urn and shield. Daniel Alexander, architect, †1846; plain wall tablet among others for the family.*

METHODIST CHURCH, St James Street. 1881. Of stone; triple traceried window towards the street with gabled hood-moulds; flanking tower with diagonal upper stage and short spire.

YARMOUTH CASTLE. Built in 1545–7, after the construction 27
of the first group of Henry VIII's Solent fortresses, such as Hurst and Southsea on the Hampshire mainland. It is essentially square in shape, with the open sea to the N, the harbour to the W and, originally, a moat on the two landward sides. A bastion – the castle's special feature – projects to the SE. The castle appears externally much as it did from the first, except that the moat has been filled and buildings

* *D.A. Alexander* specialized in warehouses and lighthouses; he designed the original Dartmoor prison, and worked on several country houses. He lived for a time in The Towers, High Street (*see* Perambulation, p. 309).

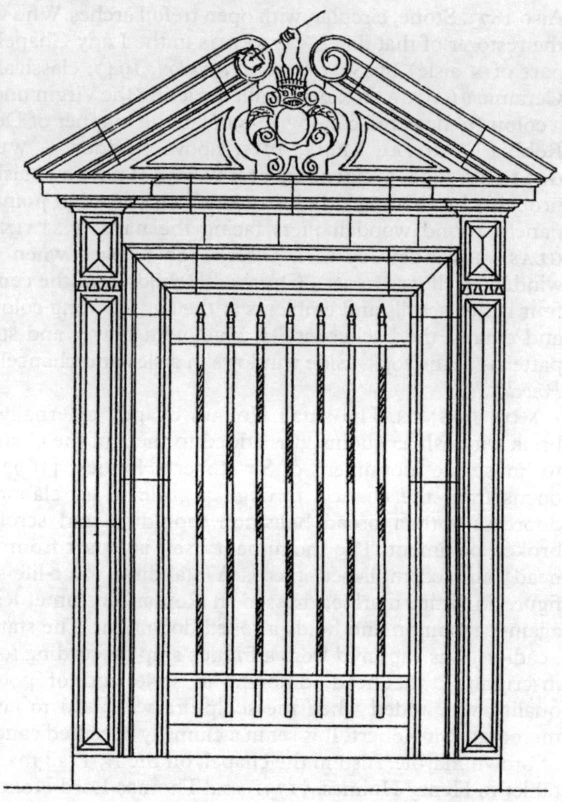

Yarmouth church, Holmes Chapel, elevation of doorway.
From Percy Stone, *The Architectural Antiquities of the Isle of Wight*, 1891

abut on the S side. The curtain walls are faced in ashlar; the original entrance, not regularly used, is on the E side and faces a hotel garden on the site of the moat. It has a four-centred arch without capitals, with the arms of Henry VIII in a panel above. The SE bastion faced the moat to its N and W; its outer two sides are canted to form an arrowhead. Bastions in this form were at the time becoming important features in European defensive architecture, but those on most of Henry VIII's earlier castles were rounded. This is the earliest extant example in England with an arrowhead form.* (As seen externally it is topped by the gable of a later upper storey.)

*The bastion was in existence in 1559; external stonework suggests that it is part of the original structure of 1545–7.

Alterations have resulted in an internal layout very different from the original. At first the curtain walls enclosed a large courtyard. In *c.* 1559–65 much of the courtyard on the N side was filled with earth to create a platform on which guns were mounted; the platform was heightened and extended *c.* 1600–9, so that the N parts of the curtain became retaining walls and parapets. In the late C17 Sir Robert Holmes moved the main castle entrance from the E to the S side. This is the entrance now used (reached from Quay Street). One passes through a modest doorway and along a vaulted passage into a part of the interior which is at first difficult to understand. It is best to turn r. into an irregular courtyard, on the S side of which is what amounted to a small house, first built in the later C16; it came to be occupied by the master-gunner. The windows facing the courtyard are early C19, but the small four-centred doorway is original. The house backed on to the SE corner of the castle, and the domestic accommodation extended into the bastion, where the ground floor, reached through a brick-vaulted passage, was fitted as a kitchen. It has a fireplace with a massive wooden lintel and a baking oven. The first floor within the bastion has a four-centred fireplace and a tiny brick-vaulted privy alcove. An attic storey was added to the house, including the bastion, in *c.* 1600 or soon after.

Further construction took place from 1632. Eight small tunnel-vaulted rooms were built in two storeys in the SW corner of the castle to accommodate members of the garrison. A new room, the Long Room, was built above them, connecting with the attic floor of the house already described. When Sir Robert formed the present entrance, he made one of the vaulted rooms into a passageway as part of the approach into the castle (*see* above); the rooms to the W became gunpowder stores. At about this time a brick-faced structure was built at first-floor level bridging the pathway within the castle – a conspicuous feature, its red brick contrasting with the surrounding stonework. It is something of a relief to pass, at upper level, from the complexity of rooms in the S part of the castle on to the open platform, now grassed, which occupies its N part – and provides seaward vistas. The parapets were altered in 1813, with copings which slope down externally, and rounded internal angles. These were the last significant alterations.

On the W side the castle now faces the ferry terminal. The W wall is that of 1545–7, heightened at the S end by the gable of the Long Room (*see* above), and modified to the N by the parapet of 1813. A massive buttress of tapering triangular section was added towards the NW corner *c.* 1610, partly blocking a gunport which went out of use when the platform behind was raised; a similar buttress round the corner faces out to sea.

PERAMBULATION

Start at the ferry terminal, with the castle to the E. The HARBOUR to the W, used intensively by yachts, dates in its present form essentially from 1843–7 when a breakwater was built across the estuary mouth; the causeway and original bridge (replaced in the C20) followed by 1860. QUAY STREET leads E, past the entrance to the castle and the GEORGE HOTEL, which backs on to the castle. It was probably built *c.* 1690 by Sir Robert Holmes, in a classical style then precocious for the Isle of Wight,* with a steep-sloped hipped roof. The seven-bay frontage has been altered since, with Late Georgian sashes and doorway, and was extended E in the later C19. There are fine interiors – e.g. the present lounge (the SE room), with tall rectangular panels, a bolection-moulded wooden fireplace, and an arched doorway with panelled spandrels. The impressive well staircase has spiral balusters, fluted angle columns and scrolled tread ends. Behind the staircase to the N are two exceptionally tall sashes, that to the W three panes by ten, and the other (less tall because of the rise of the stairs) three by eight. Are these original features in this form, or early insertions? The house first became an inn in 1764.

Quay Street leads into THE SQUARE, really a broad N–S street. The small TOWN HALL was built in 1763 by Thomas, 1st Lord Holmes. It projects from the W side of the square, of which it is the focal feature. Of red brick, with three arches that were originally open, and a hipped roof.** High Street (*see* below) leads E, and to the S is a fine view including the church. We should at first go N. The BUGLE HOTEL on the E side has a five-bay stone front with thick-framed sashes, and a moulded early C17 stone fireplace. The street ends at the PIER, which has a striking former entrance front of *c.* 1927 under a shaped gable with segmental top and concave sides; semicircular windows with radiating glazing bars flank the doorway. The pier itself is modest – built in 1876 with timber supports, ending at a small landing stage which is a fine viewpoint. Steam ferries landed here well into the C20. Set back from the street to the E is the SOLENT YACHT CLUB, a gabled building with roughcast upper storey, by *Aston Webb c.* 1898. It has been spoiled by extensions.

Back into the Square. S of the Town Hall is JIREH HOUSE, with a rough stone front, like several of the older houses in the town (Inside are C17 features including a stone fireplace). The Square narrows and continues S as ST JAMES STREET; beyond the narrowing is the tower of St James (*see* p. 304), complemented, as a landmark, by the spire of the Methodist church further S. Opposite St James is THE OLD

*Sir Robert Holmes's will of 1692 refers to 'my new house'.

**Yarmouth was a 'pocket borough' and the results of the controlled Parliamentary elections were announced from here (cf. Newtown).

HOUSE, with ashlar quoins, a datestone of 1625 and a big canted first-floor bay of *c.* 1800. THE OLD RECTORY beyond is late C18 with a variegated stone end wall.

HIGH STREET is one of the most attractive streets on the Island. It is narrow, with little traffic, and extends for about ½ m. from The Square to the open shoreside E of the town; partly commercial at the W end but otherwise residential. Building frontages are not always continuous – in many places the street lines are marked by garden walls, often backed by greenery. The houses are modest, with a few exceptions. THE TOWERS, on the E corner of a lane leading to the shore, has a simple C18 brick front with stone quoins, but seen from the lane is a taller early C19 E wing with canted N frontage under an embattled parapet; a turret, also with battlements, rises behind. This was the home from the 1820s of the architect *D.A. Alexander* (*see* St James, p. 304). NORTH HOUSE, *c.* 1860, further along the street, is an urban villa of three storeys and basement; the windows have thick architraves and the porch, with Doric columns, has small stucco lions above the corners of the entablature. THE DEACONS opposite is more local in character; of rough stone, possibly C17 but with C18 windows and door hood. Further E along High Street, beyond the turning to Basketts Lane on the r., is WESTERLY, a remarkable house of 1998–9 by *ORMS Designers and Architects*. It is a long building aligned N–S, the main section faced at each end in rough Purbeck stone with smooth quoins; the W frontage is largely taken by big-paned windows framed in timber, together with boarded panels. A broad rectangular chimneystack with flat top rises above the roof-line on this side, like a tower (the house has a single fireplace, in the main living room). The gabled street frontage, set slightly back behind a stone boundary wall, has a glazed semicircular oriel which helps to relate it to the urban scene. Altogether a successful piece of modern architecture paying a suitable tribute to a traditional context. Beyond, the street bends slightly; EASTERN COTTAGE, at the far end on the N, is C18 with dentilled cornice and keystones. Further on is open foreshore, bordered by a grassy common. About ¾ m. along the Newport road, on the r., is a series of BUNGALOWS built *c.* 1897 when this building type, derived from India, became fashionable; they have attractive wooden arched verandas and centrally placed attic storeys (somewhat belying their designation).

Former TIDE MILL, 1793, by a creek beyond the end of Mill Street to the S. Impressive; of three storeys and seven bays in red brick; all now residential (the miller's house was in the S part). This is the only former tide mill surviving on the Island; others at Wootton, at St Helens and on the Medina estuary have been demolished.

6080 YAVERLAND

Sandown

A small village just behind the beginning of the sandstone cliffs to the NE of Sandown. The manor house stands on rising ground facing out to sea, with the church to its W. Nearby is a pair of cottages, perhaps of *c.* 1800, illustrating the local vernacular: partly of sandstone and partly of brick, with thatched roofs.

ST JOHN. Until *Ewan Christian* restored it in 1887–9 this was an essentially Norman church. He added a shingled W bell-turret and half-timbered S porch which make the church seem predominantly Victorian as we approach. However, the S doorway brings us back to the mid C12. It has one order of columns and a tympanum with a strange pattern of small intersecting circles, overlain in places with larger rosettes – worn through exposure to the weather before the porch was built. The middle part of the underside of the tympanum has been cut out, as if to accommodate a door

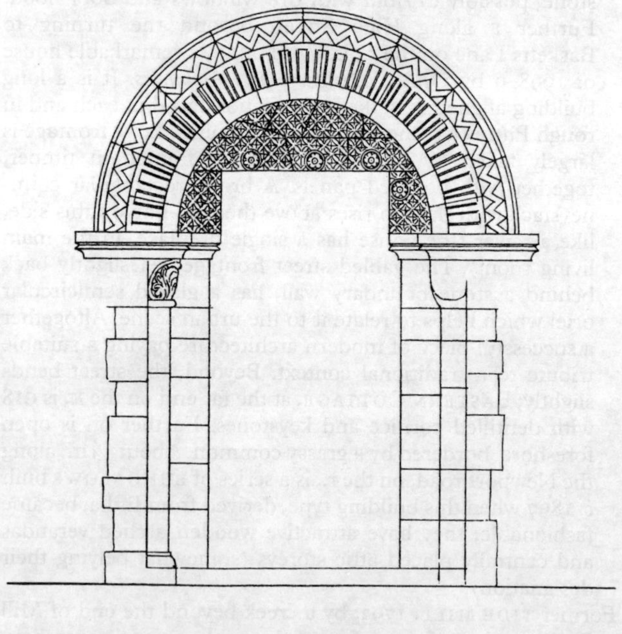

Yaverland church, south doorway, elevation.
From Percy Stone, *The Architectural Antiquities of the Isle of Wight*, 1891

at some unknown date. The arch has an odd motif of raised
radial bars, roughly carved and irregularly spaced, and also
a wide hoodmould with a single course of zigzag. Inside,
the Norman chancel arch is dominant; it must have been 12
worked, like the S door, by highly individualist masons.* It
has several courses of zigzag decoration on the outer order,

Yaverland Manor, staircase arch, elevation.
From Percy Stone, *The Architectural Antiquities of the Isle of Wight*, 1891

*The arch appears largely original, not renewed as suggested in the first edition.

a diamond pattern on the hoodmould, and a plain inner order with a roll moulding. The jambs have inset columns, the N with zigzag on its shaft, the S with chevron pattern; the capitals are curious, with small inverted trefoils over scallops. *Christian* changed the character of the interior by adding a N aisle, renewing the roofs and restoring most of the windows (which had post-Reformation wooden frames). He revealed a remarkable C13 feature which had been partly obscured: a recess in the S nave wall, which shows externally as a projection; it may have accommodated a tomb. Inside it is framed by a small arch of two orders, the inner one resting on corbels; there is a basically original two-light window with plate tracery. The chancel was extended by Christian. – REREDOS of 1891 attributed to *C.E. Ponting* of Marlborough, a strange work for an architect with later Arts and Crafts inclination; in veined marble with pinnacles, intricate cresting, and curvilinear tracery. – STAINED GLASS. By *Clayton & Bell* the E window and the plate-traceried window S of the nave. By *Hardman* the S nave windows (except the last-named). By *Burlison & Grylls* the figures of Raphael and Gabriel in the W wall, and the W aisle window.

YAVERLAND MANOR. Built in 1620 (date over door) in rough stone, and hardly altered externally except at the back.* The main (S) front has wings but no porch; there are four gables of equal size, five-light transomed windows on each floor, and mullioned openings in the gables; the clustered chimneystacks are of brick. The central doorway, square-topped and slightly moulded, is inexplicably plain. The hall was formed in the C20 through demolition of internal walls; it has a C17 four-centred stone fireplace (one of several in the house) at the W end. Leading N from the hall, and rising to ceiling height, is the timber entrance to the staircase, also dated 1620 – an important work of the Island school of p. 311 woodcarvers. The arch itself is four-centred; it is flanked by tapering pilasters with geometrical patterns, and grotesque torsos above; there are beasts and contorted pattern on the entablature. The STAIRCASE, of well form, has turned balusters and bulbous finials; three corbels carved with crouching figures support the landing. One upstairs room has simple panelling with strapwork friezes, and a fine panelled door.

p. 38 OLD RECTORY, ¼ m. S. Three-gable frontage in rendered brick, with pointed pinnacles rising from the gable ends, and canted bay windows on both floors; the porch has a gabled canopy with thick pinnacles at the sides and apex. It is attributed to *Nash*.

*Built by Edward Richards, son of a brewer who serviced ships anchored off Brading.

GLOSSARY

Numbers and letters refer to the illustrations (by John Sambrook) on pp. 322–9.

ABACUS: flat slab forming the top of a capital (3a).

ACANTHUS: classical formalized leaf ornament (4b).

ACCUMULATOR TOWER: *see* Hydraulic power.

ACHIEVEMENT: a complete display of armorial bearings.

ACROTERION: plinth for a statue or ornament on the apex or ends of a pediment; more usually, both the plinth and what stands on it (4a).

AEDICULE (*lit.* little building): architectural surround, consisting usually of two columns or pilasters supporting a pediment.

AGGREGATE: *see* Concrete.

AISLE: subsidiary space alongside the body of a building, separated from it by columns, piers, or posts.

ALMONRY: a building from which alms are dispensed to the poor.

AMBULATORY (*lit.* walkway): aisle around the sanctuary (q.v.).

ANGLE ROLL: roll moulding in the angle between two planes (1a).

ANSE DE PANIER: *see* Arch.

ANTAE: simplified pilasters (4a), usually applied to the ends of the enclosing walls of a portico *in antis* (q.v.).

ANTEFIXAE: ornaments projecting at regular intervals above a Greek cornice, originally to conceal the ends of roof tiles (4a).

ANTHEMION: classical ornament like a honeysuckle flower (4b).

APRON: raised panel below a window or wall monument or tablet.

APSE: semicircular or polygonal end of an apartment, especially of a chancel or chapel. In classical architecture sometimes called an *exedra*.

ARABESQUE: non-figurative surface decoration consisting of flowing lines, foliage scrolls etc., based on geometrical patterns. Cf. Grotesque.

ARCADE: series of arches supported by piers or columns. *Blind arcade* or *arcading*: the same applied to the wall surface. *Wall arcade*: in medieval churches, a blind arcade forming a dado below windows. Also a covered shopping street.

ARCH: Shapes *see* 5c. *Basket arch* or *anse de panier* (basket handle): three-centred and depressed, or with a flat centre. *Nodding*: ogee arch curving forward from the wall face. *Parabolic*: shaped like a chain suspended from two level points, but inverted. Special purposes. *Chancel*: dividing chancel from nave or crossing. *Crossing*: spanning piers at a crossing (q.v.). *Relieving or discharging*: incorporated in a wall to relieve superimposed weight (5c). *Skew*: spanning responds not diametrically opposed. *Strainer*: inserted in an opening to resist inward pressure. *Transverse*: spanning a main axis (e.g. of a vaulted space). *See also* Jack arch, Triumphal arch.

ARCHITRAVE: formalized lintel, the lowest member of the classical entablature (3a). Also the moulded frame of a door or window (often borrowing the profile of a classical architrave). For *lugged* and *shouldered* architraves *see* 4b.

ARCUATED: dependent structurally on the arch principle. Cf. Trabeated.

ARK: chest or cupboard housing the

tables of Jewish law in a synagogue.

ARRIS: sharp edge where two surfaces meet at an angle (3a).

ASHLAR: masonry of large blocks wrought to even faces and square edges (6d).

ASTRAGAL: classical moulding of semicircular section (3f).

ASTYLAR: with no columns or similar vertical features.

ATLANTES: *see* Caryatids.

ATRIUM (plural: atria): inner court of a Roman or C20 house; in a multi-storey building, a toplit covered court rising through all storeys. Also an open court in front of a church.

ATTACHED COLUMN: *see* Engaged column.

ATTIC: small top storey within a roof. Also the storey above the main entablature of a classical façade.

AUMBRY: recess or cupboard to hold sacred vessels for the Mass.

BAILEY: *see* Motte-and-bailey.

BALANCE BEAM: *see* Canals.

BALDACCHINO: free-standing canopy, originally fabric, over an altar. Cf. Ciborium.

BALLFLOWER: globular flower of three petals enclosing a ball (1a). Typical of the Decorated style.

BALUSTER: pillar or pedestal of bellied form. *Balusters*: vertical supports of this or any other form, for a handrail or coping, the whole being called a *balustrade* (6c). *Blind balustrade*: the same applied to the wall surface.

BARBICAN: outwork defending the entrance to a castle.

BARGEBOARDS (corruption of 'vergeboards'): boards, often carved or fretted, fixed beneath the eaves of a gable to cover and protect the rafters.

BAROQUE: style originating in Rome *c.*1600 and current in England *c.*1680–1720, characterized by dramatic massing and silhouette and the use of the giant order.

BARROW: burial mound.

BARTIZAN: corbelled turret, square or round, frequently at an angle.

BASCULE: hinged part of a lifting (or bascule) bridge.

BASE: moulded foot of a column or pilaster. For *Attic* base *see* 3b.

BASEMENT: lowest, subordinate storey; hence the lowest part of a classical elevation, below the *piano nobile* (q.v.).

BASILICA: a Roman public hall; hence an aisled building with a clerestory.

BASTION: one of a series of defensive semicircular or polygonal projections from the main wall of a fortress or city.

BATTER: intentional inward inclination of a wall face.

BATTLEMENT: defensive parapet, composed of *merlons* (solid) and *crenels* (embrasures) through which archers could shoot; sometimes called *crenellation*. Also used decoratively.

BAY: division of an elevation or interior space as defined by regular vertical features such as arches, columns, windows etc.

BAY LEAF: classical ornament of overlapping bay leaves (3f).

BAY WINDOW: window of one or more storeys projecting from the face of a building. *Canted*: with a straight front and angled sides. *Bow window*: curved. *Oriel*: rests on corbels or brackets and starts above ground level; also the bay window at the dais end of a medieval great hall.

BEAD-AND-REEL: *see* Enrichments.

BEAKHEAD: Norman ornament with a row of beaked bird or beast heads usually biting into a roll moulding (1a).

BELFRY: chamber or stage in a tower where bells are hung.

BELL CAPITAL: *see* 1b.

BELLCOTE: small gabled or roofed housing for the bell(s).

BERM: level area separating a ditch from a bank on a hill-fort or barrow.

BILLET: Norman ornament of small half-cylindrical or rectangular blocks (1a).

BLIND: *see* Arcade, Baluster, Portico.

BLOCK CAPITAL: *see* 1a.

BLOCKED: columns, etc. interrupted by regular projecting

blocks (*blocking*), as on a Gibbs surround (4b).

BLOCKING COURSE: course of stones, or equivalent, on top of a cornice and crowning the wall.

BOLECTION MOULDING: covering the joint between two different planes (6b).

BOND: the pattern of long sides (*stretchers*) and short ends (*headers*) produced on the face of a wall by laying bricks in a particular way (6e).

BOSS: knob or projection, e.g. at the intersection of ribs in a vault (2c).

BOWTELL: a term in use by the C15 for a form of roll moulding, usually three-quarters of a circle in section (also called *edge roll*).

BOW WINDOW: *see* Bay window.

BOX FRAME: timber-framed construction in which vertical and horizontal wall members support the roof (7). Also concrete construction where the loads are taken on cross walls; also called *cross-wall construction*.

BRACE: subsidiary member of a structural frame, curved or straight. *Bracing* is often arranged decoratively e.g. quatrefoil, herringbone (7). *See also* Roofs.

BRATTISHING: ornamental crest, usually formed of leaves, Tudor flowers or miniature battlements.

BRESSUMER (*lit.* breast-beam): big horizontal beam supporting the wall above, especially in a jettied building (7).

BRICK: *see* Bond, Cogging, Engineering, Gauged, Tumbling.

BRIDGE: *Bowstring*: with arches rising above the roadway which is suspended from them. *Clapper*: one long stone forms the roadway. *Roving*: *see* Canal. *Suspension*: roadway suspended from cables or chains slung between towers or pylons. *Stay-suspension* or *stay-cantilever*: supported by diagonal stays from towers or pylons. *See also* Bascule.

BRISES-SOLEIL: projecting fins or canopies which deflect direct sunlight from windows.

BROACH: *see* Spire and 1c.

BUCRANIUM: ox skull used decoratively in classical friezes.

BULL-NOSED SILL: sill displaying a pronounced convex upper moulding.

BULLSEYE WINDOW: small oval window, set horizontally (cf. Oculus). Also called *œil de bœuf*.

BUTTRESS: vertical member projecting from a wall to stabilize it or to resist the lateral thrust of an arch, roof, or vault (1c, 2c). A *flying buttress* transmits the thrust to a heavy abutment by means of an arch or half-arch (1c).

CABLE OR ROPE MOULDING: originally Norman, like twisted strands of a rope.

CAMES: *see* Quarries.

CAMPANILE: free-standing bell-tower.

CANALS: *Flash lock*: removable weir or similar device through which boats pass on a flush of water. Predecessor of the *pound lock*: chamber with gates at each end allowing boats to float from one level to another. *Tidal gates*: single pair of lock gates allowing vessels to pass when the tide makes a level. *Balance beam*: beam projecting horizontally for opening and closing lock gates. *Roving bridge*: carrying a towing path from one bank to the other.

CANTILEVER: horizontal projection (e.g. step, canopy) supported by a downward force behind the fulcrum.

CAPITAL: head or crowning feature of a column or pilaster; for classical types *see* 3; for medieval types *see* 1b.

CARREL: compartment designed for individual work or study.

CARTOUCHE: classical tablet with ornate frame (4b).

CARYATIDS: female figures supporting an entablature; their male counterparts are *Atlantes* (*lit.* Atlas figures).

CASEMATE: vaulted chamber, with embrasures for defence, within a castle wall or projecting from it.

CASEMENT: side-hinged window.

CASTELLATED: with battlements (q.v.).

CAST IRON: hard and brittle, cast in a mould to the required shape.

Wrought iron is ductile, strong in tension, forged into decorative patterns or forged and rolled into e.g. bars, joists, boiler plates; *mild steel* is its modern equivalent, similar but stronger.

CATSLIDE: *See* 8a.

CAVETTO: concave classical moulding of quarter-round section (3f).

CELURE OR CEILURE: enriched area of roof above rood or altar.

CEMENT: *see* Concrete.

CENOTAPH (*lit.* empty tomb): funerary monument which is not a burying place.

CENTRING: wooden support for the building of an arch or vault, removed after completion.

CHAMFER (*lit.* corner-break): surface formed by cutting off a square edge or corner. For types of chamfers and *chamfer stops see* 6a. *See also* Double chamfer.

CHANCEL: part of the E end of a church set apart for the use of the officiating clergy.

CHANTRY CHAPEL: often attached to or within a church, endowed for the celebration of Masses principally for the soul of the founder.

CHEVET (*lit.* head): French term for chancel with ambulatory and radiating chapels.

CHEVRON: V-shape used in series or double series (later) on a Norman moulding (1a). Also (especially when on a single plane) called *zigzag*.

CHOIR: the part of a cathedral, monastic or collegiate church where services are sung.

CIBORIUM: a fixed canopy over an altar, usually vaulted and supported on four columns; cf. Baldacchino. Also a canopied shrine for the reserved sacrament.

CINQUEFOIL: *see* Foil.

CIST: stone-lined or slab-built grave.

CLADDING: external covering or skin applied to a structure, especially a framed one.

CLERESTORY: uppermost storey of the nave of a church, pierced by windows. Also high-level windows in secular buildings.

CLOSER: a brick cut to complete a bond (6e).

CLUSTER BLOCK: *see* Multi-storey.

COADE STONE: ceramic artificial stone made in Lambeth 1769–*c.*1840 by Eleanor Coade (†1821) and her associates.

COB: walling material of clay mixed with straw. Also called *pisé*.

COFFERING: arrangement of sunken panels (coffers), square or polygonal, decorating a ceiling, vault, or arch.

COGGING: a decorative course of bricks laid diagonally (6e). Cf. Dentilation.

COLLAR: *see* Roofs and 7.

COLLEGIATE CHURCH: endowed for the support of a college of priests.

COLONNADE: range of columns supporting an entablature. Cf. Arcade.

COLONNETTE: small medieval column or shaft.

COLOSSAL ORDER: *see* Giant order.

COLUMBARIUM: shelved, niched structure to house multiple burials.

COLUMN: a classical, upright structural member of round section with a shaft, a capital, and usually a base (3a, 4a).

COLUMN FIGURE: carved figure attached to a medieval column or shaft, usually flanking a doorway.

COMMUNION TABLE: unconsecrated table used in Protestant churches for the celebration of Holy Communion.

COMPOSITE: *see* Orders.

COMPOUND PIER: grouped shafts (q.v.), or a solid core surrounded by shafts.

CONCRETE: composition of *cement* (calcined lime and clay), *aggregate* (small stones or rock chippings), sand and water. It can be poured into *formwork* or *shuttering* (temporary frame of timber or metal) on site (*in-situ* concrete), or *pre-cast* as components before construction. *Reinforced*: incorporating steel rods to take the tensile force. *Pre-stressed*: with tensioned steel rods. Finishes include the impression of boards left by formwork (*board-marked* or *shuttered*), and texturing with steel brushes (*brushed*) or hammers (*hammer-dressed*). *See also* Shell.

CONSOLE: bracket of curved outline (4b).

COPING: protective course of masonry or brickwork capping a wall (6d).

CORBEL: projecting block supporting something above. *Corbel course*: continuous course of projecting stones or bricks fulfilling the same function. *Corbel table*: series of corbels to carry a parapet or a wall-plate or wall-post (7). *Corbelling*: brick or masonry courses built out beyond one another to support a chimney-stack, window, etc.

CORINTHIAN: *see* Orders and 3d.

CORNICE: flat-topped ledge with moulded underside, projecting along the top of a building or feature, especially as the highest member of the classical entablature (3a). Also the decorative moulding in the angle between wall and ceiling.

CORPS-DE-LOGIS: the main building(s) as distinct from the wings or pavilions.

COTTAGE ORNÉ: an artfully rustic small house associated with the Picturesque movement.

COUNTERCHANGING: of joists on a ceiling divided by beams into compartments, when placed in opposite directions in alternate squares.

COUR D'HONNEUR: formal entrance court before a house in the French manner, usually with flanking wings and a screen wall or gates.

COURSE: continuous layer of stones, etc. in a wall (6e).

COVE: a broad concave moulding, e.g. to mask the eaves of a roof. *Coved ceiling*: with a pronounced cove joining the walls to a flat central panel smaller than the whole area of the ceiling.

CRADLE ROOF: *see* Wagon roof.

CREDENCE: a shelf within or beside a piscina (q.v.), or a table for the sacramental elements and vessels.

CRENELLATION: parapet with crenels (*see* Battlement).

CRINKLE-CRANKLE WALL: garden wall undulating in a series of serpentine curves.

CROCKETS: leafy hooks. *Crocketing* decorates the edges of Gothic features, such as pinnacles, canopies, etc. *Crocket capital*: *see* 1b.

CROSSING: central space at the junction of the nave, chancel, and transepts. *Crossing tower*: above a crossing.

CROSS-WINDOW: with one mullion and one transom (qq.v.).

CROWN-POST: *see* Roofs and 7.

CROWSTEPS: squared stones set like steps, e.g. on a gable (8a).

CRUCKS (*lit.* crooked): pairs of inclined timbers (*blades*), usually curved, set at bay-lengths; they support the roof timbers and, in timber buildings, also support the walls (8b). *Base*: blades rise from ground level to a tie- or collar-beam which supports the roof timbers. *Full*: blades rise from ground level to the apex of the roof, serving as the main members of a roof truss. *Jointed*: blades formed from more than one timber; the lower member may act as a wall-post; it is usually elbowed at wall-plate level and jointed just above. *Middle*: blades rise from half-way up the walls to a tie- or collar-beam. *Raised*: blades rise from half-way up the walls to the apex. *Upper*: blades supported on a tie-beam and rising to the apex.

CRYPT: underground or half-underground area, usually below the E end of a church. *Ring crypt*: corridor crypt surrounding the apse of an early medieval church, often associated with chambers for relics. Cf. Undercroft.

CUPOLA (*lit.* dome): especially a small dome on a circular or polygonal base crowning a larger dome, roof, or turret.

CURSUS: a long avenue defined by two parallel earthen banks with ditches outside.

CURTAIN WALL: a connecting wall between the towers of a castle. Also a non-load-bearing external wall applied to a C20 framed structure.

CUSP: *see* Tracery and 2b.

CYCLOPEAN MASONRY: large irregular polygonal stones, smooth and finely jointed.

CYMA RECTA and CYMA REVERSA: classical mouldings with double curves (3f). Cf. Ogee.

DADO: the finishing (often with panelling) of the lower part of a wall in a classical interior; in origin a formalized continuous pedestal. *Dado rail*: the moulding along the top of the dado.

DAGGER: *see* Tracery and 2b.

DALLE-DE-VERRE (*lit.* glass-slab): a late C20 stained-glass technique, setting large, thick pieces of cast glass into a frame of reinforced concrete or epoxy resin.

DEC (DECORATED): English Gothic architecture *c.* 1290 to *c.* 1350. The name is derived from the type of window tracery (q.v.) used during the period.

DEMI- or HALF-COLUMNS: engaged columns (q.v.) half of whose circumference projects from the wall.

DENTIL: small square block used in series in classical cornices (3c). *Dentilation* is produced by the projection of alternating headers along cornices or stringcourses.

DIAPER: repetitive surface decoration of lozenges or squares flat or in relief. Achieved in brickwork with bricks of two colours.

DIOCLETIAN OR THERMAL WINDOW: semicircular with two mullions, as used in the Baths of Diocletian, Rome (4b).

DISTYLE: having two columns (4a).

DOGTOOTH: E.E. ornament, consisting of a series of small pyramids formed by four stylized canine teeth meeting at a point (1a).

DORIC: *see* Orders and 3a, 3b.

DORMER: window projecting from the slope of a roof (8a).

DOUBLE CHAMFER: a chamfer applied to each of two recessed arches (1a).

DOUBLE PILE: *see* Pile.

DRAGON BEAM: *see* Jetty.

DRESSINGS: the stone or brickwork worked to a finished face about an angle, opening, or other feature.

DRIPSTONE: moulded stone projecting from a wall to protect the lower parts from water. Cf. Hoodmould, Weathering.

DRUM: circular or polygonal stage supporting a dome or cupola. Also one of the stones forming the shaft of a column (3a).

DUTCH or FLEMISH GABLE: *see* 8a.

EASTER SEPULCHRE: tomb-chest used for Easter ceremonial, within or against the N wall of a chancel.

EAVES: overhanging edge of a roof; hence *eaves cornice* in this position.

ECHINUS: ovolo moulding (q.v.) below the abacus of a Greek Doric capital (3a).

EDGE RAIL: *see* Railways.

E.E. (EARLY ENGLISH): English Gothic architecture *c.* 1190–1250.

EGG-AND-DART: *see* Enrichments and 3f.

ELEVATION: any face of a building or side of a room. In a drawing, the same or any part of it, represented in two dimensions.

EMBATTLED: with battlements.

EMBRASURE: small splayed opening in a wall or battlement (q.v.).

ENCAUSTIC TILES: earthenware tiles fired with a pattern and glaze.

EN DELIT: stone cut against the bed.

ENFILADE: reception rooms in a formal series, usually with all doorways on axis.

ENGAGED or ATTACHED COLUMN: one that partly merges into a wall or pier.

ENGINEERING BRICKS: dense bricks, originally used mostly for railway viaducts etc.

ENRICHMENTS: the carved decoration of certain classical mouldings, e.g. the ovolo (qq.v.) with *egg-and-dart*, the cyma reversa with *waterleaf*, the astragal with *bead-and-reel* (3f).

ENTABLATURE: in classical architecture, collective name for the three horizontal members (architrave, frieze, and cornice) carried by a wall or a column (3a).

ENTASIS: very slight convex deviation from a straight line, used to prevent an optical illusion of concavity.

EPITAPH: inscription on a tomb.

EXEDRA: *see* Apse.

EXTRADOS: outer curved face of an arch or vault.

EYECATCHER: decorative building terminating a vista.

FASCIA: plain horizontal band, e.g. in an architrave (3c, 3d) or on a shopfront.

FENESTRATION: the arrangement of windows in a façade.

FERETORY: site of the chief shrine of a church, behind the high altar.

FESTOON: ornamental garland, suspended from both ends. Cf. Swag.

FIBREGLASS, or glass-reinforced polyester (GRP): synthetic resin reinforced with glass fibre. GRC: glass-reinforced concrete.

FIELD: *see* Panelling and 6b.

FILLET: a narrow flat band running down a medieval shaft or along a roll moulding (1a). It separates larger curved mouldings in classical cornices, fluting or bases (3c).

FLAMBOYANT: the latest phase of French Gothic architecture, with flowing tracery.

FLASH LOCK: *see* Canals.

FLÈCHE or SPIRELET (*lit.* arrow): slender spire on the centre of a roof.

FLEURON: medieval carved flower or leaf, often rectilinear (1a).

FLUSHWORK: knapped flint used with dressed stone to form patterns.

FLUTING: series of concave grooves (flutes), their common edges sharp (arris) or blunt (fillet) (3).

FOIL (*lit.* leaf): lobe formed by the cusping of a circular or other shape in tracery (2b). *Trefoil* (three), *quatrefoil* (four), *cinquefoil* (five), and *multifoil* express the number of lobes in a shape.

FOLIATE: decorated with leaves.

FORMWORK: *see* Concrete.

FRAMED BUILDING: where the structure is carried by a framework – e.g. of steel, reinforced concrete, timber – instead of by load-bearing walls.

FREESTONE: stone that is cut, or can be cut, in all directions.

FRESCO: *al fresco*: painting on wet plaster. *Fresco secco*: painting on dry plaster.

FRIEZE: the middle member of the classical entablature, sometimes ornamented (3a). *Pulvinated frieze* (*lit.* cushioned): of bold convex profile (3c). Also a horizontal band of ornament.

FRONTISPIECE: in C16 and C17 buildings the central feature of doorway and windows above linked in one composition.

GABLE: For types *see* 8a. *Gablet*: small gable. *Pedimental gable*: treated like a pediment.

GADROONING: classical ribbed ornament like inverted fluting that flows into a lobed edge.

GALILEE: chapel or vestibule usually at the W end of a church enclosing the main portal(s).

GALLERY: a long room or passage; an upper storey above the aisle of a church, looking through arches to the nave; a balcony or mezzanine overlooking the main interior space of a building; or an external walkway.

GALLETING: small stones set in a mortar course.

GAMBREL ROOF: *see* 8a.

GARDEROBE: medieval privy.

GARGOYLE: projecting water spout often carved into human or animal shape.

GAUGED or RUBBED BRICKWORK: soft brick sawn roughly, then rubbed to a precise (gauged) surface. Mostly used for door or window openings (5c).

GAZEBO (jocular Latin, 'I shall gaze'): ornamental lookout tower or raised summer house.

GEOMETRIC: English Gothic architecture *c.* 1250–1310. *See also* Tracery. For another meaning, *see* Stairs.

GIANT or COLOSSAL ORDER: classical order (q.v.) whose height is that of two or more storeys of the building to which it is applied.

GIBBS SURROUND: C18 treatment of an opening (4b), seen particularly in the work of James Gibbs (1682–1754).

GIRDER: a large beam. *Box*: of hollow-box section. *Bowed*: with its top rising in a curve. *Plate*: of I-section, made from iron or steel plates. *Lattice*: with braced framework.

GLAZING BARS: wooden or sometimes metal bars separating and supporting window panes.

GRAFFITI: *see* Sgraffito.

GRANGE: farm owned and run by a religious order.

GRC: *see* Fibreglass.

GRISAILLE: monochrome painting on walls or glass.

GROIN: sharp edge at the meeting of two cells of a cross-vault; *see* Vault and 2c.

GROTESQUE (*lit.* grotto-esque): wall decoration adopted from Roman examples in the Renaissance. Its foliage scrolls incorporate figurative elements. Cf. Arabesque.

GROTTO: artificial cavern.

GRP: *see* Fibreglass.

GUILLOCHE: classical ornament of interlaced bands (4b).

GUNLOOP: opening for a firearm.

GUTTAE: stylized drops (3b).

HALF-TIMBERING: archaic term for timber-framing (q.v.). Sometimes used for non-structural decorative timberwork.

HALL CHURCH: medieval church with nave and aisles of approximately equal height.

HAMMERBEAM: *see* Roofs and 7.

HAMPER: in C20 architecture, a visually distinct topmost storey or storeys.

HEADER: *see* Bond and 6e.

HEADSTOP: stop (q.v.) carved with a head (5b).

HELM ROOF: *see* 1c.

HENGE: ritual earthwork.

HERM (*lit.* the god Hermes): male head or bust on a pedestal.

HERRINGBONE WORK: *see* 7ii. Cf. Pitched masonry.

HEXASTYLE: *see* Portico.

HILL-FORT: Iron Age earthwork enclosed by a ditch and bank system.

HIPPED ROOF: *see* 8a.

HOODMOULD: projecting moulding above an arch or lintel to throw off water (2b, 5b). When horizontal often called a *label*. For label stop *see* Stop.

HUSK GARLAND: festoon of stylized nutshells (4b).

HYDRAULIC POWER: use of water under high pressure to work machinery. *Accumulator tower*: houses a hydraulic accumulator which accommodates fluctuations in the flow through hydraulic mains.

HYPOCAUST (*lit.* underburning): Roman underfloor heating system.

IMPOST: horizontal moulding at the springing of an arch (5c).

IMPOST BLOCK: block between abacus and capital (1b).

IN ANTIS: *see* Antae, Portico and 4a.

INDENT: shape chiselled out of a stone to receive a brass.

INDUSTRIALIZED OF SYSTEM BUILDING: system of manufactured units assembled on site.

INGLENOOK (*lit.* fire-corner): recess for a hearth with provision for seating.

INTERCOLUMNATION: interval between columns.

INTERLACE: decoration in relief simulating woven or entwined stems or bands.

INTRADOS: *see* Soffit.

IONIC: *see* Orders and 3c.

JACK ARCH: shallow segmental vault springing from beams, used for fireproof floors, bridge decks, etc.

JAMB (*lit.* leg): one of the vertical sides of an opening.

JETTY: in a timber-framed building, the projection of an upper storey beyond the storey below, made by the beams and joists of the lower storey oversailing the wall; on their outer ends is placed the sill of the walling for the storey above (7). Buildings can be jettied on several sides, in which case a *dragon beam* is set diagonally at the corner to carry the joists to either side.

JOGGLE: the joining of two stones to prevent them slipping by a notch in one and a projection in the other.

KEEL MOULDING: moulding used from the late C12, in section like the keel of a ship (1a).

KEEP: principal tower of a castle.

KENTISH CUSP: *see* Tracery and 2b.

KEY PATTERN: *see* 4b.

KEYSTONE: central stone in an arch or vault (4b, 5c).

KINGPOST: *see* Roofs and 7.

KNEELER: horizontal projecting stone at the base of each side of a gable to support the inclined coping stones (8a).

LABEL: *see* Hoodmould and 5b.

LABEL STOP: *see* Stop and 5b.

LACED BRICKWORK: vertical strips of brickwork, often in a contrasting colour, linking openings on different floors.

LACING COURSE: horizontal reinforcement in timber or brick to walls of flint, cobble, etc.

LADY CHAPEL: dedicated to the Virgin Mary (Our Lady).

LANCET: slender single-light, pointed-arched window (2a).

LANTERN: circular or polygonal windowed turret crowning a roof or a dome. Also the windowed stage of a crossing tower lighting the church interior.

LANTERN CROSS: churchyard cross with lantern-shaped top.

LAVATORIUM: in a religious house, a washing place adjacent to the refectory.

LEAN-TO: *see* Roofs.

LESENE (*lit.* a mean thing): pilaster without base or capital. Also called *pilaster strip*.

LIERNE: *see* Vault and 2c.

LIGHT: compartment of a window defined by the mullions.

LINENFOLD: Tudor panelling carved with simulations of folded linen. *See also* Parchemin.

LINTEL: horizontal beam or stone bridging an opening.

LOGGIA: gallery, usually arcaded or colonnaded; sometimes free-standing.

LONG-AND-SHORT WORK: quoins consisting of stones placed with the long side alternately upright and horizontal, especially in Saxon building.

LONGHOUSE: house and byre in the same range with internal access between them.

LOUVRE: roof opening, often protected by a raised timber structure, to allow the smoke from a central hearth to escape.

LOWSIDE WINDOW: set lower than the others in a chancel side wall, usually towards its W end.

LUCAM: projecting housing for hoist pulley on upper storey of warehouses, mills, etc., for raising goods to loading doors.

LUCARNE (*lit.* dormer): small gabled opening in a roof or spire.

LUGGED ARCHITRAVE: *see* 4b.

LUNETTE: semicircular window or blind panel.

LYCHGATE (*lit.* corpse-gate): roofed gateway entrance to a churchyard for the reception of a coffin.

LYNCHET: long terraced strip of soil on the downward side of prehistoric and medieval fields, accumulated because of continual ploughing along the contours.

MACHICOLATIONS (*lit.* mashing devices): series of openings between the corbels that support a projecting parapet through which missiles can be dropped. Used decoratively in post-medieval buildings.

MANOMETER or STANDPIPE TOWER: containing a column of water to regulate pressure in water mains.

MANSARD: *see* 8a.

MATHEMATICAL TILES: facing tiles with the appearance of brick, most often applied to timber-framed walls.

MAUSOLEUM: monumental building or chamber usually intended for the burial of members of one family.

MEGALITHIC TOMB: massive stone-built Neolithic burial chamber covered by an earth or stone mound.

MERLON: *see* Battlement.

METOPES: spaces between the triglyphs in a Doric frieze (3b).

MEZZANINE: low storey between two higher ones.

MILD STEEL: *see* Cast iron.

MISERICORD (*lit.* mercy): shelf on a carved bracket placed on the underside of a hinged choir stall seat to support an occupant when standing.

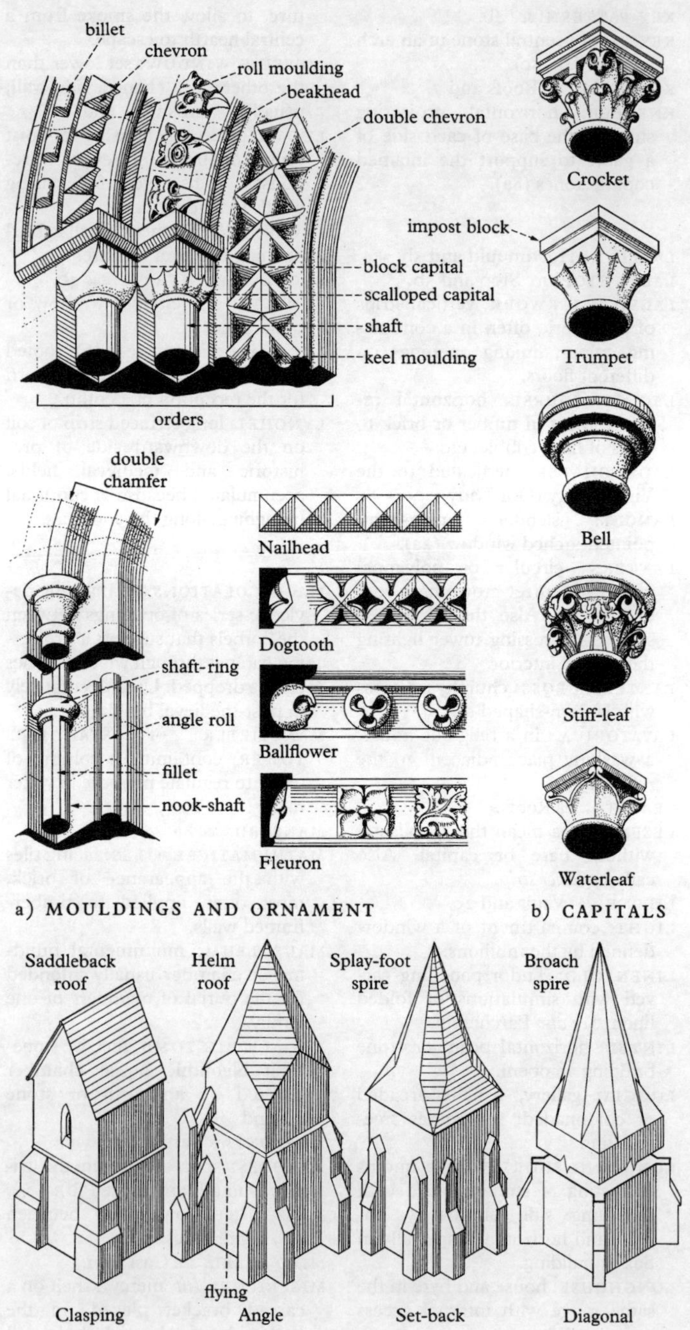
billet
chevron
roll moulding
beakhead
double chevron
block capital
scalloped capital
shaft
keel moulding
orders
double chamfer
shaft-ring
angle roll
fillet
nook-shaft
Nailhead
Dogtooth
Ballflower
Fleuron
Crocket
impost block
Trumpet
Bell
Stiff-leaf
Waterleaf
a) MOULDINGS AND ORNAMENT
b) CAPITALS
Saddleback roof
Helm roof
Splay-foot spire
Broach spire
Clasping
flying
Angle
Set-back
Diagonal
c) BUTTRESSES, ROOFS AND SPIRES

FIGURE 1: MEDIEVAL

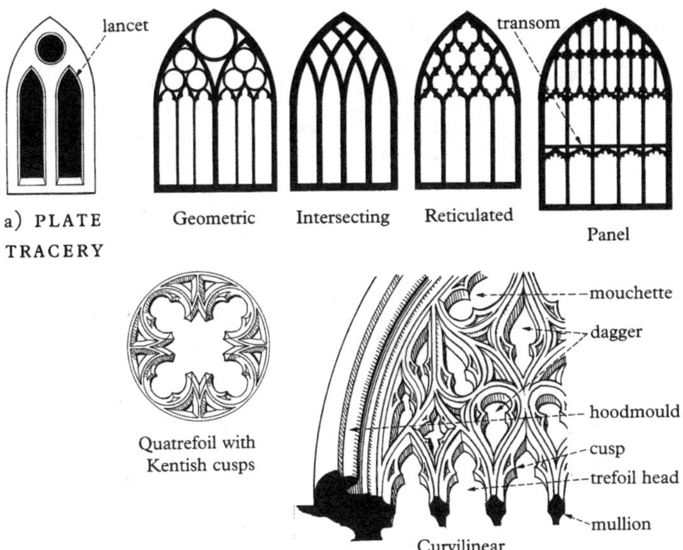

lancet
transom
Geometric
Intersecting
Reticulated
Panel

a) PLATE TRACERY

Quatrefoil with
Kentish cusps
mouchette
dagger
hoodmould
cusp
trefoil head
mullion
Curvilinear

b) BAR TRACERY

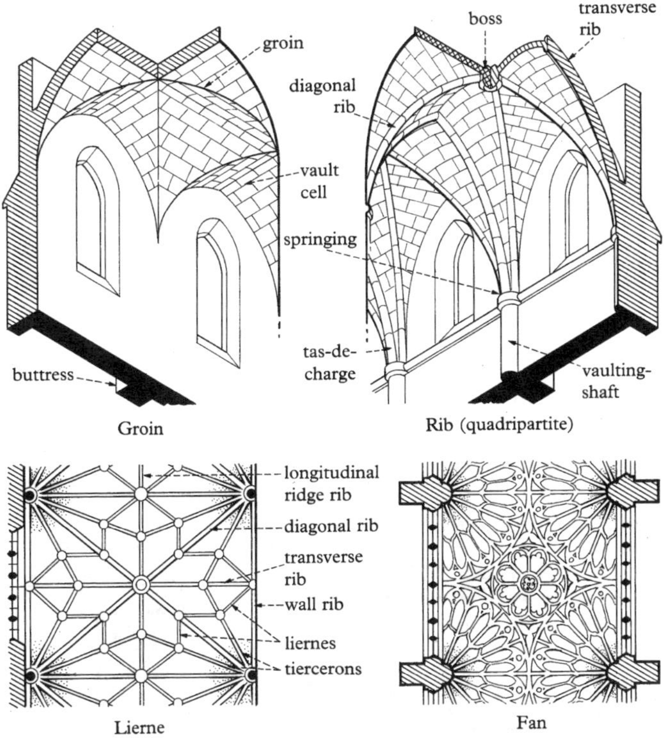

groin
diagonal
rib
vault
cell
springing
tas-de-
charge
buttress
boss
transverse
rib
vaulting-
shaft
Groin
Rib (quadripartite)
longitudinal
ridge rib
diagonal rib
transverse
rib
wall rib
liernes
tiercerons
Lierne
Fan

c) VAULTS

FIGURE 2: MEDIEVAL

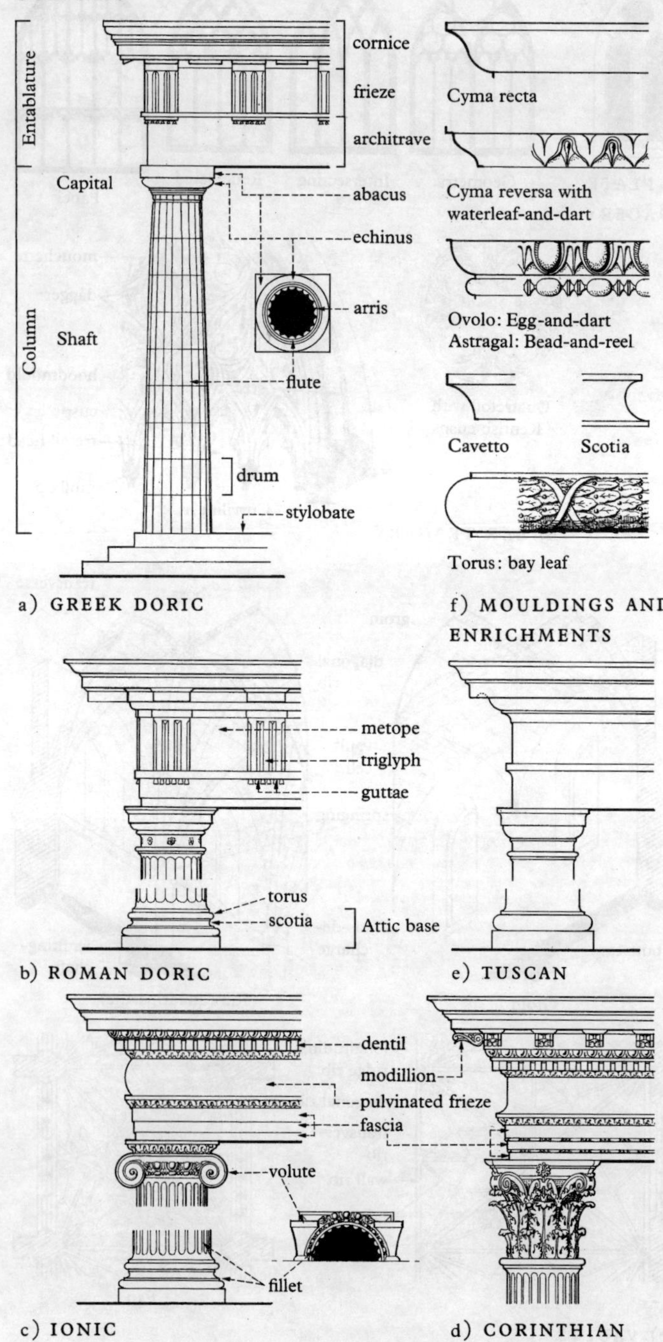
ORDERS
Entablature
cornice
frieze
architrave
Capital
abacus
echinus
arris
Column
Shaft
flute
drum
stylobate
a) GREEK DORIC
Cyma recta
Cyma reversa with waterleaf-and-dart
Ovolo: Egg-and-dart
Astragal: Bead-and-reel
Cavetto
Scotia
Torus: bay leaf
f) MOULDINGS AND ENRICHMENTS
metope
triglyph
guttae
torus
scotia
Attic base
b) ROMAN DORIC
e) TUSCAN
dentil
modillion
pulvinated frieze
fascia
volute
fillet
c) IONIC
d) CORINTHIAN

FIGURE 3: CLASSICAL

acroterion
tympanum
antefixa
column
anta
naos
naos
pronaos
Distyle in antis
Prostyle
a) PORTICO
Anthemion & Palmette
Guilloche
Key pattern
Rinceau
Husk garland
Vitruvian scroll
Console
Diocletian window
Acanthus
Broken pediment
Lugged architrave
Segmental pediment
Shouldered architrave
Venetian window
console
keystone
cartouche
blocking
Open pediment
Swan-neck pediment
Gibbs surround
b) ORNAMENTS AND FEATURES

FIGURE 4: CLASSICAL

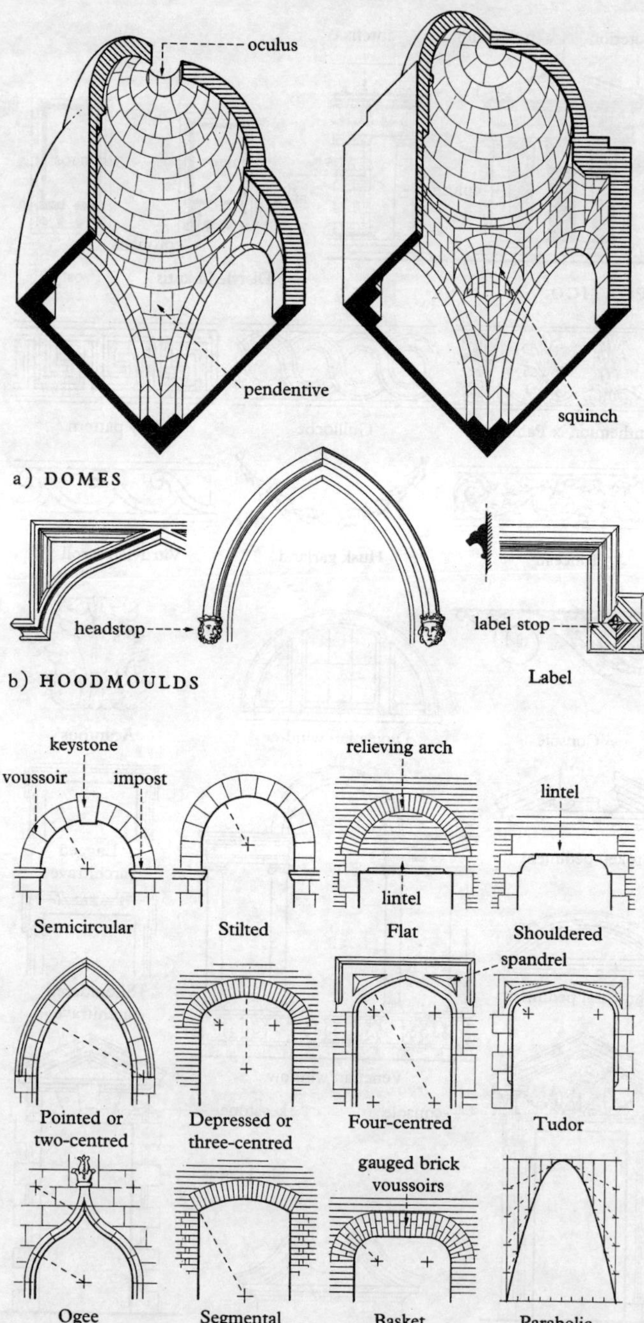

FIGURE 5: CONSTRUCTION

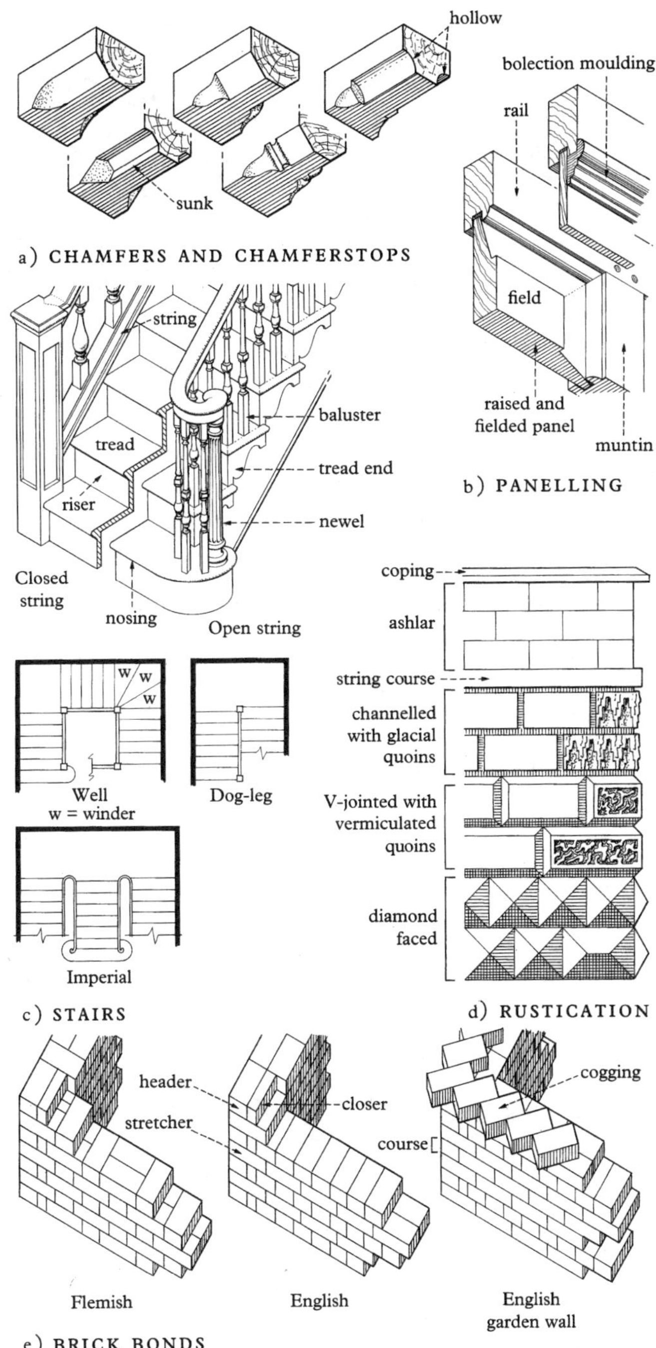

FIGURE 6: CONSTRUCTION

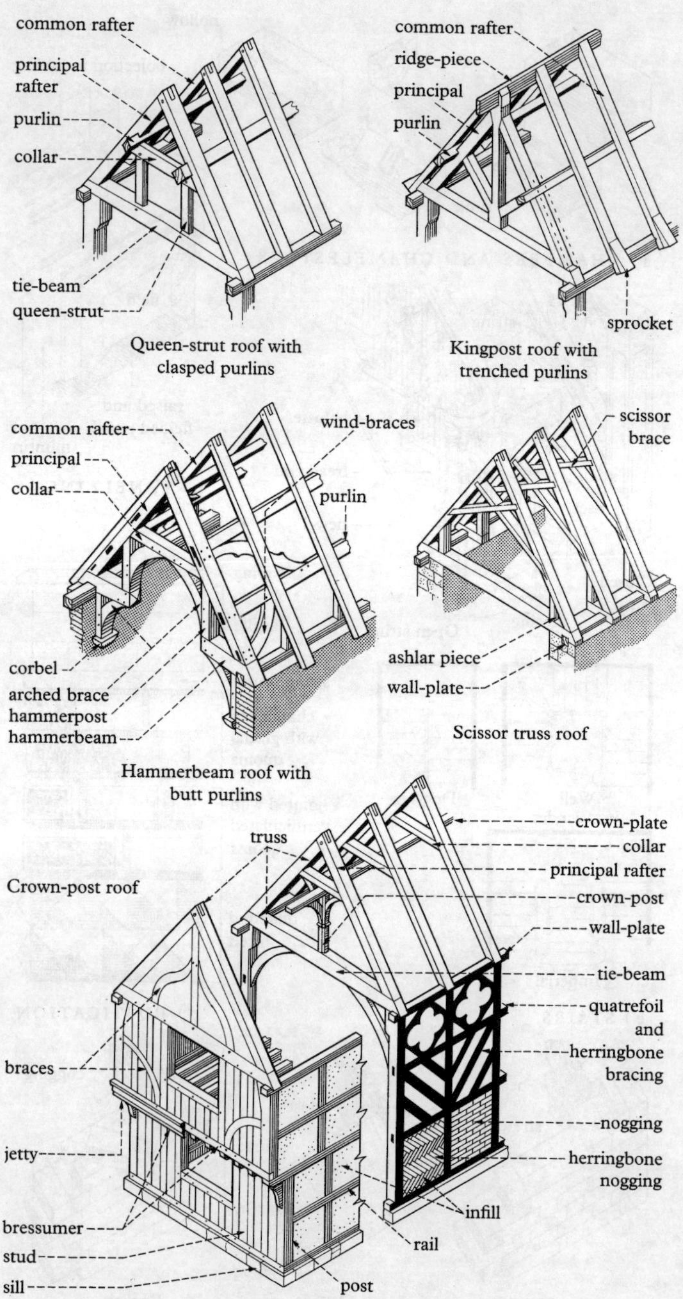
common rafter
principal rafter
purlin
collar
tie-beam
queen-strut
Queen-strut roof with clasped purlins
common rafter
ridge-piece
principal
purlin
sprocket
Kingpost roof with trenched purlins
common rafter
principal
collar
wind-braces
purlin
corbel
arched brace
hammerpost
hammerbeam
Hammerbeam roof with butt purlins
scissor brace
ashlar piece
wall-plate
Scissor truss roof
Crown-post roof
truss
crown-plate
collar
principal rafter
crown-post
wall-plate
tie-beam
quatrefoil and herringbone bracing
nogging
herringbone nogging
infill
rail
post
braces
jetty
bressumer
stud
sill
Box frame: i) Close studding
ii) Square panel

FIGURE 7: ROOFS AND TIMBER-FRAMING

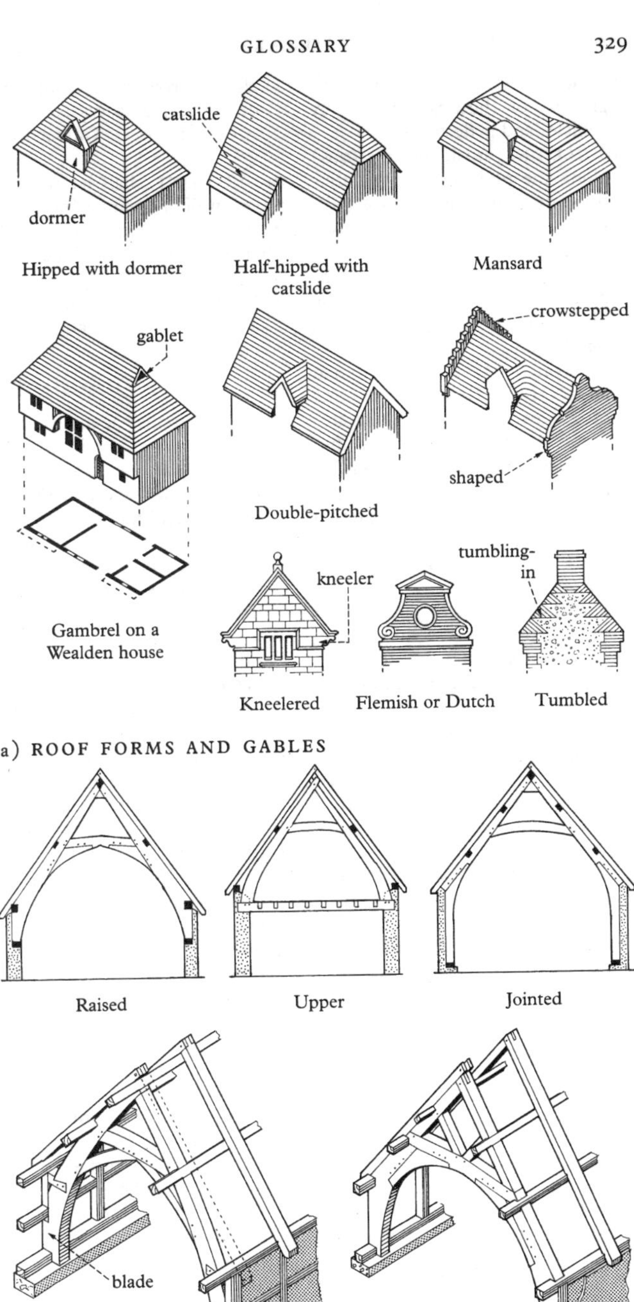

FIGURE 8: ROOFS AND TIMBER-FRAMING

MIXER-COURTS: forecourts to groups of houses shared by vehicles and pedestrians.

MODILLIONS: small consoles (q.v.) along the underside of a Corinthian or Composite cornice (3d). Often used along an eaves cornice.

MODULE: a predetermined standard size for co-ordinating the dimensions of components of a building.

MOTTE-AND-BAILEY: post-Roman and Norman defence consisting of an earthen mound (motte) topped by a wooden tower within a bailey, an enclosure defended by a ditch and palisade, and also, sometimes, by an internal bank.

MOUCHETTE: *see* Tracery and 2b.

MOULDING: shaped ornamental strip of continuous section; *see* e.g. Cavetto, Cyma, Ovolo, Roll.

MULLION: vertical member between window lights (2b).

MULTI-STOREY: five or more storeys. Multi-storey flats may form a *cluster block*, with individual blocks of flats grouped round a service core; a *point block*, with flats fanning out from a service core; or a *slab block*, with flats approached by corridors or galleries from service cores at intervals or towers at the ends (plan also used for offices, hotels etc.). *Tower block* is a generic term for any very high multi-storey building.

MUNTIN: *see* Panelling and 6b.

NAILHEAD: E.E. ornament consisting of small pyramids regularly repeated (1a).

NARTHEX: enclosed vestibule or covered porch at the main entrance to a church.

NAVE: the body of a church W of the crossing or chancel often flanked by aisles (q.v.).

NEWEL: central or corner post of a staircase (6c). Newel stair: *see* Stairs.

NIGHT STAIR: stair by which religious entered the transept of their church from their dormitory to celebrate night services.

NOGGING: *see* Timber-framing (7).

NOOK-SHAFT: shaft set in the angle of a wall or opening (1a).

NORMAN: *see* Romanesque.

NOSING: projection of the tread of a step (6c).

NUTMEG: medieval ornament with a chain of tiny triangles placed obliquely.

OCULUS: circular opening.

ŒIL DE BŒUF: *see* Bullseye window.

OGEE: double curve, bending first one way and then the other, as in an *ogee* or *ogival arch* (5c). Cf. Cyma recta and Cyma reversa.

OPUS SECTILE: decorative mosaic-like facing.

OPUS SIGNINUM: composition flooring of Roman origin.

ORATORY: a private chapel in a church or a house. Also a church of the Oratorian Order.

ORDER: one of a series of recessed arches and jambs forming a splayed medieval opening, e.g. a doorway or arcade arch (1a).

ORDERS: the formalized versions of the post-and-lintel system in classical architecture. The main orders are *Doric*, *Ionic*, and *Corinthian*. They are Greek in origin but occur in Roman versions. Tuscan is a simple version of Roman Doric. Though each order has its own conventions (3), there are many minor variations. The *Composite* capital combines Ionic volutes with Corinthian foliage. *Superimposed orders*: orders on successive levels, usually in the upward sequence of Tuscan, Doric, Ionic, Corinthian, Composite.

ORIEL: *see* Bay window.

OVERDOOR: painting or relief above an internal door. Also called a *sopraporta*.

OVERTHROW: decorative fixed arch between two gatepiers or above a wrought-iron gate.

OVOLO: wide convex moulding (3f).

PALIMPSEST: of a brass: where a metal plate has been reused by turning over the engraving on the back; of a wall painting: where one overlaps and partly obscures an earlier one.

PALLADIAN: following the examples and principles of Andrea Palladio (1508–80).

PALMETTE: classical ornament like a palm shoot (4b).

PANELLING: wooden lining to interior walls, made up of vertical members (*muntins*) and horizontals (*rails*) framing panels: also called *wainscot*. *Raised and fielded*: with the central area of the panel (*field*) raised up (6b).

PANTILE: roof tile of S section.

PARAPET: wall for protection at any sudden drop, e.g. at the wall-head of a castle where it protects the *parapet walk* or wall-walk. Also used to conceal a roof.

PARCLOSE: *see* Screen.

PARGETTING (*lit.* plastering): exterior plaster decoration, either in relief or incised.

PARLOUR: in a religious house, a room where the religious could talk to visitors; in a medieval house, the semi-private living room below the solar (q.v.).

PARTERRE: level space in a garden laid out with low, formal beds.

PATERA (*lit.* plate): round or oval ornament in shallow relief.

PAVILION: ornamental building for occasional use; or projecting subdivision of a larger building, often at an angle or terminating a wing.

PEBBLEDASHING: *see* Rendering.

PEDESTAL: a tall block carrying a classical order, statue, vase, etc.

PEDIMENT: a formalized gable derived from that of a classical temple; also used over doors, windows, etc. For variations *see* 4b.

PENDENTIVE: spandrel between adjacent arches, supporting a drum, dome or vault and consequently formed as part of a hemisphere (5a).

PENTHOUSE: subsidiary structure with a lean-to roof. Also a separately roofed structure on top of a C20 multi-storey block.

PERIPTERAL: *see* Peristyle.

PERISTYLE: a colonnade all round the exterior of a classical building, as in a temple which is then said to be *peripteral*.

PERP (PERPENDICULAR): English Gothic architecture *c.* 1335–50 to *c.* 1530. The name is derived from the upright tracery panels then used (*see* Tracery and 2a).

PERRON: external stair to a doorway, usually of double-curved plan.

PEW: loosely, seating for the laity outside the chancel; strictly, an enclosed seat. *Box pew*: with equal high sides and a door.

PIANO NOBILE: principal floor of a classical building above a ground floor or basement and with a lesser storey overhead.

PIAZZA: formal urban open space surrounded by buildings.

PIER: large masonry or brick support, often for an arch. *See also* Compound pier.

PILASTER: flat representation of a classical column in shallow relief. *Pilaster strip*: *see* Lesene.

PILE: row of rooms. *Double pile*: two rows thick.

PILLAR: free-standing upright member of any section, not conforming to one of the orders (q.v.).

PILLAR PISCINA: *see* Piscina.

PILOTIS: C20 French term for pillars or stilts that support a building above an open ground floor.

PISCINA: basin for washing Mass vessels, provided with a drain; set in or against the wall to the S of an altar or free-standing (*pillar piscina*).

PISÉ: *see* Cob.

PITCHED MASONRY: laid on the diagonal, often alternately with opposing courses (*pitched and counterpitched* or *herringbone*).

PLATBAND: flat horizontal moulding between storeys. Cf. stringcourse.

PLATE RAIL: *see* Railways.

PLATEWAY: *see* Railways.

PLINTH: projecting courses at the

foot of a wall or column, generally chamfered or moulded at the top.

PODIUM: a continuous raised platform supporting a building; or a large block of two or three storeys beneath a multi-storey block of smaller area.

POINT BLOCK: *see* Multi-storey.

POINTING: exposed mortar jointing of masonry or brickwork. Types include *flush*, *recessed* and *tuck* (with a narrow channel filled with finer, whiter mortar).

POPPYHEAD: carved ornament of leaves and flowers as a finial for a bench end or stall.

PORTAL FRAME: C20 frame comprising two uprights rigidly connected to a beam or pair of rafters.

PORTCULLIS: gate constructed to rise and fall in vertical grooves at the entry to a castle.

PORTICO: a porch with the roof and frequently a pediment supported by a row of columns (4a). A portico *in antis* has columns on the same plane as the front of the building. A *prostyle* porch has columns standing free. Porticoes are described by the number of front columns, e.g. tetrastyle (four), hexastyle (six). The space within the temple is the *naos*, that within the portico the *pronaos*. *Blind portico*: the front features of a portico applied to a wall.

PORTICUS (plural: porticūs): subsidiary cell opening from the main body of a pre-Conquest church.

POST: upright support in a structure (7).

POSTERN: small gateway at the back of a building or to the side of a larger entrance door or gate.

POUND LOCK: *see* Canals.

PRESBYTERY: the part of a church lying E of the choir where the main altar is placed; or a priest's residence.

PRINCIPAL: *see* Roofs and 7.

PRONAOS: *see* Portico and 4a.

PROSTYLE: *see* Portico and 4a.

PULPIT: raised and enclosed platform for the preaching of sermons. *Three-decker*: with reading desk below and clerk's desk below that. *Two-decker*: as above, minus the clerk's desk.

PULPITUM: stone screen in a major church dividing choir from nave.

PULVINATED: *see* Frieze and 3c.

PURLIN: *see* Roofs and 7.

PUTHOLES OR PUTLOG HOLES: in the wall to receive putlogs, the horizontal timbers which support scaffolding boards; sometimes not filled after construction is complete.

PUTTO (plural: putti): small naked boy.

QUARRIES: square (or diamond) panes of glass supported by lead strips (*cames*); square floor slabs or tiles.

QUATREFOIL: *see* Foil and 2b.

QUEEN-STRUT: *see* Roofs and 7.

QUIRK: sharp groove to one side of a convex medieval moulding.

QUOINS: dressed stones at the angles of a building (6d).

RADBURN SYSTEM: vehicle and pedestrian segregation in residential developments, based on that used at Radburn, New Jersey, USA, by Wright and Stein, 1928–30.

RADIATING CHAPELS: projecting radially from an ambulatory or an apse (*see* Chevet).

RAFTER: *see* Roofs and 7.

RAGGLE: groove cut in masonry, especially to receive the edge of a roof-covering.

RAGULY: ragged (in heraldry). Also applied to funerary sculpture, e.g. *cross raguly*: with a notched outline.

RAIL: *see* Panelling and 6b; also 7.

RAILWAYS: *Edge rail*: on which flanged wheels can run. *Plate rail*: L-section rail for plain unflanged wheels. *Plateway*: early railway using plate rails.

RAISED AND FIELDED: *see* Panelling and 6b.

RAKE: slope or pitch.

RAMPART: defensive outer wall of stone or earth. *Rampart walk*: path along the inner face.

REBATE: rectangular section cut out of a masonry edge to receive a shutter, door, window, etc.

REBUS: a heraldic pun, e.g. a fiery cock for Cockburn.

REEDING: series of convex mouldings, the reverse of fluting (q.v.). Cf. Gadrooning.

RENDERING: the covering of outside walls with a uniform surface or skin for protection from the weather. *Limewashing*: thin layer of lime plaster. *Pebble-dashing*: where aggregate is thrown at the wet plastered wall for a textured effect. *Roughcast*: plaster mixed with a coarse aggregate such as gravel. *Stucco*: fine lime plaster worked to a smooth surface. *Cement rendering*: a cheaper substitute for stucco, usually with a grainy texture.

REPOUSSÉ: relief designs in metalwork, formed by beating it from the back.

REREDORTER (*lit.* behind the dormitory): latrines in a medieval religious house.

REREDOS: painted and/or sculptured screen behind and above an altar. Cf. Retable.

RESPOND: half-pier or half-column bonded into a wall and carrying one end of an arch. It usually terminates an arcade.

RETABLE: painted or carved panel standing on or at the back of an altar, usually attached to it.

RETROCHOIR: in a major church, the area between the high altar and E chapel.

REVEAL: the plane of a jamb, between the wall and the frame of a door or window.

RIB-VAULT: *see* Vault and 2c.

RINCEAU: classical ornament of leafy scrolls (4b).

RISER: vertical face of a step (6c).

ROACH: a rough-textured form of Portland stone, with small cavities and fossil shells.

ROCK-FACED: masonry cleft to produce a rugged appearance.

ROCOCO: style current *c.* 1720 and *c.* 1760, characterized by a serpentine line and playful, scrolled decoration.

ROLL MOULDING: medieval moulding of part-circular section (1a).

ROMANESQUE: style current in the C11 and C12. In England often called Norman. *See also* Saxo-Norman.

ROOD: crucifix flanked by the Virgin and St John, usually over the entry into the chancel, on a beam (*rood beam*) or painted on the wall. The *rood screen* below often had a walkway (*rood loft*) along the top, reached by a *rood stair* in the side wall.

ROOFS: Shape. For the main external shapes (hipped, mansard, etc.) *see* 8a. *Helm* and *Saddleback*: *see* 1c.
Lean-to: single sloping roof built against a vertical wall; lean-to is also applied to the part of the building beneath.
Construction. *See* 7.
Single-framed roof: with no main trusses. The rafters may be fixed to the wall-plate or ridge, or longitudinal timber may be absent altogether.
Double-framed roof: with longitudinal members, such as purlins, and usually divided into bays by principals and principal rafters.
Other types are named after their main structural components, e.g. *hammerbeam*, *crown-post* (*see* Elements below and 7).
Elements. *See* 7.
Ashlar piece: a short vertical timber connecting inner wall-plate or timber pad to a rafter.
Braces: subsidiary timbers set diagonally to strengthen the frame. *Arched braces*: curved pair forming an arch, connecting wall or post below with tie- or collar-beam above. *Passing braces*: long straight braces passing across other members of the truss. *Scissor braces*: pair crossing diagonally between pairs of rafters or principals. *Wind-braces*: short, usually curved braces connecting side purlins with principals; sometimes decorated with cusping.
Collar or *collar-beam*: horizontal transverse timber connecting a pair of rafter or cruck blades (q.v.), set between apex and the wall-plate.
Crown-post: a vertical timber set centrally on a tie-beam and supporting a collar purlin braced to it longitudinally. In an open truss

lateral braces may rise to the collar-beam; in a closed truss they may descend to the tie-beam.
Hammerbeams: horizontal brackets projecting at wall-plate level like an interrupted tie-beam; the inner ends carry *hammerposts*, vertical timbers which support a purlin and are braced to a collar-beam above.
Kingpost: vertical timber set centrally on a tie- or collar-beam, rising to the apex of the roof to support a ridge-piece (cf. Strut).
Plate: longitudinal timber set square to the ground. *Wall-plate*: plate along the top of a wall which receives the ends of the rafters; cf. Purlin.
Principals: pair of inclined lateral timbers of a truss. Usually they support side purlins and mark the main bay divisions.
Purlin: horizontal longitudinal timber. *Collar purlin* or *crown plate*: central timber which carries collar-beams and is supported by crown-posts. *Side purlins*: pairs of timbers placed some way up the slope of the roof, which carry common rafters. *Butt* or *tenoned purlins* are tenoned into either side of the principals. *Through purlins* pass through or past the principal; they include *clasped purlins*, which rest on queenposts or are carried in the angle between principals and collar, and *trenched purlins* trenched into the backs of principals.
Queen-strut: paired vertical, or near-vertical, timbers placed symmetrically on a tie-beam to support side purlins.
Rafters: inclined lateral timbers supporting the roof covering. *Common rafters*: regularly spaced uniform rafters placed along the length of a roof or between principals. *Principal rafters*: rafters which also act as principals.
Ridge, ridge-piece: horizontal longitudinal timber at the apex supporting the ends of the rafters.
Sprocket: short timber placed on the back and at the foot of a rafter to form projecting eaves.
Strut: vertical or oblique timber between two members of a truss, not directly supporting longitudinal timbers.
Tie-beam: main horizontal transverse timber which carries the feet of the principals at wall level.
Truss: rigid framework of timbers at bay intervals, carrying the longitudinal roof timbers which support the common rafters.
Closed truss: with the spaces between the timbers filled, to form an internal partition.
See also Cruck, Wagon roof.

ROPE MOULDING: *see* Cable moulding.

ROSE WINDOW: circular window with tracery radiating from the centre. Cf. Wheel window.

ROTUNDA: building or room circular in plan.

ROUGHCAST: *see* Rendering.

ROVING BRIDGE: *see* Canals.

RUBBED BRICKWORK: *see* Gauged brickwork.

RUBBLE: masonry whose stones are wholly or partly in a rough state. *Coursed*: coursed stones with rough faces. *Random*: uncoursed stones in a random pattern. *Snecked*: with courses broken by smaller stones (snecks).

RUSTICATION: *see* 6d. Exaggerated treatment of masonry to give an effect of strength. The joints are usually recessed by V-section chamfering or square-section channelling (*channelled rustication*). *Banded rustication* has only the horizontal joints emphasized. The faces may be flat, but can be *diamond-faced*, like shallow pyramids, *vermiculated*, with a stylized texture like worm-casts, and *glacial* (frost-work), like icicles or stalactites.

SACRISTY: room in a church for sacred vessels and vestments.

SADDLEBACK ROOF: *see* IC.

SALTIRE CROSS: with diagonal limbs.

SANCTUARY: area around the main altar of a church. Cf. Presbytery.

SANGHA: residence of Buddhist monks or nuns.

SARCOPHAGUS: coffin of stone or other durable material.

SAXO-NORMAN: transitional Romanesque style combining Anglo-Saxon and Norman features, current *c.* 1060–1100.

SCAGLIOLA: composition imitating marble.

SCALLOPED CAPITAL: *see* 1a.

SCOTIA: a hollow classical moulding, especially between tori (q.v.) on a column base (3b, 3f).

SCREEN: in a medieval church, usually at the entry to the chancel; *see* Rood (screen) and Pulpitum. A *parclose screen* separates a chapel from the rest of the church.

SCREENS or SCREENS PASSAGE: screened-off entrance passage between great hall and service rooms.

SECTION: two-dimensional representation of a building, moulding, etc., revealed by cutting across it.

SEDILIA (singular: sedile): seats for the priests (usually three) on the S side of the chancel.

SET-OFF: *see* Weathering.

SETTS: squared stones, usually of granite, used for paving or flooring.

SGRAFFITO: decoration scratched, often in plaster, to reveal a pattern in another colour beneath. *Graffiti*: scratched drawing or writing.

SHAFT: vertical member of round or polygonal section (1a, 3a). *Shaft-ring*: at the junction of shafts set *en delit* (q.v.) or attached to a pier or wall (1a).

SHEILA-NA-GIG: female fertility figure, usually with legs apart.

SHELL: thin, self-supporting roofing membrane of timber or concrete.

SHOULDERED ARCHITRAVE: *see* 4b.

SHUTTERING: *see* Concrete.

SILL: horizontal member at the bottom of a window or door frame; or at the base of a timber-framed wall into which posts and studs are tenoned (7).

SLAB BLOCK: *see* Multi-storey.

SLATE-HANGING: covering of overlapping slates on a wall. *Tile-hanging* is similar.

SLYPE: covered way or passage leading E from the cloisters between transept and chapter house.

SNECKED: *see* Rubble.

SOFFIT (*lit.* ceiling): underside of an arch (also called *intrados*), lintel, etc. *Soffit roll*: medieval roll moulding on a soffit.

SOLAR: private upper chamber in a medieval house, accessible from the high end of the great hall.

SOPRAPORTA: *see* Overdoor.

SOUNDING-BOARD: *see* Tester.

SPANDRELS: roughly triangular spaces between an arch and its containing rectangle, or between adjacent arches (5c). Also non-structural panels under the windows in a curtain-walled building.

SPERE: a fixed structure screening the lower end of the great hall from the screens passage. *Spere-truss*: roof truss incorporated in the spere.

SPIRE: tall pyramidal or conical feature crowning a tower or turret. *Broach*: starting from a square base, then carried into an octagonal section by means of triangular faces; and *splayed-foot*: variation of the broach form, found principally in the south-east, in which the four cardinal faces are splayed out near their base, to cover the corners, while oblique (or intermediate) faces taper away to a point (1c). *Needle spire*: thin spire rising from the centre of a tower roof, well inside the parapet: when of timber and lead often called a *spike*.

SPIRELET: *see* Flèche.

SPLAY: of an opening when it is wider on one face of a wall than the other.

SPRING or SPRINGING: level at which an arch or vault rises from its supports. *Springers*: the first stones of an arch or vaulting rib above the spring (2c).

SQUINCH: arch or series of arches thrown across an interior angle of a square or rectangular structure to support a circular or polygonal superstructure, especially a dome or spire (5a).

SQUINT: an aperture in a wall or through a pier usually to allow a view of an altar.

STAIRS: *see* 6c. *Dog-leg stair*: parallel flights rising alternately in opposite directions, without an open well. *Flying stair*: cantilevered from the walls of a stairwell, without newels; sometimes called a *Geometric* stair when the inner edge describes a curve. *Newel stair*: ascending round a central supporting newel (q.v.); called a *spiral stair* or *vice* when in a circular shaft, a *winder* when in a rectangular compartment. (Winder also applies to the steps on the turn.) *Well stair*: with flights round a square open well framed by newel posts. *See also* Perron.

STALL: fixed seat in the choir or chancel for the clergy or choir (cf. Pew). Usually with arm rests, and often framed together.

STANCHION: upright structural member, of iron, steel or reinforced concrete.

STANDPIPE TOWER: *see* Manometer.

STEAM ENGINES: *Atmospheric*: worked by the vacuum created when low-pressure steam is condensed in the cylinder, as developed by Thomas Newcomen. *Beam engine*: with a large pivoted beam moved in an oscillating fashion by the piston. It may drive a flywheel or be *non-rotative*. *Watt* and *Cornish*: single-cylinder; *compound*: two cylinders; *triple expansion*: three cylinders.

STEEPLE: tower together with a spire, lantern, or belfry.

STIFF-LEAF: type of E.E. foliage decoration. *Stiff-leaf capital see* 1b.

STOP: plain or decorated terminal to mouldings or chamfers, or at the end of hoodmoulds and labels (*label stop*), or stringcourses (5b, 6a); *see also* Headstop.

STOUP: vessel for holy water, usually near a door.

STRAINER: *see* Arch.

STRAPWORK: late C16 and C17 decoration, like interlaced leather straps.

STRETCHER: *see* Bond and 6e.

STRING: *see* 6c. Sloping member holding the ends of the treads and risers of a staircase. *Closed string*: a broad string covering the ends of the treads and risers. *Open string*: cut into the shape of the treads and risers.

STRINGCOURSE: horizontal course or moulding projecting from the surface of a wall (6d).

STUCCO: *see* Rendering.

STUDS: subsidiary vertical timbers of a timber-framed wall or partition (7).

STUPA: Buddhist shrine, circular in plan.

STYLOBATE: top of the solid platform on which a colonnade stands (3a).

SUSPENSION BRIDGE: *see* Bridge.

SWAG: like a festoon (q.v.), but representing cloth.

SYSTEM BUILDING: *see* Industrialized building.

TABERNACLE: canopied structure to contain the reserved sacrament or a relic; or architectural frame for an image or statue.

TABLE TOMB: memorial slab raised on free-standing legs.

TAS-DE-CHARGE: the lower courses of a vault or arch which are laid horizontally (2c).

TERM: pedestal or pilaster tapering downward, usually with the upper part of a human figure growing out of it.

TERRACOTTA: moulded and fired clay ornament or cladding.

TESSELLATED PAVEMENT: mosaic flooring, particularly Roman, made of *tesserae*, i.e. cubes of glass, stone, or brick.

TESTER: flat canopy over a tomb or pulpit, where it is also called a *sounding-board*.

TESTER TOMB: tomb-chest with effigies beneath a tester, either free-standing (tester with four or more columns), or attached to a wall (*half-tester*) with columns on one side only.

TETRASTYLE: *see* Portico.

THERMAL WINDOW: *see* Diocletian window.

THREE-DECKER PULPIT: *see* Pulpit.

TIDAL GATES: *see* Canals.

TIE-BEAM: *see* Roofs and 7.

TIERCERON: *see* Vault and 2c.

TILE-HANGING: *see* Slate-hanging.

TIMBER-FRAMING: *see* 7. Method of construction where the structural frame is built of interlocking timbers. The spaces are filled with non-structural material, e.g. *infill* of wattle and daub, lath and plaster, brickwork (known as *nogging*), etc. and may be covered by plaster, weatherboarding (q.v.), or tiles.

TOMB-CHEST: chest-shaped tomb, usually of stone. Cf. Table tomb, Tester tomb.

TORUS (plural: tori): large convex moulding usually used on a column base (3b, 3f).

TOUCH: soft black marble quarried near Tournai.

TOURELLE: turret corbelled out from the wall.

TOWER BLOCK: *see* Multi-storey.

TRABEATED: depends structurally on the use of the post and lintel. Cf. Arcuated.

TRACERY: openwork pattern of masonry or timber in the upper part of an opening. *Blind tracery* is tracery applied to a solid wall.

Plate tracery, introduced *c.* 1200, is the earliest form, in which shapes are cut through solid masonry (2a).

Bar tracery was introduced into England *c.* 1250. The pattern is formed by intersecting moulded ribwork continued from the mullions. It was especially elaborate during the Decorated period (q.v.). Tracery shapes can include circles, *daggers* (elongated ogee-ended lozenges), *mouchettes* (like daggers but with curved sides) and upright rectangular *panels*. They often have *cusps*, projecting points defining lobes or *foils* (q.v.) within the main shape: *Kentish* or *split-cusps* are forked (2b).

Types of bar tracery (*see* 2b) include *geometric(al)*: *c.* 1250–1310, chiefly circles, often foiled; *Y-tracery*: *c.* 1300, with mullions branching into a Y-shape; *intersecting*: *c.* 1300, formed by interlocking mullions; *reticulated*: early C14, net-like pattern of ogee-ended lozenges; *curvilinear*: C14, with uninterrupted flowing curves; *panel*: Perp, with straight-sided panels, often cusped at the top and bottom.

TRANSEPT: transverse portion of a church.

TRANSITIONAL: generally used for the phase between Romanesque and Early English (*c.* 1175–*c.* 1200).

TRANSOM: horizontal member separating window lights (2b).

TREAD: horizontal part of a step. The *tread end* may be carved on a staircase (6c).

TREFOIL: *see* Foil.

TRIFORIUM: middle storey of a church treated as an arcaded wall passage or blind arcade, its height corresponding to that of the aisle roof.

TRIGLYPHS (*lit.* three-grooved tablets): stylized beam-ends in the Doric frieze, with metopes between (3b).

TRIUMPHAL ARCH: influential type of Imperial Roman monument.

TROPHY: sculptured or painted group of arms or armour.

TRUMEAU: central stone mullion supporting the tympanum of a wide doorway. *Trumeau figure*: carved figure attached to it (cf. Column figure).

TRUMPET CAPITAL: *see* 1b.

TRUSS: braced framework, spanning between supports. *See also* Roofs and 7.

TUMBLING or TUMBLING-IN: courses of brickwork laid at right-angles to a slope, e.g. of a gable, forming triangles by tapering into horizontal courses (8a).

TUSCAN: *see* Orders and 3e.

TWO-DECKER PULPIT: *see* Pulpit.

TYMPANUM: the surface between a lintel and the arch above it or within a pediment (4a).

UNDERCROFT: usually describes the vaulted room(s), beneath the main room(s) of a medieval house. Cf. Crypt.

VAULT: arched stone roof (sometimes imitated in timber or plaster). For types see 2c.

Tunnel or *barrel vault*: continuous semicircular or pointed arch, often of rubble masonry.

Groin-vault: tunnel vaults intersecting at right angles. *Groins* are the curved lines of the intersections.

Rib-vault: masonry framework of intersecting arches (ribs) supporting *vault cells*, used in Gothic architecture. *Wall rib* or *wall arch*: between wall and vault cell. *Transverse rib*: spans between two walls to divide a vault into bays. *Quadripartite* rib-vault: each bay has two pairs of diagonal ribs dividing the vault into four triangular cells. *Sexpartite* rib-vault: most often used over paired bays, has an extra pair of ribs springing from between the bays. More elaborate vaults may include *ridge ribs* along the crown of a vault or bisecting the bays; *tiercerons*: extra decorative ribs springing from the corners of a bay; and *liernes*: short decorative ribs in the crown of a vault, not linked to any springing point. A *stellar* or *star* vault has liernes in star formation.

Fan-vault: form of barrel vault used in the Perp period, made up of halved concave masonry cones decorated with blind tracery.

VAULTING SHAFT: shaft leading up to the spring or springing (q.v.) of a vault (2c).

VENETIAN or SERLIAN WINDOW: derived from Serlio (4b). The motif is used for other openings.

VERMICULATION: *see* Rustication and 6d.

VESICA: oval with pointed ends.

VICE: *see* Stair.

VILLA: originally a Roman country house or farm. The term was revived in England in the C18 under the influence of Palladio and used especially for smaller, compact country houses. In the later C19 it was debased to describe any suburban house.

VITRIFIED: bricks or tiles fired to a darkened glassy surface.

VITRUVIAN SCROLL: classical running ornament of curly waves (4b).

VOLUTES: spiral scrolls. They occur on Ionic capitals (3c). *Angle volute*: pair of volutes, turned outwards to meet at the corner of a capital.

VOUSSOIRS: wedge-shaped stones forming an arch (5c).

WAGON ROOF: with the appearance of the inside of a wagon tilt; often ceiled. Also called *cradle roof*.

WAINSCOT: *see* Panelling.

WALL MONUMENT: attached to the wall and often standing on the floor. *Wall tablets* are smaller with the inscription as the major element.

WALL-PLATE: *see* Roofs and 7.

WALL-WALK: *see* Parapet.

WARMING ROOM: room in a religious house where a fire burned for comfort.

WATERHOLDING BASE: early Gothic base with upper and lower mouldings separated by a deep hollow.

WATERLEAF: *see* Enrichments and 3f.

WATERLEAF CAPITAL: Late Romanesque and Transitional type of capital (1b).

WATER WHEELS: described by the way water is fed on to the wheel. *Breastshot*: mid-height, falling and passing beneath. *Overshot*: over the top. *Pitchback*: on the top but falling backwards. *Undershot*: turned by the momentum of the water passing beneath. In a *water turbine*, water is fed under pressure through a vaned wheel within a casing.

WEALDEN HOUSE: type of medieval timber-framed house with a central open hall flanked by bays of two storeys, roofed in line; the end bays are jettied to the front, but the eaves are continuous (8a).

WEATHERBOARDING: wall cladding of overlapping horizontal boards.

WEATHERING or SET-OFF: inclined, projecting surface to keep water away from the wall below.

WEEPERS: figures in niches along the sides of some medieval tombs. Also called mourners.

WHEEL WINDOW: circular, with radiating shafts like spokes. Cf. Rose window.

WROUGHT IRON: *see* Cast iron.

INDEX OF ARCHITECTS, ARTISTS, PATRONS AND RESIDENTS

The names of architects and artists recorded in this volume as working in the Isle of Wight are given in *italic*. Entries for partnerships and companies are listed after entries for a single surname.

Also indexed here are the names or titles of families and individuals (not of bodies or commercial firms) recorded in this volume as having owned property, commissioned architectural work, or visited the Island. The index includes monuments to members of such families and other individuals where they are of particular interest.

INDEX OF PLACES

Principal references are in **bold** type; demolished buildings are shown in *italic*.